OF MINIMAL THINGS

Cultural Memory
in
the
Present

Mieke Bal and Hent de Vries, Editors

OF MINIMAL THINGS

Studies on the Notion of Relation

Rodolphe Gasché

STANFORD UNIVERSITY PRESS

STANFORD, CALIFORNIA

1999

Stanford University Press
Stanford, California
© 1999 by the Board of Trustees of the
Leland Stanford Junior University

Printed in the United States of America

CIP data appear at the end of the book

Acknowledgments

Most of the essays included in this book have been published previously. "*Ecce Homo*, or The Written Body" is reprinted from *Looking After Nietzsche*, edited by L. A. Rickels, by permission of the State University of New York Press © 1990, State University of New York; all rights reserved. "Type-Writing Nietzsche's Self" appeared under the title "Autobiography as *Gestalt*" in *Why Nietzsche Now?*, edited by D. T. O'Hara, pp. 271–90 (Bloomington: Indiana University Press, 1985). I thank Indiana University Press for permission to reprint this text. "Tearing at the Texture" was first published under the title "Saturnine Vision and the Question of Difference: Reflections on Walter Benjamin's Theory of Language" in *Benjamin's Ground: New Readings of Walter Benjamin*, edited by E. Naegele, pp. 83–104 (Detroit: Wayne State University Press, 1988). I am grateful to Wayne State University Press for letting me republish this essay. The chapter "Cutting in on Distance" reproduces the essay "Objective Diversions: On Some Kantian Themes in Benjamin's 'The Work of Art in the Age of Mechanical Reproduction,'" published in *Walter Benjamin's Philosophy: Destruction and Experience*, edited by A. Benjamin, pp. 183–204 (London: Routledge, 1994). I am thankful to Indiana University Press for permission to include in this book "Floundering in Determination," which first appeared in *Commemorations: Reading Heidegger*, edited by J. Sallis, pp. 7–19 (Bloomington: Indiana University Press, 1993). "Tuned to Accord" is reprinted from *Heidegger Toward the Turn*, edited by J. Risser, by permission of the State University of New York Press © 1999 (forthcoming), State University of New York; all rights reserved. "Canonizing Measures" is reprinted here from the *Graduate Faculty Philosophy Journal* 19, nos. 2 and 20 (1997): 203–14. "Like the Rose—Without Why" was written for a special issue of *Diacritics* entitled *Heidegger: Art and Politics*, which I guest-edited with Anthony Appiah 19, nos. 3–4 (fall–winter 1989): 101–13. I am grateful to The Johns Hopkins University Press for permission to reprint this piece. The chapter "Perhaps: A Modality?" first appeared in the *Graduate Faculty Philosophy Journal* 16, no. 2 (1993): 467–84. A first version, in French, of "On the Nonadequate Trait" appeared in *Les Fins de l'homme: A partir du travail de Jacques Derrida*, pp. 133–61 (Paris: Galilée, 1981). I am thankful to the University of Minnesota Press for permission to republish "Joining the Text" from *The Yale Critics*, edited by J. Arac et al., pp. 156–75 (Minneapolis: University of Minnesota Press, 1983); copyright 1983 by the University of Minnesota, all rights reserved. "On Re-Presentation" is reprinted from *The Southern Journal of Philosophy* 32, supplement (1993): 1–18. I thank the University of Minnesota Press for permission to reprint my introduction, "Reading Chiasms," from A. Warminski, *Readings in Interpretation*, pp. ix–xxvi, 195–96 (Minneapolis: University of Minnesota Press, 1987); copyright 1987 by the University of Minnesota, all rights reserved. "A Relation called 'Literary'" was prepublished in *ASCA, Brief* 2 (Amsterdam School for Cultural Analysis, Theory, and Interpretation), pp. 17–33 (1995). The final chapter of the book, "The Felicities of Paradox," is republished from *Maurice Blanchot: Literature, Philosophy, and Ethics*, edited by C. B. Gill, pp. 34–64 (London: Routledge, 1996).

I am indebted to Judith Still for her translation (from French) of "*Ecce Homo*, or The Written Body." Very special thanks go to Leonard Lawlor, who took it upon himself in the early 1980s to translate (also from French) "On the Nonadequate Trait." I am particularly pleased to be able to include his translation in this volume. Finally, I wish to thank Dickson Tang, who assisted me in the preparation of the manuscript.

Contents

PART V. RELATION AT THE CROSSROADS

OF MINIMAL THINGS

Introduction

A full-scale philosophical discipline exclusively devoted to the study of relations—the polyadic (n-place) logic of predicates, or logic of relations—emerged only in the nineteenth century in the work of Augustus de Morgan, Charles Sanders Peirce, Gottlob Frege, and Ernst Schröder. In 1910, Bertrand Russell and Alfred North Whitehead codified in their text *Principia Mathematica* the achievements of their predecessors. Given the rather recent establishment of Russell and Whitehead's theory—contemporaneous with the reelaboration of the foundations of mathematics—it is not uncommon to encounter the belief that "relation" has achieved explicit philosophical recognition and has been given extensive theoretical treatment solely in our time. Nevertheless, the accomplishments of the logic of relations should not cloud the following fact: although antique philosophy did not have a proper term for "relation" and could refer to the topic only by way of the prepositional *pros ti*, Plato's discussion of relative predicates and Aristotle's first attempt at a classification of relatives in the *Categories* offer clear evidence of the existence of a classical theory of relations, whatever its limits may be. But it was in medieval philosophy—in a philosophical inquiry that became equipped with a set of terms for "relations" such as *respectus*, *habitudo*, *proportio*, and, especially, the Latin *relatio* (which Quintilian was probably the first to use in a logical sense)—that the topic of relation first became a prime philosophical issue.[1] Moreover, Scholastic philosophy featured an extraordinary range of strikingly diverse theories of relation. At the beginning of the fourteenth century, medieval thought even underwent a passionate debate on relations, in which realist and conceptualist theories of relation were pitted against one another. Of course, this ardent interest in the question of relation was largely theologically motivated. It was a function of the need to buttress philosophically the doctrine of the Trinity and to respond to a battery of theological questions, such as whether there is in God a real relation to his creatures. Equipped with these theological concerns bearing on philosophical theories of relation that, in addition, drew heavily on Aristotle's elaborations on the topic (particularly on his assumption that a relation is an attribute, or accident, of a subject, or substance), medieval theories of relation initially, at least, had a definitely realist thrust. Contrary to the Stoics, who held all relations to be subjective and to lack all extramental reality, medieval philosophers believed in the reality of relations. Their overall concern was what kind of extramental being to ascribe to relations. Generally speaking, the type of being that Scholastic philosophy accorded to relations is that of a thing. By "thing," however, we must not understand here something insofar as it is of itself—an absolute thing, as it were. If by conceiving of relations as "things" the Scholastics credited relations with extramental reality, they nonetheless accorded a very specific ontological status to this reality.

The general assumption that guides Scholastic reflection on relations is that a real relation is an Aristotelian attribute, or accident, one that amounts to the property, inhering in a thing, of being-toward-another. Following Aristotle, who in the *Metaphysics* speaks of relative terms as things whose very essence includes a reference to something else and who notes that things of this kind enjoy only the lowest status of being among beings,[2] medieval philosophy characterizes relations as relative things (*res relativae*). They are defined as things in this sense, whether relations are seen to be real as modes of things, that is, as things whose real being is dependent on the foundation in which they inhere, or whether relations have an accidental being of their own independent of the being of their ground. Even though this difference between dependence and independence implies a further difference in the assessment of the ontological status of real relations, still they remain, notwithstanding their nature as things, only relative things, which have less reality than their foundation; in the case where being-toward-another-thing differs from its foundation, the extramental reality of relations is, according to Duns Scotus, that of a "tiny being," or, in Richard of Mediavilla's terminology, a *minus ens*.[3] For Thomas Aquinas, a real, or categorial, relation inheres only in the subject, or foundation, of a relation, and the category of relation itself is "the weakest or least real" of all the categories. Relation is an entity, or thing, "so weak (*debilis*) that it requires for its support an entity that is 'more perfect' than itself." For this reason, Aquinas asserts, many have mistaken relations for merely intramental realities.[4] Indeed, being in the mind, as opposed to being outside the mind, is held to imply diminished being (*ens diminutum*) and has been attributed to relations, particularly to relations that are the result of comparisons.[5] Although a realist, Aquinas therefore admits that relations have the least of all being. Their ontological status is thus best described as one of minimal things. Aquinas writes, "Relatio praedicamentalis est accidens minimae entitatis" ("A predicative relation is an accident of the least being").[6] With this, the Scholastic philosopher provides a definition of relation broad enough to be shared by most of the philosophers of his time. A relation is an *ens minimum, minimum* understood as the superlative of *parvus*, and, hence, in the sense of something that is excruciatingly small, the smallest of all entities or things. As a "minimum de entitate,"[7] a relation has the ontological status of a real thing. Yet compared to substance, which exists primarily, the accidental nature of relation—regardless of whether it receives its being from the substance or possesses its own being—entails that the being this thing can claim as its own is minimal.

While the title of this book, *Of Minimal Things*, refers to the above Scholastic definition of relation, it does not follow that the ensuing studies on the concept of relation embrace the Scholastic substance/accident ontology. To a large extent, the emergence of a logic of relations in the last century results from the insight that the substance/accident ontology significantly limits the analysis of relation. But as is shown by the ongoing discussion of whether relations are internal or external—in other words, on whether they have a merely intramental reality or a mind-independent status—the question of their specific type of existence has not been resolved despite all the advances in the understanding of the logical form of relations and the development of sophisticated systems of notation for relational statements. Precisely because this controversy remains framed by the Aristotelian thesis that all objects have essential and accidental properties, or relations, issues similar to those that occupied the heated early-fourteenth-century debate between realists and nominalists continue to animate contemporary discussions of what ontological status to accord to relations. As Richard Rorty has aptly suggested, any decision for or against a particular type of reality concerning relations is so bound up with all the fundamental issues and divides in philosophy that no solution can be expected until these issues are solved.[8] Notwithstanding all the progress made by the logic of relations in finding alternatives to the classical type of analysis of relations and relative terms, the controversy over the internality or externality of relations only proves the degree to which the logic of relations remains tributary to the ontological and metaphysical assumptions that informed the first inquiries into the nature of relations by Plato and Aristotle.

If *Of Minimal Things* takes on the question of relation, the investigation is not framed by any preliminary decision concerning its ontological status. In spite of the title's allusion to the Scholastic theories of relation, relation will not be understood here as a (relative) thing, as a thing, more precisely, that is ontologically deficient compared to the existence attributed to substance. Nor is this study an investigation into entities that, because they are extramental rather than internal, enjoy at least the status of minuscule things. In what sense then do I speak here of "minimal things"? Rather than indicating a deficient mode of being or referring to things that barely have being, "minimal things" refers here, first, to the smallest, hence most elemental issues or matters of concern to philosophical thought. Relation, the title suggests, is one of the most (if not *the* most) extreme of philosophy's elemental topics. It is a minimal thing not because it is the least possible thing but because it constitutes the philosophical "thing" in the sense of issue and matter of concern at its most minute. Relation could thus be considered the most basic and simple of all philosophical problems. This is the sense in which Julius Jakob Schaaf has spoken of philosophy as intrinsically a science of relation (*Beziehungswissenschaft*). Taking up the Scholastic designation of relation as *ens minimum*, he explicitly emphasizes a positive moment contained in the expression, in addition to its characterization of relation as a deficient thing. This positive moment, he writes, "consists in this: the being of relation [*Beziehungsein*], precisely because it is an *ens minimum*, is not an object among objects, a thing among things, but reveals itself to be the trans-objective as such." Schaaf claims "to have found in the trans-objective nature of relation the starting point of philosophy," adding that "relation represents the absolutely decisive, indeed, sole category" of philosophy.[9] But it is neither only nor primarily in this sense of a founding category that I wish to understand the reference to minimal things. Indeed, by "minimal thing" I conceive of a thing more elemental than all the things that are of explicit philosophical concern, including its defining concepts.

Needless to say, compared to the "big" issues of philosophy, the question of relation already has all the appearances of a minor issue, or thing. Yet I conceive of relation not only as a thing anterior to the big topics of philosophical thought but also as a thing prior to the small things that philosophical thought has not found it necessary to privilege, even if these things can be shown to have a deciding philosophical importance. The notion of "thing" itself is such a small, or undervalued, theme, including the often deferred question of what a relation is. *Of Minimal Things* is thus not about relation as philosophy's founding category, nor about relation as the theme that defines it. In a way, it is not about relation at all. To put it differently, while this study tackles the question of relation and continuously refers to this problematic, *Of Minimal Things* also undercuts such reference. Indeed, its concern is with "something" that is more minimal than relation, with "something" from which even the thing "relation," however minimal and elementary it is in its intraphilosophical sense, derives its possibility and meaning. The seemingly minimal thing, and minor issue, to which the title draws attention is a, if not the, minimal "philosophical" problem: it is a limit-problem, an issue at the limit, to which all other questions of philosophy, large or small, are indebted and to which they must be traced and related back.

If, however, the essays of this book gesture toward a thing or things so minimal that even philosophy's minimal building blocks—that is, its prime categories, and above all the category of relation as possibly philosophy's "absolutely decisive, indeed, sole category"—have to be traced to it or them, these things cannot any longer be conceived as simple and indi-

visible elements *of* philosophy. Although I have emphasized up to this
point the elemental, or primitive, nature of the minimality of the things
in question in order to hold at bay the idea of a deficiency, diminishment,
or weakness of being, "minimal," according to its etymological and current usage, signifies a lowest, smallest, or least possible, allowable, or as-
signable amount of a quantity. Such a decrease in the being or quantity
of an entity is valued as a deficiency precisely because the least possible
marks a limit beyond which no quantity obtains anymore. Minimality
has thus the stigma of inferiority, incompleteness, and imperfection. But
minimality is not only the threshold where the diminished quantity hovers on the edge of complete annihilation; this terminal line is also the
point where the relations with a quantity's others—others that are not
simply other in the sense of opposites—manifest themselves. Minimal
things are not merely things at their barest, things at the verge of ceasing
to be things, but also things that are already something other than things.
Understood as minimal things, relations, therefore, not only hold toward
the nonrelational, whether in the sense of a deficiency of relation or in the
sense of the Absolute, but also imply a being-toward-something that is no
longer of the mode of what philosophy has always thought of as the relational. With the minimal things under discussion, a notion of relation is
envisioned that is not merely a type of relation more fundamental than
the decisive philosophical category of relation; because the notion of relation implies reference to the other or others of relation, it is also a notion of relation that no longer belongs entirely, simply, and absolutely to
philosophy. As a minimal thing, relation is reference to the others of philosophy: others that are not limited to its canonical others, such as literature, theology, or the natural sciences, and also, more disquietingly, others that are others in nonpredictable ways. The plural in *Of Minimal
Things* is irreducible. Qua minimal things, relations indeed refuse the
identity of the concept.

But what is a relation to begin with? Needless to say, the assessment
of the essence of relation differs depending on how it is understood. In
Plato and Aristotle, and throughout most of the philosophical tradition,
relation is understood primarily from the object—that is, as an objective
determination that the object possesses with respect to itself, or that is attached to it with respect to another thing. In the logic of relations, rela-

tion is conceived as a propositional function of two or more statements. Where relation is approached from the objects, a relation R can be defined as the connection between the objects x and y that obtains if the proposition "xRy," that is, "x has the connection R to y," is true. By contrast, where relation concerns logical propositions, the meaning of relation becomes a function of the classes of all the ordered pairs (or n-tuples) of objects that fulfill the expression of a relation "xRy." Yet, whereas it is generally agreed that the classical conception of relation does not satisfactorily account for the distinct ontological status of relation, the logical account of relation is not without difficulties of its own. Defining relation by way of the ordered n-tuples of individuals that can fulfill an expression of relation has, for instance, the effect of leveling the meaning of expressions of relations that can be fulfilled by the same pairs, or n-tuples, thus effectively effacing their singularity. In truth, these alternative approaches are not quite as different from each other as is often believed, because Aristotle's analysis of relations is not limited to relative terms but discusses expressions of relation as well, and because questions of ontology continue to haunt the logic of relation. Indeed, such insufficiencies have made a number of contemporary phenomenological thinkers wonder whether these theories are at all based on an adequately descriptive analysis of the phenomenon of relation. Martin Heidegger's thought in particular involves the question of whether the translation of *pros ti* as "relation" captures the original Greek sense of being-toward. "Relation," it can safely be said, is for Heidegger a subjectivist metaphysical reduction not only of the Greek understanding of being-toward, but also of the existential complexities of any comportment (*Verhalten*) and, for the later Heidegger, of the complexities of being-toward in the context of the thinking of Being.

Undoubtedly, being-toward-another—*pros ti* or *esse ad*—is the essential peculiarity of relation. But what does such being-toward-another entail? How does the thought of the other toward which the relation holds itself bear on the relation itself? Further, what are the *senses*—the directions and the ways in which it has to be taken—of such relating to something other? Is being-toward-another possible without a movement away from and ahead of the subject of the relation? Can relation be adequately thought without heeding the implication that its *relatum* lets the subject come toward it in the first place? If this is a necessity that is structurally implied in the very thought of relation, then is relation not primarily a response, a yes, to a prior invitation? More fundamentally still, does such possibilization of relation by the *relatum*, and the subject of the relation's acceptance and response to the invitation, not also suggest that relation is an occurrence, a happening, an event? Finally, what is the status of the subject from which the relation seems to originate, if relation is essentially a being-toward-something-other? And how does the nature of such an outgoing subject in turn affect the nature of relation?

For a relation to relate to something other than its subject implies being with respect to others, as the classical conception of relative terms acknowledges. What are the ramifications of this respect for the thinking of the subject of a relation? Conversely, how does the fact that the "object" of a relation is the "object" of a relation's direction toward it impact on the object itself? From early on, self-relation, or identity, has been recognized as an extreme case of relation in which its two terms coincide. At its most basic, identity has been determined as the relation that any object can and must have to itself in order for it to be what it is. Considering, however, that objects stand in relation to one another, at least some breach of their identity would seem to be required for them to be able to hold themselves, or be held, to some other thing. More importantly, does not self-identity as such include a demarcation from and, hence, a trait toward some other? Or ultimately, as in the case of the Ab-solute, or in the absence of any already constituted other, must not self-identity also include a demarcation from and a trait toward the empty place of another? If this is the case, no consideration of the notion of relation can abstract from the fact that the *relatum* to which another is held is by definition only *within* the place of the other. More precisely, in addition to being the other to which the subject relates, and independently of whether this other is the subject itself as in the relation of self-identity, the relation is not conceivable without heeding that space and place of the other—a place that can be occupied but that no host can ever saturate, and that is, by definition, a place awaiting another to come. But if the subject of a relation is dependent in this manner on the other, the subject is never at its place, either. In its place, too, there is "only" a subject to come. If, then, relation is essentially being-toward, and with respect to, something other, can relation have an essence of itself at all? Does the referring to another that constitutes relation affect relation itself, its own intelligible identity, especially if one takes into account that the other, even if it is the Ab-solute, only occupies the space of otherness? A relation, which is nothing but the trait of being-held-toward-another, is what it is only insofar as it points away from an identity of its own. The relational directedness toward something other than itself, which paradoxically provides a relation with its own identity, shows relation to the other to precede all identity. It is this further ramification tied in with the notion of relation—namely, the nonsymmetrical weighing of the other, and the place of the other, over all other moments of a relation—that no study of the issue can ignore.

But in a relation, not only does the subject tend toward the other with all the indicated implications for the subject, but also the *relatum* of the relation lets the subject come into a relation to it. There is no relation, then, without a prior opening of the possibility of the being-toward-another by which the subject is allowed to arrive "in" the place of the other. Without this gift of an opening for a subject to turn toward the other, no relation would ever be able to occur.[10] Three things, at least, follow from this. First, to rethink the notion of relation requires that one take into account the event of relation anterior to relation. Second, to rethink relation requires as well that the occurrence through which relation becomes possible no longer be understood in terms of relationality. Finally, to engage the opening event of relationality is not possible without at the same time reconceiving the traditional philosophical ways of thinking of possibilization.

The very concept of relationality carries with it a reference to the nonrelational. Philosophical reflection has taken account of this exigency: The skeptics acknowledged it by their negation in the name of the trope *par excellence*—that is, the principial (*genikotatos*) trope of relation—of what is said to be without relation, or *kath'auta*. Hegel did so by demonstrating that the Ab-solute is the highest form of relation in that it accomplishes relation to itself and thus relates relation to the nonrelational. Finally, more contemporary thinkers have heeded relationality's reference to the nonrelational by emphasizing the indivisible unity between that which is absolutely without relation (thus, isolated to the point of radically excluding any conceivable relation, including that of negation) and that which exists in relation.[11] Yet although any adequate approach to relation must take stock of this further complication, philosophy has so far addressed only the question of how the nonrelational bears on the problematic of relation, either by cutting off the relation from the nonrelational for the benefit of one term of the relation, or by seeking to do justice to the reference in question by conceiving of it as a dialectical opposition. If, as I here contend, the thinking of relation must include this relation to the without-relation, then the determination of the latter in terms of opposition can be considered only as one conception of the nonrelational, and a limited conception at that. Instead, it would seem necessary to think of this inexorable correlative of relation in terms altogether other than the relational.

Visibly, relation has with respect to substance, and its unity, a multiplying power. It secures the difference of things, their singularity. Indeed, the being-toward-other-things is an expression of things' finitude. What I have offered so far about the implications necessarily involved with the notion of relation shows that its meaning too is multifaceted. Each one of its determinations turns up further and further implications. But these ramifications and inferences do not suggest an infinite progress, and endless sequence of additional facets that consume the efforts of reflection to take them into account. For, indeed, the very fact that being-toward-another presupposes a place of the other, a place that can be occupied by the opposite, or other, of the subject (entity or self) but which is not saturated, fulfilled, or exhausted by this occupation; the fact that the identity of the subject of a relation comes to the subject only from the *relatum* and, hence, is always in waiting; and the fact that, finally, all relation involves a relation to a nonrelational that is something other than a negative modification of relationality—these very facts narrow the proliferation of the multiple implications of and cross-references to what I would like to call a "'simple' complex." As a minimal thing, relation compounds with the places that no subject, no *relatum*, and no opposite of relation can ever saturate. Yet this impossibility grants relation its logic and its status without status as a minimal thing. However, a minimal thing of such "simple" complexity is not a first thing. It certainly is not the first thing, and exclusive property, of philosophy. Rather, it is a threshold that communicates between entities, or domains, that are all in the position of others among each other. Although it is the result of a reflection on the philosophical notion of relation, the minimal thing in question does not situate philosophy with respect to *its* others. Philosophy is but one of the possible others—together with literature, theology, and the sciences, to name only a few—that the "'simple' complex" of this minimal thing ties together each time in a singular configuration.

The essays reunited in this book elaborate upon the notion of relation with a view to establishing the basic traits that make up relation as a minimal thing. Since this undertaking takes seriously the fact that relation is a being-toward-another (entity, domain, or human other), the effort implies a prior dissolution or dismantling of relation as a formal concept and of the ontology, or ontologies, under which the philosophical (formal) concept of relation has been subordinated. The first item on the agenda of a rethinking of relation is thus to free relation as *pros ti* from the *pros hen* relation, the relation to the One, and to restore the specificity and singularity of relations. As a consequence, I will approach relation in many of its shapes, shapes that, rather than being modalities of one base concept of relation, are irreducible, even though they imply and gesture in the direction of one another. Encounter, arrival, address, contact, touch, belonging, distance, accord, agreement, determination, measuring, translation, and communication are some such forms of relation. From this antiformalist, or rather aformalist, approach to relation, attention is thus given to the different ways in which being-toward-another is structured. Caesura, rhythm, and zigzag are among the types of relating that will be considered. But such consideration of relations in what is irreducibly singular about them is significant only if the ground for the diversity of relations, and their singularity, can be furnished by way of an analysis of the traits that constitute the being-toward of relation. Without such an account, all restoration of relation to its aformal intricacy remains an exercise in empiricism, that is, in an approach that is only the negative of the exigency to relate (everything) to the One. Rethinking relationality cannot consist simply in turning one's back to that demand. Rather than submitting to this demand for unification into the One, the rethinking of relation in question transforms this demand by tying into knots the cluster of traits involved in relations—that is, traits directed toward, and

stretching from, the place of the other to the place of the subject of a relation, according to a relation that combines with modes of comportment
that are no longer conceivable in terms of relation or nonrelation. These
knots qua knots hold the traits together and thus provide reasons, accounts, explications, as it were, but at the same time let themselves be undone again. These inevitably plural knots are none other than the minimal things that I have alluded to.

Given that the essays collected in this volume have been written
over a span of more than twenty years, the reader should not be surprised
to find that, although relation is their common theme, they reflect on this
issue in contexts, from perspectives, and according to styles and modes of
approach that are quite different. The earliest essays, the two contribu-
tions on Friedrich Nietzsche particularly, take up the problematic of relation with respect to questions pertaining to the self, the body, and the
name as figures of propriety (*das Eigentliche*), and with the aim of conceiving of a way of relating to the self that escapes the Hegelian dialectics
of self and other. By contrast, the essays on translatability, communicability, and reproducibility in the work of Walter Benjamin, written in
critical debate with current trends in interpreting Benjamin, elaborate on
this thinker's plight of sketching out a way of relating to the Absolute,
that is, to that which by definition precludes all relation. It is a way of relating, as we shall see, that cuts apart the ties by which concepts and the
fabric of language have sought to trap the Absolute. Most of the essays on
Heidegger discuss his attempt to foreground logical relation (and determination) and the classical conception of truth as adequation in the fundamental structures of Dasein's comportment to the world, to others, and
to itself. But these essays also follow Heidegger through some of his later
efforts to recast the concept of relationality itself, especially in light of the
other to whom (or to which) relation is said to be directed, and from
which the "subject" receives the possibility of response as a gift. How
thinkers (Edmund Husserl, Martin Heidegger, and Jacques Derrida are
the examples) relate to one another is a further angle from which I broach
the question. Finally, in the last chapters of this book, which touches on
the writings of Stéphane Mallarmé, Franz Kafka, and Maurice Blanchot,
I take issue with the relation of literature and philosophy, more precisely,
with relation as conceptual discourse and relation as fiction. The investi-

gation centers on the implications that the relation of philosophy to literature, as one of philosophy's others, has for the reworking of the concept of relationality as such.[12]

Coming into an appropriate relationship to what is to be thought, a relationship that attends to the things in question and that distinguishes thinking from all approaches that conform to pregiven programs or established methods, is not merely a function of one's mind-set or good will. Nor does sustained work and what is commonly referred to as experience suffice to secure a relation to what is in question. Indeed, if relation as we have sought to conceive of it through these essays is granted primarily by the other, it is not something that be can calculated, predicted, or secured. To come into a relation is, therefore, also a matter of chance, of luck, as it were. The essays reunited in this volume are my attempts to come into a fruitful and, especially, faithful relation to what that notion gives us to think. Only others, however, are in the position to decide whether my pursuit has succeeded.

PART I

UNTIMELY RELATIONS

1

Ecce Homo, or The Written Body

I

Of the body—the body proper—we can speak only improperly. So it will be necessary not only to talk about it in metaphors, but also to develop the discourse *of* the body, by a process of substitution, as a chain of figures in which the figure of the body itself will represent only one figure among others. Wishing to speak of the body, we can therefore speak only of quite other things, to the point where we might ask ourselves if the body does not consist precisely in those other things, in that grouping of initially heterogeneous elements. In which case the body would be dependent on a certain confusion, because it is always more or less than a body properly speaking.

This is what emerges from a text such as Nietzsche's *Ecce Homo*, an autobiographical text (but one whose deviation from the genre should be noted), a text that also functions as a self-constituting corpus, thus as a text in which the constitution of a body (*corps*) is gradually worked out, of Nietzsche's body, or more precisely of a body in which Nietzsche's name ("Nietzsche") forms an essential trait in as much as it is—momentarily—the unitary trait, if not the unifying trait, or *trait d'union* ("hyphen"). In *Ecce Homo*, indeed, the body, or rather one body, becomes readable through a chain of metaphors that are seemingly as foreign to one another as are, for instance, the book entitled *Daybreak*, a sea animal, the sun, the self, and the name of Nietzsche. How can a body, a unified body, be constituted from the starting point of these metaphors, such diverse metaphors? If each metaphor is an image of the body, it is, at the same time, only one of its traits, so that assembling these traits constitutes the body in question. It is in fact the Aristotelian question: what makes man "one" (*hen*)?—a unity on which the very name of man is founded (the denomination: man),[1] a question that should be introduced here in order to examine the principle that justifies the term "body" for the set of metaphors in question. Certainly they are not the result of that contradiction through which, as Gaston Bachelard says in *The Psychoanalysis of Fire*, "we most easily achieve originality." He goes on to say, "When it is directed towards objective knowledge, this need for originality *over-estimates* the importance of the phenomenon, *materializes* slight differences, ascribes *causes* to accidents, just in the same way in which the novelist imagines a hero endowed with an unlikely number of special qualities and portrays a willful character through a series of inconsistent actions."[2]

But although these metaphors, in Nietzsche, do not attest to contradiction, nonetheless his text exhibits clear pretensions to originality, and that these are embodied in the metaphoric chain of which we are speaking. Now, since the self of the signatory who seems to unify, to gather together the chain of metaphors (for a moment, at least), is taken up and reabsorbed by the chain itself, the question of the unifying principle is raised over and over again. The impossibility of enclosing or of closing up the question once and for all represents perhaps the major reason why we cannot talk properly about the body proper. If the organizing principle of the metaphors for the body is abolished (or is represented) in the very chain that it is supposed to totalize, then the need to keep going back to a new unifying trait opens up the discourse *of* the body to the infinite importation of metaphors that are always foreign, always improper. The impossibility of preventing the unifying trait from tumbling into the series that is to be unified bears witness to disequilibrium as an essential mark of the body, a mark whose first effect is the body's impropriety. This amounts to saying that the body does not properly belong to anyone.

The body is thus characterized by this tendency to disintegrate into heterogeneous images that, when assembled coherently, formed for a moment a unified representation. The improper side of the body, its impropriety, also entails a temporal aspect peculiar to the body, that is to say its nature as event, its "momentaneity." The body only exists for an instant—before it is again split up into its singular representations. This will have at least two consequences for Nietzsche: on the one hand the will to repetition of the divine moment in which a body was born (which thus refers back to the intimate relationship between the body and the Eternal Recurrence), and on the other hand the fixing of the moment, and of property, at the risk of seeing them turned to stone as memories, or again, as we shall see, as a handful of diamonds. In this way the body, which only really exists *in statu nascendi*, discovers the side of itself that is death.

From then on, *more than one* register will govern the thinking of the body. Let us begin then by unfolding the metaphoric chain in which, as we were just claiming, the body is caught. Emphasizing in *Ecce Homo* the affirmative character of his book *Daybreak*, Nietzsche writes as follows:

The whole book contains no negative word, no attack, no spite—it lies in the sun, round, happy, like some sea animal basking among rocks.

Ultimately, I myself was this sea animal: almost every sentence in this book was first thought, *caught* among that jumble of rocks near Genoa where I was alone and still had secrets with the sea. Even now, whenever I accidentally touch this book, almost every sentence turns for me into a net [*wird mir . . . fast jeder Satz zum Zipfel*] that again brings up from the depths something incomparable: its entire skin trembles with tender thrills of memory. The art that distinguishes it is not inconsiderable when it comes to fixing to some extent things that easily flit by, noiselessly—moments I call divine lizards—but not with the cruelty of that young Greek god who simply speared the poor little lizard, though, to be sure, with something pointed—a pen.[3]

Without claiming to exhaust this passage, let us stress a few points: these three things—the book (*Daybreak*), the sea animal, and Nietzsche—may be substituted for one another. What may be said of one is equally true of the others. The same thing is to be found under the skin of the book as in the bodies of the sea animal and of Nietzsche. The book, in fact, contains sentences like "ends" or "tails" (*Zipfel*), which allow you to bring some memory up from the depths. The book thus seems like a collection of ends or tails. Now this is equally true of the body of the sea animal and of Nietzsche himself, basking among the rocks, sharing secrets with the sea. Nietzsche tells us that this book is distinguished by its art of fixing things that easily flit by, that is the moments, the instants he calls "divine lizards." But lizards cannot be caught. You can barely get hold of them; they escape almost immediately, leaving their tails in your hand. The sea animal and the book, like Nietzsche's body, are thus nothing more than a set of broken tails, of lost tails, of dead tails. Like that other body that is largely made up of a tangle of snakes, the medusa (a jellyfish). In this way the lizards represent "divine moments" flitting by noiselessly; after they have gone, all that remains is an end, a tail left in your hand, which allows you to re-create them in memory. In order to fix them, to stop them, to catch hold of them, of their moment of presence, you must know how to use an instrument that, like the blade of a knife, cuts the vanishing moment from its full presence, leaving only, to use a term from Rousseau, "commemorative signs."[4] Of course, the instrument is not the spear of that young Greek god, in whom we recognize the Apollo Sauroktoros of Praxiteles,[5] but an instrument no less steely, that is, the point of a pen. The bodies of the book, the sea animal, and Nietzsche are thus constituted by work, by an operation of the pen that consists in fixing divine moments, of gathering together under a quivering skin a set of sentences, or tails, or phalluses, which are only ever commemorative signs of the lost actuality of that presence of a whole body. Nevertheless, in spite of, or rather because of, the cut-off, dead, and petrified nature of these instants that make up the body, this is a body that "lies in the sun, round, happy, like some sea animal basking among rocks." Paradoxically, it is that operation of the pen, fixing a set of moments by depriving them of their full momentariness, which results in the body as such: a happy pile of dead moments. And what was said of each individual sentence, that it is presented as a lizard's cut-off tail, is valid for the book, for the corpus of aphorisms, for the whole body. For Nietzsche's body itself is no more than a petrified divine instant, formed, like the book, of phrases carved in granite. It is itself no more than the product of the action of a steely point that fixes that body in its momentary nature. So it is not surprising that the body only appears as one metaphor among others, caught in the chain *book, sea animal, sun,* and so on. The body, like the book, is the effect of the pen: it is a fixed moment. But what does "fixed" mean? To what extent is fixing a property of the body? Where it appears as petrification, does it merge with the very momentariness of the body? This is what we must try to elucidate by moving to another level.

Speaking of *another of his works*, Nietzsche writes, "*Human, All Too Human* is the monument of a crisis" (p. 283). And again, "*Human, All Too Human*, this monument [*Denkmal*] of rigorous self discipline with which I put a sudden end to all my infections . . . " (p. 288).

A monument then, insofar as *Human, All Too Human* is an event marking a close, an end. Now, a sudden beginning may equally give rise to monuments. This is the case with *Zarathustra*, a monument that, Nietzsche tells us, occupies a place apart among his works ("Among my writings my *Zarathustra* stands to my mind by itself," p. 219). *Zarathustra*, indeed, put apart in this way from the rest of Nietzsche's works, is the monument erected in honor of that divine moment when Nietzsche was first struck by the idea of the Eternal Recurrence. The place where the revelation occurred was, according to Nietzsche, "a powerful pyramidal rock not far from Surlei" (p. 295). This rock itself represents the idea of the Eternal Recurrence inasmuch as, by its resistance to the elements, to the work of time, and to decomposition, it recurs ceaselessly as a new instant, as an original beginning. So the idea of recurrence appeared to Nietzsche like a petrified rock, the Eternal Recurrence being, in addition, nothing more than a pyramidal block resisting time. This contrasts, however, with what Nietzsche reports in *Ecce Homo* concerning the months preceding the encounter with the rock at Surlei: "If I reckon back a few months from this day, I find as an omen a sudden and profoundly decisive change in my taste, especially in music. Perhaps the whole of *Zarathustra* may be reckoned as music; certainly a rebirth of the art of *hearing* was among its preconditions" (p. 295). So a radical change in his appreciation of music precedes the event at Surlei, and also the erecting of *Zarathustra* as a monument. The rock, the pyramidal block in itself, does not utter a sound; it is voiceless. Consequently, if the whole of *Zarathustra* may be reckoned as music, it is something like a symphony of rocks (silent in themselves), a symphony that would make the stones dance as petrified divine moments. Notwithstanding the fact that stone is already an affirmation against time (as decadence), already a petrified formula for the affirmation of that instance in which the temporality proper to the Eternal Recurrence erupted into the temporal continuum, it must still be reconstructed into a symphony that, once again, liberates the incidental idea of the Eternal Recurrence from its stony straitjacket. The music in question is pyramidal music, for it is important that the petrified product of the incidental moment is not just any rock but a shaped block, like the pyramidal block at Surlei. This is perhaps even clearer in the following passages from *Ecce Homo*. The first refers to *The Gay Science*: "What is here called 'highest hope'—who could have any doubt about that when he sees the diamond beauty of the first words of *Zarathustra* flashing at the end of the fourth book?" (p. 293). And, in the chapter "Why I Am So Wise," explicitly with regard to *Zarathustra*: "Those who have eyes for colors will compare it to a diamond" (p. 234). A diamond, the hardest of stones and literally invincible, is a cut stone. Nietzsche represents Zarathustra, or the idea of the Eternal Recurrence that strikes him at Surlei, as durable stone, finely cut, resistant to the vicissitudes of time. The diamond that is *Zarathustra* will repeat for all eternity what happened to Nietzsche at the site of that other indestructible stone, the pyramidal block not far from Surlei. Petrified signs of divine moments.

Further support for this interpretation comes from what Nietzsche says about the nature of his words, in particular at the end of the third book of *The Gay Science*. It is here that the relationship between the originary moment and the petrification of that moment becomes clear: "Or when at the end of the third book he reads the granite words in which a destiny finds for the first time a formula for itself, for *all* time?" (p. 293). Granite words then, phrases formed out of hard crystalline material corresponding to the formulation of a destiny that is articulated for the first time *and* for all eternity! The event, the "incidental" moment, is so fleeting that it must be hewn in durable material suitable to its divine nature in order to hold it, to fix it. Only in this way will the instant appear as what resists the time of decadence. The instant when continuous time is suddenly, sharply broken by a time foreign to that temporality must be slipped into a durable atemporal material so that the instant may repeat itself, becoming eternal outside time as the recurrence of that divine moment.[6] What appears in *Ecce Homo* as a topography is the philosophical landscape, marked by the eruption of the eternal, of the untimely (*Un-*

Zeit), into historical time; as a landscape of monuments it is a landscape of "fragments of the future."

It is clear that the petrified moment also disguises the specific nature of the moment, which is the "incision" of a divine time into continuous time. The moment is indeed caught in stone, and petrifaction cannot be the true destiny of the moment. In comparison with the essence of the divine moment, the stone in which that moment is embodied is no more than, as Nietzsche says, the "ugliest stone" (p. 309). So it will need a divine artist, a sun god, Apollo in fact, the sculptor god, to intervene and cut the stone to match the divine nature of what it contains. To cite aphorism 541 of *Daybreak*, "*How one ought to turn to stone*—slowly, slowly to become hard like a precious stone—and at last to lie there, silent and a joy to eternity." Otherwise it would be necessary to release the divine moment from the stony straitjacket in which it is imprisoned. This is what Zarathustra says: "o men, in the stone an image is sleeping, the image of images! Alas, that it has to sleep in the hardest, ugliest stone! *Now my hammer rages cruelly against its prison*" (p. 309). The hammer strives to set free that image of images, the divine moment, from its prison, first by shaping the stone to match what it disguises, second by attempting to extricate the moment from the stone itself, so that the latter may recover its original nature. By wielding this hammer Nietzsche succeeded, at least once, in making the stone dance. Relating in *Ecce Homo* how he played with the instrument "man," Nietzsche writes as follows:

How often have I been told by the "instruments" themselves that they had never heard themselves like that.—Most beautifully perhaps by Heinrich von Stein,[7] who died so unpardonably young. Once, after he had courteously requested permission, he appeared for three days in Sils Maria, explaining to everybody that he had *not* come to see the Engadine. This excellent human being, who had walked into the Wagnerian morass with all the impetuous simplicity of a Prussian Junker . . . acted during these three days like one transformed by a tempest of freedom, like one who had suddenly been lifted to his own height and acquired wings. (p. 227)

The body represents a petrified divine instant, fixed by a quill or cut in stone by the artist's instrument. The body merges with the divine moment; it is but the other side of it. In Nietzsche, it is the type, the *Typus*, that corresponds to a life, to a *fatum*, to a body, which, as the Eternal Recurrence cuts into it, is transmuted into stone so that it might last beyond the vicissitudes of temporal decadence. The Greek *typos*, meaning image, image of images, model, and so on, comes from the term *typtein*, which means, among other things, to cut. The type is then indeed the cut stone,[8] a stone that encloses the image of images and whose form matches that image: a precious stone, then. *Ecce Homo* is nothing other than the attempt to constitute a body for oneself by writing oneself in granite words, by fixing the divine instants of a life, sparkling, like precious stones; it is nothing other than the effort to erect oneself as a monument by fixing oneself with the steely point of a pen. For Nietzsche himself, Nietzsche as body, is nothing other than an event, an instant in which an untimeliness outside time erupted into the time of decadence, and in which, in order to last, it had to turn to stone. This applies equally to *Ecce Homo*, in which Nietzsche's written body will form an instant, a supplementary monument in the topography that makes up the book and in which is inscribed the divine moment when the idea of the Eternal Recurrence erupted in Nietzsche's body. And so, in the last analysis, Nietzsche, his body, will have been no more and no less than an articulation of the idea that he conceived—the Eternal Recurrence itself.

II

In order to think the type-body, the cut or written body, the printed body, we shall turn our attention to another metaphorical network in *Ecce Homo*. Let us begin, for example, by taking a look at what Nietzsche says to us when he is at his lowest ebb physically, in the declining years of his life. That moment coincides with a general exhaustion (*Gesamterschöpfung*), which explains the deterioration of all his organs. That exhaustion, in fact, should be understood as a weakening of the self as totality or whole. The general exhaustion is the sign of a loss of self as totality. Now, this morbid state, one of extreme weakness, a state that also corresponds to an aberration of the instincts, is, according to Nietzsche, a preparation for a refining of the organs, inasmuch as the illness is at once the culmination of decadence and an interruption of that decadence. It is then that Nietzsche acquires "that filigree art," that skill in *grasping* both properly and figuratively, that touch for *nuances*, which, in the end, will permit him to take himself in hand and make himself healthy again. "I took myself in hand, I made myself healthy again: the condition for this—every physiologist would admit that—is *that one be healthy at bottom [dass man im Grunde gesund ist]*" (p. 224). With those fingers and that filigree art Nietzsche will reassemble the exhausted organs, organizing them into a new totality that corresponds to being healthy at bottom, in other words to what Nietzsche calls "the nethermost self" (*das unterste Selbst*), and that coincides (as we will see in the following chapter) with the name, or the type, of Zarathustra.

But that reorganization, that reassembling of the parts of the body, merges with an arithmetical operation. So we shall turn our attention briefly to that mathematical level. Nietzsche in fact *calculates* his "self," that on which the totality of his body is founded. From the outset, Nietzsche posits himself as being a totality *at bottom*, that is to say, at bottom a totality; and taking away the fact that he is a decadent, he gets to the opposite of decadence, that is to say, health. "Apart from the fact [*Abgerechnet*] that I am a decadent, I am also the opposite" (p. 224). It is already no longer Nietzsche's totality that suffers from a general exhaustion, for by means of this little operation of subtraction, Nietzsche has already got himself back in hand. He writes, "As *summa summarum* ['overall'] I was healthy" (p. 224). This is understandable, inasmuch as *summa summarum* means *apart* from decadence, but also and equally means *despite* decadence—in that health, at bottom, allows making use of decadence, transforming it into a means for health.

Let us briefly outline the calculation of the *summa summarum*. The first condition of the reconstitution of its totality is complete isolation. In complete independence the subject is able to guess what is good for him, *sich zu erraten*, and to thrive, *wohl zu geraten*. This thriving, indeed, this *Wohlgeratenheit*, becomes the necessary condition for performing the calculation in question. Nietzsche tells us about the person who is thriving:

He has a taste only for what is good for him; his pleasure, his delight cease where the measure of what is good for him is transgressed. He guesses what remedies avail against what is harmful; he exploits bad accidents to his advantage; what does not kill him makes him stronger. Instinctively, he collects from everything he sees, hears, lives through, *his* sum [*seine Summe*]: he is a principle of selection, he discards much. (p. 224)

Now a sum (*une somme*), the arithmetical product of an addition, is also (in French) the title of certain books that make a general summary of the various parts of an area of knowledge. The body as sum(mary) is also a book that constitutes this abridged body. Thus the book-body belongs to what Nietzsche elaborates under the heading of a language of signs (a semiotics). However, for the moment let us simply keep in mind that the sum of the body is the result of a selection, of an elimination (subtraction) of many things. The only things selected to go into the sum(ma) are of the sort that can be summarized in one's own sum. This occurs on condition of including in the sum(ma) only things that are marked "personal." "He is always in his own company, whether he associates with books, human beings, or landscapes: he honors by *choosing*, by *admitting*, by *trusting*" (pp. 224–25). The sum of the body is completed with a set of quite heterogeneous elements. The body is everything at once—books, men, landscapes—but homogenized by the intermediary of the index *me* or *mine*. These pronouns or possessive adjectives make a dividing line between a good and a bad proximity to things. For inasmuch as the calculation of his own sum is, according to Nietzsche, the same as a spiritual gestation, "any kind of stimulus from the outside has too violent an effect and strikes too deep." In order to keep to one side everything that could turn us aside from our task, from our giving birth to ourselves as our own type, Nietzsche appeals to Russian fatalism, which consists in slowing down all our reactions as much as possible, to the point of not reacting at all. This is how we withdraw from the continuum of time: slowly hardening until we become a precious stone, until we give birth to our body as something completely *mine*, which belongs to no one, to be exact not even to me, which is the body of our most buried *self*—such as, for instance, Zarathustra. But in the enumeration of the elements that are part of the sum(ma) of the body, we must also gather in what seems initially to belong rather to the surroundings favorable for becoming oneself, that is to say, the choice of climate, diet, and recreation. Now, with regard to diet, for example, it soon becomes clear that it can be reckoned healthy when the food is easy to digest, when it is not foreign to *me*, when on that account it can be classified as *mine*. One should note here that food that is mine can be digested quickly, so that the body, the body of the *self*, proves, in Nietzsche, to be a metabolism that recycles itself at great speed.

This body is constituted not by assimilating what is *mine* in order to store it up, but in such a way that, by the rapid rejection of what has been incorporated, it is no more than a movement of assimilation *and* expulsion. Nothing more. Only on that condition will it be granted "mobile feet." The relationship between elements classified as *mine* and the body as a rapid metabolism becomes clear during the discussion, in *Ecce Homo*, of the question of favorable place and climate. "The influence of climate on our *metabolism*, its retardation, its acceleration, goes so far that a mistaken choice of place and climate can not only estrange a man from his task but can actually keep it from him: he never gets to see it" (p. 240). It also follows that this body, characterized by its need for a rapid metabolism, is not sedentary but moves about at an accelerated tempo in an appropriate topography. Thus: "*Sit* as little as possible; give no credence to any thought that was not born outdoors while one moved about freely— in which the muscles are not celebrating a feast, too. All prejudices come from the intestines. The sedentary life—as I have said once before—is the real *sin* against the holy spirit" (pp. 239–40).

But before suggesting that these various aspects (choice of food, place, and climate) are not simply the conditions of possibility of a body with a rapid metabolism, nor simply the determining factors of the *tempo* of the metabolism, but also metaphors serving to describe, by means of certain traits peculiar to each of the various instances, the body (and, to be more exact, the spirit) itself, we shall pause for a moment on another metaphor, that of the body as *instrument*.

Now that the effects of climate and weather are familiar to me from long experience and I take readings from myself as from a very subtle and reliable instrument . . . I reflect with horror on the *dismal* fact that my life, except for the last ten years, the years when my life was in peril, was spent entirely in the wrong places that were nothing short of *forbidden* to me. (p. 241)

The body is played, like an instrument, by the effects of climate, weather, and place: they determine its *tempo*. That instrument is, however, also a book asking to be read. That is what allows us to go on to what Nietzsche says about his choice of amusements. "In my case, every kind of reading belongs among my recreations—hence among the things that liberate me from myself, that allow me to walk about in strange sciences and souls—that I no longer take seriously" (p. 242). Why are books a form of recreation for Nietzsche; why does he not take them seriously? Because Nietzsche is himself his own book, because his writing is the writing of his body. The first reader of the book-body, of the type-body, Nietzsche cannot take an interest except in books that he already considers *his*. "Otherwise I almost always seek refuge with the same books—actually, a small number—books *proved to me*" (p. 243). These books that are already proved to him are books *always already* signed by Nietzsche— more precisely, the names of the authors are all pseudonyms for Nietzsche. As much by what they demonstrate as by the names of their authors, these books are already a part of the text of the written body. These books do not slow down the accelerated metabolism of the written body. On the contrary, this body will easily assimilate and dispose of them, retaining the one fact that the books are not foreign to it but are always already itself.

Consequently, to calculate his sum also means to have space for everything in his body. "Nothing in existence may be subtracted, nothing is dispensable" (p. 272). But everything that enters this body must be marked with the index *mine*. Even the contradictory and the opposite will enter into the composition of this body provided that they are *my opposites, my contradictions*. So this writing-body, book-body, or type-body bears witness to a Dionysiac affirmation insofar as it is the field where opposing forces do battle. In other words, it is a work of art. We suggested that climate and place, diet, and so on, are not only the conditions of the body's elaboration but equally a part of it. They are a part of it inasmuch as they are metaphors. Take for instance the passage in *Zarathustra* that is cited at the end of the chapter "Why I Am So Wise": "Gone is the hesitant gloom of my spring! Gone the snowflakes of my malice in June. Summer have I become entirely, and summer noon" (p. 234). These seasons are in fact metaphors for seasons. They are seasons that have become *mine* (and are, for that reason, marked with a possessive adjective or pronoun). It is they that make up, one might say, the matter of the body, insofar as this body—a rapid metabolism—stores them only in order to expend them, borrowing from them the movement that, as metaphor for the changing seasons, becomes the circulation of metaphors of (in) the body. The writing-body, then, is a metaphorical metabolism, the metaphorical set of transformations that take place within an organism *and* the set of metaphorical transformations that constitute a body.

III

One cannot help noticing that Nietzsche describes himself as distinguished by traits (*Züge*), as being *ausgezeichnet*, as being remarkably *marked*. In "Why I Am So Wise" Nietzsche enumerates some of his traits. Here he states the last of them: "May I still venture to sketch one final trait of my nature that causes me no little difficulties in my contacts with other men? My instinct for cleanliness is characterized by a perfectly uncanny sensitivity" (p. 233). This final trait, which concerns cleanliness (*propreté*), is a trait that is Nietzsche's very own (*propre*). The cleanliness in question further implies that the traits distinguishing Nietzsche's body are proper traits, and that this is quite different from other men's bodies, which are constituted by improper traits (traits both improper and unsuitable). One could even say that the difference between Nietzsche's body and that of his contemporaries is that Nietzsche's is a body made up of proper traits or of signs, as we shall see. This body excludes any pathological trait: "There is no pathological trait in me; even in periods of severe sickness I never became pathological; in vain would one seek for a trait of fanaticism in my character" (p. 257). In the same way, he excludes all "traces of struggle," "any trace of tension," and so on (p. 258). That leads us, in accordance moreover with the sign of propriety, to make a distinction between two kinds of traits: "signs of healthy instincts" (*Zeichen gesunder Instinkte*) on the one hand and those of decadent instincts on the other. The healthy instincts characterizing Nietzsche testify that his body has a different origin. Difference is inscribed in a comparison with men honored as the *first*, whom Nietzsche considers as non-men: "When I now compare myself with the men who have so far been honored as the *first*, the difference is palpable" (pp. 256–57). A privilege, a *Vorrecht*, is associated with this other origin of Nietzsche's body, the privilege of having the supreme finesse necessary to discern all the indications of healthy instincts. Nietzsche is distinguished, then, by signs, by indices of healthy instincts: their traits characterize him as a body of signs (*ausgezeichnet*). In this capacity he possesses "a subtler sense of smell . . . than any other human being before me" for the signs of the ascent and decline of instincts. But what is the relation in fact between a body of signs and the subtle sense in question? Nietzsche writes as follows:

My instinct for cleanliness is characterized by a perfectly uncanny sensitivity so that the proximity or—what am I saying?—the inmost parts, the "entrails" of every soul are physiologically perceived by me—*smelled*. This sensitivity furnishes me with psychological antennae with which I feel and get a hold of every secret: the abundant *hidden* dirt at the bottom of many a character—perhaps the result of bad blood, but glossed over by education—enters my consciousness almost at the first contact. If my observation has not deceived me, such characters who offend my sense of cleanliness also sense from their side the reserve of my disgust—and this does not make them smell any better. (p. 233)

One can already recognize here a first difference between the two systems of signs: the healthy signs are those of a clean (*propre*) and transparent body, while the signs of bad instincts bear witness to the abundant dirt hidden at the bottom of these bodies. That dirt seems to stand in opposition to the nature of the sign itself; in that it is an obstacle to the transparent clarity, the weightlessness, of the sign, that body will not yet have become a body of signs, in fact, a body at all. Or again, as long as there is still something at the bottom (dirt, in that it is hidden), the body will not be a true body of signs. The bottom is the result of a process of sedimentation, of things that have not yet become light and transparent. Nietzsche, for his part, lays claim to a perfect transparency, and his body moves in a limpid, diaphanous element: "As has always been my wont—extreme cleanliness in relation to me is the presupposition of my existence; I perish under unclean conditions—I constantly swim and bathe and splash, as it were, in water—in some perfectly transparent and resplendent element" (p. 233). This holds equally true for mountain air: air, like water, is a clear element in which a body of signs can move about. Here there is no longer occasion to speak about a sedimented bottom; everything is transparency and weightlessness.

In addition to this subtle sense for dirt-encrusted depths, he has a sense for healthy instincts. This second sense is associated with an operation of distinction or respect, or *Auszeichnung*: "To this day I still have the same affability for everyone; I even treat with special respect [*ich bin selbst voller Auszeichnung*] those who are lowliest: in all of this there is not one grain of arrogance or secret contempt. If I despise a man, he *guesses* that I despise him: by my mere existence I outrage everything that has bad blood in its veins" (p. 258). It remains to analyze the interrelationships between these healthy signs, indeed to draw the map of the signed body. In view of our development concerning the body's gathering in of all around it, we can now have an idea of the contradictory aspect of the traits that make up its texture. They are opposed one to another. The opposing traits are organized hierarchically. In a passage that would require a lengthy commentary, Nietzsche suggests that "the organizing 'idea' that is destined to rule . . . one by one, . . . trains all *subservient* capacities before giving any hint of the dominant task, 'goal,' 'aim,' or 'meaning'" (p. 254). First of all let us note the relationship between the trait and the whole: the trait is subservient, in the service of the whole. This trait is developed in a certain order, and in such a way as to engender the whole. Here already one notices a certain order of rank among the traits. But this comes out more clearly in what follows:

For the task of a *revaluation of all values* more capacities may have been needed than have ever dwelt together in a single individual—above all, even contrary capacities that had to be kept from disturbing, destroying one another. An order of rank among these capacities; distance; the art of separating without setting against one another; to mix nothing, to "reconcile" nothing; a tremendous variety that is nevertheless the opposite of chaos—this was the precondition, the long, secret work and artistry of my instinct. (p. 254)

This order of rank among opposite terms keeps them at a distance one from another. Each new trait that becomes part of the composition of the body of signs contributes to spacing that body out (and making it lighter). Distance, as the condition of possibility of the hierarchy, prevents the body from returning to chaos. Spacing, the preventing of chaos in this body of signs, is all the more urgent in that a vast sum of traits is needed to give form to the *type* corresponding to the revaluation of values. By inscribing a set of contradictory traits in the body, organizing them so that they form a new hierarchy that literally excludes nothing, the type-body already represents on the level of the body a first reevaluation of values. The incorporation of so many traits within the type-body in fact transgresses the model of the individual hitherto prevailing, in such a way that the written body is a transgression of the volume of what it is customary to call a subject. Spacing by distance between the traits of the writing-body, of the type-body, paradoxically characterizes this body as plenitude (*Überfülle*).

There is a certain category of elements of the signed body which we have not yet mentioned. If Nietzsche, in *Ecce Homo*, can write, "Plato employed Socrates . . . as a sign language [*Semiotik*] for Plato" (p. 280), we might suspect that names can function as traits, as signs *par excellence* for the written body. Before establishing this proposition, let us first analyze how Nietzsche, in *Ecce Homo*, deals with names in general:

Philosophy, as I have so far understood and lived it, means living voluntarily among ice and high mountains—seeking out everything strange and questionable in existence, everything so far placed under a ban by morality. Long experience, acquired in the course of such wanderings *in what is forbidden*, taught me to regard the causes that so far have prompted moralizing and idealizing in a very different light from what may seem desirable: the *hidden* history of the philosophers, the psychology of the great names, came to light for me. (p. 218)

Philosophy, for Nietzsche, is bound up with the names of philosophers; philosophy, for Nietzsche, is a history of names. He can be observed to be more concerned with philosophers, with their names (their types), than with their teaching.[9] For Nietzsche, philosophers' names already contain in some way their entire philosophy. These names evince a force, a power that is not to be underestimated. One name can repress another, one name can hide another, so that Nietzsche has to take more than one name into his protection, more than one name being threatened by a greater one: "My artist's taste vindicates the names of Molière, Corneille, and Racine, not without fury, against a wild genius like Shakespeare" (p. 243). The vindication of these names, it can already be sensed, is explained by the relationship that these particular names entertain with the name of Nietzsche himself. These names are a part of Nietzsche himself; more exactly, they coincide with a certain genealogy of his. One word only with regard to that genealogy: speaking of his reading, Nietzsche writes, "It is a small number of old Frenchmen to whom I return again and again" (p. 243). Nietzsche, by means of this genealogy, bases himself in the Latin origins of French culture, in what he calls "the strong race." The names, however, that should interest us the most here are those of Schopenhauer and Wagner. What we have said about the names of the old Frenchmen is equally true of these names: they are in collusion with the name of Nietzsche. This is most visible in the case of Voltaire. *Human, All Too Human* was originally dedicated to Voltaire; this is what Nietzsche writes about it in *Ecce Homo*: "Voltaire was above all, in contrast to all who wrote after him, a *grandseigneur* of the spirit—like me.—The name of Voltaire on one of my essays—that really meant progress—*towards me*" (p. 283). Clearly it is Nietzsche's strategy to bind himself, to bind his own body to all these names: the second edition of *Human, All Too Human* no longer bears the name of Voltaire. Nietzsche substitutes his proper name for Voltaire's, and reappropriates once again his writing for himself; but this is possible only if Voltaire has always been another name for Nietzsche. That names may be substitutes for other names is in fact what may be read in the case of the names of Schopenhauer and Wagner. Nietzsche, in *Ecce Homo*, speaks of *The Birth of Tragedy* as a "practical application to Wagnerism, as if that were a symptom of *ascent*" (p. 270). He continues, "In this respect, this essay was an event in the life of Wagner: it was only from that moment on that Wagner's name elicited high hopes." The event, then, is the linking of two names, that of Nietzsche with that of Wagner. It is an event in the life of Wagner insofar as that linking elevates the name of Wagner. Nietzsche gives us to understand, however, that that connection was a mistake on his part, just as Wagner was not an ascending sign. There remains, however, the problem of knowing how a liaison between the two names had been possible. First of all let us note that *The Birth of Tragedy* was a "practical application to Wagnerism." The effect (like the fascination) of that work, that is to say, the timely effect which it enjoyed at the period, was a *zeitgemässer* effect. It follows that Nietzsche's critique of *The Birth of Tragedy*, a critique that works toward ridding it of the name of Wagner, intends to free the book of its timely aspects by showing that that work was untimely even when it first appeared.

But let us get to what makes the liaison between the names of Nietzsche and Wagner possible. Nietzsche provides a first explanation in the following manner:

I think I know better than anyone else of what tremendous things Wagner is capable—the fifty worlds of alien ecstasies for which no one besides him had

wings; and given the way I am, strong enough to turn even what is most questionable and dangerous to my advantage and thus to become stronger, I call
Wagner the great benefactor of my life. That in which we are related—that we
have suffered more profoundly, also from each other, than men of this century
are capable of suffering—will link our names again and again, eternally; and as
certainly as Wagner is merely a misunderstanding among Germans, just as certainly I am and always shall be. (pp. 250–51)

The bond between Wagner and Nietzsche is such that Nietzsche can turn
to his advantage what was most questionable and dangerous in connection with the name of Wagner, the name of decadence *par excellence*. It is
in this way that Nietzsche, being healthy at bottom, knows Wagner better than Wagner knows himself. Moreover, what Nietzsche recognizes in
the life of Wagner is pain, what might be called an *untimely* suffering. It
is this untimely suffering, in fact, that lies at the root of the relationship
between the two names. That the suffering attributed by Nietzsche to
Wagner is no more than Nietzsche's own suffering can only be justified
insofar as Wagner is only another name for Nietzsche. "That the two Untimely Ones distinguished by the names of Schopenhauer and Wagner
contribute much to the understanding of, or even to the formulation of
the proper psychological questions about, these two cases, I should not
wish to assert—excepting, as seems fair, some details" (p. 280).

   Let there be no misunderstanding about this suffering that makes
the union of these names possible: it is not the suffering of the man, Wagner, that is to say, of the empirical Wagner. It is more a question of an untimely suffering, of a trait that distinguishes Nietzsche. Notice the turn of
the phrase cited: The Untimely Ones are distinguished (*abgezeichnet*) by
the names of Schopenhauer and Wagner. These names have nothing in
common with their empirical support. Nietzsche continues, "What I was
fundamentally trying to do in these essays was something altogether different from psychology: an unequaled problem of education, a new concept of self-discipline, self-defense to the point of hardness, a way to
greatness and world-historical tasks was seeking its first expression" (p.
280). What can be read in the following passage is that the suffering that
binds together the names of Wagner and Nietzsche has nothing to do
with Wagner himself, nor with his music: "A psychologist might still add
that what I heard as a young man listening to Wagnerian music really had

nothing to do with Wagner; that when I described Dionysian music I described what *I* had heard—that instinctively I had to transpose and transfigure everything into the new spirit that I carried in me" (p. 274). So the names substituted for Nietzsche's traits, for the traits of his spirit, are names that are borrowed and reinterpreted, transposed and transfigured. Nietzsche:

> The proof of that, *as strong as any proof can be*, is my essay on *Wagner in Bayreuth*: in all psychologically decisive places I alone am discussed—and one need not hesitate to put down my name or the word "Zarathustra" where the text has the word "Wagner." The entire picture of the dithyrambic artist is a picture of the pre-existent poet of *Zarathustra*, sketched with abysmal profundity and without touching even for a moment the Wagnerian reality. (p. 274)

Several things may already be emphasized: The relationship between names, an interpretation of the other's name according to one's own instincts, is a transfiguration of reality. Wagner, as a name for Nietzsche, in no way designates the Wagnerian reality. The union of names is the translation of oneself into another name; it is, in so many words, the production of a mask. In addition, since the borrowed name has nothing in common with the true bearer of that name, the translation of one name into another coincides with the transfiguration of something timely into something untimely. And as these names that make up the body have acquired an untimely status, they can be exchanged in a rapid circulation, not for a proper name—Nietzsche, for instance—but for a name that is indeed a name for Nietzsche but does not bear any relation to the Nietzschean reality. For, as Nietzsche said, the name of Wagner *or* Zarathustra can easily be substituted for that of Nietzsche. So the name of Nietzsche ("Nietzsche") turns out to be as fictive as the name of the protagonist of the fiction *Zarathustra*.

If Nietzsche can claim that he projected his own traits onto the name of Wagner, it is because these traits are those of the fictive Nietzsche. As he says of *Zarathustra*:

> The pathos of the first pages is world-historical; the glance spoken of on the seventh page is Zarathustra's distinctive glance; Wagner, Bayreuth, the whole wretched German pettiness are a cloud in which an infinite mirage of the future is reflected. Even psychologically all decisive traits of my own nature are pro-

jected into Wagner's—the close proximity of the brightest and the most calami-
tous forces, the will to power as no man ever possessed it. (p. 275)

It is Nietzsche who is the mirage thus projected onto the names of Wagner and Schopenhauer, but it is Nietzsche only inasmuch as he is an untimely mirage, inasmuch as he is a fiction. The traits of Nietzsche—his
proper traits and those of his type—are projected onto something (Wagner and Nietzsche) that is primarily only an accidental reality. That reality gathers in traits that are fundamentally foreign to it: "This is the
strangest 'objectivity' possible: the absolute certainty about what I am was
projected on some accidental reality—the truth about me spoke from
some gruesome depth" (p. 275). The projection of one's own traits, of
oneself as a future type, presupposes an absolute certainty about what one
is. But one can be what one is only by projecting proper traits onto an accidental reality: what one is can be objectified only after an alienating
projection. Hence the necessity of recuperating that alienated self, the
obliterated name.

   "Schopenhauer and Wagner *or*, in one word, Nietzsche" (p. 277). It
is true that the fact of tying his name to that of another implies distinction. Nietzsche writes, "I honor, I distinguish by associating my name
with that of a cause or a person: pro or con—that makes no difference to
me" (p. 233). Distinction is at the same time creation of a sign for oneself,
for one's own body. This creation is, however, an alienation, and after-
wards the proper and originary name must be restored. Nietzsche tells us
this about Wagner, about his relationship with him: "What reached a decision in me at that time was not a break with Wagner: I noted a total
aberration of my instincts of which particular blunders, whether Wagner
or the professorship at Basel, were mere symptoms" (p. 286). So employ-
ing names, particularly timely, proper names, in order to make a body of
signs for oneself also represents an aberration of the instincts in that
healthy instincts are directed at the untimely. Even Nietzsche's proper
name ("Nietzsche") does not fulfill these conditions. This name does not
represent a lasting solution, for "Nietzsche" remains the name of a timely
being. However that may be, the supplementation of oneself by foreign
names cannot be avoided in the constitution of oneself as body. When,
for instance, Nietzsche attempts, in *The Untimely Ones*, to develop a concept of self-discipline and self-defense as a world-historical task, he puts

forward the names of Wagner and Schopenhauer knowing that he is essentially concerned with constituting himself. It is not enough simply to know precisely who one is before being able to project oneself onto the names of others; projection, on the contrary, is a part of the process of recognizing what one is: "Broadly speaking, I caught hold of two famous and as yet altogether undiagnosed types, as one catches hold of an opportunity, in order to say something, in order to have at hand a few more formulas, signs, means of language. . . . Plato employed Socrates in this fashion as a sign language for Plato" (p. 280). In this way other types, or their names, become the means, the signs needed to make oneself a body of signs, or even to recognize what one is (for in writing *The Untimely Ones* Nietzsche did not yet know fully who he was). Only by making use of Schopenhauer and of Wagner, in a manner that bears not the slightest relation to their reality, does Nietzsche succeed in knowing by these formulas, signs, and means what he is. But not the real, empirical Nietzsche, rather the fictive Nietzsche. "Now that I am looking back from a certain distance upon the conditions of which these essays bear witness, I do not wish to deny that at bottom they speak only of me. The essay *Wagner in Bayreuth* is a vision of my future, while in *Schopenhauer as Educator* my innermost history, my *becoming*, is inscribed. Above all, my promise!" (p. 281). The relationship between this sign language and the fictional articulation of a body is indisputable. In fact, if, as has been suggested, Nietzsche's name ("Nietzsche") is the other name for Nietzsche, the real name ("Nietzsche") being opposed to the fictional name "Nietzsche" (there is a connection to be explored between, on the one hand, the relationship between the two sides of the name "Nietzsche" and, on the other hand, what Nietzsche tells us in *Ecce Homo* about his dual descent), then that fictional name "Nietzsche," which is the name of all the other names (Schopenhauer and Wagner on this occasion), is completely separated from the Nietzschean reality, just as the name of Wagner used by Nietzsche no longer had the slightest relation to the reality of Wagner. The fictional name "Nietzsche" is as untimely as the other invented names. And that is not all. Since all these names are fictive, they have to enter into an organic exchange and so constitute the rapid metabolism whose play is that of a perfectly transparent body of signs.

Nietzsche: "I do not know any other way of associating with great tasks than *play*: as a sign of greatness, this is an essential presupposition" (p. 258). This play of the body will become unrestricted play from the moment when the names that institute the typical body have lost all relation to, all memory of, the reality they used to designate. Let us say, from the moment when the "dirty depths" have been completely eliminated from the names. This is why the process of projection and substitution does not come to a stop with the restoration of Nietzsche's proper name. Let us remember that in re-substituting his name for those of Wagner and Schopenhauer, Nietzsche owed it to himself to make his name into fiction. Now, that fictional name "Nietzsche" is still reminiscent of the real name and hence of the Nietzschean reality, of its timeliness. This is why the already fictive name of Nietzsche has to give way to names engendered by "real" fictions, as in the case of Byron's Manfred, with whom Nietzsche identified in his youth, and above all the case of the names of Zarathustra and Dionysus. Here we possess names that are entirely free of their "dirty depths." It is these entirely fictional names, then, that will have to assume the task of instituting the typic body, the type-body. This body, therefore, is nothing other than a sum of names, which are fictive, fictional, circulating, continually being exchanged. In other words, it is a text-body. For Nietzsche there is no proper body save the fictional body of a body entitled, for instance, *Zarathustra*. Now, Zarathustra is Dionysus, Dionysus being the other name for Zarathustra. But Dionysus is the name for whom?

Always lacking a name, the typic body, made up of a multitude of names, remains, finally, nameless. "Being new, nameless, hard to understand, we premature births of an as yet unproven future . . . "[10]

(1976)
Translated by Judith Still

2

Type-Writing Nietzsche's Self

Joining one heading to another, not completing one path of discourse.
—Empedocles

Upward, downward, the way is one and the same.
—Heraclitus

Nietzsche's "autobiography," his self-presentation in *Ecce Homo*, has been subjected to few treatments aside from those inflicted by philosophy.[1] In other words, this text has been considered either as literature or as an essentially philosophical piece of writing disguised under the appearances of a literary genre. According to the second of these genuinely philosophical alternatives, *Ecce Homo* has been stripped of all its aesthetic qualities, and of what belongs to Nietzsche's great style and his art of poetry, in order to lay bare the authentic experience of Being hidden beneath its delusive exterior. Martin Heidegger, undoubtedly the first to promote a philosophical reading of *Ecce Homo*, escapes this kind of logic as little as anybody else. Indeed, the few remarks on *Ecce Homo* interspersed in Heidegger's *Nietzsche* have no other purpose than to demonstrate that Nietzsche's self-presentation is a matter "neither of the biography of Nietzsche nor of the person of 'Herr Nietzsche.'" According to Heidegger, the work as work remains concealed from us as long as we leer at what is only the object of historical and psychological reporting: the "life" of the man. Only by inquiring into "Being and the world, which first ground the work," does the "work as work," rather than as an expression of Nietzsche's humanity, come into view.[2] A way in which truth grounds itself, Nietzsche's self-presentation represents for Heidegger a sort of appendix to his philosophical work by means of which he "perpetually renewed readiness for the sacrifice that his task demanded of him."[3] Since Nietzsche's self-presentation is seen by Heidegger as the essential sacrifice required by truth, *Ecce Homo* no longer pertains to literature or any literary genre of subjective and idle self-mirroring. Rather, *Ecce Homo* is the thinker's questioning of his destiny as thinker. Yet, paradoxically enough, the Heideggerian distinction between the individual and the destiny as thinker—a distinction that intersects with the one between, on the one hand, literature and philosophy, and, on the other hand, self-reflection and the business of thinking—allows for another approach to Nietzsche's work that no longer simply yields to that Heideggerian dyad. Heidegger will lend us the conceptual tools to approach *Ecce Homo* in a different way, a way that, as Philippe Lacoue-Labarthe has shown, he partially paved himself but refused to follow.[4] My question, then, is this: What if, like the systems of the pre-Socratics described in Nietzsche's *Philosophy in the Tragic Age of the Greeks*, *Ecce Homo*, too, amounted to an effort to use one's individuality, or personality, to stage conceptually the essence of Being? What Eugen Fink dismisses all too hastily as an anthropological reduction and deformation of pre-Socratic thought—namely Nietzsche's attempt to understand the pre-Socratics' systems as forms in which strong personalities articulate themselves in a manifestation that names Being in its question-worthiness—may well be the way in which *Ecce Homo* has to be approached.[5]

Undoubtedly, Nietzsche's conception of the pre-Socratic systems as realizations of the essence of Being in terms of greatness or grandeur (*Grösse*), or, more precisely, in terms of *Typus*, has historically to be retraced to the romantic ideal of a synthesis of poetry and philosophy in the form of a "new mythology," or an art of poetry (*Dichtkunst*), as it has been formulated by Hegel's "System Fragment" (1876). It has also to be retraced to Friedrich Schlegel's *Charakteristiken*, and above all to Friedrich Schelling's draft of a narrative philosophy (*erzählende Philosophie*) in *The Ages of the World* (1811–13). Yet, following Heidegger, one could argue that what the romanticism of Jena aspired to is only a more sophisticated and more conscious version of the modern attempt to think Being as *Gestalt*, the latter being, for Heidegger, the modern rendition of the Platonic *idea*. Indeed, partaking of that monumental history discussed by Nietzsche in *The Use and Misuse of History*—a history that consists in the continuum of all immortal figures (*Gestalten*) through which Being has been articulated typologically or, as Nietzsche also puts it, monographically—*Ecce Homo* has been thought to continue not only the romantic project but also, more fundamentally, the project of modernity in which the Greek notion of *eidos* is determined as *Gestalt*, and of which romanticism is but one, however important, variation.[6]

What, then, is a *Gestalt*? The *Gestalt*, as Heidegger conceives of it, is not simply the Hegelian notion of the figures or shapes of consciousness (*Gestalten des Bewusstseins*) that are, according to the *Phenomenology of Spirit*, the living incarnations of the concept, or in short, "actualized essentiality" in history.[7] Nor is it the *Gestalt* of Gestalt psychology, that is, a whole that encompasses more that the sum of its parts, and that is the source of all *Sinngebung*. If, in "The Origin of the Work of Art," Heidegger determines (as he explains himself in the Addendum from 1956), *Gestalt* from the perspective of the Greek notion of *morphe*—and the notion of *Ge-stell* as the gathering of the bringing-forth into the rift-design as bounding outline, or *peras*—*Gestalt* comes to designate truth's being fixed in place (its *Festgestelltsein*), the very mode in which truth is established (*eingerichtet*) in Being itself.[8] Undoubtedly, Heidegger's later use of the notion of *Gestalt*, for instance in "What Are Poets For?" and *The Question of Being*, differs considerably from this very general but, in fact, grounding or originary meaning. Indeed, if *Gestalt* initially translates the Greek experience of the coming forth of truth into the limits of a form, Heidegger's later use of the term is much more narrow. It refers only to the modern way in which truth is set into place, that is, to the way it is bent to the Western destiny of Being. Whereas for the Greeks *morphe* as *Gestalt* formulates the way in which Being comes forth into presence (*An-Wesen*), that is, into an appearance or aspect (*Ansehen*, or *Aussehen*), and is thus linked to the notion of *idea*, Heidegger's later use of *Gestalt* is restricted to modernity's representational (*Vorstellung*) actualization of what it conceives as Being. Although it is the modern version of the Greek *idea*, *Gestalt* also displaces this originary Greek notion of the coming into an appearance. Yet what does the modern concept of Being amount to, which the *Gestalt* serves primarily to represent (*vorstellen*), in other words, which it lets take up a position opposite a subject—the position of the object? Heidegger writes that for the moderns, the Being of being is "the incipient power gathering everything to itself, which in this manner releases every being to its own self. Being of being is the will. The will is the self-concentrating gathering of every *ens* unto itself."[9] This modern definition of Being implies, as Heidegger has demonstrated in *The Question of Being*, that all being is grounded in a conception of humanity characterized by extreme subjectivity, or in Heidegger's words, "subjectity."[10] This is a type of humanity that not only represents (*vorstellen*) being as rooted in the self-reflexive subjectivity of Being itself but also represents itself in order to set itself forth (*herstellen*). Characterized as a challenging-forth, the *Stellen* of the *Vorstellen* of Being—as well as the *Stellen* of the *Herstellen* of mankind—links the modern notion of Being, and with it the type of humanity that it presupposes, to the fate of technology as a challenging revealing. In modern metaphysics, this unconditional and hence complete unity of the activities of representation, production, and the objective character of the world takes shape as *Gestalt*. *Gestalt*, therefore, is the specific way in which the modern concept of a self-concentrating and self-reflexive Being, a Being congenital to a type of mankind that qua *subiectum* fathers all being, achieves representation.[11] In other words: if, since Descartes at least, modern metaphysics has conceived of the absolute presence of Being as self-consciousness, self-presence, and subjectivity, and if, moreover, *Gestalt* is the manner in which this presence becomes represented, it is then, historically speaking, no great surprise that the "genre" of autobiography and self-presentation turns out to be the form *par excellence* for the exposition of the modern understanding of Being. Inaugurated by Saint Augustine and Montaigne, autobiography does not conceal its relation to the Platonic determination of Being as *eidos/idea*. But in spite of its origin in the Greek notion of *idea*, autobiography is not identical to this notion. If the *idea* is the shape through which Being itself comes into an appearance, or *Aussehen*, the *idea* turned *Gestalt* in autobiography is the form through which the self-reflexivity of Being is represented (*vorgestellt*).

In order to point to the complex links that autobiography entertains with the Greek notion of the *idea*, a brief reference to Descartes must suffice here. I wish to evoke the beginning of the second part of the *Discourse on the Method*, where the subject of meditation could be shown to constitute himself according to what Heidegger calls the four horizons of Being. Held up by the winter in southern Germany, "the whole day shut up in a room heated by an enclosed stove," the *subject* Descartes turns away from the book of the world in order to study himself, and discovers that only as *one* single person is he able to make all his thoughts converge toward one and the same *ethical end*, and, consequently, attain *truth*.[12] Thus, *on, hen, agathon*, and *aletheia* govern the constitution of the subject (Descartes), who by representing himself within the horizon of these four determinations represents Being as the subjectivity of the thinking subject: *ego cogito*. One could make a similar point for Rousseau, whose obsession with transparency and sincerity can be shown to depend on the idea of a self-affection of light and whose desire for uprightness depends on the Greek notion of *stasis* as an essential determination of Being as presence.

After these all-too-sketchy remarks concerning the *Gestalt* of autobiography as the modern version of the Greek notion of *idea*, I wish to argue, in what follows, not only that the figure of Zarathustra is, as Heidegger has indicated, a *Gestalt* but that Nietzsche's self-representation in *Ecce Homo* fits that characteristic as well. But further, I hope to demonstrate that if in *Ecce Homo* Nietzsche obeys, in a first move, the logic of *Gestalt* in order to elaborate a conception of Being as type (*Typus*), that is, Being in the shape of a great personality, he subverts this representation of Being in a second move, and with it the modern notion of subjectivity and self-reflection. With this second move, a move linked to writing and the economy of his texts, Nietzsche breaks away not only from the romantic heritage but, more fundamentally, from the modern representation of Being and the form of autobiography in which Being is self-reflectively represented. Writing his self, type-writing it, to be precise, Nietzsche undercuts nothing less than representation itself, representation as *Vorstellung*, in other words, the modern, hence subjective, way of fixing Being into place.

The duality of Nietzsche's enterprise in *Ecce Homo* is manifest beginning with its subtitle, borrowed from Pindar: *How One Becomes What One Is*.[13] If this subtitle can be read as a Parmenidean interpretation of

Being as something lasting and standing in and on itself, this same subtitle also calls for a Heraclitean reading of Being as becoming. However, it is just as possible that Nietzsche may not have been concerned in his "autobiography" with these metaphysical concepts of Being as either *stasis* or becoming.[14] Indeed, I will argue that from the start Nietzsche operates in the interval between these two complementary metaphysical determinations of Being. Contrary to Heidegger's forceful argument that the thought of "the eternal return of the same" attempts to escape Platonism only to remain caught in its simple reversal, Nietzsche, in his intent to elaborate the time and space of this *great thought*, stages *another* notion of history, of time and space beyond what governs the metaphysical duality of Being and becoming. As we will see, the great thought of the eternal return of the same also undermines the very notion of the *Gestalt* and, in the same stroke, the genre of autobiography. With the thought of the eternal return of the same, we thus face the need to rethink self-presentation.

I

To avoid being mistaken for someone else, or even for his own work and, in particular, for some of its Hegelian overtones (and thus perhaps for Hegel himself),[15] Nietzsche decides to narrate his life, more precisely, to tell *himself* his life.[16] This self-revelation, or revelation of oneself to oneself, clearly continues and repeats the autobiographical gesture of Descartes's second meditation.[17] Yet this enterprise, which grew to maturity at a very particular moment in Nietzsche's life and which finds expression at a singular juncture in the text of *Ecce Homo*—namely on the intercalated leaf between the preface and *Ecce Homo* "properly" speaking[18]—results from conflicting forces and soon enough reveals itself to be self-contradictory. Seeing himself under pressure to declare who he is, Nietzsche experiences this necessity as an inevitable condescension and a fatal descent (*Niedergang*) opposed to the instincts of distance. This interplay between necessity and the pride of the instincts in the attempt to reappropriate his former work and to make up or complete his life through self-presentation, rather than to assure a contemporaneity with himself and his fellowmen, leads only to an ever greater dissimilarity with himself and to an even greater distance with regard to his own self. However, the fatal failure of autobiography—a catastrophe due to Nietzsche's *Gegensatz-Natur*—is not simply an unsuccessfulness. Indeed, what Nietzsche accomplishes as a result of this impossibility of reappropriating himself and of recognizing himself by himself, thus failing in becoming a self-consciousness, is an *untimely* (*unzeitgemässe*) relation to himself. This is a relation of noncontemporaneity with oneself, hence of nonidentity, in which the constituted self is not merely a self out of season, presenting itself at the wrong time, or a premature self in advance of its time, but a self that is not present to itself, and that, by relating to itself in a temporality distinct from that of the present now and its modalities, forever differs from itself. The different possible readings of *Ecce Homo*'s subtitle—*How One Becomes What One Is*—will furnish evidence if this.

On the one hand, this subtitle demands, as aphorism 263 of *Human, All Too Human* intimates, that one should become what one already is. Yet Nietzsche also declares that "to become what one is, one must not have the faintest notion *what* one is" (p. 254). Consequently, to become what one is precludes all forms of self-knowledge. Instead of a model for becoming oneself, *nosce te ipsum* ("know thyself") is for Nietzsche the ruin of the self. Thus: "where *nosce te ipsum* would be the recipe for ruin, forgetting oneself, misunderstanding oneself, making oneself smaller, narrower, mediocre, become reason itself" (p. 254). The "Know thyself" is dangerous because it represents a *contradictio in adjecto*. Nietzsche expresses consequently, in *Beyond Good and Evil*, his "unconquerable distrust of the *possibility* of self-knowledge."[19] But such self-knowledge is dangerous as well because it drains the *what* of what one is, that is, one's "essence," by fixing it into an identity.[20] Obviously, made into the *telos* of one's becoming, such objective knowledge of oneself, rather than helping one become what one is, would require that one become different from oneself. The "Know thyself" clearly expresses the desire to become another and not oneself. Becoming another, however, is something that must be resisted if one is to become what one is. Nietzsche writes: "I do not want in the least that anything should become different than it is; I myself do not want to become different" (p. 255). To become what one is is to become the *same*. Such becoming is achieved by way of a *return* of what one is. Since this is a becoming that excludes self-consciousness, hence, the process of reflexive determination, what one is occurs only by way of a sudden intrusion of the "organizing 'idea'" into the whole of consciousness (p. 254), interrupting the continuity of its surface and the flow of subjective time. What unexpectedly irrupts into the self, in a manner that must be qualified as *untimely*, is nothing less than the self-*same*. The return of the same, its re-petition, is the nonreflexive yet not, for that matter, immediate mode of becoming what one is. It follows from this that the Parmenidean reading of the subtitle, a reading that privileges Being over becoming, becomes modified and turns into a determination of Being as a *same* that is not identical to itself but that stands, because it relates to itself in the mode of repetition, in a nonreflexively mediated relation to itself. The Parmenidean concept of Being thus gives way to the repetition, or return, of the same.

On the other hand, the subtitle of *Ecce Homo* allows for a Heraclitean reading, which, rather than emphasizing Being, shows Being to be a modification, if not a modality, of becoming. When urging the reader not simply to comprehend the word "Dionysian" but to comprehend *oneself* in this word (pp. 272–73), Nietzsche suggests that the Dionysian puts an end to the immobility of Being. For this is a comprehension that is not without the touch of the "genius of the heart," and "from whose touch every one walks away richer . . . richer in himself, newer to himself than before, broken open, blown at and sounded out by a thawing wind, perhaps more unsure, tenderer, more fragile, more broken, but full of hopes that as yet have no name, full of new will and currents, full of new dissatisfactions and undertows" (pp. 268–69). Indeed, to read the subtitle *How One Becomes What One Is* in a Heraclitean fashion implies an "affirmation of passing away *and destroying*, which is the decisive feature of a Dionysian philosophy; saying Yes to opposition and war; *becoming*, along with a radical repudiation of the very concept of *being*" (p. 273). In sum, then, what does this subtitle mean when read in a Heraclitean vein? Besides putting into question all possible freezing of becoming into individual beings and into motionless Being in general, the subtitle indicates the way of one's becoming "the eternal joy of becoming [itself], beyond all terror and pity—that joy which includes even joy in destroying" (p. 273).[21] The subtitle *How One Becomes What One Is*, therefore, inquires into the ways in which all petrified individual forms are liquified, in which Being as frozen and immobilized becoming is dissolved, and in which one becomes becoming itself. It now should be clear: to become what one always already is is to become the eternal joy of becoming. With this second reading of the subtitle, the *same* that one must become and that one can only hope to become by excluding all self-consciousness is to be understood as becoming itself. Becoming is the *same* that proceeds from repetition, or return. Since it bars all self-reflexivity, such sameness is no longer that of the *self*same, but that of a self*same* that qua becoming relates to itself in the mode of repetition.

Consequently, both the Parmenidean (or, for that matter, Platonic) and the Heraclitean readings of *what* one is to become, taken by themselves, are incorrect. Indeed, if the same that one must become has to be free from all becoming to meet a Parmenidean interpretation, the fact that this sameness is a function of repetition, or return, and that it excludes all self-knowledge undercuts the possibility that this sameness will ever reach a motionless and self-sufficient being-with-oneself in identity. By contrast, a strictly Heraclitean reading of this selfsame sustains Heidegger's objection that Nietzsche raises becoming to the status of everlasting Being. Nevertheless, such a conception of becoming, one that amounts to a simple inversion of Platonism, is equally problematic. As Aristotle established, there is no such thing as an essence of becoming. More importantly, Nietzsche's determination of becoming as a return, or repetition that bars self-knowledge, does not allow for the transformation of becoming into a self-identical entity like Being. The *same* that one is to become does not have the structure of an ideality that relates to itself in full accordance with itself. Precluding all modes of self-consciousness and self-affection, the same is no longer of the order of a presence. It is no longer present to itself. Instead, the same relates to itself in untimely repetition. With this the two alternative readings collapse. *How One Becomes What One Is—Ecce Homo*, for short—is the exposition of a notion of the *same* characterized by an absence of all self-referring and self-reference. Unable to avoid the pleonasm, Nietzsche calls this same (a becoming in the mode of return) the eternal return of the same.[22] It no longer represents a speculative or reflexive relation to oneself, or of the selfsame to itself, but a kind of relation to "oneself" that, because it is a relation of return or repetition without a knowledge of what one is, never proceeds from, or produces, a self.

II

Needless to say, such a definition of the *same*, that is, of a notion of nonreflexive "self"-reference, encounters formidable problems as to its conceptualization. Furthermore, nothing could be more resistant to the habits of language than the expression of such a relation. But this barely conceivable "self"-reference of a nonidentical same finds its "expression" in the way texts are arranged and staged. The mise-en-scène of a text such as *Ecce Homo* is the place where this *same* is at work and where it can be apprehended. Yet, since spatiality has always served to illustrate the concept of time, the text's spatial arrangement renders manifest the specific temporality not only of the text but of its "object" as well: the nonreflexive *same*. It can easily be shown that *Ecce Homo* stages the two classical concepts of time: first, its representation as "the unconditional and infinitely repeated circular course of all things" attributed to Heraclitus (pp. 273–74), and second, the representation that time is linear and continuous, a conception that is Aristotelian in origin. Yet the becoming that characterizes the *same* obeys neither mythical-cyclical nor historical-linear time.[23] Nor does the temporality of becoming yield to the dialectical matrix. Instead, this becoming is to be understood through the temporality of repetition and the affirmation of chance that Nietzsche's concept of repetition invokes. Taking up a Nietzschean image, becoming can be compared to a repeated casting of the die that forever shows the figure six.[24] Distinct from the Hegelian synthetic notion of time, the temporality of the nonidentical *same* takes place in the interval between the linear and circular representations of time, an interval that defies all representation. Unable to conceptualize this *Untime* (*Unzeit*) of the interval, unable also to represent it as such, *Ecce Homo stages* this unheard-of time as the space or interval, of Nietzsche's double origin.

According to the aphorism entitled "Personal Providence" from *The Gay Science*, Nietzsche, in order to mark off his "innermost history, [his] . . . becoming" (p. 281) from all linear narrative of events, writes *Ecce Homo* in the space where his "own practical and theoretical skill in interpreting and arranging events has now reached its high point."[25] The first sentence of the first chapter of *Ecce Homo* opens with the riddle of Nietzsche's double origin, which we will now have to discuss in some depth:

The good fortune of my existence, its uniqueness perhaps, lies in its fatality: I am, to express it in the form of a riddle, already dead as my father, while as my mother I am still living and becoming old. This dual descent, as it were, both from the highest and the lowest rung on the ladder of life, at the same time a *decadent* and a *beginning*—this, if anything, explains that neutrality, that freedom from all partiality in relation to the total problem of life, that perhaps distinguishes me. (p. 222)

Nietzsche starts tracking his history as a history with a double origin from the moment at which he becomes aware that to recover from his sickness he must return to his "nethermost self" (p. 287). This return is coupled with a developing interest in medicine, physiology, and the natural sciences. At the expense of the (in truth, decadent) preoccupation with history, this interest, as we have seen in the previous chapter, is supposed to further an active "ignorance *in physiologicis*," through which a rearrangement of his personal history becomes possible in terms and for the benefit of his nethermost self. Let me, then, follow Nietzsche through this exploration of his buried nethermost self.

First, we need to recall the unusual beginning of Nietzsche's career as a writer. He states: "This beginning is exceedingly strange. I had discovered the only parable and parallel in history for my own inmost experience—and thus became the first to comprehend the wonderful phenomenon of the Dionysian" (pp. 271–72). It is a strange beginning, indeed, for it reveals that the actuality of Nietzsche's life has a pendant in the past. This similarity of the two temporal moments of past and present, but especially the parallelism of Nietzsche's experience and the Dionysian, explains his penetration of the phenomenon of the Dionysian itself. Further, the coincidence in question shows history to be double. On the one hand, there is a repetition or return of the past—Dionysian, or Heraclitean, history. On the other hand, there is history properly speaking, history as linear—the Apollonian and Socratic fall-away from cyclical, or Dionysian, history. But both histories are double as well. Linear history is decadent history, and cyclical history is predicated on becoming *and* destruction. Dionysus has a double origin: twice born, once from the womb of the princess Semele, once from the leg of Zeus. Nietzsche's origin, parallel to the Dionysian phenomenon—its parable (*Gleichnis*)—is similarly a double origin.

In section 3 of "Why I Am So Wise," Nietzsche evokes "this *dual* series of experiences" that proceeds from the double origin. In this particular context, he explains the double nature of these experiences by his descent, which involves a double nationality. "My ancestors were Polish noblemen: I have many racial instincts in my body from that source." "Yet my mother, Franziska Oehler, is at any rate something very German" (p. 225). According to Nietzsche, his father, Karl Ludwig Nietzsche, "was full of deep reverence for the Prussian king Frederick William IV. . . . I myself, born on the birthday of the above named king, on the fifteenth of October, received, as fitting, the Hohenzollern name *Friedrich* Wilhelm" (p. 226). German by virtue of the name—"perhaps more German than present-day Germans"—and Polish because of his descent and instincts, Nietzsche claims to have "a 'second' face in addition to the first."[26] In every respect, he is a *Doppelgänger* (p. 225). Yet Nietzsche's duplicity is not exhausted by this double descent. In order to examine thoroughly the enigma of his fatality, let me consider what he tells us about his father:

My father, born in 1813, died in 1849. (p. 226)

My father died at the age of thirty-six: he was delicate, kind, and morbid, as a being that is destined merely to pass by—more a gracious memory of life than life itself. (p. 222)

I consider it a great privilege to have had such a father: it even seems to me that this explains whatever else I have of privileges—*not* including life, the great Yes to life. (p. 226)

Merely a reminiscence of the future—of Nietzsche's future *life*—the father withers away as soon as he has engendered his son. Yet the legacy bequeathed by this dearly beloved father is double. Nietzsche owes his life to his father. But his father's heritage is a "*wicked* heritage . . . at bottom, [a] predestination to an early death" (p. 287). Still, when "selflessness" and "sense of duty" paved the way for Nietzsche's decadence, this wicked heritage turned out to be a remedy. Indeed, his sickness detaches him from decadent life and gives him the means to come to his own aid. Thus a tentative reading of the enigma of the double origin becomes possible. Dying as one's own father amounts to giving birth to oneself. As the wicked heritage—the "predestination to an early death"—becomes transformed into a life-giving remedy, Nietzsche gives *life* to himself by dying as his own father. Yet what does it mean for Nietzsche still to be living and becoming older as his mother? A mother's role is to carry a child for the full term. But not yet due to be born, his time not yet having come, he will remain, as his mother, indefinitely pregnant with himself. If, as Pierre Klossowski suggests, Nietzsche does not father himself because he dies as his own father, neither is he his own mother, because he does not give birth to himself.[27] As Nietzsche holds, "I live on my own credit: it is perhaps a mere prejudice that I live" (p. 217).

Insofar as Nietzsche stands on the highest rung on the ladder of life, the further role of the father is to take that life from him. The wicked heritage, and the death as one's own father, impedes all possible becoming from the outset. But this misfortune is also what allows Nietzsche to short-circuit the process of linear decadence. Deprived of the possibility of a continuous climb from the lowest to the highest rung on the ladder of life, Nietzsche escapes altogether the time of decadence, that is, linear historical time. As he himself as his own mother carries himself endlessly for the full term, he grows old "at the same time a *decadent* and a *beginning*." More succinctly, since Nietzsche is already dead as a beginning capable of development to its end, Nietzsche remains an eternal beginning, a beginning that is already its own *end*. Congenitally deprived of linear development and decline, Nietzsche enjoys the privilege of a life in which he *repeats* himself *eternally* as the *same*, a life of becoming. By taking place *in* and *as* the interval of *beginning* and *decadence*, this repetition, or return, of oneself as a stillborn beginning, and as a selfsame that does not wish to become different, opens a third space.[28] Before any further exploration of this space, I note that Nietzsche characterizes it as a neutral space. Although the interface of Nietzsche's *Doppelnatur*—opened up, for instance, by the interruption of the flow of time in sickness—generates a state of "fullness and [the] self-assurance of a *rich* life," as well as a space rich in perspectives "toward *healthier* concepts and values" (p. 223), it is not a dialectical space. Nor is it a place where complementary or self-contradictory doubles resolve into nullity or abstract nothingness. Instead, Nietzsche's dual descent, which provides him with the most subtle smell for the "signs of ascent and descent"—"I know both, I am both" (p. 222)—qualifies this intermediary space of the return of the same as a space of neutrality, or rather, impartiality, toward "the total problem of life."

III

To understand this remarkable space better, I focus on a figure that at first may be mistaken for a sublation of the *Doppelblick*. Having stressed that he is at the same time a decadent and its opposite, Nietzsche remarks: "This *dual* series of experiences, this access to apparently separate worlds, is repeated in my nature in every respect: I am a *Doppelgänger*, I have a 'second' face in addition to the first. *And* perhaps also a third" (p. 225). The *Doppelgänger* possesses a second face. His insights into the world are "fruitful and terrible at the same time" (p. 289). *Ecce Homo* ties this double sight to the month of January, to which Nietzsche pays homage. Nietzsche conceived of *The Gay Science* during this month—a month dedicated in Roman chronology to the god Janus, who, as *Ianus bifrons*, is a deity of beginnings (and endings). As a guardian of doors and gates, and a patron of beginnings and endings, Janus looks simultaneously forward and backward. Yet Nietzsche locates a third eye in the interface of this two-faced figure—a theatrical, tragic eye.[29] Regarded as a doorkeeper and a guardian of gates, Janus's statue stood where two roads met. But does the *Doppelgänger* not also simultaneously walk a double road? Rather, is his place not precisely at the intersection of two roads, there where a third road begins? In *Ecce Homo*, Nietzsche suggests as much when he recalls the very conception of his *Zarathustra*:

Mornings I would walk in a southerly direction on the splendid road to Zoagli, going up past pines with a magnificent view of the sea; in the afternoon, whenever my health permitted it, I walked around the whole bay from Santa Margherita all the way to Portofino. This place and this scenery came even closer to my heart because of the great love that Emperor Frederick III felt for them; by chance, I was in this coastal region again in the fall of 1886 when he visited this small forgotten world of bliss for the last time.—It was on these two walks that the whole of *Zarathustra I* occurred to me, and especially Zarathustra himself as a type: rather, he *overtook me*. (pp. 297–98)

At the intersection of two ways, as it were—the way leading upward and the way leading downward and around the bay—as well as in the interval of the times of the rising and the setting sun, Nietzsche is being overtaken by Zarathustra. The time of Zarathustra coincides with the "great noon" that Nietzsche invokes. In *Ecce Homo*, he defines this "great noon" as a task:

My task of preparing a moment of the highest self-examination for humanity, a *great noon* [*grosser Mittag*] when it looks back and far forward, when it emerges from the dominion of accidents and priests and for the first time poses, *as a whole*, the question of Why? and For What?—this task follows of necessity from the insight that humanity is *not* all by itself on the right way. (p. 291)

Similar to his illness, which suspends the necessarily decadent flow of time and thus allows Nietzsche to repeat, renew, and bring back (*Wiederholung*) the nethermost self, the "great noon" and the "right way" represent breaks in the continuum of space and time during which the *type* of Zarathustra becomes impressed on Nietzsche. This fork in the road—a momentary caesura of the way upward and the way downward, both of which are the *same* way—leads us back to the riddle of Nietzsche's double origin left in abeyance. Indeed, the solution to that riddle at the beginning of the text of *Ecce Homo* is the condition not only for our ability to enter and read Nietzsche's text but also for our understanding of what it may mean to find oneself (*Selbstfindung*) through repetition.

Tentatively, the riddle's solution can be transcribed as follows: I have killed myself as my father so as to be able to commit incest with my myself as my mother, but as my father I prevent myself from being born. However, to contextualize the solution of this riddle, a series of events following the death of Nietzsche's father needs to be recalled. We know already that he died at the age of 36. Yet "in the same year in which his life went downward, mine too, went downward: at thirty-six, I reached the lowest point of my vitality—I still lived, but without being able to see three steps ahead" (p. 222). If Nietzsche's father died in 1849, and Nietzsche reached the lowest point of his life before renouncing his professorship at Basel in 1879, exactly 30 years separate his father's death from his own temporary blindness. Incidentally, this low in Nietzsche's life is not without relation to reading. He writes: "I have seen this with my own eyes: gifted natures with a generous and free disposition, 'read to ruin' in their thirties" (p. 253). Turning away from reading thus leads Nietzsche out of the state of decadence: "My eyes alone put an end to all bookwormishness—in brief, philology: I was delivered from the 'book'; for years I did not read a thing—the greatest benefit I ever conferred on my-self" (p. 287). This blindness—during which Nietzsche is unable to see three steps ahead, and which he experiences 30 years after his father's death, at the precise moment when he reaches his father's age, 36—is also, I argue, a kind of self-punishment for having slain himself as his own father and for having committed incest with himself as his own mother. At the fork in the road, in the interface of the way upward and the way downward, and at the moment when Nietzsche looks both forward and backward, that is to say, at the moment when he finds himself as the same, Nietzsche *repeats* all the moments of the triangular oedipal configuration. The oedipal triangulation, which necessarily structures the becoming of the subject in a genealogy predicated on continuous and cumulative time, would thus also seem to be vital to one's becoming a type. What does this repetition stand for? What does the fact that even in becoming a type it cannot be circumvented indicate? Does it simply mean that there is no difference in essence between a self-conscious subject encrusted in a ge-nealogy and a type who dismisses any apology?[30] Is the moment of medi-ation the same in both cases? Does the third space, the unusual space of the interval, become absorbed by this triangulation? These are some of the questions we must ask. But before I can begin answering them, a further investigation of Nietzsche's temporary blindness is necessary.

This loss of sight, which prevents Nietzsche from seeing more than three steps ahead, is connected to three days of migraines during which Nietzsche excels in dialectics: "In the midst of the torments that go with an uninterrupted three-day migraine, accompanied by laborious vomiting of phlegm, I possessed a dialectician's clarity *par excellence* and thought through with very cold blood matters for which under healthier circum-stances I am not mountain-climber, not subtle, not *cold* enough" (pp. 222–23). If Nietzsche reminds us right away that he considers "dialectic as a symptom of decadence; for example in the most famous case, the case of Socrates" (p. 223) (similar, indeed, with its three operative steps, to the three-day migraine, the vision reduced to three steps, and the triangular configuration), then the book *Dawn*, to which Nietzsche gives birth dur-ing these three days, announces necessarily a *new* beginning. But what is this new beginning that comes about only through, and as, a repetition of triple steps and triangular figures?

Even though this figure three is a figure of closure that presides over the movement of speculative thought in a totalizing perspective, Nietzsche makes this figure turn upon itself and transforms it into a sign of liberation. Heinrich von Stein, who came to visit Nietzsche for three days, is a case in point. Nietzsche recalls, "This excellent human being, who had walked into the Wagnerian morass with all the impetuous simplicity of a Prussian Junker . . . acted during these three days like one transformed by a tempest of freedom, like one who has suddenly been lifted to his own height and acquired wings" (p. 227). Nor should one forget in this context the following passage, also from *Ecce Homo*: "With a dithyramb like the last one in the third part of *Zarathustra*, entitled 'The Seven Seals,' I soared a thousand miles beyond what was called poetry hitherto" (pp. 265–66). At once symptomatic of decline and of ascent, the new beginning is born from the superior and exceeding excellence of the very repetition of these threefold figures. If Nietzsche enjoyed "a dialectician's clarity *par excellence*," it is precisely because by its repetition, dialectics becomes a liberating force. The new beginning takes shape through and as a repetition of the totally mediated and speculatively closed tertiary figures. Only through the repetition of these totalizing tertiary figures is it possible to displace their decadent limitations and implications and to open up the space—the third space—of the same. I recall that all these triple and tertiary figures presuppose an intermediary space—the space of the interval—in which they tie into one the interval's respective *relata*, or foundations. However, in the capacity of totalizing figures, both the number three and the threefold of the triangulations are blind to this intermediary space. They are, therefore, blind as well to their repetition in the space and as the space, in which their possibility is rooted, a repetition that is a return of the same, insofar as, precisely, this repetition displaces these figures' mastering power.

Such blindness of dialectics can be witnessed, for example, in the arguments that Eugen Fink advances to support the claim that the third part of *Zarathustra* represents the central part (*Herzstück*), the mean, the middle (*die 'Mitte'*) of the work. According to such arguments, this third part is "the natural end of the work," that is, the part in which Zarathustra-Nietzsche returns for the third time "in order to find himself as the essential middle [*wesentliche Mitte*] of his thinking," and the part that, hence, concludes "the step-by-step development of Nietzsche's central thought." Indeed, Fink argues that in comparison to that third part, the fourth part of *Zarathustra* is simply derivative and inferior.[31] But is this truly the case? Is Fink's assessment of the third part as a concluding part correct in the first place? Instead of being the dialectical end-term of the quest for the self-identity, self-appropriation, and self-reflection of the thinker, is this so-called "essential middle" not precisely a beginning of something new? What if this third part were in fact already the superior repetition of all the speculative moments and movements that culminate in the parousia of the self, and thus the beginning of a resolutely nontotalizing repetition of those very same tertiary figures, a repetition, in short, that stages the space itself from which all the totalizing operations spring forth by covering up that intermediary expanse? Originating in repetition, the "essential middle" of *Zarathustra* would then no longer be an "essential" middle. Furthermore, to the extent that the threefold figures are subject to repetition, the medial and mediating function and the concept of the middle itself become irretrievably connected to repetition. And finally, given that repetition is a nonreflexive mode of "self"-reference, repetition is revealed as the degree zero of all reflective and speculative mediation. Is it not in such a light that not only the third but also the fourth part of *Zarathustra* need to be judged? A dithyramb, a hymn to Dionysus in short, concludes the third part of this book. With this dithyramb Oedipus takes off his mask, as it were, and steps forward as Dionysus. Oedipal triangulation and dialectical figuration open up to their infinite repetition through which they abdicate their former closing power. No need, consequently, to look for a fourth way, a way out of the "essential middle," oedipal genealogy, self-conscious subjectivity, and so on. Such a way is already present in the third way, as the difference that prevents the latter from returning into an identity of its own. The third way is always already a fourth way. If this is true, the fourth part of *Zarathustra* can in no way be derivative. Instead of following a successful and definitive exposition of Nietzsche's central thought, this fourth part is the repetition of the new beginning accomplished by part 3. It is the same.

Undoubtedly, the "object" of a repetition and the repeated "object" stand in a relation to each other. They share a sphere of commerce that prevents the repetition of the same from being immediate (*unmittelbar*).

But if the recurrence of the same presupposes a common medium of sorts, this does not mean, for that matter, that it is a medium of speculative mediation. What is repeated and its repetition do not relate in terms of difference. What is repeated is affirmed in totality. It is not repeated as a negative determination, hence as, in essence, a moment of a whole, system, or concept. In spite of the fact that the referent of a repetition and its repetition partake in a shared sphere of commerce and in spite of the fact as well that the repetition of the same is not immediate, what is to be repeated and the repetition thereof do not entertain, in Hegel's terms, a reciprocal relation of reflexive determination (*Reflexionsbestimung*). Since the repeated and its repetition do not relate as differences, their relation is free of all specular properties. Therefore, neither is it a relation of identity. In such repetition, the repeated recurs as the same.

Rather than initiating an end-oriented process whose end coincides with the speculative point of departure of the process, the affirmation through repetition of the threefold figures constitutive of self-identical entities—the oedipal triad and the dialectical triad—is not processual. Even though nonimmediate, the affirmation through repetition effects a collapse of the (speculative) difference between beginning and end. The what of a repetition, repeated in its totality without being determined in relation to another, hence negatively, is an aborted beginning, stillborn so to speak, divested of its potential to become the starting point for a possible development. Here, beginning and end are the same. In the absence of all reflexive determination between the repeated and its repetition, between beginning and end, mediation makes room for repetition and the recurrence of the same. With it one reaches the end of all development, and all exposition (*Ausführung*).

At stake here, then, is something other than a quest for the transcendental possibility of mediation, reflection, and identity. By signifying, on the one hand, that all three presuppose repetition as a nonreflexive relation and, on the other hand, that the affirmation of the repeated as the same breaks down the process of mediation, Nietzsche literally practices a nonreflexive discourse. In *Ecce Homo*, he no longer discursively and argumentatively—"argument" being taken here in a narrow logical sense—inquires into grounds, reasons, or conditions of possibility. But *Ecce Homo* is not Nietzsche's new beginning *of* philosophy—it is not to begin with a beginning, as defined, for example, at the outset of Hegel's *Science of Logic*.[32] It is neither a *philosophical* beginning nor a beginning of philosophy. As a nonreflexive, nonspecular relation between the affirmed "self"*sames* of beginning and end; as a degree-zero exchange that excludes any mirroring and specular reflection by way of one's (or any entity's) negative, or other, the notion of repetition central to Nietzsche's thought in *Ecce Homo* leaves the horizon of the determinations of consciousness, subjectivity, and history, and with it modern philosophy's self-understanding. However, as repetition of philosophy, Nietzsche's discourse is the *same* as philosophy. Such sameness makes all the difference, even though philosophy and Nietzsche's repetition thereof are not distinct like differences. Nor is their relation to be taken as one of nonidentity. In other words, by relating to itself in the mode of a return, a discourse such as *Ecce Homo* is divested of self-identity, the identity that philosophy gives to itself.

A "selfsame" that bars reflexive mediation is a type. The notion of type, however, requires resistance to the possibility of self-appropriation. As we have seen, the *Gestalt* of autobiography is a mode of specular self-appropriation. It is the very medium of exposition of the modern concept of Being as self-present subjectivity. By using the discourse of self-presentation in *Ecce Homo* to elaborate a nonreflexive "self"-same, or type, Nietzsche seeks to overcome both the form of autobiography and the concept of Being that it promotes. But if self-presentation (*Selbstdarstellung*) in autobiography strives to raise the self-appropriating self to self-presence, the renunciation of speculative mirroring in the repetition of the "self"-same not only thwarts self-presence but also announces the limits of representation as *Vorstellung* and opens up the problem of *Darstellung* as such.

Unable to recognize what is at stake in Nietzsche's self-presentation, the humanist critic is reduced to accusing Nietzsche, in Heidegger's words, of "exorbitant subjectivity [and] endless and tormented self-mirroring."[33] Yet what Nietzsche undertook by imitating, in *Ecce Homo*, the modern genre of autobiography is an attempt to sketch out the end of subjectivity and its correlative notion of Being as the self-present subject.

(1979)

PART II

INTENDING THE NONRELATIONAL

3

Tearing at the Texture

The history of the criticism to which Walter Benjamin's writings have given rise is the story of many friendships. Whether he has been linked up with Hegelian thought, coupled to the theology of the Jewish religion of revelation, tied to romantic linguistic philosophy, paired off with historical materialism, or even related to Lutheran theology, the critics have primarily sought to appropriate Benjamin's thought for their own philosophical viewpoint.[1] Yet Benjamin, as is well known, did not fraternize easily. As reserved as he was, how could he have held all those views, or been all those things that critics have suggested? Undoubtedly, Benjamin's philosophical allegiances that critics have pointed out have significantly contributed to our understanding of this complex author. If Benjamin, as Gershom Scholem has insisted time and again, was indeed a philosopher—a metaphysician—it ought to be possible, in principle, to assign a definite place to his writings in the history of philosophical thought.[2] But can Scholem's characterization of Benjamin as a philosopher (and hence the possibility of assigning his affiliation) simply be taken for granted? How is one, indeed, to explain the lack in Benjamin's writing of almost everything usually associated with the philosophical enterprise: a homogenous conceptuality, canonized rules of argumentation, and reference to the traditional set of problems? Bernd Witte has convincingly argued on this basis that Benjamin is no philosopher at all.[3] Benjamin's

total disregard for any form of sustained conceptuality and argumentation, as well as the elitist and esoteric if not idiosyncratic nature of at least
Benjamin's early writings—an aspect that Witte is so far the only one to
have systematically explored—runs counter to the philosophical requirement of transparency and systematic exposition of arguments. In addition, what Witte calls Benjamin's authoritarian and hypertrophic subjectivism irreducibly resists the claim to universality to which philosophy
must measure up. From this perspective it is ultimately impossible to tie
Benjamin to any of the philosophical currents that characterized his time.
And yet he had, undoubtedly, something at stake with philosophy. Until
the debacle regarding his habilitation dissertation, Benjamin even flirted
with the idea of becoming a university teacher of philosophy. Moreover,
most of his work up to that point is obviously of philosophical inspira-
tion. In view of this paradoxical situation, rather than choosing between
Scholem's and Witte's positions on Benjamin, should one not first explore
Benjamin's relation to philosophy in general? Instead of trying to discover
one more philosophical debt that would link this author up with an established brand of philosophical thought, it might be appropriate to begin by inquiring into the importance that Benjamin gave to philosophy
and into the modalities of such valorization. To do so I will consider some
of Benjamin's writings that are commonly referred to as his metaphysical
and historico-philosophical work; in short, writings of that period in his
life that stretches from 1915 to 1926. Since during those years Benjamin's
thought was still maturing, it is difficult to approach the period as a
whole. Nevertheless, many motifs of a philosophical bearing characterize
his writings at that time, offering clear testimony to sustained and persistent philosophical concerns. Benjamin himself suggests such a continuity
of views and interests when he claims, in a letter to Scholem, that the
"Epistemo-Critical Prologue" of *The Origin of German Tragic Drama* not
only replaces his earlier essay "On Language as Such and the Language of
Man" but expresses its original intentions perhaps more effectively.[4]

    Before analyzing some of these persistent motifs, let me emphasize
that, notwithstanding Benjamin's often obscure and idiosyncratic writing,
the essays and larger works of the period in question also reveal considerable philosophical refinement. Such subtlety, however, does not consist in
technical refinement; rather it touches not only on philosophically ele-

mentary distinctions but, above all, on the difference that philosophical distinction makes in the first place. It is my contention that when Benjamin broaches questions of philosophy, this concern with the difference philosophy makes is what occupies him primarily. "Fate and Character" is a case in point. In this essay, in which the author is primarily concerned with establishing the total divergence of the two concepts—"where there is character there will, with certainty, not be fate, and in the area of fate character will not be found"—Benjamin shows himself fully aware of the philosophical implication of such an operation.[5] Fate, he explains, is a connection (*Zusammenhang*); more precisely it is "a nexus of meaning" in which the natural life in man is indiscriminately "coupled to cards as to planets." It is a weave or net of ensnaring threads (*Verkettung*) in which the possibility of difference is destroyed (pp. 202, 204). Such nondifference in weblike interconnectedness "corresponds to the natural condition of the living," or, in other words, to "the demonic stage of human existence," we are told (pp. 203–4). Webs of whatever sort, because they make difference impossible, are mythical in essence. In the essay on Goethe's *Elective Affinities*, Benjamin notes that without difference, all of existence succumbs to the power of nature and its concept, which, free of boundaries, expands monstrously. Without a sovereign principle or limits, "the life of the myth . . . imposes itself as the sole power in the domain of existence" (p. 316). Where character is understood to be, as is commonly the case, "a network that knowledge can tighten at will into a dense fabric" made up of "finer and closer connections, until what looked like a net is tightened into cloth," it can then become, as Benjamin remarks, erroneously connected to fate (pp. 204–5). To make character a function of a weft is to endow it with the same mythical indifference that already distinguishes fate. Character, for Benjamin, can be clearly demarcated from fate only if it is defined not by the immense complexity of a tightly woven cloth but, on the contrary, by an exclusive character trait that cuts apart the knots of fate. If distinguished by "the brilliance of its single traits," character stands in radical opposition to the interconnectedness and entanglement of fate, causing it to be "liberating" in all its forms (pp. 205–6). The importance that Benjamin attributes throughout his writings to the tragic hero is based on a similar principle. By proudly recognizing that he is better than the gods with whom he has been chained up, this hero instigates a myth-shaking difference by which he rises from what is termed "the mist of guilt," or in other words, from the realm of mythical and natural interconnectedness. Through this eye-opening insight into man's distinction from the gods, a difference is made by which boundaries are assigned to myth and nature. Benjamin can, therefore, consider the tragic hero as the prototype of the philosopher who dispels natural and mythical indifference in an act of setting himself apart by raising his head higher. Distinction and difference are rooted in an act of demarcation by which the interlacings of myth are shattered in the name of a radical heterogeneity—truth. In his essay on Goethe, Benjamin writes: "In Greece genuine art and genuine philosophy—as distinct from their inauthentic stage, the theurgic—begin with the departure of myth, because art is not based on truth to any lesser extent than is philosophy, and philosophy is not based on truth to any greater extent than is art" (p. 326).

In what follows I would like to show that the concept of difference—of a difference that breaks up the continuum of the mythical chain—is a persistent concern of Benjamin's thought. But in analyzing this philosophical motif *par excellence*—it is indeed through difference that philosophy comes into the world—I shall also be able to reflect on the limits of philosophy from the perspective of truth that Benjamin adopts. From the start, let me emphasize that the act through which the tragic hero raises his head above the mythical interconnectedness of guilt is not simply a purely mental act of abstraction. The difference he inaugurates—the limits he draws—is the result not of pure cognition, meditation, or contemplation but of a hubristic reflection that culminates in self-confident recognition that he is better than his gods. The difference that the tragic hero brings into the world is rooted in an act of revolt; it is a very practical act of cognition. Instead of proceeding through philosophical abstraction or reduction, the tragic hero achieves difference by destroying the interwoven threads of the mythical web, or by violently breaking up the mythical web of the realm of mere appearance. Difference, in short, is based on an act as concrete as a revolt, a violent exhaustion (*Aufzehrung*) or burning up, by what Benjamin will later call "The Destructive Character." This difference is thus not simply philosophical. As the tragic hero's hubristic act shows, it is artistic and religious as well.

To bring Benjamin's treatment of philosophical difference more clearly into view, I will briefly consider "On Language as Such and the Language of Man," "The Task of the Translator," and some aspects of the "Epistemo-Critical Prologue." From the start it is necessary to emphasize that Benjamin's elaborations in the essay "On Language as Such" do not fall into any of the traditional philosophical modes of discussing this issue. This is of capital importance considering that throughout the period of Benjamin's writing that we are concerned with here, the pilot science for the coming philosophy he envisioned was to be a theory of language. All his developments of language have a double thrust. They intend to dismantle both an instrumentalist understanding of language—what he calls the bourgeois theory of language—and a theory of language that takes the word to be the essence of the thing, or in short, what he calls mystical linguistic theory. Roughly speaking, Benjamin distinguishes his own investigation of the nature of language from the two views on language discussed in Plato's *Cratylus*, that is, against the two theories on language that have informed all philosophies of language hitherto. Critics such as Winfried Menninghaus have argued that by dismissing as insignificant language's utilitarian function, and by inquiring into the nonsignifying nature of language, Benjamin became a structuralist before that doctrine's time.[6] Richard Wolin, by contrast, contends that Benjamin's criticism of the receptive and cognitive aspects of language is a result of a "long-standing Kabbalistic doctrine of language as the divine substance of reality."[7] As I shall argue, Benjamin's theory of language is based neither on insight into the structure of linguistic representation nor on the assumption of a definable divine linguistic substance. Benjamin leaves those alternatives behind.

All language, Benjamin insists, communicates primarily a mental meaning (*geistige Inhalte*). But language does not communicate such mental content by way of serving as an agency for it. Rather, this content is communicated in unmediated fashion *in*, and not *through*, the medium of language. Although content is communicated in language, it does not coincide with the linguistic medium in which it is expressed. It is something quite different from that medium. Benjamin notes, "the distinction between a mental entity and the linguistic entity in which it communicates is the first stage of any study of linguistic theory" (p. 63). What, then, is the specific object that language communicates? Benjamin writes, "As communication, language communicates a mental entity—something communicable per se [*eine Mitteilbarkeit schlechthin*]" (p. 66). The mental content distinct from the linguistic entity in which it is communicated is thus communicability itself. In itself, that is, as an expressive medium, language communicates communicability. It is the primary content of language and, for Benjamin, the true and sole object of a philosophical theory of language. Yet apart from a very brief reference by Derrida to the issue of communicability in Benjamin, not one of the leading Benjamin critics has bothered to shed light on this intriguing notion.[8] Thus Benjamin's theory of language remains obscure. The same must be said of Benjamin's concept of translatability, which informs his entire theory of translation. It has not to my knowledge drawn any attention from Benjamin scholars.

One might, at first, be tempted to understand communicability as simply the (condition of) possibility of communication. Since Benjamin also notes, however, that "languages have . . . no speaker," and that communicability is communicated not *through* but *in* language, communicability is obviously not a Kantian formal condition of possibility (p. 63). Its characteristics are not subjective. Thus communicability, if it may be related to the traditional concepts of possibility at all, is rather of the order of a real possibility (*dunamis*) of potency in language. As we will see below, it is indeed an objective characteristic of language as language. But rather than speculating on the status of communicability, let me return to the text of "On Language as Such" to clarify this concept's meaning.

After establishing that the mental being that communicates itself in language is not outwardly identical with the linguistic being in which it is expressed, Benjamin remarks: "Mental being [*geistige Wesen*] is identical with linguistic being only insofar as it is capable of communication [*mitteilbar*]. What is communicable in a mental entity is its linguistic entity" (p. 63). The communicable, consequently, is that part of a spiritual being that is linguistic, that part that is expressed in unmediated fashion in the spiritual being's communication. What this means is that what is being communicated is primarily language itself, language (*Sprache*) being understood here in a strictly verbal sense as relating exclusively to language as act. The communicable *per se* is, thus, language's language, or communicability. This is the spiritual content *kath' exokhen* ("par excellence") in language. When Benjamin writes, "The answer to the question '*What* does language communicate?' is therefore 'All language communicates itself'" (p. 63), he does not contradict his earlier statement regarding the difference between language as linguistic being and the content expressed in it qua linguistic medium. "Itself" indeed designates a "substance" different from the specific language in which the communication occurs. This substance is language's communication itself, the very act and fact that it speaks. Beyond the Cratylian alternatives of understanding the word either as a means to designate things different from it or as expressing immediately the essence of things themselves, communicability refers to the speech act in the word. This communicability, language's act of communication in a verbal sense, is for Benjamin the fundamental problem of all philosophy of language. It is the communicable *per se*.

What I have said up to this point about communicability as the object *par excellence* of the theory of language may seem simply trivial. Upon further scrutiny, however, this impression may dissolve and the triviality of communicability may reveal itself as similar to those essential simplicities with which philosophy is concerned. Although communicability has the look of a philosophical condition of possibility, it designates only language's communication itself. Why, then, does Benjamin still cast language's communication of *itself* in terms of possibility? At the beginning of the essay "On Language as Such" Benjamin contends, in order to insinuate at the outset that communicability is not simply a philosophical category, "that we cannot imagine anything that does not communicate its mental nature in its expression" (p. 62). A linguistic theory for which communicability is the object *par excellence* has indeed, as he claims, an "intimate connection with the philosophy of religion" (p. 66). Communicability, understood as language's communication of itself as communicating, is, in things, "the residue of the creative word of God" (p. 74), and is thus oriented by the horizon of this divine source. Rather than being a category of possibility, communicability is constituted by things' yearning to relate to the origin of their creation in the Word. In language, in a verbal sense of their expression, things communicate that they are of divine origin. It shows them in a process of wanting to communicate, to be heard, and to be redeemed. This then is the point where one can grasp the specificity of communicability. It marks the difference it makes to be able to speak—a difference that shows everything created to have its truth in the divine Word. But such yearning, such intention in language, is not subjective. It is not the things themselves that yearn to be heard; only that part of them that is spiritual, already linguistic—the residue of the·creative word—does so. Communicability is, thus, an *objective* (metaphysical) category that designates the difference that expression or language makes to the extent that as expression and language it communicates all by itself its difference. Yet language makes such a difference only by marking itself off against something else. Communicability, consequently, implies a motion of breaking away from, of separation. It represents a tendency or intention only to the extent that it is a part of a flow that leads away from a given condition. This condition is that of the world of appearances (*Schein*). For Benjamin, language is characterized in depth by a tendency of pointing away from that realm, thus making a difference.

To understand better this difference-producing function of communicability and hence the status of this category itself, I turn to "The Task of the Translator." From the start, let me emphasize that the law of translation that Benjamin formulates in this essay is as objective a law as the one that we have seen determine language's expressive function.

Just as communicability indicates a yearning of language to be heard as expressing communication itself, independently of all symbolic and utilitarian functions of language, so translatability, as an objective category of the work of art, points beyond the original itself. Rather than aspiring to a fulfillment of the original, translatability indicates the work of art's search for a fulfillment in something other than the original itself. Translatability, as a call in the work of art, calls for a liberation of the work of art from itself. Benjamin remarks, "No translation, however good it may be, can have any significance as regards the original" (p. 254). On the contrary, a translation implies a displacement, even a disregard of the original's sense, as we shall see. The objective possibility of translation, a possibility that is also a call for it, can thus best be described as an inner limit of the work of art, or again, as a structural feature that, within the work itself, points beyond it. Translatability is the means by which the work of art rises above itself, above its own linguistic enmeshments. It is an operator of sorts, of difference, and not what one could commonly call an essence.

According to Benjamin, the language of works of art differs from that of ordinary language to the extent that it is no longer simply referential and intentional. As Benjamin's strong criticism of intentionality reveals, intentions for him belong to the world of appearances and phenomena.[9] They are a function of natural and subjective ends by which words become chained up with things external. In this sense ordinary language is thoroughly natural language since it is governed by mythical interconnectedness. While artistic language breaks with these natural and, thus, mythical properties of language, the work of art has not therefore already transgressed all of language's mythical interconnections. Its language is still characterized by a certain natural relation between its content and itself, a relation that Benjamin describes as forming "a certain unity in the original, like a fruit and its skin" (p. 258). A poet's effort, Benjamin reminds us, is directed "solely and immediately at specific linguistic contextual aspects [*sprachliche Gehaltszusammenhänge*]." Therefore, the work of literature and poetry finds itself still "in the center of the language forest [*innerer Bergwald der Sprache*]" (p. 258). As similar images in *The Origin* (or the Goethe essay) reveal, where Benjamin refers to the "wooded interior" of the symbol—probably a reference to Baudelaire's poem "Correspondences"—the image of the language forest serves to stress the literary work's symbolic aspect, which is to say, its being constituted by a natural unity based on natural relations between sign and content.[10] Now, translatability represents in the work of art the objective call for overcoming this still-natural unity rooted in mythical linguistic relations. Translatability is, in the work of art, the yearning to break the symbolic relations that constitute it as a mythical web—or, for short, as a text. Translations, if they are to be successful, must indeed achieve this goal. As Benjamin's stress on literal, verbatim translation clearly shows, a translation that measures up to a work of art's demand for translation not only disregards content and sense but destroys the original's *structures* of reference and sense communication as well. Whereas the language of the original destroys language's bond to empirical intentions, a translation destroys the art work's natural linguistic unity "root and branch [*Stumpf und Stiel*]" (p. 258). It faces the "wooded ridge" of language from the outside, Benjamin remarks (p. 258). Because the language of translation undoes language's functions and structures for imparting sense, and with this all natural linguistic relations, the language of translation stands in a relation of disjunction (*Gebrochenheit*) to its content (p. 258). It is characterized by broken natural or symbolic relations, or, to refer to another of Benjamin's images, by a relation of discrepancy. Indeed: "Whereas content and language form a certain unity in the original, like a fruit and its skin, the language of translation envelops its content like a royal robe with ample folds. For it signifies a more exalted language than its own and thus remains unsuited to its content, overpowering and alien" (p. 258). Like the royal robe, language in translation represents nothing but the power of language, language *in actu*, independently of all content it may impart and of the structures that make such communication possible.

Translatability is, in the work of art, that structure that points away from its still-natural linguistic unity and weblike quality, toward language itself. It is, within the artwork's language, the structure directed beyond its own symbolic language and its entanglements, "at language as such, at its totality," "*Intention auf die Sprache als solche*," says the German text, intention being understood this time in a radically nonsubjective and nonempirical fashion (p. 258).[11] This structure, immanent to the language of the original, calls for a departure from that language toward pure language—language beyond its utilitarian and symbolic functions, beyond the burden of extralinguistic meaning and the structures upon which it rests; which is to say, toward the difference that language as language makes. Thanks to this structure the work of art raises itself above textual, weblike, and hence mythical interconnectedness to communicate that within it, language speaks, or that within it, a difference has been set forth.

Because of its direction (*Richtung*), a translation is not called upon by the original work of art for the sake of that work itself, but rather for the benefit of pure, or divine, language itself. The difference that translatability makes is a difference determined by this objective intention toward what Benjamin calls the "afterlife" of the works of art, or again, toward what is thoroughly on the other side of natural life and its connections.

Yet what does this nonphenomenal and pure state of language, at which art's demand for translation aims, represent? And what is its relation, finally, to the original itself? Translation, Benjamin writes, "ultimately serves the purpose of expressing the innermost relationship of languages" (p. 255). He continues, "Languages are not strangers to one another, but are, a priori and apart from all historical relationships, interrelated in what they want to express." But languages are not akin to one another as far as their words, sentences, and linguistic structures are concerned, nor are they related through the content that they individually impart:

> Rather, all suprahistorical kinship between languages consists in this: in every one of them as a whole, one and the same thing is meant. Yet this one thing is achievable not by any single language but only by the totality of their intentions supplementing one another: the pure language. Whereas all individual elements of foreign languages—words, sentences, associations—are mutually exclusive, these languages supplement one another in their intentions. (p. 257)

What Benjamin establishes here as "a law [that] is one of the fundamental principles in the philosophy of language" (p. 257), namely, that all singular languages intend one and the same thing (*eines und zwar dasselbe*), had already been thematized in the earlier essay "On Language as Such" under the name of communicability. The latter stipulated that language, qua language, qua linguistic medium, communicates only the unmediated communication of its own communicating. And just as this medium-related quality presupposes a distancing from language's instrumental functions, so language's intention toward pure language becomes manifest only if languages become thoroughly denaturalized. Such denaturalization of natural language—the task *par excellence* of translation—is achieved by translation's focusing not on a language's intended objects but on the mode of its intending, or on what the Scholastics called *modus significandi*—the mode, or intention, of meaning (*Art des Meinens*).[12]

By finding in his own language those tendencies or intentions toward pure language that transcend its own natural condition, the translator produces "in that language the echo of the original" (p. 258). In this, his enterprise resembles the Adamic naming language as described in "On Language as Such." As Benjamin establishes in this essay, man can name things only because they communicate their expression, their linguistic being to him. What they express is their communicability, their each-time-singular intention to communicate: "Their language passes into man" when man contemplates (*Anschauen*) things and names the singularity of their expression (p. 72). A name is the proper name, so to speak, of things' intention or mode of signification. In other words, in thus calling by their name the each-time-singular mode in which things yearn to speak, man completes language as communication *in actu*, by naming it. The name names language's each-time-particular mode of communicating, its mode of expression. Hence Benjamin can state that the name "is the innermost nature of language itself. The name is that *through* which, and *in* which, language itself communicates itself absolutely. In the name, the mental entity that communicates itself is *language*. Where mental being in its communication is language itself in its absolute wholeness, only there is the name, and only the name is there" (p. 65). He can conclude, therefore, that one "can call name the language of language (if the genitive refers to the relationship not of a means but of a medium)" (p. 65). It is of interest to note that Benjamin, in "On Language as Such," also calls man's naming language—which is both receptive and spontaneous—translation; it is "receptive to language" (*sprachempfangend*) to the extent that it listens to "the language of things themselves," and independent to the extent that in naming, it names itself as language (p. 69). That is to say, in translation as in naming, the intent to communicate, as well as its each-time-specific mode of meaning, is named, and thus raised to an autonomy of its own.

The "Translator" essay reproduces this same movement of language, a movement that names what language yearns to communicate, and that does so in setting itself off from all of language's natural and mythical qualities. A translation, I have said, focuses on what in the original is of the order of intention toward the divine, and difference-creating Word (independent of the content intended), and, more precisely, on the overall mode of its language as language. In its own language it establishes a correspondence to the mode in which the original speaks by activating what in its language breaks with the latter's natural condition. A translation, therefore, can be said to be "directed at language as such." In philosophical terms, a translation seems to be based on what the Scholastics called *intentio secunda (formalis)*. Rather than focusing on the object intended in the initial intention, translation—and naming as well—cognitively reflects on the *ens rationis* that is the primary act of intending itself (*actus intellectus reflectus, id est quo aliquid per reflexionem cognoscimus*).

Indeed, in naming the singular modes in which things express themselves, things become known to man: "Only through the linguistic being of things can he get beyond himself and attain knowledge of them—in name" (p. 65). By translating, in the original, the intention toward pure language, this intention is also reflected upon and made known. In naming as well as in translation, communicability and translatability—or the structures within language that yearn for a liberation from its natural and mythical interconnectedness and weblike quality—are cognitively appropriated. The name as well as a translation reflect on difference, on the difference that in language itself permits language to overcome its own mythical entanglements.

The reference above to the philosophical issue of *intentio secunda* is a reference not to one particular philosophical problem but rather to philosophy itself. Philosophy constitutes itself in the act of a distancing reflection as a rational entity, different from the immediate, from being, and so on, and as an entity concerned with exploring and assessing its own difference in the attempt to secure its autonomy in self-foundation. Naming and translating, because they reflect cognitively on difference, are of the order of philosophy. Benjamin himself makes the connection, at least as far as translation is concerned. The "divination and description" of pure, or divine, language is, he writes, "the only perfection for which a philosopher can hope." Yet such pure language, the language of truth, "is concealed in concentrated fashion in translations." Therefore not only are translations intrinsically philosophical, but "there is [even] a philosophical genius that is characterized by a yearning for that language which manifests itself in translations" (p. 259).

But such cognitive reflection of difference as it occurs in the Adamic act of naming, in translation, and in the task of the philosopher has its intrinsic limits. Indeed it does not, for Benjamin, escape all mythical predicament. Let me first remark that a translation in principle cannot "possibly reveal or establish" the pure language intended by the non-natural tendencies of artistic language (p. 255). Although the translator's task is spurned by "the great motif of integrating many tongues into one true language," his intention remains "ideational," that is, regulated by this idea in a Kantian sense (p. 259). All a translation can hope for is to "represent it [the one true language] by realizing it in embryonic or in-

tensive form [*darstellen, indem sie es keimhaft oder intensiv verwirklicht*]."
The mode of representation in question, a mode "of so singular a nature
that it is rarely met with in the sphere of nonlinguistic life" (a mode, by
the way, that originates in chemistry) allows only for an "intensive—that
is, anticipative, intimating—realization" of the hidden relationship between the languages (p. 255). What is true of translation, that it "is only a
somewhat provisional way of coming to terms with the foreignness of
languages" since "an instant and final rather than a temporary and provisional solution to this foreignness remains out of the reach of mankind,"
is valid for Adamic naming language, and for philosophy as well (p. 257).
Although man, in "On Language as Such," is shown to be "the speaker of
language" since "he speaks in name," this only "vouches for the fact *that
language as such* is the mental being of man," and not for the one realizing language as such in naming, that is, the divine word itself (p. 65).
Adam's naming language, which answers things' language, is, notwithstanding its importance, only one moment of "the uninterrupted flow
of . . . communication [that] runs through the whole of nature, from the
lowest forms of existence to man and from man to God" (p. 74). Philosophy too, and its thought of difference, is only one rung on the ladder
leading to what Benjamin terms doctrine (*Lehre*), which is concerned
with the divine, or pure difference itself.[13]

     As Benjamin knew very well, the translation by name of the differ-
ence that things communicate to man in their expression, as well as a
translation's articulation of what in the original's language hints at the
hidden kinship of languages, establishes a community between two
spheres that needs an ultimate grounding in a higher sphere. However
perfect the language may be into which the less perfect language is translated, "the objectivity of this translation" must be guaranteed by God, he
reminds us (p. 70). Indeed, as Benjamin argues in "On Language as
Such," it is only because the divine word created things, which thus contain as a residue "the germ of the cognizing name," that man can name
things in the first place (p. 70). Benjamin demonstrates a fine philosophical sensitivity when he declares that man's task of naming things "would
be insoluble were not the name-language of man and the nameless language of things related in God and released from the same creative word,
which in things became the communication of matter in magic commu-

nion, and in man the language of knowledge and name in blissful mind" (p. 70). For naming and translation to be possible, a prior "identity of the creative word and the cognizing name in God" must, indeed, be assumed (p. 70). The identity of the creative and at the same time cognizing divine word—this ultimate community—is the condition of possibility of all expression and all naming, or translation.

In his "Program of the Coming Philosophy," where, in the name of a unitarian approach to the question of the ultimate ground, Benjamin takes a critical stand against the Kantian division between epistemology and metaphysics, or again, between criticism and dogmatic philosophy, Benjamin had already severely criticized the Kantian philosophical notions of experience and cognition. Yet the metaphysics targeted in this essay still envisioned the possibility of a higher form of specifically philosophical cognition and experience in which the "absolute, as existence," God for short, could be encountered in unmediated fashion (p. 109). Although such concepts of experience and cognition already turn philosophy into the doctrine of religion with its immediate absolute certainty of the absolute, Benjamin continued to think the latter as cognitively apprehensible in systematic unity. But by the time of his later work—*The Origin of German Tragic Drama*—Benjamin had given up hope that mere thought could conceptually come to grips with the fundamental identity and unity of the ultimate ground. In the Goethe essay, Benjamin had established that the unity of philosophy, its system, is in no way within the reach of philosophical questioning (p. 334). Truth, he states in "The Epistemo-Critical Prologue," "is devoid of all intention, and certainly does not itself appear as intention. Truth does not enter into relationships, particularly intentional ones." Its mode of existence is that of "an intentionless state of being." The prior identity that, as seen, must underlie both poles of a translation process can no longer be approached philosophically since, as he writes, "truth is the death of intention."[14] All attempts to come to grips with it cognitively, by attempting to ensnare truth in the "spider's web" of thought "as if it were something which came flying in from outside," show philosophy still to be in the grips of myth.[15] Cognition is still intentional and relational, and thus mediated by natural desires and ends. Benjamin writes: "Knowledge is possession. Its very object is determined by the fact that it must be taken possession of—even if in a transcendental sense—

in the consciousness."[16] Knowledge, because it is reflective, is still a function of natural subjectivity. The systems it weaves, in which everything becomes linked to the subject, are mythic webs that allow for no difference. The Adamic naming gesture, the task of the translator and of the philosopher as well, are thus limited to being moments in a higher scheme because naming, translating, or reflecting difference presupposes an underlying prior unity, which they themselves cannot hope to bring about. But it is not so much because of their status as moments that all three orders are limited; it is, rather, the fact that they are still cognitive, and hence fundamentally incapable of truly setting difference free.

Truth, or the prior identity, not only escapes the reach of cognitive appropriation but also does not relate intentionally to what it embraces, itself included. It does not relate to itself in a relational manner, since all such relation would, according to Benjamin, still be mythical. For the same reason, truth is not of the order of *intentio recta*, the intention of intention, nor for that matter the order of the language of language. The reflexivity characteristic of *intentio recta* only distinguishes man's naming language, as well as the status of translation and philosophy, each of which is a mere moment in the flow of communication of difference that runs through all of creation toward God.

Although naming, translating, and philosophizing are constituted by the *telos* of the creative word and the hidden kinship of languages, they cannot by themselves bring that unity about or cognize it. In spite of the fact that communicability and translatability point away from the mythic web of language toward the difference of nonphenomenal "Otherness," the philosophical activity of naming and reflecting these difference-producing tendencies remains caught up in what it yearns to transgress. In other words, the structures of transcending immanent to language, the structures that create difference by pointing away from language's empirical and mythical entanglement, that is, those of translatability and communicability, are unable to achieve the pure difference that they aim at and presuppose. However decisive the transcending power of the linguistically immanent structures of difference may be, they remain finite. They are not different enough, not as radically different as an absolute ground by right ought to be. Their transcending and difference-creating power, and the objectivity of these structures are themselves in want of an ultimate justification and legitimation by the absolute Otherness of truth. But they cannot hope to bring this sanctioning about on their own terms. It is a legitimation that only truth itself can grant, in its own time and on its own terms. And since truth is not relational, intentional, or based on reflection, such granting cannot, for Benjamin, be of the order of grounding available to philosophy, such as the order of the modes of legitimation or justification. Since Benjamin conceives of truth as radically different, and in total disjunction from that of which it might be the truth, such demand for grounding by the structures of difference that are communicability and translatability can only take place through their radical *redemption* (*Erlösung*), more precisely, detachment or release from the prisonhouse of language.

Communicability and translatability, as we have seen, come closest to being philosophical concepts of difference. But this proximity is for Benjamin also what constitutes their limit. They are still epistemological concepts of difference, and still in want of a redeeming relation to truth, which thought is unable to provide. The difference from the embroilments and enmeshments of nature and myth that they achieve, however decisive it may be, is not yet radical. The difference-producing thrust of these structures depends, as far as its possibility and effect are concerned, on a difference so radical that it escapes the spiderweb of thought. Philosophical difference, for Benjamin, is thus a function of a difference that escapes its grasp, but a difference that it must nonetheless presuppose, even though by itself philosophical difference is unable to secure this difference's legitimizing function. Because of philosophy's limitations in disrupting the tightly woven web of myth by establishing a fully objective difference that would escape the empirical and the subjective (or rather, because of philosophy's limitations in securing, in immanent fashion, the transcending thrust of the difference that philosophical difference makes with respect to myth, the empirical, and the aesthetic), philosophy itself must call for legitimation by a higher instance, namely, by the doctrine of truth. Yet it is not in the power of philosophy to secure for itself an answer to its pledge.

I cannot hope to solve here the question whether this inability of the philosophical concepts of difference to secure their own legitimation truly implies an irreducible relation of philosophy in general to theological concepts, as Benjamin seems to suggest, or whether such a problematic is not rather due to Benjamin's inability to sound the intellectual possibilities of philosophy, along with a perhaps too-narrow Kantian concept of philosophy as criticism. What I can try to show is that the flaws of the philosophical concepts of difference are not, for Benjamin, simply shortcomings. Indeed, in spite of their finite nature, they contain, paradoxically, not the promise that eventually they will strike a difference but only that the chance that such difference is within the range of their possibility. To show that this is the case, I will return one last time to the internal limits of the structures of difference discussed above.

It is not in the power of these structures, however objective they might already be, to break away once and for all from the empirical and aesthetic web of language toward divine language. All they achieve is a *caesura* in the realm of mythical entanglement. A caesura, Benjamin tells us, does not lead to a complete separation of what it divides; as an instance of critical power a caesura only prevents the parts and levels in question from becoming mixed (pp. 340–41). A caesura keeps them simultaneously together and separate. Benjamin illustrates such caesural difference when discussing the relation of a translation to the sense of the original, with the following simile:

> Just as a tangent touches a circle lightly [*flüchtig*] and at but one point—establishing, with this touch rather than with the point, the law according to which it is to continue on its straight path to infinity—a translation touches the original lightly and only at the infinitely small point of sense, thereupon pursuing its own course according to the laws of fidelity in the freedom of linguistic flux" (p. 261)

For a translation to correspond to the demand for translation in the original, it must disregard, or rather, touch the original's sense in such a manner that a movement away from sense is inaugurated. The disregard of sense must not be absolute; such difference in translation would be abstract, false, erring difference. True philosophical difference is achieved in the fleeting touch of what is to be disregarded, in fidelity to what is to be abandoned. A caesura thus seems to yield to the philosophical demand *par excellence*—that genres as different as the universal and the particular, the empirical and the transcendental, are not to be mixed—of which Benjamin has shown himself fully aware in his criticism of Friedrich

Schlegel's attempt to conceive of the unity of art (first thought as an idea in the Platonic sense as *proteron te phusei*) as itself a concrete work of art (p. 167). But the difference between that philosophical law itself and Benjamin's use of it is striking. For Benjamin, the universal or transcendental is not, as we have seen, a given or something that could be thought in its unity, and that could thus be clearly marked off against the empirical or the particular. Benjamin's concept of difference is based on the assumption that the radically differing pole of philosophical difference or opposition is not at hand. Lacking the radical and nonphenomenal Other, all that thought can do is touch on what is in order to move away from it. In this motion alone, in a differing in an active sense, can the Other, truth, or originary difference be anticipated. Benjaminian difference, as it is formulated in such concepts as communicability and translatability, is thus a difference that realizes in perhaps a fundamental way the philosophical demand not to mix genres. By fleetingly touching the webs of language (which allow for no difference) in a disrupting movement away from them, thought produces difference, and with it, the empty space of the Other of myth. Although the difference thus created does not imply clearly divided realms (nor a constituted Other), it anticipates the possibility of the radical otherness of truth whose thinking does not fall into the powers of man.

In short, the difference with respect to the interlacings of language in the grips of myth and nature, which Benjamin seeks to conceptualize, is a difference not between already constituted poles or realms. Still, the philosophical requirement not to mix remains a must, or better, becomes even more pressing since in the mythical absence of difference the demand not to mix turns into the more fundamental demand for difference in the first place. Benjamin's concept of difference inscribes in itself the impossibility to distinguish immanently between the profane webs of language and language's total Other; but the demand for difference becomes, then, all the more urgent. In the absence of the total Other— "Other" to a point that it must necessarily be absent from the mythical webs of language if it is to truly make a difference—of an Other so beyond man's finitude and his natural condition that it can only be termed the sacred, the fleeting touch that touches to break away is the sole means to instigate difference. This finite difference, however, points at the radical difference that alone can make it meaningful, and that alone can grant significance to the fundamental philosophical law not to mix.

As mentioned, from a philosophical viewpoint, communicability and translatability are finite concepts of transcending and difference. As such they might seem to mix the incommensurable dimensions of the universal and the particular. But that such mixing does not occur is shown by the fact that Benjamin's notion of language—not unlike Kant's notion of the sublime, which only negatively represents the realm of ideas—refers to that same ideal realm by violently destroying language's aesthetic and structural characteristics. In precisely this manner, communicability and translatability avoid mixing domains. In aesthetic considerations, reference to theological concepts does not imply any *metabasis eis allo genos* ("a mixing of genres"), as Benjamin remarks in *The Origin of German Tragic Drama*, but serves instead to demarcate levels in the first place so that the theoretical paradoxes that distinguish these considerations can be solved. In the same way, the finite concepts of difference, rather than implying an illegitimate confusion of levels of thought, secure their distinction by likewise representing (*darstellen*) what pertains to "the higher domain of theology," in the very destruction of the networks of language.[17] Such destruction, as discussed above, makes the difference.

This concept of difference, then, is not simply a philosophical concept. Benjamin agrees with Kant that reference to the absolute ground as absolutely Other is inevitable. He also agrees with Kant that such a ground cannot be known in its difference from objects of nature. Thought cannot hope to conceptualize it, or realize it in consciousness. Yet Benjamin refuses, not only in "Program of the Coming Philosophy" but throughout his writings, to go along with Kant's injunction to keep criticism and metaphysics separate. For Benjamin to conflate the two realms is not to indulge in empiricism, or what amounts to the same, in the leveling demonic forces of myth; on the contrary, such conflation serves only to realize difference in the first place. Benjamin proceeds from the assumption that actual reference by (critical) philosophy to the higher domain of the ground is what endows philosophy with its distinguishing trait. Although it cannot think the ground, it actually anticipates it in the existent. In that sense critical philosophy is for him always already theology, but not theology, of course, in a positive sense. Benjamin's concept of difference is not a pure philosophical concept inasmuch as it implies actual reference to "the higher domain of theology"; neither is it a purely theological concept since what has been established regarding philosophy as a cognitive undertaking is valid of theology as a positive discipline as well.

Benjamin's thought of difference cannot be cast in terms of any particular philosophy and thus cannot be appropriated for any particular brand of thought. The paradoxical nature of his intellectual enterprise, permitting multiple appropriations, may well stem, on the one hand, from his accepting, seemingly unconditionally, the Kantian concept of philosophy while refusing the Kantian requirement of distinguishing the critical and the dogmatic, and on the other hand, from his not opting for a Hegelian solution of that difference (and in this sense Benjamin is also very much like Kierkegaard). But Benjamin seems to be specifically concerned with the fundamental question of how philosophy in general is to make a difference. Reference in philosophy to the "higher domain of theology" seems, for Benjamin, to make such difference possible. But at the same time, this constitutive reference to the absolute Other of myth and the entanglements of language is also what strikes, with irreducible finitude, philosophy's attempt to raise itself above the web of language. Or rather, it causes such attempt to become utterly idiosyncratic.

For such a position as the one outlined, a position based on a tension between philosophy and theology, there is, it seems to me, a name in Benjamin's writings. In *The Origin of German Tragic Drama* it is called "saturnine vision."[18] Such vision, such a theoretical glance, realizes reference to the Absolute, to that which is completely separated from the entanglements of myth and the mythical interconnectedness of language, not by cognitive abstraction but by "close touch" with what is, that is to say, by violently tearing its texture to shreds. This vision's transcending glance reaches beyond the realm of interconnectedness only to the extent that it stands under the sign of the natural powers and their mythical entanglements that it seeks to overcome. Saturn is the planet under which Benjamin was born.[19] The demonic powers it symbolizes limit any order of existence to and within the plane of the profane and temporal. Yet the infinitely small, or almost insignificant, disruption that such vision under the sign of the most earthy planets produces in the tightly woven web of

the demonic forces of fate is, because it exists (as opposed to merely phenomenal and cognitive nondifference), anticipatory of the *being* of the
ideas—or to use another of Benjamin's expressions, the being of the "indivisible unity," or, rather, as the German original puts it, "the crackless
[*sprunglose*] unity of truth."[20]

(1986)

4

Cutting in on Distance

Walter Benjamin's meditations on art and art criticism represent a continued debate with all the major positions punctuating the development of modern aesthetics. Yet although Benjamin's texts critically take up Enlightenment, *Sturm und Drang*, Kantian, romantic and idealist reflections on art, the aesthetic position—if it still is one—from which Benjamin levels his critique is difficult to ascertain. In light of this difficulty, the fact that only Kant emerges relatively unscathed from this debate becomes significant. By means of an analysis of "The Work of Art in the Age of Mechanical Reproduction," I wish to argue that Benjamin's understanding of art can best be approached by tracing its principal statements back to motifs in Kantian aesthetics.[1] First and foremost, Kant's detachment of the beautiful and the sublime from the object seems to have been Benjamin's model for the transformed perception of art that he delineates throughout his 1935 essay, a perception free from the authority of the object. It is common knowledge that in the *Critique of Judgment*, Kant develops a conception of the beautiful and the sublime in which beauty and sublimity no longer are attributes of objects but rather refer back—in the reflective judgment constitutive of the judgment of taste—to the subject, or more precisely, to the experience of pleasure or displeasure arising from the agreement of the faculties in a free play constitutive of the possibility of cognition in general, or their disagreement revelatory of the subject's suprasensible destination. In thus detaching the beautiful and the sublime from the object, Kant occupies a singular position in the history of aesthetics, at odds both with his Enlightenment predecessors, for whom objects are beautiful if fashioned according to conventional rules of taste, and with the idealists, for whom art objects are beautiful and sublime because in them the idea has taken on sensible shape. Still, although Benjamin continues this nonobjective aesthetics in "The Work of Art," all the philosophemes that sustain Kant's foundation of aesthetics here undergo significant transformations. Indeed, the Kantian notions of subject, object, and reflective judgment emerge thoroughly altered in Benjamin's treatment. And yet, beyond all these transformations, the exposition of Benjamin's debt to Kantian objectives helps to situate the significance of Benjamin's provocative thesis that the loss of the aura in the age of mechanical reproduction allows the work of art to assume a political function. Moreover, paradoxically, it also serves to sketch out the limits, for Benjamin, of aesthetics—not simply its end but also its restriction to being a domain from which anything transcendental is ostensibly absent.

If in the Third Critique Kant can dispose of the object and concentrate on purposiveness with respect to form alone, it is because the judgment of taste is a pure judgment of taste only if it is neither interested in nor intrigued (as is the teleological judgment) by the existence of the object. Free beauty is pleasurable because its perception assures the subject of its cognitive ability in general, and is achieved only where the judgment of taste has kept in check sensuous charm and moral connotations, both of which rest on the presence of the object. Benjamin's separation of the effects of art on its beholder in the age of mechanical reproducibility from the work of art's phenomenal character coincides with his massive critique of the aura. By following Benjamin through the various facets of the process in which the aura is repudiated, both his similarities to and his differences from Kant should become tangible.

From the start, let me emphasize that for Benjamin the loss of the aura in mechanically reproducible art is not something to be deplored, as some of his Frankfurt School interpreters in particular have held. Nor is there a double response—positive toward the work of art, negative toward the human being—to be detected in "The Work of Art," or anywhere else for that matter—as Susan Buck-Morss, for instance, sees it.[2]

Undoubtedly, as long as the full implications of this decay of the aura in modern times remain unclear, it is pointless to discuss the beneficial or detrimental aspects of the loss in question. It must be admitted, however, that certain "values" linked to the auratic make it difficult—especially when the elimination of the singular human being's aura is shown to be a function of his transformation into a mass being—to argue that Benjamin could indeed have endorsed its radical destruction. These "values" happen to be those of uniqueness, singularity, and authenticity, and they explain to a large extent the ambivalence evident in Benjamin's treatment of the aura. Yet in order to glimpse what the thesis of the loss of the aura is supposed to establish, it is necessary to interrogate what uniqueness, singularity, and authenticity mean for Benjamin. This done, little doubt will remain that Benjamin must reject both the aura of art objects and the aura attributed to the human being.[3]

Benjamin unambiguously endorses the radical reversal that comes with the technical reproducibility of art, and that totally separates the new art forms from those that make up the continuum stretching from ritual art in mythic times to secular, autonomous art in bourgeois culture and society. He subscribes to this event without nostalgia. The "comprehensive liquidation" of "the traditional value of the cultural heritage," which goes hand in hand with the loss of the aura, is even viewed as a cathartic event.[4] Indeed, "for the first time in world history, mechanical reproduction emancipates the work of art from its parasitical dependence on ritual," Benjamin holds (pp. 224; 481). With ritual and cult values radically severed from the artwork, a new era arises—a "crisis and renewal of mankind" (pp. 221; 478)—in which art is "based on another practice—politics" (pp. 224; 482). It is an entirely positive event for Benjamin—a liberating event, an event in which mankind is reborn—and Benjamin celebrates it without regret.[5]

He writes, "We know that the earliest art works originated in the service of a ritual—first the magical, then the religious kind" (pp. 223; 480). Originally, artworks were "instruments of magic" that were "meant for the spirits," he holds (pp. 225; 483). The link of the work of art to its function in cult is so fundamental that even where the cult value has become secularized, as in the cult of beauty, its ritualistic basis "is still recognizable as secularized ritual" (pp. 224; 480). For Benjamin, "it is significant [*von entscheidender Bedeutung*] that the existence of the work of art with reference to its aura is never entirely separated from its ritual function"(pp. 223–24; 480). *L'art pour l'art*, one of the last reactive movements in art against the advent of truly nonauratic, that is, ritual-free art is a case in point. In mechanically reproducible art this essential link between art and cult is thoroughly cut. Art in the age of mechanical reproducibility is an art that no longer has even a secular ritualistic function. The crisis is radical: stripped of its cult value in both a magical, religious sense and a secularized sense, art has become entirely profane, free from all such dependencies.

But what constitutes the aura? It is highly significant that in order to explain what this concept implies for historical objects such as artworks, Benjamin has recourse to the aura of natural objects. Indeed, with this move, the aura is shown to be something that *fundamentally belongs to the order of nature*. I quote:

> The concept of aura which was proposed above with reference to historical objects may usefully be illustrated with reference to the aura of natural ones. We define the aura of the latter as the unique phenomenon of a distance, however close it may be. If, while resting on a summer afternoon, you follow with your eyes a mountain range on the horizon or a branch which casts its shadow over you, you experience the aura of those mountains, of that branch. This image makes it easy to comprehend the social bases of the contemporary decay of the aura. (pp. 222–23; 479)

Benjamin's distinction between historical and natural objects is not one between two different kinds of the auratic. Quite the contrary,

> the definition of the aura [of natural objects] as a 'unique phenomenon of a distance however close it may be' represents nothing but the formulation of the cult value of the work of art in categories of space and time perception. Distance is the opposite of closeness. The essentially distant object is the unapproachable one. Unapproachability is indeed a major quality of the cult value. (pp. 243; 479)

The aura is identical; we have a phenomenon of the order of nature in each case. If Benjamin continues to distinguish between the aura of natural and that of historical objects, it is for other reasons. Depreciation of the here and now through reproduction affects objects of nature as well as those of art, yet "in the case of the art object, a most sensitive nucleus—

namely, its authenticity—is interfered with whereas no natural object is vulnerable on that score" (pp. 221; 477). The difference between natural and historical objects concerns indeed this "most sensitive nucleus," not a qualitative difference as regards their aura. As is obvious from the context, the nucleus in question, that is, the artwork's authenticity, corresponds to its authority to institute a tradition, that is, a *continuity* between its own unique existence and everything to which it becomes subject throughout the time of its existence (pp. 220; 475). The difference between objects of nature and artworks concerns the latter's power to inaugurate a cultural heritage, tradition, and history.[6] Yet, although the nucleus characteristic of artworks is termed most vulnerable to the destructive effects of reproducibility, here too Benjamin knows no regret. The history, tradition, and cultural heritage to which artwork give rise, and through which the authority of the original holds sway, are flatly said to have their origin in cult. He writes, "Originally the contextual integration of art in tradition found its expression in the cult" (pp. 223; 480). The difference between natural and historical objects is thus a difference not between their auras but between their powers: historical objects such as artworks have the power to extend the power of nature into the realm of the social and human. Tradition, heritage, history, with their value of continuity, are forms of natural, mythical interconnectedness.

But let us return to the definition of the aura, since it alone will explain the ease with which Benjamin is ready to relinquish it together with all the values attached to it. "We define the aura [of natural objects] . . . as the unique phenomenon of a distance, however close it may be [*als die einmalige Erscheinung einer Ferne, so nah sie sein mag*]." Harry Zohn's translation is here in need of correction. Benjamin defines the aura as the unique *appearance* (*Erscheinung*), or appearing, of a distance (*einer Ferne*), that is, not merely spatial remoteness or an open space, as the clause "however close it may be" indicates, but *substantive*, if not substantial, distance. What comes into appearance here is distance as "something" distant or unapproachable. First, then, auratic objects are appearances, that is, manifestations according to the forms (or categories, as Benjamin incorrectly writes) of space and time (the reference to Kant's pure forms of intuition is obvious), of a distance, a remoteness, of "something" that is beyond, that transcends the phenomenal. All appearing (of the suprasensible, or the noumenal, supposing that such a thing were possible) is necessarily a singularizing manifestation. Appearances in the Kantian sense are always singular (and merely give rise to a manifold). Auratic objects, for this reason, are *unique*, singular appearances of the distance in question. That this distance must be read as "something" distant is further supported by Benjamin's reference to the substratum of the artwork's uniqueness (*vom Substrat seiner Einmaligkeit*, pp. 244; 481). The uniqueness of the appearance is rooted in a substratum, an existing support or ground, underpinning what of it comes into view as a singular object. Distance is such a substratum spreading or laying itself underneath its unique phenomenal existence in the auratic object. With this we are in a position to pinpoint Benjamin's understanding of uniqueness and singularity (*Einmaligkeit* and *Einzigkeit*) insofar as they represent qualifications of the auratic object whether natural or historical. Uniqueness and singularity are a function of the phenomenal appearing, in space and time, in a here and now (*Hier und Jetzt*), of something nonphenomenal, something distant that transcends the phenomenal. The "one element [*eines*]" that constitutes the auratic work of art is "its presence in time and space [*das Hier und Jetzt des Kunstwerks*], its unique existence at the place where it happens to be" (pp. 220; 475). The uniqueness of the artwork, its quality of being *one*, is thus clearly a function of sensibility, in Kantian terms, or of its being an object of nature, nature however, having for Benjamin connotations of fallenness, entanglement, and fate. I also note that the very appearing of a distant substratum explains why works of art are *authentic* (*echt*) and have *authority*. Benjamin writes, "The presence [*das Hier und Jetzt*] of the original is the prerequisite to the concept of [its] authenticity." But the original, singular object that is the work is also endowed with authority, and it has this authority *as* object, that is, as an appearance in space and time of a distant substratum. (See pp. 220; 476 and 221; 477.) But in order to get a better grasp of why such a unique appearance of a distance is endowed with authority, we must return to the appearing substratum itself.

Benjamin claims that "the uniqueness of the phenomena which hold sway in the cult image [*die Einmaligkeit der im Kultbilde waltenden Erscheinung*] is more and more displaced by the empirical uniqueness of the creator or of his creative achievement" (pp. 244; 481). In other words, the unique appearance of a distance in the cult object is that of an appearance that holds sway in it. In the auratic object, the unique appearance of a substratum is at work, and reigns in it. The cult object, but also the work of art as a cult object, not only is an instrument of magic meant for the spirits but also is inhabited by the appearance of a substratum that is actively at work in it. Such an object inhabited by a reigning substance is truly an *object*, or *Gegenstand*. It is set against the beholder, at a distance from him, unapproachable. Unapproachability is, indeed, the defining characteristic of the cult object, whether belonging to ritual or to art. (Yet such unapproachability does not exclude but rather implies attraction by the cult object. Benjamin, putting forth the example of the mountain range on the horizon to illustrate his definition of aura as the unique phenomenon of a distance, might very well have had the following verse by Goethe in mind: "und wenn mich am tag die ferne blauer berge sehnlich zieht" (literally, "and when during the day the distance of blue mountains longingly draws me"). With this, another aspect of Benjamin's definition of the auratic object as a unique appearance, as shaped according to the categories of space and time, by the here and now, comes into view. After making the distinction between the cult and exhibition value of artworks, he notes, "what mattered [for the works of art as cult objects] was their existence [*dass sie vorhanden sind*], not their being on view" (pp. 224–25; 483). The auratic is thus linked to the being present as object, or thing, of the distance. It is a function of this materialization of distance, its being effective in the shape of a present object. This objective quality is intimately linked to the auratic. Objects as defined in this context are the unique material appearances of a distance that, like a power, holds sway in them. What the nature of these powers might be is not explicitly stated in "The Work of Art." Yet Benjamin gives us a hint in a footnote in which he credits German idealism, Hegel in particular, for having anticipated the distinction between the cult and exhibition value, as well as this link between object and the appearing in it of something noumenal. In this footnote Benjamin quotes the following passage from Hegel's *Philosophy of History*: "Worshipping . . . is concerned with the work as an object [*Ding*], for it is but a spiritless stupor of the soul [*ein geistloses Verdumpfen der Seele*]" (pp. 245; 482). What comes into appearance as a thing or object can therefore also only be of the order of the spiritless, dazzling, stupefying power, in short what Benjamin elsewhere, especially in the essay on Goethe's *Elective Affinities*, designates as the opposite pole to spirit (*Geist*), namely that which is of "spectral [*geisterhaften*] origin." The spiritless, the spectral—not only in the form of the deceased who bar the way of the living but especially in the form of the superhuman, demonic forces, the dark powers of myth, the thirsty shadows—is associated in the Goethe essay with the chthonic element, the stagnant waters, the magnetism of the earth core.[7]

Yet the aura is not only the coming into presence of what Benjamin characterizes at one point—in "A Small History of Photography," while describing a picture of Dauthendy, the photographer's wife—as "an ominous [*unheilvolle*] distance" in which the gaze becomes absorbed (*saugend an eine unheilvolle Ferne geheftet*).[8] Its own structure has traits that betray its belonging to the order of nature and myth. The aura is the web itself, a tissue spun from the here and the now to produce the appearance of a distance. "A Small History of Photography" asks:

What is the aura, actually? A strange weave [*Gespinst*] of space and time: the unique appearance or semblance of a distance, no matter how close the object may be. While resting on a summer's noon, to trace a range of mountains on the horizon, or a branch that throws its shadow on the observer, until the moment or the hour become part of their appearance—that is what it means to breathe the aura of those mountains, that branch.[9]

The phrase "until the moment or the hour become part of their appearance," which is absent from the otherwise very similar passage in "The Work of Art," shows the aura to be constituted as a web in which space and time (*Augenblick, Stunde*) are interwoven so as to create the conditions for a mountain range or a branch to become the unique appearance of a distance. All by themselves insignificant, space and singular moment when woven together transform these mountains and that branch into the singular coming into presence of a distance entirely different in kind from that of the far-off mountains or the nearby branch.

To sum up, then, the auratic is the attribute of the thing, or object-like appearing of something beyond appearances, that thus becomes effective, actual, real. As such a materialization of a distance become power, the auratic object, whether belonging to cult or to art, is authentic and has authority. It has authority in that powers hold sway in it. It is always unique and singular because in it a distance has taken on a concrete appearance. It is thus not surprising that Benjamin would reject, along with the auratic work, "values" such as singularity, uniqueness, and authenticity, since in essence they are nothing but the result of the appearing as thing or object of a spiritless substratum that thus acquires a power to hold sway. Benjamin writes, "the unique value of the 'authentic' work of art has its basis in ritual, the location of its original use value" (pp. 224; 480). Nor, therefore, should it come as a surprise if Benjamin celebrates, along with the disappearance of the aura, the decay of the object in contemporary art.[10]

But before taking up that issue, the lack of any essential difference between the auras of objects and of human beings remains to be established, as does the fact that Benjamin mourns the loss of neither. In section 6 of "The Work of Art"—the section mainly referenced by Susan Buck-Morss and others to claim a concomitant negative valorization by Benjamin of the decay of the aura—Benjamin argues that although photography displaces cult value all along the line, it does not give way without resistance. He then writes:

It retires into an ultimate retrenchment [*ein letzte Verschantzung*, that is, a temporally last form of retrenchment, before it will have been displaced for good]: the human countenance [*Menschenantlitz*] . . . The cult of remembrance of loved ones, absent or dead, offers a last refuge for the cult value of the picture. For the last time the aura emanates from the early photographs in the fleeting expression of a human face [*Menschengesichts*]. (pp. 225–26; 485)

Undoubtedly this passage, in its melancholic beauty, seems to display a sentimentality and nostalgia that one would deem appropriate under the circumstances. But is this not merely the honorable if less than comfortable sentiment of a reader unaware that what Benjamin describes is a cult—the cult of remembering loved ones in pictures that have become the *objects* through which they look at us? First, it must be noted that the importance that Benjamin attributes in this section to Atget's photography clearly shows him to favor without regret an art that has entirely eliminated cult value for the benefit of exhibition value. "A Small History of Photography" is even more explicit. "He [Atget] initiates the emancipation of object from aura which is the most signal achievement of the latest school of photography," Benjamin remarks. Atget's pictures, he adds, remove "the makeup from reality"; "they pump the aura out of reality like water from a sinking ship." This achievement, prefiguring surrealist photography's "salutary estrangement between man and his surroundings," is largely the result of the emptiness and the absence of mood (*stimmungslos*) characteristic of his pictures.[11]

But more important is the fact that Benjamin does not valorize the human face, as have several of his interpreters. To make this point, it is useful to look once again to "A Small History of Photography." Here Benjamin argues that the aura or "atmospheric medium" that hovers about the people in early photographs, and that lends "fullness and security to their gaze even as it [the gaze] penetrated that medium," endows the human face (and likewise the folds of the protagonists' frock coats, into which the aura has seeped) with immortality.[12] In these early portraits, "the human countenance had a silence about it in which the gaze rested," because the portraiture of this period still sheltered the reproduced from contact with actuality. "Everything about these early pictures was built to last," Benjamin writes. They convey "an air of permanence," and assure immortality to the portrayed not only as members of a rising bourgeois class but as *living* human beings.[13] As the photography essay states, the aura of the human countenance in early photography is technically conditioned—it is indeed a function of "the absolute continuum from the brightest light to darkest shadow," of the prevailing darkness and the penumbral tone of the early photographs.[14] But the aura stems as well from the ideological nature of these photographic subjects—imperialist bourgeoisie—and in particular (here I return to "The Work of Art") from the fullness, security, and rest that photographs lend to the face in its mere natural singularity. If, in this latter essay, Benjamin evokes the aura of the pictured human face, he thinks primarily of the faces of absent or dead loved ones (*fern* or *abgestorben*). The early photographs portray singular living beings now absent or dead, that is, beings in whose countenances *mere life*—natural, biological life—has taken on phenomenal shape. The aura of the human being, whether in pictures or in real living persons, is a function of the unique and singular appearance as thing of something for which Benjamin, continuing a tradition that originated in Aristotle, knows only contempt—*das blosse Leben*, mere natural life. Such life, Benjamin asserts in the essay on Goethe's *Elective Affinities*, is life that has become guilty (*verschuldetes Leben*).[15] As the singularizing shining forth of mere life, the human face is not essentially different from the unique and singular objects that are the coming into appearance of a distance.[16]

Benjamin's analysis of the difference between the actor on stage and the actor in front of the camera (*Apparatur*) in section 9 of "The Work of Art" is a case in point. He writes:

> For the first time—and this is the effect of the film—man has to operate with his whole living person, yet forgoing the aura. For aura is tied to his presence [*Hier und Jetzt*]; there can be no replica of it. The aura which, on stage, emanates from Macbeth, cannot be separated for the spectators from that of the actor. However, the singularity of the shot in the studio is that the camera is substituted for the public. Consequently, the aura that envelops the actor vanishes, and with it the aura of the figure he portrays. (pp. 229; 489)

The camera, unlike the eyes of stage viewers, allows nothing to appear or shine into singularizing presence. No distance can manifest itself here in the unique shape of a thing, human body, or face. Indeed, Benjamin's whole discussion of what happens to the actor who represents himself to the camera presupposes that time and space, here and now, are no longer the forms that frame or shape what the camera "eye" registers. Camera pictures are free pictures, detached from the outset from all space and time and thus also reproducible from the outset. The images are completely stripped of anything that could make them appearances. The passage quoted above links the aura of the actor to the presence, here and now, on stage, of "his whole living person." On stage, the whole *living* person comes into an appearance for the spectators. The aura that surrounds the actor is a function of this singularizing phenomenalization of the mere life that animates his whole person. Before the camera, by contrast, life loses its phenomenalizing power; it forgoes its ability to create appearances and, hence, aura.

To conclude the preceding attempt to define "aura," it must thus be remarked that if Benjamin, without hesitation or regret, rejects the singularity of both objects and human faces, it is because the human face, too, is an object in the sense discussed above—an objectified distance.

Consequently, the singularity that he relinquishes is in his eyes entirely mythical and deserving of no redemption. Rooted in what Benjamin elsewhere calls "mythical boundary-setting [*mythische Grenzsetzung*],"[17] the singularity of the human face as it shows itself in the melancholic portraits of the early photographs is infinitely different from the human face as it is said (in the essay on photography) to figure in the best of the Russian films or in the work of August Sanders. Yet if Benjamin celebrates the human face in these films or photographs, he does so precisely because it is no longer auratic. The human face that appears on film "with new and immeasurable significance . . . [is] no longer a portrait," he writes. It is the "anonymous physiognomy" of people "who have no use [*keine Verwendung*] for their photographs."[18] No longer representative portraits (*repräsentative Portraitaufnahme*), these pictures of human faces exhibit, on the contrary, the social provenance, role, and function of the pictured and train their beholder "to read facial types," an ability that is, according to Benjamin, "of vital importance" given the "sudden shifts of power such as are now overdue in our society." Benjamin adds: "Whether one is of the left or the right, one will have to get used to being looked at in terms of one's provenance. And one will have to look at others the same way."[19] In these latter pictures of the human face, aesthetic distinctions have irrecoverably made room for social functions. But even more radically distinct from the representative portraits of individuals of the bourgeois class or the auratic pictures of absent or dead beloved ones—radically different because without even a negative link—is the singular, lonely creature before God. As a reading of Benjamin's essay on Goethe's *Elective Affinities* would demonstrate, the moral singularity of such an individual is the only one that counts for Benjamin.

From everything developed above, it should be obvious that Benjamin's criticism of auratic art includes its status as an object—the authority of the artwork as a present thing. If Benjamin claims that art in the age of mechanical reproducibility assumes a political function, it is because this art has succeeded in ridding itself of the spell that the phenomenal actualization of a distance casts on its beholder. Indeed, the traditional artwork is constituted, according to Benjamin, by "an alluring appearance or persuasive structure [*lockender Augenschein oder ein überredendes Klanggebilde*]" (pp. 238; 502), that is (in more precise translation), by an enticing appearance or a sound formation that talks the beholder into doing something against his better judgment. These unmistakably magical qualities of the auratic work get the viewer entangled in the work itself, rob him of his freedom, and bring him under the influence of the powers that dwell in the work as thing. By contrast, the nonauratic work of art is no longer a thing, and hence it allows the spectator a very definite autonomy. Indeed, as Benjamin's analyses demonstrate, the change in perception brought about by film permits the viewer to "reflect" himself, as it were, into himself. But before further refining this point, let me first address Benjamin's contention that dadaism is the art form that "promoted a demand for the film" (pp. 238; 502).

All art, Benjamin holds, produces the conditions for its own overcoming by creating a demand that can "be fully satisfied only later. The history of every art form shows critical epochs in which a certain art form aspires to effects which could be fully obtained only with a changed technical standard, that is to say, in a new art form" (pp. 237; 500–501). In these critical epochs—not unlike the *dies critica* that designates the turning point in the course of an illness—a given art form points beyond itself, toward another art that is capable of superior techniques and that fulfills the demand and promise created by the first. Needless to say, this thesis is not to be measured against empirical facts. It is a historico-philosophical thesis that rests on the assumption that artworks are not in essence self-sufficient. Yet works of art as cult objects, objects that are a singular manifestation here and now of a distance, repress the artwork's essential tendency to be overcome by another work or form of art and by ever more radical technical possibilities. Indeed, artworks critically call for their being transcended by technique, and above all by mechanical reproducibility. However, it is only in photography and film that this essential feature of all art is truly set free. According to this scheme, dadaist art created a demand that only film came to fulfill.

What is it then in dadaism that helps us situate film? Dadaism, Benjamin holds, produced works that prohibit all contemplative approach to them. In dadaist works, the aura of their creation is destroyed. But although the dadaists branded their creations as reproductions, they did so "with the very means of production" (pp. 238; 502). This limit is overcome by film. The fundamental reason why the dadaist creations no longer allow for contemplation is their shock character. The dadaist work of art is "an instrument of ballistics. It hit the spectator like a bullet, it happened to him, thus acquiring tactile quality," Benjamin asserts. With this latter quality, he continues, "it promoted a demand for film, the distracting [*ablenkendes*] element of which is also primarily tactile, being based on changes of place and focus which periodically assail the spectator" (pp. 238; 502). He concludes, "By means of its technical structure, the film has taken the physical shock effect out of the wrappers [*aus dieser Emballage befreit*] in which Dadaism had, as it were, kept it inside the moral shock effect" (pp. 238; 503).[20] In film, something held back by dadaist art is fully liberated. But, as we still have to see, this is also a liberation from something and for something.

Indeed, what precisely is it that happens in shock? In shock, the viewer becomes diverted from the object that causes the shock. With this, the possibility of contemplation (*Versenkung*) or concentration (*Sammlung*) in front of the object comes to a stop. Instead, the beholder becomes preoccupied with reacting to the shock to which he has been subjected. Through the violent shake that the dadaist work produces in the spectator and with which he must come to grips in one way or another, the work itself deflects from itself, from the thing or object that it is. It distracts the viewer from its singular appearance and diverts him toward what at first would seem to be some sort of subjective reflection on, or *Durcharbeitung* of, the violent disturbance that has occurred to him. With dadaist art, and even more so with film since its distracting element rests on structural features such as cutting and montage, the object character of the artwork recedes entirely, and thus a radical diversion from what attracts—the singular object of the auratic work with its luring and enticing qualities—has effectively been achieved.[21] An aesthetics of shock is thus nonobjective. In it the object has become diverted and deflected. It thus has all the allure of Kantian aesthetics, with its subjective bent. Yet, despite the striking similarities, is the subject who seeks to come to terms with his experience of shock the Kantian subject, and does he achieve his goal in a process of reflection or judgment?

Auratic works of art lure the spectator into a state of concentration and contemplation, more precisely into immersing himself in the object. Benjamin writes: "A man who concentrates before a work of art is absorbed by it [*versenkt sich darein*]. He enters into this work of art the way legend tells of the Chinese painter when he viewed his finished painting" (pp. 239; 504). Yet such absorption by the work presupposes that its viewer be an individual subject. The cult value of the work, Benjamin emphasizes, demands not just "that the work of art remain hidden" but also that it can only "be viewed by one person or by a few," "the priests in the cella," or the private art collector (pp. 225; 483–84). Concentration, contemplation, absorption presuppose a single spectator, or very few, who in front of the authentic, authoritative artwork lack the power to control themselves or each other. The moviegoer, by contrast, is no longer the *one* viewer. It is a mass public, a collective subject from the start. For the mass of individuals in the movie theater, concentration on or contemplation of the artwork is out of the question. First, what they relate to is, as said before, no longer a thing that could lay claim to authority. Moreover, the content viewed by these moviegoers is not the representation of some spellbinding exotic reality (geographical or social) but, as Benjamin's emphasis on Russian movies demonstrates, *themselves* as actors and workers at work.[22] Second, contemporary man, Benjamin insists, relates in a critical fashion to what he views. He writes, "it is inherent in the technique of the film as well as that of sports that everybody who witnesses its accomplishments is somewhat of an expert" (pp. 231; 492). Film invites what Benjamin terms "a progressive reaction." This reaction "is characterized by the direct, intimate fusion of visual and emotional enjoyment with the orientation of the expert. . . . With regard to the screen, the critical and the receptive attitudes of the public coincide" (pp. 234; 497). This critical attitude, entirely at odds with the contemplative attitude demanded by auratic art, is the ownmost property of the mass individual, more precisely, of the mass audience. Indeed, as Benjamin claims, mass individuals check their reactions against one another. He contends that "individual reactions are predetermined by the mass audience response they are about to produce, and this is nowhere more pronounced than in the film. The moment these responses become manifest they control each other" (pp. 234; 497). Third, the subject who seeks to come to grips with the effects of shock experienced in film—Benjamin characterizes the movie theater as a training ground for acquiring the transformed mode of perception required by modern life—is thus an autonomous subject of sorts. As a mass, the film audience is in control of itself; it checks and collectively tests its reactions to shock—shock produced by a work that no longer exercises any authority over its beholder. Free from all domination, this collective subject, testing against one another the success of each individual in dealing with shock, reflects itself into a free, independent subject that gives itself the rule, as it were. This is the source of the "great social significance" (pp. 234; 497) that Benjamin attributes to a nonauratic art form in which the object has been successfully repelled. If with these new media, art assumes a new function—a political role, to be precise—it is because art has become the training ground for the proletariat, or rather the masses, to constitute itself as a collective subject by developing all by itself the necessary skills to survive in contemporary society.

Yet what sort of autonomy is it that the moviegoers achieve in the dark depths of the movie house? Has this collective subject the substantial unity of the Cartesian, or the merely formal unity of the Kantian subject? Does the reflection upon self that comes with the repulsion of the object grant the subject an awareness of his cognitive and suprasensible abilities? Can this process of coming to terms with the shock effect even be understood as a reflective coiling upon self? To answer these questions, however schematically, the effects brought about by the violent disturbance of shock needs to be addressed. As Benjamin puts it, referring to the effects of the film images, "the spectator's process of association in view of these images is indeed interrupted by their constant, sudden change. This constitutes the shock effect of the film" (pp. 238; 503). Or, to refer to the photography essay, the camera's images "paralyze the associative mechanisms in the beholder."[23] In other words, the effect caused by shock is precisely the hampering of a subject's constitution of itself, its ability to cohere with itself so as to form a center. Benjamin quotes Georges Duhamel as a witness for this loss of all inner continuity with self: "I can no longer think what I want to think. My thoughts have been replaced by moving images." Whereas the spectator "can abandon himself to his associations" before a painting, "before the movie frame he cannot do so" (pp. 238; 502). It comes therefore as no surprise that Benjamin characterizes the new mode of participation of the mass audience in the movies as one of distraction (*Zerstreuung*). Not only does art in the age of mechanical reproduction deflect from the object, distract it, as it were, but further the collective subject of the critical reception of the new art forms is a distracted beholder. His associative mechanisms are interrupted by shock, and although he responds to the shocks that assail him through "a heightened presence of the mind" (pp. 238; 503), he does so in a distracted manner. The collective subject, consequently, is neither a substantial nor a formal center that would ground its autonomy. It is a distracted subject in all the senses of the word. Yet compared to the individual who lets himself be immersed in the auratic work, or who in front of it weaves an equally mythical identity for himself while abandoning himself to his associations, this distracted collective subject and its behavior toward art is, according to Benjamin, the answer to the questions that humanity faces today. The new kind of behavior that issues from the mass's matrix (*neugebohren hervorgeht*) is undoubtedly a form that appears first in the "disreputable form" of distraction as diversion, or entertainment, Benjamin admits (pp. 239; 503). Similarly, the new subject that collectively emerges with the loss of the aura coincides, at first, with what one contemptuously and condescendingly refers to as the masses. But this much is clear: both this distracted behavior and this centerless subject are credited by Benjamin with representing a solution to the problems of his time. The heightened presence of mind of this collective subject is not self-consciousness (individual or class consciousness). When Benjamin notes that, in contrast to the traditional viewer who becomes absorbed by art, "the distracted mass absorbs [*versenkt in sich*] the work of art" (pp. 239; 504), it is not only to stress the scattering of the work of art as object in the mass and its replacement by the shock effect, but to characterize the mass's state of mind as so permeable that paradoxically it cushions against all attack.[24] But, perhaps more significantly, this remark forces us to conceive of the state of mind of the distracted mass, as set up by Benjamin, along lines akin to the classical divide between high and low culture. According to this opposition, the state of mind of the masses is characterized by absentmindedness, habitual modes of thinking, and unfocused, incidental relating to its surroundings. It is separated by a gulf from the self-consciousness of the (bourgeois) individual. Indeed, what Benjamin valorizes in the masses coping with shock are precisely these despised states of mind. Philosophically speaking, such a mental disposition is empirical consciousness.

As distinct from the transcendental unity of consciousness, or pure apperception, which secures the thoroughgoing identity of a manifold in intuition, "empirical consciousness, which accompanies different representations, is in itself diverse [*zerstreut*] and without relation to the identity of the subject," Kant states in the First Critique.[25] This distracted consciousness is unable to combine coherently a manifold of intuitions into one consciousness, because it lacks the ability to represent in its synthetic efforts the identity of consciousness in the consciousness of the manifold intuitions themselves. Empirical consciousness is not only diverse and distracted in the different representations that it may accompany but also distracted *in itself*, and thus is in no situation to secure self-coherence, or self-identity, authoritatively. Its distracted nature prevents it from having any authority, any leverage, even regarding itself. In *Anthropology*, Kant defines distraction as follows: "Distraction (*distractio*) is the state of diverting attention (*abstractio*) from certain ruling ideas by means of shifting to other dissimilar ideas. If the distraction is intentional, it is called dissipation; if it is called involuntary it is absentmindedness (*absentia*) [Abwesenheit *von sich selbst*]."[26] The distraction described by Benjamin is of the second kind. It is involuntary and causes an absence from self. Although autonomous after repelling the authority of the auratic object, the collective subject of the mass audience does not constitute itself as a unifying subject. Its rejection of authority in distraction goes so far as to deprive even itself of any authority. This rejection of self-authority is a constitutive feature of the masses, as analyzed by Benjamin. Their distraction, he insists, is habitual.

In his discussion of distraction, Kant remarks, "the reading of novels, in addition to causing many other mental discords, has also the consequence that it makes distraction habitual".[27] This is not the place to discuss the relation between novel and film,[28] but as we have seen, the mode of perception fit for viewing this latter kind of art is a distraction entailed by the structural aspects of that art form. Moreover, the reading of fiction, according to Kant, not only makes distraction habitual but "makes for habitual absentmindedness [*Geistesabwesenheit*] (lack of attention to the present)."[29] It also bereaves the subject of self-presence (Abwesenheit *von sich selbst*). Yet, while these characteristics of distraction are discredited by Kant, Benjamin approves of them wholeheartedly where they characterize the mass audience reaction to the shock effect of the film. Indeed, this critical achievement is accomplished not merely in a state of distraction but by habit as well.

As Benjamin's discussion of architecture would seem to suggest, the kind of relation to art that becomes dominant with film is in truth a liberation of the modes of reception of buildings by the masses since time immemorial, modes repressed by auratic art. Since the beginning of architecture, the masses have appropriated buildings, not through "attentive appropriation" but by habit. It "occurs much less through rapt attention than by noticing the object in incidental fashion" (pp. 240; 505). Such habitual ways of appropriation determine both the tactile and optical reception of works of architecture. This mode of reception of art culminates in the masses' consumption of films, and has, according to Benjamin, "canonical value. For the tasks which face the human apparatus of perception at the turning points of history cannot be solved by optical means, that is, by contemplation, alone. They are mastered gradually by habit, under the guidance of tactile appropriation" (pp. 240; 505). Indeed, the thrust of Benjamin's argument is that the problems he refers to have been successfully solved only when they have been mastered "in a state of distraction [since this] proves that their solution has become a matter of habit. Distraction as provided by art presents a covert control of the extent to which new tasks have become soluble by apperception" (pp. 240; 505). In these times, the only problem solving that has a chance of succeeding is that which occurs in incidental fashion but has become habitual, hence repetitive and reproducible and not unique or singular, and which consequently does not focus or concentrate on what causes the problems. Only the masses are up to these tasks, Benjamin claims. "Individuals are tempted to avoid these tasks," presumably because of the fatal attraction exercised by the causes, or objects, of these problems. Against them the individual, acting alone, cannot protect himself. Only in conjunction with other individuals in a mass can he develop the repetitive habitual modes of reaction that prevent him from falling prey to the spell of what obtains here and now. In the movie theaters, the mass audience practices distracted and habitual problem solving. "The film makes the cult value recede into the background not only by putting the public in the position of the critic, but also by the fact that at the movies this position requires no attention. The public is an examiner, but an absent-minded one," Benjamin concludes (pp. 240–41; 505). This distracted critic gives no direct attention to the film as an art object; in passing, he cushions the shocks he receives by a heightened presence of the mind and habitual modes of handling them, modes that have been rehearsed and practiced with other mass individuals in front of the movie screen. He is a critic who has successfully cut himself free from the spell of the aura and its object. They have lost all authority over this collective subject, who has also dismissed the authority of a self. This distracted critic is the first citizen of a world without magic.

In his Epilogue, Benjamin denounces fascism's attempt to pervert the revolutionary possibilities of film by pressing the apparatus "into the production of ritual values" (pp. 241; 560), an effort that would re-aura-tize art while abolishing the aura "in a new way": the fascist way, through gas warfare. But aside from noting this single, aberrant exception, Benjamin ends his essay with the emphasis on a world become resolutely profane. In this world without aura or magic, the power of myth and fate has been overcome in all its forms—ritualistic and secular. It is a stupendous transformation of the world that Benjamin describes, in which all forms of transcendence bastardized by myth have been evacuated from the realm of the present. It is a world so free that it has become empty. The aesthetic of shock expresses this loss of distance as the very texture of what exists for the artworks. It is an aesthetics in which distance has made room for total proximity, and it remains, therefore, confined as well within the limits of what it depicts. Divorced from all transcendentalism, it has become empirical, at the limit of a discipline.

A strange silence hovers about this world emancipated from myth. No circumstantial reasons such as Benjamin's temporary affiliations with historical materialism, his friendship with Brecht, or his financial dependence on Adorno and Horkheimer can explain the total silence about the Other of the profane. But silence speaks. In its utter profanity and blankness, the world void of myth points to what it cannot name, that from which the very meaning of "profane" remains suspended.

(1992)

PART III

COMING INTO RELATION

5

Floundering in Determination

Thought as well as proper life in language are "especially prone to succumb to the danger of commonness," Heidegger writes in *What Is Called Thinking*. If this is so, it is because thought and language have a tendency to drift away into the obvious or self-evident—into ordinary thinking and the common meanings of words. Common terms easily take the place of proper terms—of the words inhabited by language and thinking (*gewohnte Worte* as opposed to *gewöhnliche Worte*). More precisely, common terms, as if driven by frenzy, usurp "the place of language properly inhabited and of its habitual words." Yet, says Heidegger, such "floundering in commonness [*Taumel im Gewöhnlichen*] . . . is not accidental, nor are we free to deprecate it. This floundering in commonness is part of the high and dangerous game and gamble in which, by the essence of language, we are the stakes."[1] Consequently, thought cannot simply push aside current meanings of words in favor of the proper ones. It must face this floundering in its very inevitability, and in such a manner that it can show that these words and thoughts are not unrelated to the words of language inhabited by thinking. As we will see, Heidegger conceives of the relation in question as one in which customary signification is rooted in the originary meaning of a word or thought (and, conversely, as one of falling away from that decisive meaning). Yet does this attempt to come to grips with the inevitable slide of language successfully reverse its course? Or is the manner in which floundering in commonness comports with genuine thought perhaps more insidious, more complex, than the possibility of retracing the original significations of common words or thoughts would make it seem? What if precisely the possibility of getting ahead of the game, of resisting the floundering in commonness, would perpetuate that very same floundering? Or what if thought's chance of coming into its own by leading the common terms back to their proper and inhabited meanings would depend not only on a reproduction but perhaps also on a multiplication of commonness? It is true that such multiplication of common terms and thoughts in the very process of their overcoming could be a (partly or totally) calculated game. Yet the proliferation of commonness may also escape all strategy and no longer be accountable in terms of what has hitherto been called *common*, ordinary. Indeed, such a proliferation of ordinary meanings results, as suggested, from the very attempt to assess the same logic that rules the binary opposition of the common and the proper. Hence, the question arises as to what relation "properly" exists between the manifold ordinary terms that have to be resorted to in order to retrace the ordinary back to the original, and the very process of derivation itself. In addition, one may wish to ask, is such proliferation necessary, accidental, or neither? Should one perhaps also regard the nature of this proliferation itself as floundering precisely because it may well no longer be a simple opposite to genuine thought, if, indeed, successful thought does not go without it?

These are among the questions on which I would like to elaborate in this chapter, which I conceive of as an inquiry of sorts into the mood of *Being and Time*. However, a warning is called for at this point. I will engage the questions alluded to from a quite specific angle by concentrating on one term only, on its inescapable floundering in common meaning, and on Heidegger's "inability" to secure a proper meaning for it. The term in question is "determination" (*Bestimmung*). Since I must also limit myself, for reasons of space, to the first half of *Being and Time*, I will have to forgo the exploration of this term's temporal, destinal, historical implications until another occasion.

When used in philosophical discourse, by Kant for instance, the expression *Bestimmung*, as Heidegger notes in *The Basic Problems of Phenomenology*, is "not arbitrary [*beliebig*] but is terminologically defined:

determinatio." The immediate source for this term in Kant is Alexander Baumgarten, yet its history reaches back through Christian Wolff and Gottfried Wilhelm Leibniz to Scholasticism and antiquity, Heidegger adds.[2] In the conceptual history of "determination" that Heidegger is concerned with, the term denotes a formal-apophantic category. A determination is a predicate of what in the grammar and general logic pertaining to assertions is called a subject.[3] It enlarges the concept of a thing—that is, its what-content (and not a thing in its empirical manifoldness). Through determination, a thing (or rather its concept) becomes demarcated from another thing. *Omnis determinatio est negatio* ("Every determination is a negation"), Spinoza wrote, and with this set the framework within which the formal-apophantic category of determination had to be understood. Since the eighteenth century, *Bestimmung*, which translates the Latin *determinatio*, has had, in the technical language of philosophers writing in German, the meaning of a conclusive fixing or settling of the content of concepts by demarcating them with the help of marks, characteristics, or predicates from other concepts. Wherever the notion of *Bestimmung* appears in a philosophical text, it is thus not, as Heidegger aptly remarks, an arbitrary concept or word, and that is true as well for the text of *Being and Time*. Yet although Heidegger's elaborations focus in that work on the formal-apophantic nature of *Bestimmung*, he has already broadened the scope of this notion beyond its meaning in the tradition I have alluded to, so as to include within its horizon predication not only of the what-content of the *concept* of things but of *things* in their actuality, existence, or extantness as well. The notion in question is thus treated as a category of epistemological realism, in addition to its serving to assert the nature of essences or possible things. Undoubtedly, this extension of the scope of the notion in question responds to specific historical reasons, in particular to Heidegger's debate with neo-Kantianism. Yet considering the perspective of fundamental ontology that informs Heidegger's discussion of *Bestimmung* in *Being and Time*, the broadening of that notion may have still another, and perhaps more essential, purpose.

A first definition of *Bestimmung* is given in *Being and Time*, when Heidegger proceeds in chapter 13 to describe knowing of the world (*Welterkennen*) as a mode in which being-in is exemplified. Knowing, he writes, is "a way of determining the nature of the present-at-hand by observing it." Heidegger tells us here that the act of making determinate is primarily an interpretative perception (*Vernehmen*) constituted by an addressing oneself to something as something and discussing it *as such*. Therefore, determination presupposes "a *deficiency* in our having-to-do with the world concernfully." Indeed, determination is based on a "fixed staring at something that is purely present-at-hand," on an attitude toward the world, in other words, that becomes possible only if all ordinary ways of relating to the world have been blended out. Something like *Bestimmung* can become envisioned only if the world is encountered in such a way that entities present-at-hand reveal themselves "purely in the *way they look*."[4] At first, determination as an interpretative perception is non-propositional. However, what is perceived and "made determinate can be expressed in propositions, and can be retained and preserved as what has thus been asserted" (p. 89).

It is while discussing assertion as a derivative mode of interpretation both in chapter 33 of *Being and Time* and in the Marburg lectures of winter 1925/26, published as *Logik: Die Frage nach der Wahrheit* (Logic: The question of truth), that Heidegger refines this definition of *Bestimmung*, its characteristics and presuppositions, but especially the ontological realm in which it obtains. In the analysis of assertion, determination becomes defined as a mode of "pointing out" (*Aufzeigung*, or *Aufweisung*) in which something present-at-hand is predicated of something that itself is present-at-hand. As assertion, determination is a mode of discovering (*Entdecken*), of *apophansis*. Yet what it discovers—what it makes thematic, as Heidegger says in *Logik*—is the present-at-hand as present-at-hand. Thus predicative, or determining, assertion is a restricted mode of discovering. Heidegger writes in *Being and Time*:

It is not by giving something a definite character that we first discover that which shows itself—the hammer—as such; but when we give it such a character, our seeing gets *restricted* to it in the first instance, so that by this explicit *restriction* of our view, that which is already manifest may be made *explicitly* manifest in its definite [*in seiner Bestimmtheit*] character. In giving something a definite character, we must, in the first instance, take a step back when confronted with that which is already manifest—the hammer that is too heavy. In "setting down the subject," we dim entities down to focus in "that hammer there," so that by thus dimming them down we may let that which is manifest be seen *in* its own definite character as a character that can be determined. (p. 197)

But thus focusing in on a thing as something present-at-hand, which paves the way for any access to properties or the like, not only dims down or blends out the thing's nature as something ready-to-hand but also covers up readiness-to-hand entirely (p. 200). In his lectures of 1925/26, Heidegger adds that in determining-letting-something-be-seen as merely present-at-hand, the proper character of Being of this something (in this case its readiness-to-hand) withdraws. Giving the example of a piece of chalk, he remarks, "if the determination: this piece of chalk is white, is made in conformity with the meaning that determination and assertion have in asserting, then this way of letting this thing be seen is possible only on the basis of a *re-concealing* [*Wiederverbergens*] of the piece of chalk as a with-what of one's dealings."[5] By reconcealing the way we have been relating to the piece of chalk in our unthematized everyday dealings with it, and by thus purely *concentrating* on its presence-at-hand, we make it possible to let this piece be seen from characteristics that are drawn from the object itself and that are themselves present-at-hand. Heidegger writes, "In determining assertion the as-what from which the determination takes place, namely white, is drawn from the given about-what itself."[6] This mode of predication, in which the characteristics that let something be seen assertively are drawn from the thing itself, is what Heidegger calls *Bestimmung*. Determination as assertion is constituted by "communication," or speaking forth. Of "communication" in which one makes assertions, Heidegger notes in *Being and Time* that it "is a special case of that communication which is grasped in principle existentially" (p. 205).

The very fact that in determining assertion the "what" that is said of something is "drawn *from that* which is present-at-hand" reveals that the as-structure that characterizes assertion as a derivative mode of interpretation "has undergone a modification." Since determining assertion becomes possible only when the ready-to-hand is veiled as ready-to-hand, so that properties or the like can come into view, the "as" "in its function of appropriating what is understood . . . no longer reaches out into a totality of involvements" (p. 200). Compared to the "as" of an interpretation that understands circumspectively—the primordial existential-hermeneutical "as"—the "as" in determining assertion has been leveled to "just letting one see what is present-at-hand, and letting one see it in a definite way. This leveling of the primordial 'as' of circumspective interpretation to the 'as' with which presence-at-hand is given a definite character is the speciality of assertion." This derivative "as" that constitutes the structure of determining assertion is called the apophantic "as" (p. 201). Determination, therefore, is not a primary discovering. In *Logik*, Heidegger emphasizes that "assertive determination never determines a primary and originary relation to what is." Because it is derivative, stemming from the originary as-structure of circumspective understanding—the result of a leveling modification of this as-structure—it can never "be made the guiding thread for the question regarding Being." "Determination," he concludes, "is itself as well as its whole structure a derivative phenomenon."[7]

If determination is thus a restrictive mode of discovering that presupposes modified structures of understanding and a reduction of the world to the present-at-hand, what then is the status of the word *Bestimmen* in the discourse of *Being and Time*? Indeed, not only does Heidegger demonstrate the derivative character of determination as a concept and a mode of interpretation, but he continues in that work to make use of the terms *bestimmen* and *Bestimmung* (as well as numerous words of the same root) in a variety of ways. I shall address the status of the notion of *bestimmung* in *Being and Time* by suggesting that it is not merely a question of stylistics, and not simply a theoretical question, but a question concerning the *Stimmung* (the mood and/or the coherence) of Heidegger's discourse. Heidegger, while discussing the leveling of primary understanding in determining assertion in his 1925/26 Marburg lectures, makes a distinction that may give us a lead on the question of the word *Bestimmen* in the work of 1927:

When I say: This piece of chalk is white, then this assertion about something with which I am dealing is not an assertion that as such would primarily relate (as far as its content is concerned) to my dealings. If I said, while writing: The chalk is too hard . . . then I would make an assertion *within* my performance [*Verrichtung*], within writing. . . . This assertion: "The chalk is too sandy," is not only a determination of the chalk, but at the same time an interpretation of my behavior and of not being able to behave—of not being able to write "correctly." In this assertion I do not wish to determine this thing, that I hold in my hand, as something that has the properties of hardness or sandiness, but I wish to say: it *hinders* me in writing; thus the assertion is interpretatively related to the writing activity, i.e. to the primary dealings of writing itself, i.e., it is assertion as interpretation of being-in—as being-alongside.[8]

Undoubtedly, when Heidegger, in *Being and Time*, engages the problem of *Bestimmung* as one that has served as the guiding thread for the question of Being from Greek antiquity to Husserl, as well as for the sciences, his conclusion that *Bestimmung* is a derivative phenomenon primarily relates to the subject matter under discussion. But this assertion is made as well in the process of developing, arguing, and writing *Being and Time*, and is thus also, and especially in consideration of what this work is all about—the question of Being—a statement regarding his argumentative and writing performance. That *Bestimmung* is a derivative phenomenon, then, comes to mean that assertive determination is an obstacle in trying to come to grips with the question of Being while writing *Being and Time*. Indeed, if the determining mode of assertion is not appropriate for dealing with the question of Being, this mode, as well as the word *Bestimmung* itself, inhibits (*hemmen* is Heidegger's word) the very performance of elucidating the question of Being. Yet, as we shall see, *Bestimmung* as a term, if not as a concept, is all over *Being and Time*, and thus the question arises as to the status and function of this term in the production of Heidegger's work. Why must Heidegger continue to use the philosophical language of *Bestimmung*; how do the uses of that term relate to what he has himself established about this notion; and how does Heidegger's own explicit or implicit account of his continued use of the term do justice to its manifold appearances or occurrences in *Being and Time*? These are among the questions that I would like to touch upon in the following.

Heidegger, in *Being and Time* (but elsewhere as well), makes frequent and seemingly innocent use of the terms *bestimmen*, *bestimmt*, and *Bestimmung* in their common meaning of "to define," "to characterize," "to qualify." Certainly, on repeated occasions he makes an arbitrary (*beliebig*) use of the term *bestimmt*. He employs it as well in the sense of "certain," "specific," or "determined," for instance when he writes: "These Others, moreover, are not *definite* [*bestimmte*] Others" (p. 164). And at times, *bestimmt* has the meaning of "intended" or "destined for," as when we read "that along with the equipment to be found when one is at work, those Others for whom the 'work' is destined [*bestimmt*] are 'encountered too'" (p. 153). In all these cases, the term is used in a casual, ordinary way.

A definitely more technical use of *Bestimmung* occurs in Heidegger's text when the task of phenomenological description or interpretation becomes characterized as one of determining the structures of its objects (in paragraph 14, for example). In this latter case, *Bestimmung* means *in die Bestimmtheit bringen*, "to give definiteness to," or "to raise to a conceptual level the phenomenal content of what has been disclosed" (pp. 117, 179). Although *Dasein*, the object of the phenomenological analysis of *Being and Time*, is thoroughly different from objects present-at-hand, Heidegger continues to characterize his whole investigation as an *existentiale Bestimmung*, as an attempt to exhibit the *Grundbestimmungen des Daseins*. But even more questionable is a third type of reference to the concept of determination.

The structures that constitute the meaning of Being are said to "lie beyond every entity and every possible character [*seiende Bestimmtheit*] which an entity may possess" (p. 62). Hence the meaning of Being "demands that it be conceived in a way of its own, essentially contrasting with the concepts in which entities acquire their determinate signification [*Bestimmtheit*]" (p. 26). But not only does Heidegger characterize phenomenology as the *Bestimmungsart* of Being; he also seeks to make Being itself determinate, and that according to the essential determinative structures for the character of its Being (*seinsbestimmende*) (p. 38). At stake in such an analysis is Being's originary *Sinnbestimmtheit* (its "temporal determinateness"), which has to be made thematic in an overcoming of "the very indefiniteness [*Unbestimmtheit*]" in which vague and average understanding holds Being, by means of a return to "those primordial experiences in which we achieved our first ways of determining the nature of Being [*Bestimmungen des Seins*]."[9]

One may perhaps wish to object here that this use of the word and notion of *Bestimmung* with reference to what the analytic of *Dasein* is to achieve and to Being itself is not to be taken literally, that the term is used in quotation marks, so to speak. Yet although in *Logik* he had clearly stated that Being is not an object for any possible *Bestimmung*,[10] in *Being and Time* Heidegger does not make the slightest effort to counter possible misunderstandings that could result from his talk about *Seinsbestimmung* and *Seinsbestimmungen*, as opposed to his hyphenation of the word (*Be-stimmung*) in *What Is Philosophy?* for instance. Supposing that in the con-text of the question of Being, the notion of determination should have another, more originary signification than in its current and metaphysical use, it never becomes distinguished from its metaphysical double. Why this neglect in a work that prides itself on reaching beyond the established philosophical and scientific distinctions even at the price of neologisms? In determination, one recalls, something (present-at-hand) is character-ized in terms of properties drawn from this something itself. It is a mode of assertion that lets something be seen from itself. Is Heidegger's neglect of the specific meaning that determination ought to have when used with reference to Being perhaps rooted in an unresolved problem regarding the phenomenological characterization of, on the one hand, what shows *itself by itself*—Being, first and foremost—and on the other hand, the letting-be-seen of what is present-at-hand by means of determinations drawn ex-clusively from that which is given in such a manner? Has Heidegger in-deed fully clarified, in *Being and Time*, the relation between the wealth of demarcating traits that come into view when what shows itself to a phe-nomenological glance is allowed to show itself by itself, and the "abun-dance of things which can be discovered by simply characterizing them [*ein neuer Reichtum des im reinen Bestimmen Entdeckbaren*]" in the theo-retical glance by which the world becomes dimmed down to the unifor-mity of what is present-at-hand? (p. 177). In any case, the very fact that Heidegger has relegated the concept of determination to the derivative domain of the present-at-hand, and to a mode of letting-be-seen in terms of characteristic properties drawn from the thing itself, requires that the "improper" references to this concept in *Being and Time* be somehow ac-counted for.

In *What Is Called Thinking?* Heidegger remarks that the common meaning of a word that has usurped the word's proper meaning is "not totally unconnected and unrelated to the proper one. On the contrary, the presently customary signification is rooted in the other, original, de-cisive one."[11] Yet the technical meaning of *Bestimmung* that Heidegger has limited in a categorical way to the sphere of the present-at-hand is at best *Bestimmung*'s proper metaphysical sense. It is, as we have seen, a mode of relating derived from a more fundamental mode, and thus there is nothing originary to it. *Bestimmung* as a philosophical *terminus technicum* is just as common as its customary signification. But is there then a proper signification of *Bestimmung*, a signification in which that word would *properly* be thought and inhabited? It must be noted here that the derivation and limitation of *Bestimmung* in *Being and Time* does not yield a proper meaning of that word. No fundamental meaning of *Bestimmung* is produced in this work to account for the juxtaposition of the different usages of that word by showing them to be derived from that word's proper meaning.[12] As a result, a certain disparity seems to prevail between the various occurrences of the word in question in *Being and Time*, a disparity that would be considerably complicated if one were to include in this investigation the additional and major signification of *Bestimmung* as vocation or destination. If, however, all these manifold usages of *Bestimmung* (and its variants) can be related, it is certainly not because of some more originary meaning of the term. Another law than that which commands the relation of the improper to the proper must regulate their distribution. Let me recall that assertive determination is a derivative mode of interpretation, one that presupposes and replaces the more primordial mode of interpretation in circumspective understanding. Understanding and state-of-mind (*Befindlichkeit*) are the two constitutive ways in which Dasein *is* its "there" and are equiprimordial with discourse (*Rede*). State-of-mind is one of the basic ways in which Dasein's Being is disclosed to it as its "there." Such disclosure takes place in what is called "our mood, our being-attuned [*Stimmung, Gestimmtsein*]" (p. 172). Heidegger writes, "In having a mood, Dasein is always disclosed moodwise as that entity to which it has been delivered over in its Being; and in this way it has been delivered over to Being which, in existing, it has to be" (p. 173).[13] Such disclosure, Heidegger adds, is not knowledge in the sense of being known *as such*. The "that-it-is" disclosed to Dasein in its being-attuned does not express "ontologico-categorially the factuality belonging to presence-at-hand." Whereas the latter "becomes accessible only if we ascertain it by looking at it," the "that-it-is" disclosed in Dasein's state-of-mind by contrast has to be conceived "as an existential attribute [*existenziale Bestimmtheit*] of the entity which has being-in-the-world as its way of being." In being-attuned, Dasein "is always brought before itself," not as beholding itself but as "finding itself in the mood that it has" (p. 174). In this prereflexive and precognitive mode of finding itself, Dasein experiences its *thrownness*, that is, the facticity of always already being its own "there," not as such, not abstractly, but in a specific way, as belonging to a determined world and as being alongside determined intraworldly things. This "that-it-is" in which Dasein finds itself in the mood that it has (*als gestimmtes Sichbefinden*), and "which, as such, stares it in the face with the inexorability of an enigma" (p. 175), represents, by its very facticity, the matrix for existential-hermeneutical understanding (according to the as-structure), as well as for its derivative, apophantic interpretation. In being-attuned, Heidegger continues, Dasein has, in every case, already disclosed *"being-in-the-world as a whole, and makes it possible first of all to direct oneself towards something"* (p. 176). But if being-attuned permits directing oneself toward something in the first place, it is because Dasein encounters the world in such a way that what it encounters can *matter* to it (*von innerweltlich Begegnendem angegangen werden kann*). Only because, in being-attuned, the world is experienced as a world that can "affect" us can understanding be primarily circumspective, and under given circumstances can be "just sensing something, or staring at it" (p. 176).

In other words, *Stimmung* is the condition not only of the possibility of circumspective interpretation but of its modification and leveling in determining assertion as well. Without the primordial disclosedness of *Stimmung*, or *Gestimmtheit*, and its matricial structures, no such thing as *Bestimmung* would be possible. *Stimmung*, in a sense prior to all psychology of moods, that is, in the sense of a fundamental *existentiale*, is thus the original, decisive thought and word upon which *Bestimmung* (the thing and the word) are based. With *Stimmung* we thus seem to have found a proper and fundamental mode of "awareness" to which the technical philosophical term *Bestimmung* as well as the customary term *Bestimmung* can be connected according to a scheme of deduction; still, it is not a proper meaning of *Bestimmung*. Even where *Bestimmung* is properly understood (as in *Being and Time*, but especially in *The Question of Truth*), it never becomes a proper word, a word inhabited by thought (a *gewohntes Wort* as opposed to a *gewöhnliches Wort*). Thus, although with *Stimmung* we have in principle a proper deduction of the possibility of *Bestimmung*, the problem I alluded to remains. There is no proper use of

Bestimmung that would justify Heidegger's speaking of *Seinsbestimmung* or of *Bestimmungen des Seins*. The disparity remains.

Let me add at this point that with the derivation of *Bestimmung* from *Stimmung*, Heidegger has also accounted for the possibility of *stimmen* in the sense of *Übereinstimmung*, and thus for the question of truth as *homoiosis* or *adequatio*. Propositional truth is rooted in the accord between a determining assertion and what it is about. But since determining assertion is based on a definite modification of the primordial hermeneutical as-structure of interpretation, "truth, understood as agreement, originates from disclosedness" (p. 266). In the explicit exhibition of the derivative character of the phenomenon of *Übereinstimmung* (chap. 44, section b), Heidegger secures his derivation by demonstrating that this phenomenon is, in the same way as *Bestimmung*, limited to the realm of the present-at-hand; not only is *Übereinstimmung* a relation between two terms that are both present-at-hand, but further, the relationship of agreement in *Übereinstimmung* is present-at-hand itself (p. 267).

Yet if truth as agreement is a function of determining assertion that itself is rooted, as far as its possibility is concerned, in the *Gestimmtheit* of state-of mind (as well as in understanding), *Gestimmtheit* or *Stimmung* must be conceived as a primordial way of *Beziehen*, *Bezug*, relationship. Indeed, the three essential determinations of *Stimmung*—Dasein's thrownness or facticity, the disclosure of its being-in-the-world as a whole, and the fact that something can "matter" to it (its *Angänglichkeit*)—constitute existentially Dasein's openness to the world. In *Stimmung*, in the attunement of a state-of-mind, Dasein, which experiences *itself* always already factically (knowingly or not), is shown to be capable of being "affected" by the world and of directing itself toward things in a world that in every case has already been disclosed to it. Dasein's being-attuned in a state-of-mind is the existential a priori of all possible linkage, connecting, or relationship.

For lack of time and space I must forgo here the temptation to show that Heidegger's understanding of *Stimmung* in *Being and Time* is a recasting of Kant's notion of transcendental apperception from a fundamental ontological perspective. Such a demonstration would have to be based on the discussion of transcendental aesthetics in his 1925/26 Marburg lectures. "All determination and all thinking is a connecting of a given manifold,"

Heidegger remarks here.[14] And "Determination is synthesis, synthesis is gathering together [*Zusammennehmen*] in a unity."[15] Heidegger makes these statements with respect to formal intuiting, and asks consequently, what it is that ultimately makes a connecting of the manifold possible? Such connecting by intuition and understanding is possible only if there exists something like unity in general. For Kant, this unity, Heidegger writes, is the transcendental unity of apperception—that is, "the originary a priori of all connecting, that is, of all determining, and hence the a priori of the possibility of determining the manifold as such."[16]

Stimmung is, existentially speaking, the most primordial unity that *Being and Time* resorts to, an originary mode of relating, from which *Bestimmung* as a restricted mode of discovering and truth as *Übereinstimmung* follow. As such, *Stimmung* is at once the enabling condition of logical determination and truth as agreement, of all characterization, definition, description, and so on—that is, the arbitrary common meaning of *Bestimmung*—and the enabling condition of all *stimmen* (about which Heidegger only speaks disparagingly as indicative of a merely formal mode of relating and correctness). This concept of *Stimmung* will be replaced by Heidegger later on with the less subjective notion of *Grundstimmung*,[17] but in particular by the notion of *Stimme*, in the sense of the (*lautlose*) *Stimme des Seins*. What is true of *Stimmung*, namely, that it must be understood beyond all psychology of moods, is also true of *Stimme*—although the original basic meaning of the verb *bestimmen* in Middle High German has been "to name by voice, to fix by voice."[18] The *Stimme* toward which Heidegger retraces the possibility of determination and truth as accordance is not primarily voice. *Stimme*, as Heidegger uses it, must be understood verbally, actively, as minimal cohering, minimal agreeing. As he will say later, *Stimme* puts into *Stimmung*, which itself disposes thought to co-respond appropriately to what speaks to it. Needless to say, what thus becomes *gestimmt*, attuned to Being, whether in *Stimmung* or in thinking, can always also become articulated linguistically. With this I circle back to the question of Heidegger's use of the term "determination" in *Being and Time*. The expansion of the term to include epistemological predication of things now appears to have provided Heidegger with a sufficiently generalized backstage to be able to derive all forms of determination (philosophical, epistemological, and commonsensical) from one primordial unity—the unity of attunement. It is a derivation that takes the form of a grounding through exhibition of the modifications that the originary unity undergoes in the various types of determination.

If it is a general principle, as Heidegger claims in chapter 29, that from an ontological point of view one must "leave the primary discovery of the world to 'bare mood,'" then even the "purest *theoria* has not left all moods behind" (p. 177). But not only theory, that is, not only the conceptual grasp of a world dimmed down to the uniformity of the present-at-hand, but philosophy as well, as he notes in *What Is Philosophy?* is attuned. And so is Heidegger's *Being and Time*. This work, to take up the language from the Cerisy conference of 1955, is attuned to the "voice," the *Stimme* of Being. Its task is, as Heidegger notes from the outset, to lift Being out of its forgottenness and to reawaken an understanding of the meaning of the question of Being. *Being and Time* corresponds to the "voice" through a very definite mood, undoubtedly. But also, and primarily, through a very definite sort of cohering, of having a unity in a specific way. One way in which *Being and Time* achieves this unity is by exhibiting *Stimmung* as what sets the term(s) for determination. But does this a priori synthesis account for all determinations, as well as for the manifold ways in which *Stimme* is said, in particular in Heidegger's text? Has Heidegger, indeed, explained his continued use of the term and concept of *Bestimmung* with respect to the question of Being with this model of originary cohering? Undoubtedly, from *Stimmung* all other (determined) forms of determinations have been successfully derived. But is such essential derivation capable of accounting for the problem that I have tried to point out? The improper, or more precisely, *common* use of a word such as "determination" in formulations like *Seinsbestimmungen* or *Bestimmungen des Seins* remains an inhibition (*Hemmung*) to thinking— to thinking nothing less than the ways in which Being attunes. Apart from the technical meaning of *Bestimmung*, no proper meaning of the word can come to the rescue of the philosopher. Yet Heidegger uses it, as he does so many other variations of the word. Inescapably, he *must* do so, and thus must flounder in commonness. However, the thinker would have to account for such floundering by exhibiting the slide of language between the proper and the improper. But what if no habitual meaning of determination is to be found? The model of essential derivation to which *Stimmung* yields in *Being and Time*, and which makes it such a powerful synthetic tool, seems to be either too finely or too loosely knit a synthesis to account for the paradoxically inevitable improper use that Heidegger must make of the term in question. What becomes visible here is that such improper reference to *Bestimmung* in the context of the question of Being can only be accounted for if the manifold forms of determination are no longer gathered together according to the traits of letting-something-be-seen *from itself, as itself,* or from the negative modalities thereof. In other words, a model must be found other than that by which determination is properly a pointing out of essences (or of things *as such*)! The limits of the originary synthesis of *Stimmung* would even come more poignantly into view were one to emphasize the numerous terms that Heidegger summons in *Being and Time* and that have a root part: *stimm-*. From both a subject-related and a performative perspective, all these words and notions contribute to the thought of *Stimmung*, and ultimately to that of Being. My point here is not, as one might easily infer, to fault Heidegger's achievement in *Being and Time*, and especially not to insist upon the linguistic limits to properly expressing something that has already been properly thought. Rather it is to argue that the development in all rigor of something like an originary synthesis that would account for all forms of determinations cannot but flounder, not merely because of its inevitable recourse to improper usage of the terms to be derived, but also because of a variety of ways in which these terms must be used that do not fall under the binary oppositions that organize the various stages in the deduction. Still, the very idea of an originary synthesis calls upon us to think together this inescapable floundering and what in such floundering is positively achieved.

Yet Heidegger's evocation of a floundering in commonness as part of the high and dangerous game of thinking and speaking does not master the diversity and disparity of all the ways in which *Stimme* is being said. The binary opposition of the proper and improper, of the habitual and the common meaning of words, and perhaps of philosophical thought and common sense cannot serve to bring order to the manifold in question. If thought flounders when trying to come to grips with determination, it is because the very necessity of formulating an originary synthesis such as *Stimmung*, for instance, cannot avoid producing a proliferation of what precisely has to be derived—a plurality of not only improper but sharply different notions of determination (and of notions expressed by root-related words)—different because of tone, style, tense, and, in particular, levels of argumentation. A certain lack of coherence thus comports with the coherence that *Stimmung* makes. This incoherence, which the philosophical schemes of derivation and binary opposition fail to master, must nonetheless be accounted for.

Stimmung as the ultimate a priori of all connecting would indeed have to be the starting point for such an elucidation of the way or ways in which *Stimmung* itself comports with a certain incoherence. It is an incoherence that, unlike the improper, does not stand in a symmetric relation to its opposite, and that thus escapes binary determination. Hence the kind of accounting that I call for cannot consist in tying originary *Stimmung* up with such things as *Stimmungslosigkeit*, *Verstimmung*, and so on, which Heidegger, in chapter 29, has effectively accounted for. Nor can it be a question of linking *Stimmung* to some equiprimordial disunity, discord, disharmony, and so forth, *if* these values continue to receive their meaning from within the horizon of unity, harmony, accord, and so on. Rather, it is a question of tying *Stimmung* as originary synthesis and its successful derivation of *Bestimmung* and *Übereinstimmung* to the floundering of thinking; not only to the improper, common use of *stimm*-related terms but to all the major irreducibly different occurrences of *stimm*-related terms that result from the phrase regimens (to use a Lyotardian term) and the metaleptical shifts in argumentation that are required in demonstrating the originarity of *Stimmung* in the first place. Such floundering does not take place in improperness or impropriety. It is a floundering congenital in the dangerous game of thought Heidegger talked about. If this game consists in establishing *Stimmung* as the originary synthesis for all possible *Bestimmung*, to tie this game up with the manifold and heterogeneous occurrences of *stimm*-related words in *Being and Time* would then mean to think the becoming of *Stimmung*, the coming into its own of originary *Stimme* from a beyond not only of its synthetic achievement, its character of state-of-mind, but also of its possible verbalization. Beyond the minimal cohering of *Stimmung* and *Stimme*—in their *Erstimmung* or *An-stimmung*, perhaps—a mesh of relations would thus emerge that would no longer be simply attuned, synthetic, or originary. Rather than seeking some sort of accordance, some even deeper *stimmen* between *Stimmung* and the manifold "voices" in Heidegger's text, the accounting in question would instead have to take the form of a weave—of what Heidegger, on several occasions, has referred to as a *Geflecht*.

(1989)

6

Tuned to Accord

Common sense and a venerable tradition of philosophical thinking are in full accord about the essence of truth: truth consists in accordance. Whether it is ordinary or philosophical consciousness that makes a statement about the truth of a matter, in each case the criterion for truth is agreement, concordance, accordance. Both common sense and technical philosophy speak in one voice of this accord of truth between itself and what thus is said to be its essence. Indeed, it is a truth about truth that is "immediately evident to everyone" or, more precisely, obvious and universally valid.[1] Yet universality and the "obviousness which this concept of truth seems to have but which is hardly attended to as regards its essential grounds" (p. 121) are, according to Heidegger, the result of a protective, self-securing isolation of this determination of truth from "the interpretation of the essence of the Being of all beings, which always includes a corresponding interpretation of the essence of man" (p. 121). Although in "On the Essence of Truth" Heidegger claims that between common sense—and with it, the tradition of thinking that not only accords with it but even provides a ground for the commonsense understanding of truth—and philosophy (in a strict sense), there is no transition, no possible communication; he does not wish to refute common sense and what has "long been called 'philosophy.'" "Philosophy can never refute common sense, for the latter is deaf to the language of philosophy. Nor may it even wish to do so, since common sense is blind to what philosophy sets before its essential vision," he writes (p. 118). But what *is* possible is to lift the commonsensical and "philosophical" concept of truth as accordance above its isolation, and to relate it to an interpretation of the whole—the Being of all beings. In short, what is possible for thought is a one-way approach to the commonsensical concept of truth as accordance, by which this concept, without common sense's knowledge, becomes grounded in the order of Being. It is this approach that Heidegger has set out to make in "On the Essence of Truth."

The traditional criterion for the truth, then, is accordance. *Accordance* renders *Übereinstimmung*, which in turn translates the Greek *homoiosis* or *orthothes* and the Latin *adaequatio*. In ordinary, everyday speech, one says *es stimmt*, "it is in accord," or simply "it is true." Truth, consequently, is "what accords, the accordant [*was stimmt, das Stimmende*]" (p. 119). Such *stimmen* is at least dual, and refers to the *Übereinstimmung*—or as Heidegger also says, to *Einstimmigkeit*, that is, unison, unanimity, consonance, agreement, and so forth—of, on the one hand, "a matter with what is supposed in advance regarding it and, on the other hand, . . . of what is meant in the statement with the matter" (p. 119). Everyone agrees—layman and philosopher alike—that truth is what accords. All have come to the agreement—univocally—that this definition of truth is in accord. Heidegger undoubtedly knows that *stimmen* also has the meaning of casting a vote, of having a voice, of exercising a political franchise. Indeed, the usual (and metaphysical) concept of truth has juridical and political connotations. Something's being in accord is based on a unanimous casting of votes, on a ringing of all voices in unison. Truth as accord is the result of an egalitarian leveling of voices that celebrate the consonance—that is, absence of heterogeneity—between matter and meaning or between matter and proposition. In short, the essence of the universally valid and self-evident concept of truth as accordance is justice in the sense of *Gerechtigkeit*: what is in accord is nothing less than "correct" (*richtig*) and "right" (*recht*).[2]

Having argued that accordance is dual, Heidegger also reminds us of the hierarchy of ontological and logical dependence between the two modes of the common concept of truth. Indeed, propositional truth (*Satzwahrheit*) rests, by right, on material truth, on the ontic truth of what is (*Sachwahrheit*) that is, on things' accordance with their idea or concept. This duality and hierarchy of accordance—in full agreement with classical philosophical exigencies, yet forgotten by positivist truth theories that restrict truth to propositional truth—hints, for Heidegger, at a complication of the very idea of unison that characterizes truth. As we shall see, this complication arises from the determination of accordance as correctness. Heidegger writes, "Both concepts of the essence of *veritas* have continually in view a conforming to [*Sichrichten nach*] . . . and hence think truth as *correctness* [*Richtigkeit*]" (p. 120). Correctness, as a criterion of truth in the ordinary sense, presupposes that in the unison between proposition and thing, the proposition and the thing be *directed, oriented, turned toward* one another. Conformity is not possible without a *conforming to*. Nothing could be more banal than the discovery of this directedness, one may object. But after scrutinizing this apparently self-evident and unquestioned implication of truth as correct accordance and consonance, Heidegger will in fact be led to relativize and foreground the traditional concept of truth. What, then, is this directedness at the heart of accordance and correctness? To answer the question, we must follow Heidegger through his discussion of the ways in which the two modes of accordance—material and propositional truth—relate to one another.

Material truth, Heidegger notes, is a function of the Christian theological belief that things have been created by God in conformity with the idea that He conceived of them. If a thing can be said to conform to its idea in the divine intellect—if it is *idee-gerecht*, that is, correct (*richtig*), just and justified—it can be said to be true. The same conformity must also be expected from the human intellect as an *ens creatum*. It achieves such conformity in accomplishing

in its propositions the correspondence of what is thought to the matter, which in its turn must be in conformity with the *idea*. If all beings are "created," the possibility of the truth of human knowledge is grounded in the fact that matter and proposition measure up to the idea in the same way and therefore are fitted to each other [*aufeinander zugerichtet*] on the basis of the unity of the divine plan of creation. (p. 120)

The directedness that is at the heart of the conformity of matter and proposition to the idea is thus a function of a prior destination of one for the other, of a prior fitting of matter and proposition to their divine conception. Without such original directedness of matter and proposition to the idea within the unity of the divine plan of creation, no proposition could hope to achieve any accordance whatsoever. Heidegger remarks, "Throughout, *veritas* essentially implies *convenientia*, the coming of beings themselves, as created, into agreement with the Creator, an 'accord' with regard to the way they are determined in the order of creation [*ein 'Stimmen' nach der Bestimmung der Schöpfungsordnung*]" (p. 121). Consequently, accordance (*Stimmen, Übereinstimmung, Einstimmigkeit*), whether of material or propositional truth, is grounded in the "being destined for one another" (*Bestimmung*) of matter and idea, matter and proposition, according to divine plan. There is no possible accordance without a prior "being directed to one another" of the items that make up the accord, and without the end in view that such a destination represents. Furthermore, no correctedness is possible without a certain justness, rectitude, righteousness, by which justice is done—in the last judgment—to the goals or ends (*Bestimmung*) of the divine creation and its order.

It is essential to remark here that this theological account of the "being fitted for one another" of matter and idea, matter and proposition, continues to hold true for all secular notions of truth as long as they are based on accordance. Any concept of truth constituted by *Übereinstimmung*, or simply by *Stimmen*, presupposes directedness toward one another of what are to accord with one another, within the horizon not so much of the *telos* of a plan of creation as of a world order in general. Further, when secularization has reached its climax, it is the possibility of a universal planification, or ordering into a plan, of all objects that underlies truth as accordance. In a radically secularized world, truth as accordance presupposes, indeed, the ontological possibility of a universal subjectibility to ends, not just to a particular end or to multiple ends; the possibility of absolutely everything lending itself to ends. In short, all accordance rests on destination, or in general terms, on what one might call destinability. All *Stimmen* as *Übereinstimmen* presupposes *Bestimmung* by an order, or more generally, by the possibility of yielding to order. The prefix *Be-* of *Bestimmung* confers the directedness toward an end upon the consonant agreement of the *Stimmen* through which truth rings.

With these developments, which correspond to section 1 of "On the

Essence of Truth," Heidegger seems to have rounded out his discussion of the traditional concept of truth—of ordinary *and* metaphysical truth. This conception of truth is called a particular (*diese*) "definition [*Bestimmung*] of the essence of truth" (p. 121). Is this to say that truth, understood as accordance, is an interested determination of truth in which truth becomes subjected to an end? If so, does this mean that there are other possible determinations of truth's essence? And how, then, should we understand "determination" or "destination" in this case? Finally, could what Heidegger says here about the usual conception of truth mean that there might possibly be a determination of truth that is not a determination of it, and in which truth is not suspended from an end, but which is, for all that, not undetermined (*unbestimmt*)? Is there a determination of truth that would altogether escape the logic of *Bestimmung* in the double sense of determination and destination?

In the following section, Heidegger inquires into "the inner possibility of accordance." It is the *first* of three steps by which he interrogates the usual determination of the essence of truth as *Übereinstimmung*, or more simply as *Stimmen*, as to its conditions of possibility and foregrounds it in a more elementary conception of truth. Yet has not Heidegger answered that question with the reference to the *ens creata* and the divine plan—to the *Bestimmung* in the perspective of the order of creation? Have not metaphysics and theology put to rest the question of the possibility of the determination of truth as accord, by arguing that that determination is based on the mutual destination for one another of matter and idea, matter and proposition, within the horizon of the divine plan? What both disciplines (which according to Heidegger are ultimately one and the same) establish is that accordance is a function of matter and idea's, and matter and proposition's, being fitted to each other on the basis of a *Bestimmung* (determination/destination) by the divine order of the creation. But what Heidegger seeks to clarify is the *inner possibility* of such being-fitted-to, and hence of accordance. This is a quest that is eminently *philosophical*, as opposed to the metaphysical and theological determination of the essence of truth. It is a quest that perhaps no longer seeks to *determine* the essence of truth, if determination is also, and always, a determination by an end.

Before embarking on an analysis of Heidegger's inquiry into the inner possibility of truth as accordance and correctness, let me stress the unbridgeable gap that remains between the metaphysical/theological account of truth and the philosophical attempt to question its inner possibility. As Heidegger notes at the beginning of the essay, common sense—and both metaphysics and theology are of that order—is deaf to the language of philosophy. Common sense cannot be refuted; but without its becoming aware of it, it can be foregrounded. One consequence of this single-tracked approach is that everything that has been said about the relation of *Stimmen* and *Bestimmung* with respect to the common concept of truth will, because that discussion is still "unphilosophical," be marked by a certain heterogeneity compared to the truly philosophical elaborations on the inner possibility of *stimmen*. A certain discrepancy, perhaps a discord (*Verstimmung*), between the commonsense and the philosophical treatments of *stimmen* as accordance will distinguish Heidegger's text. In order to inquire into the inner possibilities of accord, Heidegger's approach has to be out of tune with metaphysic's statements on accord; more precisely, it has to sustain the discord in such a manner that the philosophical foregrounding of the metaphysical statements of accordance becomes possible. Otherwise, the metaphysical determination of truth would be replaced by just another determination.

Let us recall that Heidegger's insistence on investigating the inner possibility of accordance is a response to the certainty with which both ordinary thinking and metaphysics, but especially the sort of thinking that restricts truth to propositional truth, take this possibility for granted. Although this kind of thought can lay claim to a venerable tradition, its determination of truth as the accordance of statement with matter is what makes the question of the meaning of "accordance" a pressing issue. This question is all the more urgent since what are said to be in accordance are entirely dissimilar things—matter and proposition. How can accord exist between things as heterogeneous as matter and proposition, and if accord can occur, what is the meaning of such according? A relation of accordance between such things as matter and proposition, Heidegger remarks, is only conceivable as a relation of presentation, in which the presenting statement expatiates upon the matter *as* presented. Presentation (*Vor-stellung*) is not representation (*Vorstellung*). As "that perceiving which does not take beings in passively, but which can actively give to itself what is present as such in its outward appearance (*eidos*) by gazing up at it," presentation is *noein*,[3] and has to be demarcated from all philosophical and physiological theories of representation. But to let "a thing stand opposed as object," as is the case with presentation, presupposes an open region, a domain of relatedness and opposedness, which a presenting statement must traverse before meeting the object that stands against it. In turning to this region, a region unthematized not only by the dominant brand of thinking that limits truth to propositional truth but by the theological and metaphysical explications of the possibility and reason for accordance, Heidegger embarks on a philosophical analysis, strictly speaking. This open region, without which no presentative statement could possibly relate and be in accord with a presented thing, "is not first created by the presenting but rather is only entered into and taken over as a domain of relatedness" (pp. 123–24). As Henri Birault has remarked, it is "the openness of an opening that no intentional relation could institute and that all our comportments presuppose."[4] The presentative traversal of the openness of the open region in question is "the accomplishment of that bearing [*Verhältnis*] which originally and always comes to prevail as a comportment [*Verhalten*]," Heidegger writes (p. 124). This presenting comportment is one of many possible modifications of comportment, which he defines as the "open relatedness [*offenständiger Bezug*]," in general of man or *Dasein*, "to something opened up *as such* [*ein Offenbares* als ein solches]" (p. 124). But within this openness to beings (opened up as such), which characterizes comportment in general, a presenting comportment relates only—just as all other forms of comportment relate "according to the particular perspective that guides them" (p. 123)—to the particular way in which a thing is (*wie es als dieses ist*). Indeed, things do appear in the mere openness of their appearance to comportment; they appear always as these particular things (as what they are) according to the perspective that all comportment brings with it and that determines *how* things are. As for the presenting proposition, things become presented in it "with regard to what they are and how they are" (p. 124). In the openness of a presenting comportment, what is presents itself as it is (*selbst vorstellig wird*) to a presentative statement (*vorstellendes Aussagen*). The latter, Heidegger continues, "subordinates itself to the directive [*Weisung*] that it speak of beings *such-as* [*so-wie*] they are. In following such a directive the statement conforms [*richtet es sich*] to beings. Speech that directs itself accordingly is correct (true) [*richtig*]" (p. 124).

To sum up: presentative statement, and with it, the possibility of truth as accordance, presupposes—to the extent that it is first and foremost a comportment (an *act* of relating)—an open region in which it can stand open, not merely to what shows itself pure and simple but to the particular way in which things take their stand. Such a presentative statement can achieve accordance only if it conforms itself to the directive that things that present themselves as such give to the presenting proposition. This, then, is the point where the *inner* possibility of accordance comes into view. Accordance as a presenting comportment rests on the statement's being directed toward something that itself (and from itself) instructs the statement as to what and how it (the thing) is. In short, by focusing on the open region as a domain of relatedness, it becomes clear that accordance (*stimmen*) presupposes—and this is its inner possibility—that a concordance occurs, between the being *directed toward* (*richten*) of the statement and the *indicating* or *ordering* (*Weisung*) by the thing that is to be presented. Truth as accordance thus requires the possibility of an accord *more originary* than the one between statement and the thing as it is. Truth will not occur if the directional traits of *richten* and *weisen* do not accord. These traits are the particular modifications of the general traits that characterize comportment as such—as to holding oneself in (*sichhalten*) an openness in which one holds on to (*sich an . . . halten*) something that presents itself by itself (*das selbst vorstellig wird*)—and that obtain for presenting comportment. Without the possibility of the "synthesis" of these traits, there can be no accord between a statement and the thing it presents.

The inner possibility of accordance is thus the synthesis of the more fundamental accord between the trait that causes the proposition to respond to the particular way in which a thing is and the equally particular trait by which a thing indicates what and how it is. But precisely because this inner possibility of adequation rests on the more originary accord of *specific* (and actually very determined) directional traits, another question arises as to the ground of this inner possibility. What are the *general* conditions of the being-fitted-to-one-another of *richten* and *weisen*, without which a statement could not hope to secure the accord between itself and what it represents? Heidegger will answer this by elaborating on the *second* step in which the traditional characterization of the essence of truth as accordance becomes foregrounded. He asks: "Whence does the presentative statement receive the directive to conform to the object and to accord by way of correctness? Why is this accord involved in determining [*warum bestimmt dieses Stimmen mit*] the essence of truth? How can something like the accomplishment of a pregiven directedness occur? And how can the initiation into an accord [*Einweisung in ein Stimmen*] occur?" (p. 125).[5] We recall that the inner possibility of accordance established the minimal synthetic conditions for a comporting statement to relate adequately to something *opened up as such* in the specific mode of its whatness. The minimal synthesis was that of the directedness (*sich richten*) of the statement and the pregivenness of a direction (*Vorgabe einer Richte*) by the thing to be represented. The new question centers around the *donation* and the *reception* of the directive to conform to the object. The answer to this question ought to yield the *ground*, which is also the *essence*, of what enables as its inner possibility something like accordance.

If statement as comportment is possible only to the extent that "[when] standing in the open region, it adheres to something opened up *as such*" in its very specificity (p. 124), then the ground for the enabling possibility of accordance resides in stating comportment's "*being free* for what is opened up in an open region [*zum Offenbaren eines Offenen*]" (p. 125). In other words, in order to be given a directive, stating comportment must already have "entered freely into an open region for something opened up which prevails there and which binds every presenting." Statement must have freed itself for a binding directedness "by *being free* for what is opened up in an open region." No directive can occur, and no directed response to it can take place, without a being free for being given a directedness. What Heidegger calls freedom here is the being *free for* what is *opened up* in the open region of comportment. It is thus the enabling countertrait to the trait of directing oneself to what gives directedness in the open region as a domain of relatedness. To *yield to* a directive is possible only if one is *open*, or *free for* being bound by what is opened up as such. Conversely, it must be said (although Heidegger does not make this move explicitly) that for a thing (i.e., something opened up in an open region of comportment) to point out its mode of presentation, the thing must be drawn to, must be free for, being said as it is. It is the enabling countertrait to the trait of pointing out, by which a thing gives its directedness to statement. Such being-free-for, and the corresponding being-drawn-to-being-said, are the two countertraits, to those of *richten* and *weisen*, that represent the ground or essence of (correct) accordance. This double being-free-for, or more precisely, the finely tuned accord of these two freedoms—which are directed against one another and which embrace one another in the open region—is the essence of truth as correspondence. Truth as accord is grounded in a *stimmen* of these two countervectorial traits, traits more originary than those that make up the synthesis of the inner possibility of accordance. As the ground of truth as correspondence, this is a *stimmen* more originary than that which makes up its inner possibility.

In the section entitled "The Essence of Freedom," Heidegger sets out to further refine the notion of freedom, that is, of being *free for what presents itself* in the open of an open region, a freedom he characterizes as "letting beings be" (p. 127). Freedom, as the ground of truth as correspondence or accordance, he argues, can serve only as "the ground of the inner possibility of correctness . . . because it receives its own essence from the more original essence of uniquely essential truth [*der einzig wesentlichen Wahrheit*]" (p. 127). The twice-double accord of the directional and counterdirectional traits, which makes truth as accordance possible and grounds it, will consequently depend on a gift that it receives from that more originary and unique truth.[6] By inquiring into how freedom, as the ground of the inner possibility of truth as accordance, receives its own essence from a more originary conception, if not happening, of truth—of a truth that does not primarily reside in correspondence and that escapes (to some extent at least) the logic of *Bestimmung* in its double meaning of definition and destination because the very meaning of these terms depends on this truth's occurrence—we shall encounter the *third* step by which the classical notion of truth will be foregrounded.

Freedom, as the ground of the possibility of truth as correctness, is the being free for what is opened up in an open region (*das Offenbare eines Offenen*). Such freedom lets beings be the beings they are, since it responds to the things that *present themselves* in the open region of comportment. Yet in this response and "subsequent" letting-be, the freedom in question shows itself to be engaged "with the open region and its openness [*das Offene und dessen Offenheit*] into which every being comes to stand, bringing that openness, as it were, along with itself" (p. 127). In other words, for accordance to be possible—that is, for a proposition to be able to direct itself according to the directive given by the thing to the thing—not only must the proposition be free for what presents itself in specificity (for its *was sein* and *so sein*); but it must also, and primarily, relate to the open region itself in which (as which) the presencing-as-such of the thing occurs. For there to be an accord between statement and matter, statement (as a modification of comportment, that is, as open relatedness, *offenständiger Bezug*) must from the start be open or free, not so much for what is in the open as for the openness of the open itself. It must from the start be free to accommodate, not the thing in its specificity itself but the openness of what is opened up in the open. Without being bound by the openness of the opened up, a statement could not possibly hope to come into accord with what presences itself as such in an open region. As open relatedness, comportment is engaged with disclosedness first and foremost. But Heidegger writes:

> To engage oneself with the disclosedness of beings is not to lose oneself in them; rather, such engagement withdraws [*entfaltet sich in einem Zurücktreten vor*] in the face of beings in order that they might reveal themselves with respect to what and how they are and in order that presentative correspondence might take its standards from them. As this letting-be it exposes itself [*setzt sich aus*] to beings as such and transposes [*versetzt*] all comportment into the open region. Letting-be, i.e., freedom, is intrinsically exposing [*aus-setzend*], ek-sistent. Considered in regard to the essence of truth, the essence of freedom manifests itself as exposure to the disclosedness of beings. (p. 128)

Qua open relatedness, all stating comportment is thus necessarily engaged with the disclosedness as such of beings. It is grounded in the freedom that, as letting-be (*Seinlassen*), is an engagement with (*Sicheinlassen auf*) the openness of the open. But at the same time, and according to the same "logic" of letting-be, this freedom for the openness of the open is also freedom for what is disclosed in the open. It withdraws (*Zurücktreten vor*) in order to expose itself to what is disclosed as such. In this free retreat, engagement with the openness of the open makes room for the beings as such that take their stand in this open. It makes room for beings in their disclosedness, so that they can show themselves in themselves and from themselves. An ever more refined accord thus seems to characterize the third step of the foregrounding of truth as accordance. Provisionally, I construe it as the accord between the traits of letting-be/withdrawing, on the one hand, and disclosure as such (of things in what and how they are), on the other hand.

Before further elaborating on this latter accord (which, after those seen at the heart of the inner possibility and the ground of truth as correctness, is an ever more original essence of truth), it may be appropriate to reflect for a moment on the status of this (as yet not completed) new accord. Heidegger's terminology—"inner possibility," "ground," or "essence," and now "the more original essence of uniquely essential truth"—would seem to aim at deeper and deeper syntheses. One can expect this more original essence and the accord that constitutes it to be the ultimate condition of truth as accordance. The question that thus arises concerns the criteria by which it is decided that *the* final condition has been established, that is, the inner possibility and the ground of truth as correctness. Freedom for what is opened up in its singularity, as the ground of the inner possibility of accordance, seems to be (in conformity with established rules of thinking) a deeper, truly fundamental enabling reason. Yet what can be the meaning of an essence "more originary" than essence, of a more fundamental foundation, supposing, as one must, that Heidegger does not indulge in a *regressus ad infinitum*? It certainly cannot be an essence, ground, or foundation in the traditional sense. Heidegger suggests as much when he claims that freedom as the ground of truth has its own essence in uniquely essential truth, that is, in the far-from-ordinary concept of truth as unconcealment. But that the accord exhibited in the third step of foregrounding is not another, still-deeper synthesis can be gauged from the fact that although it exhibits the *fundamental* implications inherent in the very determination of statement as comportment—that is, of an open relatedness in an open region—it does nothing more than formulate the *hidden implications* under which the inner possibility and the ground of truth as accordance become meaningful in the first place. It does not add a new possibility or ground to the previous ones, but recasts them in terms of the engagement with the openness of the open that the very conditions of accordance require. Presentative concor-

dance can take its standards from beings, and beings can present themselves on their own terms, only if such comportment is, in its freedom for
what is opened up as such in the open region, freedom for the open region and its openness, or for things' self-revealing. This engagement with
disclosedness is not a more profound ground for accordance but the
framework without which the inner possibility of truth as correctness and
its ground in freedom could not be what they are. Yet an accord that can
be shown to resonate through the accords that make up the inner possibility and the very ground of truth as correspondence is certainly not a
condition of possibility or ground anymore. It is an accord, by contrast,
which is required in order to speak of inner possibility and ground in the
first place, and of accord and accordance as well. But there is perhaps still
another reason why this latter accord is dissimilar to those that constitute
inner possibilities and essences.

Heidegger hints at such a dissimilarity when, toward the end of section 4, he notes that if truth is primarily freedom, that is, engagement
with disclosedness, then covering up, concealment, and distortion are
equally primordial possibilities of truth. In short, if, as we have seen, the
more originary essence of freedom as the essence of truth harbors an accord, then it must also be inhabited by a certain dis(ac)cord. We shall
thus have to pursue our analysis of the more refined accord, which we
have seen orchestrating both the inner possibility and the ground of
truth. This ever more refined accord must accord, it would seem, with a
trait that accounts in an essential manner for the possibility of covering
up, namely, un-truth.

At the beginning of the section entitled "The Essence of Truth,"
Heidegger claims that freedom, as disclosive letting beings be, is "engagement in the disclosure of being as a whole as such [*des Seienden im Ganzen
als einem solchen*]" (pp. 130–31). Similarly, the last paragraphs of the previous section had contended that the experience of unconcealment is that of
Being as a whole (p. 129). The exposure to the disclosedness of beings, in
which freedom as letting beings be is rooted, is exposure to, and disclosure
of, what all beings qua beings imply, that is, Being as a whole, the openness as disclosed openness as such. Now Heidegger writes that any comportment, to the extent that it is open (*offenständiges Verhalten*), "flourishes
[*schwingt*] in letting beings be" (p. 130). It flourishes thus in the essence of

freedom as a disclosure of beings in their being, and consequently, in the disclosure of Being as a whole as such. Each and every mode of comportment toward beings, Heidegger holds, is "already attuned [by freedom] . . . to being as a whole [*hat die Freiheit alles Verhalten schon auf das Seiende im Ganzen abgestimmt*]" (p. 131). The ever more refined and more essential accord (between disclosive letting-be and the corresponding showing itself as such of beings) that we have seen to be required for a more originary thinking of the possibility of truth as accordance and its ground thus appears to derive its more fundamental status from the fact that it articulates the most universal condition for every mode of open comportment, as comportment toward a particular being. The condition that it sets forth is that each and every particular mode of comportment has to be attuned to Being as a whole, that every comportment must flourish according to the tune of Being, so to speak. Such attuning is called "being attuned (attunement) [*Gestimmtheit* {*Stimmung*}]." Attunement—which, as Heidegger remarks, is not a psychological mood—"draws up [*hebt hinein*] into beings as a whole" (p. 131).

Attunement explains why no relation to a thing can ever be free of a (historical) relation of awareness of the whole of the open in which this thing takes its stand, and why all relation to the thing is thus originally and always an open comportment. Consequently, stating, although it does nothing but assert the accord between what is said of a thing and the thing as it presents itself, is, because it is a comportment, attuned "in a way that discloses beings as a whole." The limited accord achieved in propositional truth presupposes that a universal accord (a being-attuned to beings as a whole as such, to the disclosedness of Being) flourishes in it. Thus there is no accordance without such a universal accord achieved in the (always historical) attunement of comportment to being in its disclosedness. No *Übereinstimmung* without *Gestimmtheit*, no *stimmen* without the *Stimmung* that, prior to all modifications of comportment and all modes in which a thing can present itself as such, secures the openness of the disclosedness of Being as a whole within which beings can relate to one another.[7]

Heidegger writes: "Letting beings be, which is an attuning, a bringing into accord, prevails throughout and anticipates all the open comportment that flourishes in it [*Das stimmende Seinlassen von Seiendem greift durch alles in ihm schwingende offenständige Verhalten hindurch und greift ihm vor*]. Man's comportment is brought into definite accord [*durchstimmt*] throughout by the openness of being as a whole" (pp. 131–32). The universal attunement in question strikes (as one strikes an accord), or stretches (as one stretches an octave, for instance), through the open comportment that swings, vibrates, oscillates in it (according to the rhythm of the accord). It anticipates (*greift ihm vor*) all comportment, Heidegger notes, and thus emphasizes the antecedence of the attunement in question. Through it, all of man's comportments have always already been attuned (*abgestimmt*) to the openness of Being as a whole that pervades it (*durchstimmt*) from the start. Now if the openness of Being as a whole is the being-attuned or attunement in which all open comportment, and in particular, stating comportment, flourishes, then it is not only what precedes all possible accordance (and the latter's inner possibility and ground) but what precedes it as an ever more refined accord. Although, in the attempt to foreground truth as accordance and its dependence on a destination according to the order of creation (*Übereinstimmung* and *Bestimmung*) in the inner possibility and the ground of truth as correctness, Heidegger did not construe these enabling conditions himself in terms of an accord of the vectorial traits discussed above, still, when dealing with the openness of the open and with truth in the essential sense of *aletheia* (that is, with the final presuppositions or implications of the traditional concept of truth), he has recourse to terms—*Gestimmtheit, Stimmung*—that not only mean being-attuned, or mood, but also echo "accord." With the fundamental being-attuned of all comportment to being as a whole, with this disclosedness, which is openness as such, upon which something as narrow as the accordance of proposition and matter rests—with all this, a background melody, or rather a rhythm, comes into sight that is indistinguishable from the openness of Being as a whole. "From the point of view of everyday calculations and preoccupations this 'as a whole' appears to be incalculable and incomprehensible. It cannot be understood on the basis of the beings opened up in any given case, whether they belong to nature or to history," Heidegger writes; and he adds, "Although it ceaselessly brings everything into definite accord [*ständig alles stimmend*], still it remains indefinite, indeterminable [*das Unbestimmte, Unbestimmbare*]" (p. 132). From the point of view of everyday thinking, science, and metaphysics, such attuning that allows for accordance must remain indeterminable. For a thinking engaged in determination, what makes accordance possible must necessarily escape determination. To speak of the whole that attunes as something indeterminate or indeterminable is to speak of it metaphysically, or—what amounts to the same thing if we follow Heidegger—to speak of it in a most common and unconsidering manner. But if what ceaselessly brings everything into accord by attuning it to Being as a whole as such appears undetermined and indeterminable, the reason for this may also be that what brings into accord cannot itself be an accord anymore in the usual sense. It itself, perhaps, no longer accords. It accords, perhaps, without according (itself). But because this originary attuning is undetermined or indeterminable, it is not a fleeting, unfathomable, or vague concept. Indeed, what ceaselessly *accords* everything can achieve such a task with the help of very precise and definite means. We must therefore try to grasp with all possible rigor—and that means, by its constitutive traits—the necessarily indeterminable and perhaps no longer simply accorded accord on which accordance depends.

As already noted, being-attuned as something indeterminable "coincides for the most part [*fällt . . . zusammen*] with what is most fleeting and most unconsidered" (p. 132). The two reasons advanced—the inability of metaphysics and common understanding to think of it otherwise, and the specific ontological status of being-attuned—bring about in a concerted action this collapse of what ceaselessly accords into the indeterminable and the most common. By becoming determined as the indeterminable, what ceaselessly puts everything into accord becomes concealed. But this concealment is a self-concealment. As that which lies at the origin of all accord, what ceaselessly accords must withdraw from what it brings harmoniously together. It achieves such withdrawal as the undetermined and indeterminable, both of which are inevitable counterconcepts to determining thought within the latter's sphere. If originary attunement is lost in the indeterminable, it is because it loses itself in allowing for the possibility of accord in the sphere of the determinable. The indeterminable is in that very sphere the proxy, the phantom image, of originary attunement, in which image it is lost as well. Heidegger can thus claim that "what brings into accord is not nothing [not something trifling, trivial, fleeting, etc.] but rather a concealing of beings as a whole." He explains: "Precisely because letting-be always lets beings be in a particular comportment which relates to them and thus discloses them, it conceals beings as a whole. Letting-be is intrinsically at the same time a concealing" (p. 132). For accordance between a particular statement and a particular matter to be achieved, and for the particularity of a being to show itself in and from itself, that without which a particular being could not reveal itself in its very particularity, namely its appearing as such (beings as such as a whole), must withdraw. The withdrawal of Being as a whole is coeval with the actualization of Being as such in letting-be. The dissimulation of what makes it possible for a particular being to present itself as such, in what it is and how it is, is the necessary condition for the very presence of that being itself.[8] This necessary dissimulation in letting-be, the inevitable withdrawal of Being as a whole in the coming into their own right of singular beings, also affects the accordance on which truth as correctness rests. Accordance is also always singular, and thus its being-attuned to beings as a whole must necessarily become dissimulated too. What is opened up as a singular accord obfuscates the openness, the being-open by which it becomes accorded. As a result, what ceaselessly accords everything must necessarily comport with the trait not only of withdrawal, concealment, retreat, but also of a certain discord. What ceaselessly accords puts out of accord. The necessary eclipse of the according whole of being as such in letting a particular being be is also, and inevitably, the event of discord, of the war among beings.[9] The ultimate accord, which attunes all human comportment to seek accordance between itself and what it lets be, can thus only be an accord very much unlike those that, as we have seen, render possible and ground truth as correctness. The ultimate accord must be one whose constituting trait cannot but comport with the countertrait of discord. But how are we to think the unity or economy of such a complex? Can it still have the nature of an accord?

In the following section, "Untruth as Concealing," Heidegger argues: "The concealment of beings as a whole, untruth proper, is older than every openedness of this or that being. It is also older than letting-be itself which in disclosing already holds concealed and comports itself toward concealing" (p. 132). Older than letting-be is "the concealing of what is concealed [*die Verbergung des Verborgenen*] as a whole, of beings as such, i.e., the mystery [*Geheimnis*]" (p. 132). What Heidegger calls "the one mystery" is not just the exact counterpart of disclosedness or the openness of the open. Being as a whole as such attunes and accords everything ceaselessly. But Being as a whole as such, the openness of Being, is wrenched from concealedness. It is "derived" from Being's concealedness. The concealing of this concealedness—the mystery—is older than all letting-be, and this also implies that it does not comport with the disclosure of disclosedness in a symmetric fashion. It does not harmoniously accord with it in a unitary synthesis. The concealing of concealedness, indeed, refers what ceaselessly accords, Being as a whole, not to a definite or determined trait that would be the bipolar correspondent to the according trait (and which could lend itself to entering into accord with the according trait), but to an abyssal trait. The mystery names the inner limit not only of truth as correspondence but of truth as *aletheia* as well. All disclosing letting-be, with the inescapable dissimulation of Being as a whole that goes with it, is itself "dependent" on the concealing of what is concealed.[10] This concealing is, as Heidegger puts it, "the fundamental occurrence [*Grundgeschehen*]" on which letting-be and the withdrawal of Being that accompany it hinge (p. 134). Although this concealing is the ineluctable abyss, or blind spot, that accompanies truth as *aletheia* (and by extension truth as *adaequatio* or *homoiosis*), it is also older than truth, not only because singular accordance presupposes the withdrawal of Being as a whole to which it must be attuned, but because the disclosure of Being as a whole itself entails that it be wrenched from concealedness. The concealing of what is concealed—of Being as a whole—is the dissymmetric (and abyssal) countertrait to which that which ceaselessly accords—Being as a whole—relates. The ultimate synthesis, then—the third, but perhaps fourth, fifth, sixth step in Heidegger's attempt to foreground truth as accordance—is no longer an accord, strictly speaking. It is certainly not the accord of accord and discord. Rather, in it the accord comes to stand in a relation to its limit. What attunes and accords ceaselessly is not inhabited by discord. There is no *Verstimmung* intrinsically linked up with the enabling accord of *Gestimmtheit*. The dissymmetry of this ultimate synthesis precludes the possibility that any simple opposite of *Stimmung* should enter into a relation to it. This dissymmetry also precludes the possibility that the limit of *Stimmung* should be thought by way and in terms of a (linguistic, etymological) derivative of the notion of *Stimmung*. Heidegger recognizes as much when he shows the limit of accord to be the mystery of the concealing of the concealed—*Geheimnis*. Neither a name nor a concept can hope to designate this strange arrangement. *Stimmung* and *Geheimnis* are names in a Heideggerian sense. For the economy of their interrelatedness, however, Heidegger could not find a name. That is why he left it unnamed. But name and concept do not exhaust the linguistic means for thinking and spelling out the disposition of the traits that make up the ultimate accord that is no longer an accord. To think and spell it out, it is perhaps necessary to turn around and take up once again the analysis whose very premises lead Heidegger to search for names for both the fundamental occurrences of concealing and what rests on it—*aletheia*. To think this unnamable and unconceptualizable accord that is not an accord, it would perhaps be necessary to displace the whole style of Heidegger's analysis. But that would perhaps also mean to no longer being able to keep intact the distinction between philosophy on the one hand and metaphysics and ordinary thinking on the other. Such a displacement would involve shaking up the manner in which Heidegger conceived of the relations that exist between these types of thinking. And finally, a question, modalized by probability as well: would such an undertaking, if possible and successful (if that could still mean something here), still be thinking? Would the spelled-out accord that is no longer an accord be an accord that has been thought?

(1989)

7

Canonizing Measures

As a discipline, that is, a department of knowledge and learning, philosophy must inevitably have a system of rules or a method for the maintenance, proper conduct, and transmission of its specific task. But philosophy's task not only is to be executed in an orderly fashion but is itself constituted by a set of rules, the rules of orderly or disciplined thinking. As a branch of knowledge and instruction, the discipline "philosophy" thus has its own proper canon. Without the canon of its elected books, the harmonic ordering of its corpus, and the strict rules to be observed not only in learning or teaching it but in philosophizing as well, philosophy would not be recognizable as a discipline.[1] For these are what give it its identity. Hence, this canonicity, in particular the domain of established fundamental rules for thought within it, profoundly affects our understanding of philosophy. Indeed, depending on what these rules are said to be (and to what level of thinking they pertain), the discipline of philosophy fans out into the diverse definitions that it has been assigned historically.

It is not unimportant for what is to follow to mention that the meaning of "canon" as the entirety of a discipline's fundamental rules derives from the Greek word *kanon*, which itself originates from the Semitic word *quanae*. Yet, whereas *quanae* merely designates the reed from which baskets are woven and measuring rods are made, the word in its Greek cast becomes dominated by its figural meaning. The referential emphasis shifts from the material out of which measuring rods, plumb lines, or beams of scales are manufactured to the measuring rod's form, its straight line or shape, and thus to the measuring instrument itself. Further, with this shift away from the material to the form of the rod, the term *kanon* acquires the additional meaning of infallible standard, model (as with the statues of Polyclitus), or desirable aims that are thus raised to the status of *kriteria*, that is, means for judging or trying (by a court of judgment or tribunal, for instance). Although the notion of a canon is commonly associated with the attempts, beginning in the early Middle Ages, to secure the literary tradition of the schools, the juridical tradition of the state, and the religious tradition of the church,[2] it has been a *terminus technicus* in Greek philosophy to refer to the criteria for the discovery of the foundations of knowledge, the distinction between what is true and false, and what is good and evil. The echo of this early philosophical use of "canon" is still clearly perceptible in Kant's critical philosophy. But in this essay, I will not be concerned so much with the explicit thematization of canon and canonicity in (historical) philosophy as with the ways in which canon as standard, rule, and principle is constitutive of philosophy as such, insofar as it conceives of itself as a discipline.

Philosophy is a discipline only if it yields or measures up to its standard. But what is this standard in most general terms? When Epicurus uses the term "canon" to circumscribe logic as a system of rules for the production and examination of cognitions, when Epictetus identifies philosophy as the establishment of a canon for correct acting and knowing, when Kant defines logic and pure reason as the canon of a priori laws or principles of thought without which there can be no correct (or legitimate) use of our cognitive faculties, it becomes evident that they wished philosophy to be understood in a certain, very determined way—either as a theory of knowledge (Epicurus), as a doctrine for the proper conduct of life (Epictetus), or as the "general art of reason [*eine allgemeine Vernuftkunst*]" (Kant).[3] But independently of these specifically historical standards that help the discipline of philosophy achieve determined goals, what does "canon" do for philosophy as philosophy, and how does it affect our understanding of philosophy itself?

At this point it is necessary to reflect briefly on the ground rules, the bare necessities required by philosophical thought to be such thought in the first place, rather than science or literature, for instance. Although likely to invite misunderstanding, the following extremely schematic characterization of the nature of the formal ground-structures of philosophical thinking must suffice here: philosophical thought, I suggest, is essentially transcendental synthesis. Beyond historical configurations, this fundamental form of thinking (which overlaps with the method of thinking), establishes philosophy as a specific discursive practice in its own right and serves as a criterion to demarcate it from other branches of knowledge. Beyond the technical Kantian and Husserlian sense of "transcendental synthesis," beyond the characterization of philosophy from a transcendental-logical perspective as intertwined categorial, affirmative, and self-positing synthesis,[4] and thus also beyond the conception of judgment as the prototype of synthetic thought, I understand "transcendental synthesis" to mean the elemental and elementary constitution of the *as such* of the world (the world *as* world) by way of the difference that irrupts into the world in the experience of wonder (or anxiety). At its most fundamental, philosophical thinking is thus the inauguration of the concept *of* the world—of a difference of the world from itself that, once attributed to the world, sets the condition for all synthetic knowledge about the world. This characterization of philosophical thought, however, does not yet provide a standard, a canon properly speaking. It does not yet serve to institute philosophy as a disciplined and disciplinized discursive praxis. The inaugurating transcendental synthetic experience of the *thaumazein* turns into a standard or canonic rule only under a given condition, namely that the elementary exigency of a radical break with world-immediacy is not purely met. Indeed, although philosophy has from its inception in Greek wonder claimed this exigency of thinking the *as such* as its own, it has conceived of it in substantial terms (as *ousia*, for instance), thus committing a category mistake of colossal proportions, as gigantic as the *gigantomachia tes ousias* ("the battle of the gods and giants about Being") itself.[5] In consequence, the exigency against which philosophical thought must be measured has always given in to the tendency to mistake the *as such* of the world for the world itself, to understand the whole in terms of something that it comprises. This confusion, or *metabasis eis allo genos* ("confusion of genres"), of the *as such* with entities, that is, with instances capable of causal origination, authority, and disciplinization above all, is the condition under which the ground rules of philosophical thinking can turn into the canon for philosophy as a discipline, and endow philosophy with the power to punish and discipline any other discourses simply by judging them to be science, literature, or something else. The category mistake in question makes it possible to speak of the elementary exigencies and fundamental forms of philosophical thinking as a standard, a canon for thought as philosophical thought, in the first place.

In this essay, I would like to inquire into the status, or fate, of canonicity in that kind of contemporary philosophy—sometimes incongruously labeled "postmodern"—in which the concern with thinking produces a critical distinction and opposition between (philosophical) thought and traditional disciplinary philosophy. Heidegger thematizes this passage from the discipline of philosophy (which in all its abstraction—or more precisely, because of its abstraction—remains unsevered from commonsense thinking) to the craft of thinking as a *Wandlung des Denkens*. However, *Wandlung*, translated as change, mutation, transformation, transubstantiation, fails to capture the very manner in which this passage from disciplined philosophizing to thinking occurs. *Wandlung* must be understood here from its etymological roots in Old High German: *wanton*, to turn (around), belongs to the verb *wintan*, to wind. Rather than a continuous development, *Wandlung* implies for Heidegger a breaking out and away from everything traditionally associated with philosophical—abstract and conceptual—thought. The change of thinking that he evokes "apparently remains on the path of metaphysics. Nevertheless, in its decisive steps . . . it accomplishes a change [*Wandel*] in the questioning that belongs to the overcoming [*Uberwindung*] of metaphysics."[6] *Wandlung des Denkens* thus refers to a turning away, a rebounding from, and a leap out (*Sprung*) of disciplinary thinking, thus emphasizing a sharp discontinuity in thinking's *relationship* to the tradition of the philosophical discipline. If the transformed kind of thinking that characterizes "philosophy" from Heidegger to Derrida is thus characterized by a marked departure from the procedures handed down within the discipline—including the steps requisite for continuous development—this change must also affect the fundamental exigencies of philosophical thought, its standard, or canon. We ask: what happens to canon and canonicity when thought extracts itself (in a relation of continued implication) from the philosophical? To sketch the beginning of an answer to this question, I will briefly analyze some passages from " ... Poetically Man Dwells ... "

Although Heidegger discusses only poetic dwelling in this essay, the proximity between poetry and thinking suggests that, after due allowances, everything established about poetic dwelling will be true of thinking dwelling as well. What then does Heidegger say in " ... Poetically Man Dwells ... " that might pertain to my question regarding canonicity and canon in postphilosophical thought? Heidegger sets out to claim that what is usually called the existence of man has to be understood in terms of dwelling. "Dwelling" does not in this case refer to "merely one form of human behavior alongside many others"; rather it refers to what may be *the* "basic character of human existence [*des menschlichen Daseins*]."[7] Understood essentially, dwelling characterizes the human being's mode of being in the between of sky and earth. Like the fundamental structure of being-in-the-world analyzed in *Being and Time*, dwelling has eminently ethical, or rather proto-ethical connotations—as will become evident as soon as the mode of "relationship" that dwelling has to both sky and earth comes into view. Poetry, Heidegger continues, is what "causes dwelling to be dwelling. Poetry is what really lets us dwell [*eigentliches Wohnenlassen*]" (p. 215). It is capable of letting-dwell precisely because poetry is a measuring (*Messen*), Heidegger adds. Indeed, it is a measuring that has "its own *metron*, and thus its own metric" (p. 221). What does this *metron* consist in that serves as a measure for poetic measuring, and thus dwelling? What is this standard against which letting-dwell must be judged? And what is a measure to begin with?

A measure (*metron, mensura, Mass*) is either an ethical, aesthetical concept or one pertaining to the philosophy of nature. In my analysis of Heidegger's essay I will only be concerned with its ethical meaning. Werner Marx has defined the essential traits of the traditional, that is, onto-theological conception of measure as follows:

Measure is a "standard measure" that contains as such the demand of an ought. Preceding the measuring act, it has the mode of being of a "transcendence." At the same time, it has the "power" to determine the human being "immanently." Therein lies the deciding significance of a measure, namely its "binding obligingness." It has the power to remain the "same" in different situations, and as such it has the characteristics of "obviousness" and "unambiguity."[8]

In the essentialist perspective characteristic of our Platonic and Judeo-Christian heritage, the measure for ethical behavior is constituted either by a canon of the cardinal virtues or by virtue as a mean (*meson*) or *frugalitas* comprising all other virtues, or by the emerging domination of human being's rational nature over its animal nature. Traditionally, measure's possible effectiveness as a standard for responsible, ethical behavior is guaranteed in that it takes on the form of a canon of teachable rules, laws, and injunctions that endow it with an indisputable objective reality. Considering Heidegger's anti-Platonic and anti-essentialist position, his reference to the notion of measure in " ... Poetically Man Dwells ... " should, in principle, presuppose a redetermination of the traditional concept in question.

Poetry is a measuring, Heidegger notes, in that it takes the measure of man with respect to what he calls the dimension dealt out to him, that is, the between of heaven and earth that "man spans [*durchmessen*] . . . by measuring himself [as mortal] against the heavenly" (pp. 220–21). But poetry's measuring is not just one measuring act among others. Indeed, since in poetry the measure is taken for man's dwelling in the between of earth and sky, the taking of measure that occurs in poetry is the primordial measure-taking subsequently applied in every measuring act. Poetry, Heidegger writes, is the measure-taking (*Mass-nahme*) "by which man first receives the measure for the breadth of his being" (p. 222). By virtue of its primordial nature, such measure-taking is not comparable to all further acts of measuring; it is "a strange measure for ordinary and in particular also for all merely scientific ideas, certainly not a palpable stick or rod" (p. 223). Nor is it a rule or standard in the habitual or even philosophical sense. The measure that Heidegger is discussing here is not canonical; it does not take the form of a canon of virtues and rules and does not lend itself to disciplinary measures. But to realize fully the strangeness (*befremdlich*) of this measure, and the extent to which it differs from traditional conceptions of measure, it will be necessary to return to Heidegger's text.

I recall that for Hölderlin, the author of the poem from which Heidegger has taken the title of his essay, the measure against which man measures himself as a mortal in the between of earth and sky is the godhead. But Heidegger specifies: the godhead is a measure for the mortals that span the dimension of the between only insofar as the godhead is the Unknown One. He writes, "for Hölderlin God, as the one who he is, is unknown and it is just as *this Unknown One* that he is the measure for the poet" (p. 222). This means that Heidegger conceives of measure-taking in terms of the structure of aletheic concealment in disclosure. Indeed, "something that man measures himself by must after all impart itself, must appear. But if it appears, it is known. The god, however, is unknown, and he is the measure nonetheless" (p. 222). If the appearing godhead is to be the measure for mortals, it can only be insofar as he appears *as* the one who conceals himself and remains concealed or unknown. But if the godhead reveals himself as a measure only if he appears as the *Unknown One*, the measure contains in Heidegger's terms a mystery (*Geheimnis*). With this Heidegger's notion of measure shows itself to lack the essential features of "obviousness" and "unambiguity," as well as those that pertain to the enduring identity of the idealities that traditionally constitute a measure. Heidegger adds: "Not only this, but the god who remains unknown, must by showing *himself* as the one he is, appear as the one who remains unknown. God's *manifestness*—not only he himself— is mysterious." The mystery thus pervades the very manifestness of the measure, as opposed to *what* manifests itself as measure (god); the very appearing of god must occur in such a way that it shows only withdrawal in the openness of the open of what comes to the fore. It is thus not god properly speaking who is the measure for man, but *the way* in which god as the unknown *becomes manifest as withdrawn*. We read:

The measure consists in the way in which the god who remains unknown, is revealed *as* such by the sky. God's appearance through the sky consists in a disclosing that lets us see what conceals itself, but lets us see it not by seeking to wrest what is concealed out of its concealedness, but only by guarding the concealed in its self-concealment. Thus the unknown god appears as the unknown by way of the sky's manifestness. This appearance is the measure against which man measures himself. (p. 223)

The *metron* of poetic dwelling is a mode of appearing that lets us see what conceals itself (god, the heavenly, the immortals) in such a way that the concealed remains concealed. The strange (*befremdlich*) *metron* that Heidegger talks about thus reveals its intrinsic ethical implications. It is a mode of appearing in which the unfamiliar, the alien, is allowed to reveal itself as alien in the familiar (*Vertrauten*). Exemplified by god's appearance as the unknown, this *metron* preserves "the darkness and the silence of what is alien" in its appearing. It lets the alien reveal *itself*, but reveal itself *as* alien, *as* other, in short, "*as* that which conceals itself" (p. 225). In measuring himself against such a measure—in a measure that lets be as other—man dwells on earth, in the dimension that *as mortal* is assigned to him. If this measure looks strange, and estranges, this is because, in contrast to the traditional ethical law (primarily concerned with the human being's harmonious fitting into the whole of what is), it is opened up to strangeness—in a radicalization of what already had been sketched out as Dasein's structure of being-in. It is opened up to strangeness in that it lets what is strange freely demarcate itself from the familiar and thus be itself as such: strange and other.

This *metron* is the standard of poetic dwelling. Dwelling is dwelling only if it yields to the measure taken by poetry. But, as Heidegger's "Letter on Humanism" recalls, poetry "is confronted by the same question, and in the same manner, as thinking." Thus when toward the end of that text Heidegger asks, "Whence does thinking take its measure?" it becomes obvious that, in a way similar to poetry, thinking dwelling occurs only when it rests in the measure taken by thought. The measure for thought—or as he also puts it, "the sole matter of thinking"—is "to bring to language ever and ever again . . . [the] advent of Being which remains, and in its remaining waits for man." The saying of Being, more precisely, "the fittingness of the saying of Being, as of the destiny of truth, is the first law of thinking—not the rules of logic which can become rules only on the basis of the law of Being."[9] The *metron* or law for thinking, like the measure for poetry, is not a canon, a rule or stick, a standard or principle. It is, in both cases, much less and much more than a canon. Whereas a standard sets the rules for a discipline, such as literature or philosophy, the *metron* represents the measure of poetry (*dichten*) and thinking (*denken*). Whereas a standard's features are authoritatively applied from outside to a realm of human activity (such as cognition or poetic activity), the *metron* is immanent to poetic or thinking dwelling. It is such dwelling only if it rests in the measure in question. A *metron* comes to stand or to bear, in the very process, happening, or occurrence of such dwelling. It is nothing independently of the active happening of poetry and thought. The measure for thought and poetry cannot therefore be taken in the sense of being clutched or grasped, in order to be applied or imposed. The measure is taken in a gathered taking-in (*gesammelten Vernehmen*), in Heidegger's words, that is, in a hearing-response to what is disclosed as concealed (p. 223). The measure is taken in a response that is both responsive and responsible. It can consequently be said that the taking of the measure obeys as well the law of granting a stay, an *ethos*, to what remains sheltered in concealment.

But how does this *metron* for thinking and poetry relate to the canon, the traditional standards, the exigencies of the disciplines? What commerce exists between it and the canon of the discipline of philosophy in particular? Moreover, if, as I argued, "transcendental synthesis" is at the basis of the canonical laws of philosophy, what happens to the exigencies of transcendentality and synthesis in what Heidegger emphatically calls thought or thinking? Do transcendentality and unification become altogether obsolete in postphilosophical thought, that is, in a thought that calls for "less philosophy, but more attentiveness in thinking; less literature, but more cultivation of the letter"?[10]

If the rules of logic can become rules only on the basis of the law or *metron* of Being, then the *metron* for thought is not unconnected to these standard rules of the disciplines. It stands in a grounding relation to them. For the *metron* to delimit these latter rules in a gesture that is indeed more philosophical than interdisciplinary is not to overthrow them. They are merely shown to derive from the *metron* through restriction, and only through this derivation they can serve the legitimate yet limited interests of the specialized tasks proper to the disciplines. Undoubtedly, their authority is breached when they are shown to result from a restriction of the law or *metron* of thinking and poetry, but at the same time, this demonstration provides the disciplines with a new kind of legitimation. The relation between the *metron* and the rules of the disciplines is not exhausted, however, by describing it in terms of a grounding relation. As I have argued, the *metron* for poetic and thinking dwelling is immanent to dwelling itself. In other words, it cannot rigorously be detached from dwelling by some metadiscourse and raised to the status of a transcendence. Yet, of this *metron* of poetic and thinking dwelling we cannot but speak *as if* it was a transcendence, a measure, or a canon in the traditional sense. This difficulty—that the *metron* is not a canon yet cannot be conceived of or talked about except by being raised above its immanence in poetic or thinking dwelling—can be dealt with provisionally by taking the following lead from Jean-François Lyotard. Resorting, in *The Differend*, to the Kantian distinction between determinant and reflective judgments, he characterizes the stakes of philosophical thought (in post-philosophical thinking, if you wish) as directed toward "discovering its (own) rules rather than . . . supposing their knowledge as a principle."[11] In other words, the law of thinking, its *metron*, has to be understood as a reflective law rather than as a principle. It can only be incessantly discovered, since it is not a law that is fixed once and for all. It can only be reflected upon, in the occurring of philosophical thinking, as a law, to use a Heideggerian formula, that is always only on the way to itself. The *metron* of thought is not frozen into canonicity. It is a canonical law only in a process of approximation. Hence, when the law of thought turns into *a law*, thinking ends, and the disciplines begin. When the reflective determination of the measure of thinking and poetry comes full circle, the measure becomes transformed into a canon. In the canons of the disciplines, thinking has abandoned the reflective search for its immanent rule. All that is left, in that case, of the ethical dimension of the *metron* of poetic or thinking dwelling is the individual and specialized disciplines' demand that their standards be specific, and that they take the singularity of the domains they govern into account.

The foregoing developments about the relation between *metron* and canon implicitly contain an answer to the question regarding the role of the transcendental in the measure of thought. But before articulating this response, I shall make another brief detour through Heidegger's discussion of "measure" in " ... Poetically Man Dwells ... " He writes: "The measure taken by poetry yields, imparts itself—as the foreign element in which the invisible one preserves his presence—to what is familiar in the sights of the sky. Hence, the measure is of the same nature as the sky" (p. 226). Although the sky (along with everything beneath it) is the element of the appearing and disclosure of the unknown godhead, the familiar sights (*Anblicke*, or images, as Heidegger also calls them) remain foreign, incommensurate with the invisible one even when he is revealed as the one who conceals himself. Conversely, the godhead's disclosure as the invisible in the radiance of the sky is itself a foreign ingredient in the familiar. In transcending the familiar sights, the godhead could be said to be a transcendent entity, and hence man's absolute and decisive measure in the traditional onto-theological sense. Hölderlin might still have understood the godhead in this fashion. But as we have seen, for Heidegger, it is not the godhead who is the measure, but "*the way* in which the god who remains unknown, is revealed *as* such by the sky." Yet this measure is said to be of the same nature as the sky. The measure's celestial nature, however, does not imply that it would have the mode of being of a transcendent essence. "The sky is not sheer light," we are told. "The radiance of its height is itself the darkness of its all-sheltering breadth" (p. 226). Thus, when Heidegger agrees with Hölderlin that there is no measure on earth, it is not in order to associate the measure in a traditional manner with the heavenly. If the measure were of the earth, it would, first of all, be a measure lacking the exigency of "universal" bindingness. But as Heidegger explains, we deny an earthly character to measure primarily "because what we signify when we say 'on the earth' exists only insofar as man dwells on the earth and in his dwelling lets the earth be as earth" (p. 227). Such a measure, however, rather than having the mode of being of a transcendence, is something transcendental. But if it is, as Heidegger repeatedly notes, a strange measure, this is also because the transcendentality of this measure, which articulates a preserving disclosure, is of an unheard-of nature. Since Kant, to speak of transcendentality is to imply finitude. The transcendentality invoked by Heidegger, however, is no longer subjectivist, and hence the finitude that goes with it would also be of a different sort than that of Kant. The measure for poetic dwelling is of the same nature as the sky, the familiar sights of man, the topos of the celestials, and yet it contains the foreign as foreign, which has imparted itself to the element of light. It is inhabited by the darkness from which what appears shines forth, and back into which it withdraws. What causes the measure to be slightly different from what it applies to is that it lets be as withdrawn, as sheltered, as unknown. But such letting-be of the disclosure of the alien *as such*, which sets poetic dwelling radically apart from ordinary dwelling, is also what makes poetic dwelling irreducibly finite.

In the discussion of how *metron* relates to canon, the *metron*'s transcendentality and its finitizing reference to a transcendens was already implied. If I now circle back to that discussion, I do so in order to exemplify yet another decisive feature of poetry's and thought's dependence on transcendentality. When I advanced with Lyotard that thought (or for that matter, poetry) is rooted in reflective judgment, in a judgment that seeks the universal rule for a given manifold, I also understood poetry, or thought, to approximate this rule infinitely. This lack of, or resistance to, a final standardization or canonization was said to be constitutive of the *metron*. After what I have just elaborated, it is evident that the *metron*'s transcendentality is thus constituted not by such things as an exhaustive set (or canon) of categories or other idealities (say in the Husserlian sense), but by the endless spanning of the dimension, and in particular, of the difference that separates man from and ties him to the other, the foreign, the alien. To let the other be *as* other in poetic or thinking disclosure is not only to transcend the familiar (and to prepare a stay for the alien), it is also to remain unflaggingly in the gesture of transcending, preserving it from crystallizing into a substantialist or subjectivist perspective, into, for example, categories, or conditions of possibility. The transcendence or the transcendental of poetry or thought escapes the category mistake I referred to earlier, and hence their *metrons* resist canonization.

But what about unification, synthesis? As we have seen, the measure is taken in a *gesammelten Vernehmen*. *Gesammelt* here means collective, collected, gathered, and refers to the hearing that responds to the appeal of what speaks. But the measure for poetic dwelling and thinking dwelling is collective in yet another sense. It gathers into one, it lets be together and near, the familiar and the foreign that estranges. Needless to say, such a gathering of the familiar and the alien cannot be a synthesis or a unity in the usual philosophical sense. In the togetherness of the familiar and the foreign, the foreign is allowed to be the foreign that it is. Its heterogeneity remains. Yet it is referred to; it is allowed a stay. In this gathering union of the familiar and otherness as otherness, the ties and relations are as tightly knit as in any synthetic whole. And yet, in the gathered unity in question, unification itself remains deferred. It takes place, it occurs—unflaggingly—but without consummation in a whole or totality.

In short, then, beyond the disciplines and their canons, beyond philosophy and its standards, thought and poetry encounter the *metron* for a mode of thinking and poetry that allows for no canon. Such modes of thinking and poetry do not give rise, therefore, to disciplines. The measure given by such a *metron* to thinking and poetry, the metric it provides for their movement (*Gang*), is one of steps (*Schritte*), if not of leaps (*Sprünge*), of the decisive steps of questioning that, in the case of thinking, at least, mark its measured course, its way.

(1989)

8

"Like the Rose—Without Why"

The French philosopher Alain's poignant observation that philosophy is just as little a politics as it is an agriculture, could easily be made to include ethics. If ethics is understood as a doctrine of prescriptive norms for human behavior, it is not necessarily part of philosophy. Nonetheless, the absence of an ethics in this sense from the work of a variety of contemporary thinkers has been turned into a means to challenge their philosophies. It is as if a philosophy could prove itself only if it became extended in a concrete set of precepts for acts of obligation or duty. Such an ideological, or more profoundly, technological misconception of what philosophy is about inspired Heidegger's young friend (as well as many other friends and foes afterward) to ask him, soon after *Being and Time* appeared: "When are you going to write an ethics?"[1] Yet considering the very topic of *Being and Time*—the thinking of Being—such a question or request demonstrates not only confusion but, as Reiner Schürmann argues in *Heidegger on Being and Acting: From Principles to Anarchy*,[2] "the confusion par excellence." Indeed, "to expect *Seinsdenken*, thinking of being, to provide principles for action as Aristotelians sought to derive the principles of moral and institutional theory from a first philosophy, or as philosophers in early modernity divided general metaphysics into branches of special metaphysics, . . . amounts to confusing the ontic with the ontological" (pp. 286–87). As Heidegger has repeatedly stressed, the analytic of Dasein is not an anthropology; its sole goal is to come to grips with the meaning of Being as Dasein qua Dasein implies it. As one could show, the fundamental ontological perspective of the analytic of Dasein is not without some ethical (or rather, *proto-ethical*) dimension: Heidegger's elaborations on the being-in and being-alongside the world as *existentiale* constitutive of Dasein's fundamental structure of being-in-the-world show, right from the start, his engagement with the originary (Greek) meaning of ethics as "dwelling" and "being accustomed."[3] Schürmann, however, limits Heidegger's concern with political and ethical questions—with praxis—to his writings after the *Kehre* (his philosophical turning). Still—and let us be clear about this from the beginning—not only does the question of action enter Heidegger's later thinking from "an entirely different angle" than is customary in traditional formal derivations of the schemes of praxis from those of theory (p. 293), but further, the modes of action that Schürmann shows Heidegger to be concerned with have an entirely different status than actions have in traditional practical philosophy. Schürmann speaks of them as constituting a practical a priori—a priori in a sense to be elucidated hereafter. For all these reasons, the practical philosophy that seems to transpire in Heidegger's later work is still not the ethics that his young friend had requested. It is something much more simple than an ethics, and poorer, yet at the same time more fundamental than a system of guidelines for moral behavior or for a better future.

However, although Heidegger's later writings (unlike *Being and Time*) provide the adequate context to raise the question of action, this does not mean that a full-fledged practical philosophy could be found there. On the contrary, Heidegger more often than not elides the radical and political consequences of his later thought for action, and refuses to render them explicit. *Heidegger on Being and Acting* has the undisputed merit of having followed up, for the first time, and in a systematic fashion, on all of Heidegger's hints regarding practical philosophy, and of having drawn the consequences of his insights into the nature of thought for such a philosophy. An enterprise of that kind, needless to say, does not go without a certain violence, as Schürmann readily acknowledges. Indeed, as the author's developments around the concept of deconstruction (in the Heideggerian sense of *Abbau*)[4] suggest, such violence against

Heidegger's oeuvre (his texts) in its empirical, ontic, historical form is warranted if it brings into view what is public and political about them. Yet what is more public and political than precisely the question of action and activity in Heidegger's texts? Schürmann's attempt to formulate the consequences of Heidegger's thought for a practical philosophy, consequences on which Heidegger in his texts has generally refused to elaborate, requires a certain interpretive twist. This violence is epitomized, first and foremost, in reading Heidegger against the grain, *à rebours*—that is, backward, from and through his later writings. Although reading what comes before with the help of what comes afterward is just another type of finalist reading, Schürmann's retrospective reading strategy has a potential for undoing the teleocratic structures of reading in the first place. That such may be the case, however, could only be argued from a perspective thoroughly familiar with Heidegger's late philosophy.

I

The notion of *Kehre*, of the turning, is usually understood to refer to Heidegger's relinquishing of fundamental ontology in the name of a history of Being. But this notion is also, and more importantly, a phenomenological concept, which thematizes a chance or possibility that arises when the valuations of all the essential positions in their extreme forms throughout the history of metaphysics are concentrated and united in technology. If technology is understood in this manner, it becomes the terminal position in Western metaphysics; and because it reunites the latter's extreme positions, the closure of metaphysics. Yet if technology permits a glance at the history of Western thought as a closed destiny, thought has already risked itself beyond the metaphysical closure (and thus technology can also be said to ruin the very principles that it embodies). With this possibility of conceiving of metaphysics as a closed thinking, technology appears as a chance—as the chance of approaching metaphysics from another domain of thinking in which thinking is no longer subject to principles. Indeed, as Schürmann demonstrates in following up on Heidegger's developments about the history of Being, metaphysics is not a unified, homogeneous field of thought but the nonlinear genealogy of successive fields of intelligibility governed each time by different principles. The chance that the terminal figure of meta-physics offers for thought and, as will be seen, for praxis is a liberation from principles—the chance of an-archy. How does Schürmann, then, conceive of such an-archy in thinking and acting? An-archy, as he under-stands this term, has nothing to do with the historical anarchism of, say, Mikhail Bakunin (which, like the nineteenth-century movements of ni-hilism, was based on a deeply humanist and rationalist doctrine). Nor does Schürmann wish to promote disorder pure and simple. To do so in the name of an originary an-archy would merely lead to an inversion, and thus to instauration of hierarchy.[5] Although at times he risks formulations that may lend themselves to such an interpretation,[6] the developments regarding an-archical thought and praxis in Schürmann's study clearly show that such thought—that is, *thought* in the first place—comprises both a principle and what is beyond the principle, *arche* and *an-arche*. An-archical thought and praxis are not, we shall be reminded, without a certain Parmenidism!

Much of *Heidegger on Being and Acting* is devoted to establishing a phenomenology of the epochal principles—that is, an archaeology or ge-nealogy of these principles. Obviously, such an undertaking sounds more like Foucault than like Heidegger, even the Heidegger from the history and destiny of Being. But although Schürmann has "recourse to an assortment of terms not all of which are to be found in Heidegger" (p. 21)—and some of which clearly originate with Foucault—his pointed critique of the latter's archaeology shows Schürmann to be involved in a very different enterprise. Foucault's archaeology, according to Schürmann (e.g., pp. 318, 345), is merely regional, because it is limited to describing the phenomenon of the emerging epochs in terms of knowledge. But what is an epochal principle in the first place? It is both the *principium*, the foundation that provides reasons, and thus a matter of knowing, and the *princeps*, the authority that dispenses justice, and thus a matter of act-ing. As such, a principle is both the beginning and what commands or rules; in short, what gives an epoch its cohesion (p. 25). An epochal prin-ciple is constitutive of what is called "economy of presence," in which words, things, and actions are interconnected each time in specific ways. As already noted, the archaeology of epochal principles extends to the realm of acting as well. It is not merely restricted to the domains of cog-

nition. In order to understand how epochal principles have also been constitutive for acting, one has only to clarify how the tradition has conceived
of the relation between theory and praxis. Traditionally, praxis has always
been legitimized by theory. To the question "What is to be done?"
philosophers have replied by relying "on some standard-setting first whose
grounding function was assured by a 'general' doctrine, be it called ontology or something else" (p. 1). Practical philosophy, Schürmann argues,
has always borrowed its prime scheme from first philosophy, namely "the
reference to an *arche*, articulated according to the attributive *pros hen* or
the participative *aph'henos* relation. Theories of action not only depend in
general on what prevails as ultimate knowledge in each epoch but, furthermore, they reproduce the attributive-participative schema as if it were
a pattern" (p. 5). This schema springs from philosophy's attempt to
achieve knowledge in the domain of the sensible. Without referring the
sensible manifold to some One, no knowledge or verification of the sensible is possible. Since the Greeks conceived of the political as translating
"an ahistorical order, knowable in itself, into public organization, for
which that order served as an a priori model and as a criterion for a posteriori legitimation" (p. 39), speculative philosophy has remained the father
of practical philosophy. Its categories have been not *sui generis* but derivative from philosophy's doctrine of substance. The formal identity between the two is constituted by "the principial reference as such, the *pros
hen*" (p. 38), that is, the relation to the first, the one, a relation that both
grounds and gives a telos to all acting. Hence the history of the epochal
principles—what Schürmann also calls "referential history" (p. 43)—is,
inevitably, a history "where the *principia* set themselves up as *tele*, as the
ends for man, for his doing and his speculating" (p. 42).

Principles that are both foundational and teleocratic organize the
specific economies of presence that make up referential history. Consequently, they can be understood as a priori principles. Yet these principles
arise and fade away, and therefore are not transcendental a prioris, but
rather "factual a priori(s), finite" (p. 57). The genealogist, as Schürmann
determines him, seeks to conceptualize this rising and waning, this coming into presence and withdrawing of economic arrangements of presence (of words, things, and actions) that are encompassing each time, but
precarious as well since they pass away. However, a phenomenology of

epochal principles cannot as such content itself with a mere description of these finite and ontic a prioris that for a limited time found, govern, and link together words, things, and actions. Such a phenomenology must inquire into the beginning of the principles that are arch-present in their respective epochal orders of presence. It must follow the trail and conceive of the arising, the coming about, the birth, or the origin as such of what is, qua principle and telos, more present than the presence it orders and organizes. In sum, a phenomenology of epochal principles has to inquire into the "presencing" of the temporary principles, that is, into the coming into presence of foundations that are all present themselves (or even arch-present, if they are construed as they generally are, as the *causa sui* of an epoch), and thus, in essence, not different (except in degrees of presence) from what they arraign. The phenomenology in question is necessarily a phenomenology of presence investigating the origin of presence. Indeed, Schürmann's study is centered around this capital methodological distinction between origin and ground or foundation. "As 'presencing' the origin is not a ground, not a fundament," he writes (p. 90). Although it is not always easy, as the author reminds us, to distinguish clearly between *arche*, principle, and origin, the attempt to conceive of the emerging of the factual a prioris of the economies of presence must take off from an analysis of the concept of origin in its Aristotelian form as *arche*. It is here that one must begin, because the Aristotelian concept of *arche* stands at the beginning of the Western conception of origin.

In his analysis of this concept, Schürmann closely follows Heidegger's hint, in *Pathmarks*, that Aristotelian physics is the hidden foundational book (*Grundbuch*) of Western philosophy—thus of Aristotle's *Metaphysics* as well, where the philosophical definition of *arche* as beginning and rule takes shape. The Aristotelian notion of *arche* is, indeed, a kinetic paradigm of origin. Its philosophical meaning is derived from Aristotle's analysis of the origin of (sensible) movement, and is a function, as the joining of "beginning" and "rule" shows, of a previously constituted metaphysics of causes (p. 99). Moreover, as an analysis of *arche*'s antonym—*telos*—demonstrates, artisanal production, in particular the art of architecture, is the true domain in which ends are to be realized. Consequently, Schürmann can conclude, "The notion of *arche*, then, proves to be generally kinetic and more specifically technical" (p. 103). In part 3,

"The Origin Is Said in Many Ways," he continues this history of how origin is understood in the tradition by focusing on Duns Scotus, and on what happens when *arche* becomes translated as *principium*. The origin manifests itself during the epoch of Latin philosophy via reason, the law of the mind; and rather than ruling over becoming (movement), the origin now rules a hierarchical order. When origin becomes *principium*, the Greek idea of origin as beginning is covered over "for the sake of retaining pure domination." But the locus where origin can show itself has changed as well. Human fabrication "has lost its paradigmatic role in the constitution of knowledge. Another site now functions as the center of things knowable and renders fabrication and know-how secondary, derivative. The domain from which the medievals understand the origin is no longer man-made change, but *gubernatio mundi*, the government the supreme entity exercises over things" (p. 112). For Duns Scotus the supreme entity is the Divine Substance, which governs what is called "the essential order" (p. 110). This new epochal position of origin as *principium*—and this is characteristic of the Latin Middle Ages—reflects the observation of a religious heritage. It comes to an end when the rule of a sovereign entity—God—is replaced by the rule of evident truth. This new reversal in the thinking of origin was inaugurated by Leibniz, argues Schürmann. In Leibniz's *Monadology*, "the essential order dominated by a *princeps* is replaced by the logical order dominated by a *principium*" (p. 112). With this reversal, "to speak of a principle no longer means to follow the course of a kinetic trajectory nor to follow the lead of a religious transmittal. Rather, it means to confine oneself to the realm in which human knowledge is the principal, the principial, problem" (p. 112). More precisely, with this new reversal, the mind's representation of facts becomes the issue. Such representation is shown to be rooted in the principle of sufficient reason, that is to say, in an axiom, a linguistically articulated law. A principle, henceforth, "is the starting point, the origin, of an argument," and thus one can conclude that with the reversal brought about by Leibniz, "the origin has been transferred from the field of essential causes to the field of causes that regulate representation" (p. 113).

The three epochs of principial thought described here clearly evidence that the history of what has been taken to be the origin represents a series of principles that are fundamentally "ultimate ontic referents"

(p. 114). The major punctuations of what was thought as the first are sensible substance with Aristotle, divine substance in the Middle Ages, and the human subject who posits principles of reason during the Age of Enlightenment, that is, the Age of Modernity. But origin as "presencing," as the mere coming into presence of an epoch, can never be something present. That by which a whole economy of presence abruptly surges forward is, rather, as Heidegger put it, "nothing." To think what opens a field of presence, an epoch, it is thus necessary to reach beyond the conception of origin as *arche* and principle. The outline of the history of the various ways in which the origin has been cast from Aristotle to the moderns suggests, indeed, that in the course of this history the origin has been constantly covered up by the ultimate ontic principles. Three tasks follow from this: first, to deconstruct the different stamps of origin in the history of Western thought; second, to engage the Heideggerian notion of *Ur-sprung* as precisely the thought of the mere surge of presence; and finally—the major task—to elaborate on the "logic" that governs the becoming *arche* or principle of the origin.

Schürmann, taking his lead from Heidegger, dispatches the first task by confronting, in particular, Aristotle with the pre-Socratic's understanding of origin and by pointing out that traces of this understanding pervade his *Physics* and *Metaphysics*. But the thrust of this deconstruction lies in the underlying assumption that a colossal category mistake stands at the beginning of the Western quest for the first. Indeed, Aristotle's discovery that the *pros hen*—a schema that, as Schürmann notes, "rightfully pertains only to the *Physics*"—can be applied to all domains and to all branches of philosophy causes all philosophy since Aristotle to speak "with the voice of a physicist." Yet "this totalitarian sweep of the relation-to-one" that opens the history of the epochs of principial thought (pp. 42–43)—a sweep that affects all acting and thinking in general by transposing the ideas of causality and finality or goal-directedness from the domain of artisanal making to all other domains—is a *metabasis eis allo genos* (p. 256). With this confusion of levels of thought, which started in Aristotle's extension of *Physics* to *Metaphysics* and by which the thinking of the One becomes obstructed, begins the long errancy of the rich history of Western thought as one of arising and waning principial epochs. For the whole of European philosophy, the ascendancy of the idea of substantialism at the root of the triumph of *Physics*—the triumph of a domain of sensible reality—has been an invariant. As a consequence, the One could be conceived only by bringing substantialist criteria to bear on it.

The discussion of Heidegger's notion of *Ur-sprung*—the second task required by the attempt to free "origin" from its systematic coverings-up—serves to conceptualize the notion of origin that is to be retrieved from and through a deconstruction of the history of thought. This effort attempts to conceive of origin not as a *principium* or foundation but as the (multiple) presencing signified by the etymological meaning of the word *oriri*, "coming forth." Origin, in this sense, means origination. It coincides with what Heidegger terms the event proper, or the event of appropriation (*Ereignis*). This event of presencing is "nothing" but the pure phenomenal showing-forth in all its contingency, fortuitousness, and instability. As Schürmann stresses, origin in this sense of "the ahistorical, always instantaneous emergence of presencing," or more simply in the sense of *there is*, is the answer that Heidegger gives to the traditional philosophical astonishment (constitutive of philosophical thought) that there is something rather than nothing (p. 130). As we will see, this answer is not just one more in the history of answers to the opening question of philosophy. It is an answer that opens a new register for thought.

Finally, a thinking that seeks to recover such a meaning of origin needs to understand why origin in the sense of simple origination could be covered up in the first place. What are the enabling conditions under which origin as mere phenomenal showing forth could turn into something like an *arche* or *principium*, that is, into "ontic substitutes," or objectivations of the *originary* "under the guise of arch-present entities?" (p. 148). Schürmann writes: "The transmutation through which presencing institutionalizes itself into principles that rule and justify action is the ill fate of origin. As pure emergence, the originary is essentially fragile, finite, no sooner recognized than ready to turn into a principle" (p. 147). If the location of metaphysics is to be established, and if "the relapse from an understanding of the origin as *event* into its *principial* comprehension" is to be forestalled (p. 147), it is imperative to get a hold on the reasons for this necessary and, as Heidegger has argued, inevitable ill turning of the origin. With the closure of metaphysics, both issues become possibilities for thinking. Schürmann, in what undoubtedly represents a most impressive achievement, proceeds to analyze the conditions under which presencing turns into presence, *originary origins* into *original origins*, in part 4, "Historical Deduction of the Categories of Presencing." This deduction also provides the conceptual tools for answering the correlative question of how presencing becomes history.

Heidegger is not, and cannot be, a systematic thinker—his thought is situated at the boundary of metaphysical thought. Systematic thinking belongs intrinsically to metaphysics as a quest for legitimizing foundations. Yet the "rigorous reading" of Heidegger that Schürmann proposes (not without a polemical twist in the direction of tranquilizing poetic and religious readings) emphasizes, for the first time to my knowledge, a dimension of Heidegger's late thought, for which it is difficult to find another word than "systematic."[7] "Systematic" here means not simply that Heidegger's philosophical enterprise is coherent but that it is interlinked in all parts, yet without forming a whole in the traditional sense. (On what level of thought such "systematicity" can—and must—be achieved even in Heidegger's borderline thinking will be indicated hereafter.) It is precisely in the central part on the deduction of the categories of presencing that Schürmann's book confronts us with this "systematic" aspect of Heidegger's later thinking.

To *think* originary presencing it is not enough to repeat the key word "showing-forth." Magic incantation and invocation of master words does not replace differential thought and what it alone can achieve. By contrast, Schürmann's project, in the central part of his book, of a categorization of originary presence—of establishing with respect to presencing a network of categorial functions—accomplishes a thinking articulation of the phenomenon of pure surging-forth into presence, or as he also calls it, of the an-archic origin. If this origin is to be established in its own right, and with respect to what *by right* distinguishes it, then the thinking of this origin is a legitimation. Yet "since the originary appears only in differing from the original; since the event of appropriation (*Ereignis*) can be thematized only through the reversals in historical destiny (*Geschehen*)" (p. 157), this legitimation must, inescapably, take the form of a deduction. If Schürmann speaks in this context of categories rather than of schemata, transcendentals, or topoi, it is because he wishes to emphasize the coming into presence, the manifestation, or the historical self-articulation of be-

ing as presencing, in other words, the singular angle under which the originary shapes itself differently each time. Indeed, in this sense, "category"
recovers its prephilosophical meaning of "manifesting" (p. 161). The categorization that Schürmann attempts in this part of his book seeks to free
the formal continuities, the invariants, "according to which the many networks of epochal presence have differed from presencing." He finds these
categories in what Heidegger had called *Grundworte*, and classifies them
in three classes, which have six categories each. Space does not permit me
to do justice to this extremely powerful and exemplary articulation
through which Schürmann wishes "to wrest originary presencing from
the original shifts in presence" (p. 162). A few words must suffice.

The three classes of categories that Schürmann shows to be opera-
tive in Heidegger's later works are *prospective*, *retrospective*, and *transitional*
categories. This distinction is a function of the movement of the analytical
glance at the whole of the history of Being. Reading this history from its
inception in pre-Socratic thinking, one obtains the prospective categories,
which are modes of saying the coming into light of presence as well as its
withdrawing: *eon*, *physis*, *aletheia*, *logos*, *hen*, *nous*. Reading from the history's conclusion, or closure—from metaphysic's end in technology—one
gains access to the retrospective categories. In a truly striking if not
provocative interpretation of Heidegger's writings on Nietzsche, *Heidegger
on Being and Acting* demonstrates that although these writings speak formally about Nietzsche, materially they are about technology. Rather than
taking his retrospective categories directly from what he has established
about the end of metaphysics, Heidegger substitutes the Nietzschean discourse for the technological economy at the end of metaphysics, Schürmann argues. Thus, the will to power, nihilism, justice, the eternal return
of the same, the transmutation of all values, and the overman become
transmuted so as to speak of technology and to denote the categories of
the economy of closure. What these retrospective categories make evident
is that the essence of technology, the germ of metaphysics' completion and
death, has always already inhabited Western thought from Plato on. In
order to describe the shifts and crises between eras, that is, the phenomenon of reversal as such, Heidegger proposes the following transitional categories: ontological difference / world and thing, there is / favor, unconcealment / event of appropriation, epoch/clearing, nearness/fourfold, and

corresponding/thinking. These categories appear to function bifocally since they serve "to indicate the step from the actual to the potential, or the transition to *the other* arrangement that may begin with the technological turning" (p. 206). Indeed, as Schürmann remarks, "only these categories allow us to hold together the entire system which organizes, on one hand, the concepts of *arche* and *principium* as well as their phenomenological 'truth,' the original and the originary, and, on the other, the oppositions accompanying the distinction between metaphysical and non-metaphysical thinking" (p. 204). Although they do not allow one to escape simply from metaphysics, they allow thinking to conceive of thinking, as well as of praxis, and the relation between the two in a new, nonmetaphysical way.

The deduction in question—a project that becomes feasible only under the condition that metaphysics has come to its closure in technology, and thus into view as a whole—a deduction through which the origin manifests itself as presencing or as the event of appropriation, requires "a type of thought other than that which traces the reversals of historical principles." Moreover, it requires a "turning in the way of thinking" itself (p. 29). But not only of thinking; of political praxis as well. At the fringe of metaphysics, when *Ereignis* becomes a possibility for thought, the possibility of a thinking and an acting emerge that would no longer be subject to a unifying *pros hen*—an-archic thinking and acting.

II

The eternal return of the same, seen as a retrospective category, describes how technological metaphysics (and all the disciplines—scientific and literary—that depend on it) is a countermovement against the whole of Western philosophy and at the same time its ultimate figure. What makes the way in which Schürmann analyses this and the other retrospective categories so interesting to me is that it clearly exemplifies what happens to thought when the closure of metaphysics becomes effectuated in technology. Read as a category of closure, the eternal return of the same is indicative of the collapse of all the received dualities at the end of metaphysics. If "real distinctions" have been "the backbone of metaphysics," these distinctions become reduced "to technological onedimensionality" or indifference in the era of closure (p. 195). The eternal return indicates the becoming one of all differences. Yet if such a collapse into one of all differences, and all constructs of otherness, is rendered epoch-ally possible by technology, thus shaking metaphysics in its most funda-mental exigencies, it is because this possibility of the impossibility of dif-ference has been prepared for a long time. Indeed, the doctrine of difference constitutive of metaphysics is itself rooted in "the Platonic re-versal where *eon* turned into the difference between *to estin* and *to ti es-tin*" (p. 194). In other words, the annulment of difference at the end of metaphysics confirms the beginning of metaphysics as the reduction of premetaphysical difference, verbal-nominal difference, or ontological dif-ference. The flattening of thought, its loss of depth and motility at the end of metaphysics, is thus, a function of the loss of transcendence in metaphysical transcendence.

The transmutation of all values, interpreted as a retrospective cate-gory, reveals that the becoming illusion of all the supreme values of West-ern metaphysics in the era of technology and the converse valuation of what is empirically verifiable—the manipulable and the manufacturable (that is, the sensible)—occur through a reenactment of what is constitu-tive of metaphysical thought: hierarchical distinction. In Schürmann's words, "The technological transvaluation, first understood by Nietzsche, *inverts* the high and low established at the beginning of metaphysics—and thereby renders it the greatest homage, permuting from within, from bottom to top, the valuative game" (p. 197). Like difference and indiffer-ence, the beginning and the death of metaphysical thought are intimately interconnected. If all the fundamental values of Western philosophy be-come illusions in the era of metaphysical closure, it is because "estima-tion, the preference for one region of entities over others, the attribution of rank," is a constitutive ingredient of metaphysics—and its fatal agent as well (p. 198). Indeed, the backbone of metaphysics, namely the dis-tinction between a world of being and a world of becoming, a distinction that is itself derived from "the forgottenness of the differential One" (p. 198), is the patron difference between what is high and what is low. The elevation of the low to the rank of the only true reality in technology thus confirms metaphysics in its role as an estimating approach rendered possible by the initial forgetting of the ontological difference.

In the face of this abolition of difference and valuation of the low as a consequence of an essential indifference to ontological difference in metaphysics, the question arises about the nature of thought at the fringe of the tradition. "The very issue for thinking is presencing as it differs from systems of presence," Schürmann remarks (p. 258). Its issue then is, as we have seen, something extremely contingent, fragile, and unstable. But regarding the forgetting of the differential One operative not only in the indifference to difference in the last phase of metaphysics but in metaphysical difference as well, how does thought at the closure of Western thought do justice to difference? To sketch an answer to this question, I shall first draw out some major characteristics of such thought from Schürmann's developments:

1. The principal gesture of thought is transcendental, and is thus geared to exhibiting a prioris. "Heidegger renovates the transcendental problematic," says the author (p. 296). As a matter of fact, the prime task of the phenomenology of presence is, as discussed above, a deduction of categories and their systematic interrelatedness (thought achieves "systematicity" on this level, and perhaps on this level alone). Such a deduction, however, clearly has a transcendental look. But Heidegger, and Schürmann as well, not only conserve transcendentalism and its quest for a prioris but also recast it entirely. Schürmann speaks of a postmodern transcendentalism (p. 74). Such a transcendentalism would be dissociated from subjectivism. In contrast to the transcendental method, postsubjectivist transcendentalism no longer yields any regulatory focal point or foundation (the conditions of possibility of knowing, or the universal essences of a sense-giving subjectivity), as has been the case with Kant, Husserl, and even the early Heidegger. The transcendentalism of thought at the borderline of metaphysics situates the conditions and the a prioris elsewhere than in man, namely in what comes to light of the event of appropriation in the epochal *Geschehen*. But in his elaborations on the transitional category of ontological difference / world and thing, Schürmann hints at an even more radical recasting of transcendentalism in Heidegger's later thought. Indeed, if the later Heidegger substitutes the relation of world and things to that of Being and beings, he dismisses the ontological difference, and with it the issue of difference as transcendence. Ontological difference stands here for "the oppositions between the One

and the many, being and entities, being and thought, all oppositions inherited from Parmenides" (p. 210). The dismissal of these oppositions, which helped metaphysical thinking to conceive of the essence of what is, becomes necessary at the closure of Western thought since the transcendence (being, substance) and the reduplication (being as being) now appear to miss the simple presencing. What had been the very condition for Western thought's appropriateness to presence—its gesture of transcending and of reduplicating what is *as such*—shows itself to be based on the forgetting of the question of difference, the question in whose form presencing first came into view. Although one must still call thinking at the fringe of metaphysics "transcendental" in spite of the fact that "transcendental" obfuscates the difference that the issue of thought—presencing—makes (by transcending entities and incorporating difference into the transcending), thought conserves transcendentalism's formal frame.

2. The issue to which thought responds at the borderline of metaphysics is presencing, the originary, as opposed to the economies of presence, the original. As discussed above, showing forth is the most precarious object that thought can have. It can be beheld only through its various modalities, but as soon as a modality of presencing has occurred and is past, it is lost forever. It is thus characterized by "extreme finitude" (p. 17), as is thought that responds to presencing. In addition, presencing (itself) has no history, no destiny. This absence of finality in presencing leads to a repeal of the reign of goals in thinking (first and foremost, by ceasing to be cognitive). Thinking, we read, "does not have any contents, properly speaking, to pursue. . . . Thinking lacks any external end" (p. 257). Multiplicity is a function of presencing's essential finitude. Once thematized, it "proves to be irreducibly manifold. . . . It shows that prior to the binary struggle between veiling and unveiling, presencing de-centers the process of manifestation" (p. 144). The thought that corresponds to such manifoldness in presencing is, consequently, irreducibly plural and dispersed.

3. Yet such finitude, plurality, and absence of ends does not imply that thought, or presencing for that matter, would lack all identity. Undoubtedly, the simple showing forth that thinking reaches out for in a "transcendental" move is not *one* origin. Still, the originary unfolding has a unity of its own. Schürmann speaks of this unity as a Parmenidean

unity, as the Parmenidean unity of the event of appropriation. But the unique event of coming into presence—"the One as an economic event" (p. 76)—allows for no henology, since it is not a foundation or center to which what comes into presence could be related according to the *pros hen* schema (p. 144). The unity of this originary Oneness that thought at the turning must respond to "is no more than the simple event of any phenomenon's 'coming-about'" (p. 144). It is one only formally, and as the (nonexhaustive) system of the categories shows, is made up of only directional traits. But what is true of presencing is valid for thought that answers to it as well: an-archic thought thinks presencing only if it follows the originary leap into presence in such a way that it accounts for the constellation of truth in which all things present are gathered. Without a certain Parmenidism, thought cannot respond.

Let me circle back to the question of difference. Thought at the turning—where all difference reveals itself as intrinsically indifferent—thought whose issue is presencing itself, responds to the differential One covered up not only by metaphysical difference but by ontological difference as well. Such thought is plural, since it answers to the always novel and contingent surge of presence. But thought is the thinking of this differential One only to the extent that it thinks this One in the unity of its emerging. In conceiving of the event of appropriation as the simple event of the showing forth of any phenomenon, thought thinks what philosophy has not been able to think: the mere "there is" in its singularity and precariousness. But such thought of the leap into presence is also, and necessarily, the most empty thought, empty of content. Thought that centers exclusively on the originary is, as Schürmann stresses after Heidegger, poor if compared to technological metaphysics. Merely to follow the emerging from absence into presence is a modest task. Yet the modesty of this task should not blind us to the fact that it is an unheard-of response to the traditional philosophical wonder of why there is something rather than nothing.

The type of thinking that becomes possible with the closure of metaphysics is a type that, because all original origins (the principles) have run out, can answer to the originary surge of presence itself. Yet the withering of the epochal principles that the originary revealed itself as, provides thought at the turning with the chance of avoiding all *metabasis eis allo genos.* Rather than thinking the originary in terms of what covers it up, thought would, finally, be able to think the originary in its own unique singularity and finitude. Such a thinking, free of all category mistake and beyond the confusion of levels of thought, is a kind of thought that in its very singularity and contingency would achieve what thinking in metaphysics has been unable to do but which has always been the dream of philosophy—to be a discourse about what is possible, and to hold itself as discourse in the very dimension of the possible.

So much for thought. What about acting after the break? What "other acting" corresponds to the "other thinking"? The provocative thesis of *Heidegger on Being and Acting* is that "the other acting" is not the symmetric counterpart of thought, as it has traditionally been in practical philosophy. The guidelines for acting after the turning do not follow as usual from what has been established about an-archic thought. Although such acting can only be an-archic itself, since all principles have withered away, this anarchism does not proceed from an ascendance of theory over praxis. On the contrary, as Schürmann convincingly demonstrates, for the later Heidegger, a certain acting becomes "the transcendental condition for thought" (p. 233). With this the traditional relation between thinking and acting has become inverted. He writes, "The practical a priori for understanding fully that deterioration and its virtualities inverts the sequence of condition and conditioned in which the tradition has placed thinking and acting" (p. 244). This inversion is in fact a subversion of the ancient distinction between theory and praxis: If "Heidegger *makes action deprived of* arche *the condition of the thought which deconstructs the* arche," then Heidegger inscribes himself, as Schürmann remarks, "in a tradition entirely different from that of Aristotle" (p. 7). But what sort of acting makes up such a practical a priori? Such acting must, in the same way as thought in the age of closure, respond to the event of appropriation and be open for presencing—in Heidegger's terminology, *resolute* presencing—in its coming to pass. The different modes of acting that Schürmann analyzes—*Gelassenheit* and *Abgeschiedenheit*, for instance—show this a priori acting to be free from all ends. By virtue of its responsive nature to the aletheio-logical constellations, this acting is responsible acting. And, finally, by its unattachment, such acting challenges current business, anticipating another path or destiny, another constellation beyond the present one. But the acting that constitutes the a priori for the thinking of presencing at the turning is not just any acting. Although *Gelassenheit, Abgeschiedenheit,* and so forth, are concrete modes of behavior, their status is that of a transcendental a priori for a thought that articulates and enacts the possible as possible. Being without goal, as well as being unattached, the acting before all thinking responds to the event of presencing by maintaining its potentialities in suspense. It is an acting at the limit of acting in that it affirms the play without consequences of the merely potential, the "sheer superabundance with no purpose or end" of the event itself (p. 18).

Since a discourse on the practical a priori does not tie acting to the conceptual pivot of the relation to the One, it is not properly speaking a practical philosophy. Practical philosophy is, by definition, derived from a first philosophy. Nonetheless, the discourse in question is one on acting, but *in advance* of all norms. Schürmann writes, "From the transcendental 'subject' of Idealism, to the *Dasein* of the Existential Analytic, to the 'thinking' of the Topology of being, the discourse on man progressively deprives itself of the very possibility of approving or condemning, and especially of commending, concrete behavior, whether individual or collective" (p. 208).

Heidegger's lack of interest in the immediate and concrete future of mankind is well known, and, as Schürmann remarks, "runs quite deep" (p. 208). And, indeed, all that Heidegger seems to have envisioned for the destinal break with metaphysics is an economy "whose only time structure is originary," trusting "that the event could become our sole temporal condition, one without principial overdeterminations" (p. 273). Yet in such an economy of the originary, everything—action, thoughts, and things—"perdures" in its mere showing forth as (manifold) possibility. It is goalless, hence without aim and without why. It is as if the economy of the originary represented the concrete realization of the transcendental realm of the conditions of possibility for the phenomenal, but of this realm alone without the phenomena that it makes possible. But what makes such a comparison inappropriate is that in the economy envisioned, the distinction in question no longer obtains.

From the simple point of view of presence, everything in such an economy of the originary is like the rose of which Heidegger writes, after

Angelus Silesius, that it "flowers because it flowers" (p. 259). In *The Essence of Reasons*, Heidegger speaks one more time about the "rose—without why." The simile serves to point at the most hidden essence of man, yet he adds immediately: "We cannot however pursue this thought any further here" (p. 38). That this thought *can* be thought, that it can even become the (perhaps multiple) element for thought as such—in which thought comes into its essence(s)—is the thesis around which Schürmann's argument develops, and is what his book, unmistakably, succeeds in proving.

(1989)

9

Perhaps: A Modality?

> . . . as a "perhaps" of pure chance, in the uncertainty of "the exception,"
> not necessary but the absolutely un-necessary, a constellation of doubt
> which only shines in the forgotten sky of perdition.
> —Maurice Blanchot, *The Space of Literature*

In his caustic and cutting review of one W. T. Krug's critiques of Fichte's conception of the "I" in *The Science of Knowledge*, Hegel identifies the thrust of Krug's objections as the attempt to demonstrate that the system of transcendental idealism "is not one bit better than the synthetism of [Krug's]" own self-proclaimed "fundamental philosophy."[1] Indeed, if Krug can at all suggest a similarity between his own dabblings in philosophy and Fichte's thought, and even claim to have overcome the alleged difficulties of transcendental idealism in his new philosophy, it is due to his confusing Fichte's transcendental conception of the "I" with his own empirical understanding of it. According to Hegel, while Krug objects to the limitations of the "I" in transcendental philosophy, he does so not in view of a possible liberation of that "I" from such limitation but in order to "find within it a license for the infinite manifold of the limitations of empirical consciousness." In Krug's reempiricized transcendental philosophy, his own synthetism, in which "an infinite manifold of limitations of consciousness is posited," appears indeed as the more radical of the two systems of thought. Yet as if this claim were not pompous enough, Krug further holds that Fichte's transcendental philosophy is merely the symbolic anticipation of his own new system. Reporting on how Krug seeks to bring order into the bewildering manifold of the limitations thus posited in consciousness, Hegel notes that Krug wishes to link the singular and multiple cognitions in the uniting point of a principle, but not a principle from which the content of the cognitions could be derived. The cognitions are rather linked to the principle "in a manner similar to a vault in which everything is related to the keystone as its highest and ultimate uniting point, although this point cannot, at the same time, contain within itself the foundation of the vault." Now this very conception of what a principle is to achieve prompts Krug, according to Hegel, who quotes from Krug's writings, to think that "*perhaps* this is what *The Science of Knowledge* has in mind when it put the proposition I = I at the head of its investigations, and that this A = A is a symbolic representation of the before mentioned harmony." And Hegel sarcastically concludes, "This *perhaps* does credit to Mr. Krug's caution; most certainly he did not wish to assert anything of the kind."[2]

In the following I shall speak of this adverb *perhaps*. Grammatically, *perhaps* represents a modality in which assertions in the enunciatory process are put into suspension. It expresses possibility with uncertainty, mere possibility, that is, possibility for which there is no or only scant evidence, and characterizes discourses that are vague, imprecise, unrigorous, and, more generally, like those of everyday speech. This is the discourse of common sense that Hegel, in his review of Krug, terms *gemeiner Menschenverstand*. The grammar of the term reflects the logical and philosophical assessment of the modality in question. From the perspective of the certitude of the *cogito* and its judgmental operations, *perhaps* signifies, without exception, a deficit of knowledge, if not a total lack of cognition. Since the modality *perhaps* will be discussed hereafter in regard to a German text, it is appropriate to recall briefly the linguistic history of its German equivalent *vielleicht*. Originating in the middle High German *vil lithe*, *vielleicht* draws together in one linguistic compound the different meanings of *sehr leicht* (facile), *vermutlich* (presumably) and *möglicherweise* (possibly). In older German one still hears the word's connection with *sehr leicht*, and consequently, more often than not, it designates an expectation that is certain, rather than a simple possibility. This connection, however, is entirely lost in the contemporary use of the word. According to Jacob and

Wilhelm Grimm, "*vielleicht* [therefore only] names the assumed possibility that an assertion corresponds to reality, or that something will occur or happen."[3] Like *perhaps*, *vielleicht* marks statements as devoid of certainty, merely based on conjecture, amounting to a rough guess, or even the product of mere chance. For this word there is thus, at least in principle, no place in a discourse, like that of philosophy, that seeks certainty and rigor. It belongs rather to ordinary language and its associated modes of thinking. Indeed, if *perhaps* could at all play a modalizing function with respect to certain of Krug's propositions, it is because for Hegel and the discourse of knowing, Krug's "fundamental philosophy" is not a philosophy to begin with. He has made "empirical consciousness into the principle of his speculation," Hegel claims.[4] Hence, the philosophical convictions expressed in his new philosophy amount to nothing else than popular representations and opinions of the common human intellect. Hegel's castigation of Krug's ratiocinations as mere representations of ordinary consciousness finds ample justification in the opinions expressed by the latter. But it is in particular the presence in his discourse of the modalizer *perhaps* and a host of others that express uncertainty, limitation, restriction, reservation, and so on, that compels Hegel's judgment. As Hegel shows, "quite," "more or less," "largely," "almost," "from time to time," and many other such terms unmistakably establish Krug's discourse as belonging to ordinary, everyday speech, to a discourse devoid of the certainty of knowing.[5]

Hegel's sulfurous denunciation of Krug's recourse to the modalizing term *perhaps* in a discourse of philosophical ambitions, is, of course, not incidental. This denunciation is, indeed, representative of philosophy's appraisal in general of that term. Although one may perhaps wish to object that the long tradition of skepticism and empiricism, not to speak of theology, vindicates the role of this modalizer in knowledge, such knowledge is not strictly speaking knowledge but of the order of presumption, know-how, instrumental reason, or faith. As a German proverb has it, *Vielleicht ist eine halbe Lüge*, perhaps is a half-lie. Half-truths, however, have no place in a discourse that prides itself on its rigor and precision. In short, then, *perhaps* is not a *philosophical* term; it does not belong to philosophy's vocabulary. With this, the fate of *perhaps* seems to be sealed for good. Determined as it has been by the certitude of the *cogito* and the discourse of judgmental cognition, nothing else can be said about it, or on its behalf.

Perhaps! Beyond the distinction between ordinary and philosophical discourse, opining and knowing, natural and formalized speech, thinking perhaps holds in reserve another use of *perhaps*. Although the modalizer in question, weighed as it always has been in the balance of the *cogito*, is not only negatively determined but determined according to the standard of modalizers of the certitude of cognition, is it not conceivable that *perhaps*, rather than signifying a deficit of knowledge and certitude, could possibly also be the qualifier for a kind of thinking that is no longer cognitive, without being for that matter of the order of the nonpropositional or subpropositional commonly attributed to ordinary speech? What if *perhaps* would modalize a discourse that no longer proceeds by statements yet is no less rigorous than the discourse of philosophy?

Take for example Heidegger's essay on "The Nature of Language" from 1957–58, which, in sharp contrast to his other writings, makes abundant use of the term in question. For instance, after evoking the various translations of "Tao" that have been suggested as alternatives to the superficial-sounding "way"—namely, reason, mind, meaning, *logos*—Heidegger writes:

Yet *Tao* could be the way that gives all ways, the very source of our power to think what reason, mind, meaning, *logos* properly mean to say—properly, by their proper nature. *Perhaps* [emphasis mine] the mystery of mysteries of thoughtful Saying conceals itself in the word "way," *Tao*, if only we will let these names return to what they leave unspoken, if only we are capable of this, to allow them to do so. *Perhaps* [emphasis mine] the enigmatic power of today's reign of method also, and indeed preeminently, stems from the fact that the methods, notwithstanding their efficiency, are after all merely the runoff of a great hidden stream which moves all things along and makes way for everything. All is way.[6]

Is Heidegger's recourse to the modalizer *perhaps* in this meditation on the non-Western notion of *Tao* still the same sort as the one that Hegel so forcefully denounced in his review of Krug? Is it simply the mark of ordinary talk, empirical consciousness, or sloppy argumentation? Presumably not! Yet assuming that the recourse to the modalizer *perhaps* is not a sign here of unrigorous argumentation, could it not just be a rhetorical device, not for the suspension of assertions but for suspense? Considering that *perhaps* is used in conditionals (*if only* . . .), is it perhaps merely a literary device in a text that, moreover, seeks the neighborhood of the poetic, forecasting, in the form of hypotheses, what in due time will be thoroughly demonstrated? Although not expressing possibilities combined with uncertainty, the status of the modalizer in question would in this case play a determined role in the elaboration of the text's argument but, as a merely rhetorical device, would remain exterior to the thought process itself. However, can things be that simple? What about Heidegger's claim that *perhaps* the alien word "Tao" could be "the very source of our power to think what reason, mind, meaning, *logos*" mean, that is, what thinking means?

Apart from the fact that the quoted statements occur in lectures "underway on the lookout for a possibility of undergoing an experience with language" (p. 92), the very nature of the conditional in which they occur bestows upon the modalizer an unheard-of complexity. The mystery of mysteries said to be, *perhaps*, hidden in the word "way" is that of thoughtful Saying. If this is the case, *perhaps* may well be the modality of thoughtful Saying itself, a mode not exterior but intrinsic to Saying. Moreover, what Heidegger tells us on this occasion is that the possibility that the mystery of thoughtful Saying may be hidden in the word "way" arises only if we are capable, that is, if we have the possibility (*vermögen*), of letting names such as reason, spirit, meaning, *logos*, return into their unspoken. Consequently, the *perhaps* is conditioned by a possibility itself. *Only if* we have the possibility of letting certain names return into their unspoken, *only then* does there arise, *perhaps*, the possibility that the mystery of thoughtful Saying might be concealed in the word "way"! Finally, is it not significant that the possibility expressed by the *perhaps* in this case is one not of revelation but of concealment, and takes place only if the key words themselves are allowed for their part to become sheltered in their unspoken. In short, only if we let what we believe these words say return into their unspoken, let them say what they mean from their proper nature, then, perhaps, the word "way" will itself reveal a hidden nature. *Perhaps*, rather than indicating a possibility with uncertainty or being simply a rhetorical device, modalizes here the way in which something relates to its unspoken and to what Heidegger calls the mystery of mysteries. *Perhaps* signifies the mode in which something becomes sheltered in the mystery, and honors this mystery by letting it be the mystery that it is. Obviously, in the context of the passage analyzed, *perhaps* performs a function entirely different from the usages in ordinary language or in philosophy. Moreover, its role appears to be intrinsic to a certain thinking, to what Heidegger had called thoughtful Saying.

It has been remarked, by Ute Guzzoni in particular, that the "categories" to which the later Heidegger has recourse are, as "compared to those of the philosophical tradition, marked by an entirely different character: they are of an onticity and concreteness that implies a fundamentally new manner of generality."[7] I intend to argue as well that they take up what in the eyes of traditional philosophy represent the very signifiers of ordinary, everyday language. Nevertheless, these signifiers do not enter Heidegger's discourse unchanged. They certainly do not operate in it according to the functions assigned to them by traditional grammar, that is, by metaphysics. Take, for instance, Heidegger's redefinition in "The Nature of Language" of the term "only": "The 'only' here does not mean a limitation, but rather points to . . . pure simplicity" (p. 93). But it is with the word *perhaps* that I will be concerned. I will proceed to a further exploration of its new role in Heidegger's text, not through additional refinement on the word's status in a sentence such as the one already commented upon, but by reflecting on the gesture of thought in which it occurs, and, perhaps, must occur.

I already pointed out that unlike all other texts by Heidegger, "The Nature of Language" makes profuse use of the modalizer *perhaps*. It must be noted as well that in this text, Heidegger revises his long-standing definition of the essence of thinking as questioning. For the first time, indeed, thinking is said here to be primarily a listening. He states: "the authentic attitude [*Gebärde*] of thinking is not a putting of questions—rather, it is a listening to the grant, the promise [*Zusage*] of what is to be put in question" (p. 71). Calling up his assertion in "The Question of Technology" that "questioning is the piety of thinking," Heidegger now claims, "the true stance of thinking cannot be to put questions, but must be to listen to that which our questioning vouchsafes—and all questioning begins to be a questioning only in virtue of pursuing its quest for essential being [*sondern das Hören der Zusage dessen sein muss, wobei alles Fragen dann erst anfragt, indem es dem Wesen nachfragt*]" (p. 72). Thus it may well be that this foregrounding of thinking as questioning in listening and the abundant recourse to the *perhaps* are not unrelated. But let us first turn to these three lectures that make up the essay "The Nature of Language," which, in Heidegger's words, are "intended to bring us face to face with a possibility of undergoing an experience with language" (p. 57). As a "thinking experience"—"the true experience with language can only be a thinking experience" (p. 69)—the experience with language is not an attempt to question the essence of language in terms of a ground and foundation. Nor is it a metalinguistic, scientific, that is, cognitive approach to language. As Heidegger puts it in "The Way to Language," we cannot know the nature of language—"know it according to the traditional concept of knowledge defined in terms of cognition as representation." "If to know means to have seen something in the wholeness of its nature, seen it in the round," then we cannot know the nature of language. Indeed, what distinguishes language from all other objects is that "we are not capable of seeing the nature of language in the round because we, who can only say something by saying it after Saying, belong ourselves within Saying," Heidegger writes. He concludes, "Thus we always see the nature of language only to the extent to which language itself has us in view, has appropriated us to itself" (p. 134). The same point is made in "The Nature of Language," where he states that although "we speak and speak about language. What we speak of, language, is always ahead of us. Our speaking merely follows language constantly. Thus we are continually lagging behind what we first ought to have overtaken and taken up in order to speak about it. Accordingly, when we speak of language we remain entangled in a speaking that is persistently inadequate" (p. 75). As a consequence of language's being always ahead of our speaking about it—since we have to speak in order to speak about it—language does not let itself be thematized and methodically approached. For a scientific, that is, cognitive approach to language, this is necessarily an unsolvable tangle precisely because science requires thematization and method. But what Heidegger calls a thinking experience in "The Nature of Language" is intended to solve nothing less than this intricate tangle.

Although "thinking is not a means to gain knowledge" or an instrument "to promulgate reliable information concerning the nature of language" (p. 70), the thinking experience sought with language does not, for that matter, belittle or ignore the achievements of metalinguistic cognition. But, as Heidegger notes, if we are to put questions to language regarding its essence, language must already have addressed us and granted us its nature. "Inquiry and investigation [*Anfrage und Nachfrage*] here and everywhere require the prior grant [*Zuspruch*] of whatever it is they approach and pursue with their queries. Every posing of every question takes place within the very grant of what is put in question" (p. 71). It is with this speaking of language itself, which has the floor just as little in everyday speaking as in scientific statements, that Heidegger seeks a thinking experience in "The Nature of Language." On the way to that experience Heidegger proceeds not, as it may seem, by means of mere intuitions and mystic living experiences but on the contrary through a series of statements or propositions, theorems that are each time recontextualized so as to hear what transpires through the grant of language, that is, of language itself.[8] Yet of such thinking experience, Heidegger says right at the beginning of his essay that it is a question of chance or luck: "Whether the attempt to bring us face to face with the possibility of such an experience will succeed [*glückt*], and if it does, how far that possible success [*vielleicht Geglückte*] will go for each one of us—that is not up to any of us" (p. 59). From the start, such an experience with language itself, with its address and grant, is modalized by a *perhaps*. Whereas the thematic and methodical approach of science and philosophy not only yields "certain insights, and information about language" (pp. 58–59) but also has the certainty of succeeding in knowing the object that it has in front of itself, a thinking experience lacks this certainty altogether. Compared to the self-confidence of science, its self-determined decidedness, a thinking experience is strangely passive. To make an experience with language, Heidegger suggests at the beginning of the essay, is simply not in the power of the subject. Experience, as understood here, means to become stricken, overwhelmed, and consequently transformed. It is supposed to be a *thinking* experience, but as we shall see in a moment, thinking too, is not to be determined from itself, that is, in a subjectivist manner. Whether such an experience may succeed is therefore a question of luck.

If "The Nature of Language" seeks to prepare the conditions for such an experience with language in the neighborhood of thinking and poetry, it is because "the attempt rests upon the supposition [*Vermutung*] that poetry and thinking belong within one neighborhood" (p. 80). "Neighborhood" implies that each one—thinking and poetry—is only what it is next to, in the proximity of the other, and in a region they both share. Yet if thinking cannot be determined in and from itself alone, if it must be determined in relation to its other (and vice versa), thinking cannot be *ratio*, "calculation in the widest sense" (p. 70). It does not ground in itself, it does not have the certitude of the *cogito*. What thinking is and what it is to achieve remain dependent, as it were, on thinking's neighbor, its other: poetry. With this an essential uncertainty, one not of the order of empirical approximation, necessarily distinguishes thinking, and especially the thinking experience. It is in this context in the essay that Heidegger's talk of "supposition" (*Vermutung*) becomes significant. Deriving from the German verb *vermuten* ("to suspect, to assume, to suppose, to presume"), *Vermutung* is to be understood as a tentative supposition, assumption, conjecture, or opinion, as the thought of something probable, or in keeping with the facts.[9] In German law, *Vermutung* has the sense of either *praesumtio facti*, meaning that it may suffice as proof for a case and not require any presentation of evidence to substantiate it, or *praesumtio iuris*, meaning that it may require such evidence in the case of a grounded supposition or hypothesis. But commonly the term *Vermutung* refers to assumptions that are only presumed, conjectured, surmised. A thinking based on suppositions is akin to ordinary, everyday conjecturing and devoid of all rigor. What is thus assumed is only *vermutlich*, probable, possible, perhaps. Until raised to the status of a working hypothesis, for which there is already grounded evidence, there is no place for suppositions in a propositional discourse, in a discourse with scientific or philosophical pretensions. But "The Nature of Language," and to a lesser extent some of the other essays in *On the Way to Language*, make frequent use of the term.

From what we have already seen, Heidegger's suppositions cannot ultimately be grounded suppositions in the sense of scientific or philosophical hypotheses. It is just as unlikely that they would represent unmodified incursions of ordinary thinking or sloppy language in his own meditations. For a better grasp of how to conceive the status of these suppositions, let us take another example. Heidegger remarks, "despite the fact that since the early days of Western thinking, and up into the late period of Stefan George's poetic, thinking has thought deep thoughts about language, and poetry has made stirring things into language," language has not been given voice "in its essential being." He then observes, "We can only conjecture [*vermuten*] why it is that . . . the being of language nowhere brings itself to word" (p. 81). The reasons Heidegger offers to explain why language's speaking has always been overheard point to the propositional treatment of language in philosophy. "There is some evidence that the essential nature of language flatly refuses to express itself in words—in the language, that is, in which we make statements about language," he claims (p. 81). But even so, language "holds back its own origin and so denies its being to our usual notions"; it effectively speaks "the withholding of the being of language," thus putting itself "into language nonetheless, in its most appropriate manner" (p. 81). So why have philosophy and poetry not been able to respond to this manifestation of language? The reasons must lie deeper than philosophy's (and, poetry's?) propositional nature. "We may avoid the issue no longer," Heidegger asserts. "Rather, we must keep on conjecturing [*vermuten*] what the reason may be why the peculiar speech of language's being passes unnoticed all too easily. Presumably [*vermutlich*] part of the reason is that the two kinds of utterance [*des Sagens*] *par excellence*, poetry and thinking, have not been sought out in their proper habitat, their neighborhood" (p. 81). Only if philosophy and poetry are advised as to the neighborhood that prevents them from being rooted in themselves independently of all relation to an Other does the chance arise for a thinking and a poetic experience that would do justice to language itself.

Like all the other examples of such conjecturing that could be cited from "The Nature of Language," the one just dealt with shows to what extent Heidegger's thinking persists in suppositions and in making further conjectures on the basis of what had been inferred from merely, it would seem, presumptive evidence. Although Heidegger seems to suggest on one occasion—while discussing the kind of hint that the guide word "The being of language: the language of being" offers to thinking in order to achieve the neighborhood with poetry—that conjecturing is a preliminary approach to "a thought-worthy matter for which the fitting mode of thinking is still lacking," conjecturing is not reducible to something ultimately to be superseded by thinking (p. 96).[10] But even so, although these conjectures do not enjoy the status they have in philosophical or scientific discourse, they are not for the same reason deficient modes of thinking. Instead of revealing a relaxation of standards, a slippage into mere opining and belief, conjecturing is here intimately linked to the thinking experience itself. Supposition is the peculiar mode of a thinking that, rather than questioning (in our case) the essence of language, is receptive to the address, the grant, and the promise of language (prior to any particular content conveyed). It is thinking itself, and not opining, that arrives at suppositions. Heidegger writes, "if the nearness of poetry and thinking is one of Saying, then our thinking arrives at the assumption [*dann gelangt unser Denken in die Vermutung*] that the occurrence of appropriation acts as that Saying in which language grants its essential nature to us" (p. 90). Presuming, or conjecturing, is not just one of thinking's possible modes; rather, in the neighborhood of poetry, the thinking experience proceeds primarily in this mode, characterizing thinking in its essence. At the end of "The Nature of Language," after recasting once again the guide word for his approach to language, which now reads "It is: the language of being," Heidegger recalls the last lines of George's poem, in whose neighborhood he sought the possibility of a thinking experience with language. The last line is: "Where word breaks off no thing may be." Heidegger concludes, "now, thinking within the neighborhood of the poetic word, we may say, as a supposition [*denkend, vermutend sagend*]: An 'is' arises where the word breaks up" (p. 108). Undoubtedly, what Heidegger wishes to say in this passage—in which he steps back from the word and its sound, which for George gives being, to the soundless, the stillness, from which both the word and the "is" arise as gift—is that authentic thought (*eigentliches Denken*) can proceed in the mode of presumption once it is in the neighborhood of the poetic. But *denkend, vermutend sagen*, shows conjecturing to be a mode of thinking in its own right, a mode of thinking that in essence is conjectural. Rather than excluding supposition or relegating it to a secondary mode, thinking here embraces it. Having noted that thinking and poetry are two wholly different kinds of Saying, Heidegger remarks, "we should become familiar with the suggestion [*wir möchten uns mit der Vermutung befreunden*] that the neighborhood of poetry and thinking is concealed within this farthest divergence of the Saying" (p. 90). Thinking, in the neighborhood in question, all ears to the address of language, stands in an amiable relation to supposition.

It certainly seems appropriate to limit thinking to conjecture with respect to what eludes any possible knowledge, and indeed language, for Heidegger, is just such an object. But unlike other unfathomable objects, language is not unknowable because it exceeds the range of our faculties, assumed or established. It follows that the conjectural thinking in question is a far cry from those other modes of thought—skeptical, empiricist, or theological—likewise restricted to supposition. If the recourse to conjectural inferring in the face of noncognizable objects is, in the last resort, a futile attempt to transgress the boundaries assigned to our faculties, the peculiar impossibility of knowing the nature of language is, paradoxically, an advantage. It "is not a defect," Heidegger claims, "but rather an advantage [*Vorzug*] by which we are favored with a special realm [*in einen ausgezeichneten Bereich vorgezogen sind*], that realm where we, who are needed and used to speak language, dwell as *mortals*" (p. 134). What this passage tells us is that the impossibility of stepping out of language to "look at it from somewhere else" in order to know it is an advantage in that we are drawn forward into the dwelling place that constitutes our humanity. "In order to be who we are, we human beings remain committed to and within the being of language," Heidegger remarks (p. 134). But such being drawn forward is an advantage in another sense. The impossibility of knowing language provides for the chance, the stroke of luck, that conjectural thinking might be more than just an idle attempt to grasp what cognitively does not let itself be appropriated. At the beginning of the essay "Language," Heidegger wonders whether the answer to the question "In what way does language occur as language?"—namely, "Language speaks"—is "seriously, an answer?"

Presumably [*Vermutlich schon*]—that is, when it becomes clear what speaking is. To reflect on language thus demands that we enter into the speaking of language in order to take up our stay within language, i.e., within *its* speaking, not within our own. Only in that way do we arrive at the region in which it may happen— or also fail to happen [*glückt oder auch missglückt*]—that language will call to us from there and grant us its nature.[11]

By taking up our stay in the speaking of language, the chance presents itself that language may grant us its nature. This is the chance that language gives thinking in the mode of conjecture—the chance of becoming a response to language's nature—if thinking dwells in the realm that it cannot master. But it is only a chance. This uncertainty that conjectural thinking may indeed correspond to the nature of language is, however, the condition under which thinking has at least a chance to correspond to the nature of language. Without the risk of failing, the risk of slipping into the banality of everyday presumptions or assumptions backed at best by scant evidence, conjecturing as a mode of thought would have no chance of saying the nature of language. Yet if this is so, if the possibility of a correspondence between thinking and language requires such unpredictability, it is because the uncertainty in question is an essential one.

Before taking up the specific reasons for this uncertainty, and the ensuing chance that it presents for a thinking experience in the mode of conjectural thinking, I recall that what such a thinking experience invites us to think is, in Heidegger's words, an imposition. In "The Nature of Language" Heidegger contends that the guide word for the experience sought with language, recast as "The being of language—the language of being," is nothing less than "an imposition. If it were merely an assertion, we could set out to prove its truth or falseness. That would be easier by far than to endure the imposition or make our peace with it [*uns in sie zu finden*]" (pp. 76–77). "Imposition" translates the German *Zumutung*, an unreasonable request, an appalling demand, an affront. For ordinary thinking, and philosophical and scientific thinking as well, the guide word is an imposition in that it is not a (verifiable or falsifiable) proposition. It is not even a sentence. After an additional transformation of the guide word into "The being of language: the language of being," Heidegger notes that the colon preceding the second phrase must point "to something which we, coming from the first turn of the phrase, do not suspect [*nicht vermuten*] in the second; for the second phrase is more than just a rearrangement of the words in the first" (p. 94). Not only are the two turns of the phrase not inversions, but their forms differ. By virtue of the total lack of symmetry between the two phrases, propositional thinking is unable to suspect or to glimpse something on the other side of the colon that would speak about the nature of language. The guide word is such an imposition for propositional thinking because it does not allow that thinking to infer anything from it. Yet the transformed guide word, "The being of language—the language of being," might be seen as simply an imposition by Heidegger upon his readers. He states: "The demand [*Zumutung*] that we experience this sentence thoughtfully would seem to stem from the lecture imposing it on us. But the imposition comes from another source" (p. 77). In other words, although the guide word is definitely an imposition on ordinary and scientific propositional thinking and might even be suspected of representing an arbitrary imposition by Heidegger, it is an imposition in still another sense. Just as the demand to think that "nearness and Saying [are] . . . the Same" is, according to Heidegger, "a flagrant imposition [*eine arge Zumutung*]" that "must not be softened in the least" (p. 95), so the imposition that the guide word represents is not to be dulled in the least. If, indeed, thinking must endure the imposition, it is because only the inability to suspect from the first turn of the phrase what the second holds makes the guide word a guide word.

What then can it mean to thinkingly experience, or to endure the imposition of the guide word? What is that which, without being able to suspect it from the first phrase, we must nonetheless allow to impose itself on us if the guide word is to give us a hint as to the nature of language? Before proceeding, I must again recall that in "The Nature of Language," thinking for Heidegger is first a listening. As a listening, thinking is attentive to the arrival of what it seeks to approach. If what one approaches must first come in our direction, then thinking must be most fundamentally an openness to what comes toward us. In the case of language this implies that thinking must first be a listening not to the content of linguistic utterances but to the address of language itself and what is said in such address, in other words, to the Saying of language. Heidegger writes: "If we put questions to language, questions about its nature, its being, then clearly language itself must already have been granted to us [*dann muss uns doch die Sprache selber schon zugesprochen sein*]. Similarly, if we want to inquire into the being of language, then that which is called nature or being must also be already granted to us" (p. 71). Prior to any inquiry into the nature of language, language must "first promise itself to us [*zuvor uns zusagen*], or must already have done so. Language must, in its own way, avow to us itself—its nature" (p. 76). Indeed, language *is* in essence such avowal. "Language is active as this promise [*Die Sprache west als dieser Zuspruch*]" (p. 76). This prior promise or grant, or more precisely, this address of language—its *Zuspruch* or *Zusage*—is, in Heidegger's words, the thoughtworthy (*das Denkwürdige*), in short, what thinking as listening must attend to in the first place. Reflecting on this gift by language through a meditation on George's poem—whose last line runs, "Where word breaks off no thing may be"—Heidegger holds that with this giving by language before all being, we "are struck by the sight of something other [*Anderes*]" (p. 87). Language as the prior grant or promise, as the Other to "the slumber of hastily formed opinions" (p. 87) of common sense and of philosophy as well, is the thoughtworthy *par excellence*. Just as George's poem says this Other in its own way, in a way different from philosophy (*ganz Anderes auf andere Weise gesagt*), thinking must say this Other in still another way (p. 89). If the transformed guide word represents such an imposition, it is precisely because its other and its true source (*kommt anderswoher*) is this Other, the thoughtworthy, that cannot be suspected or inferred syllogistically from the first segment of the guide word. If language is first and foremost promise, grant, address, it is essentially an Other that as Other does not let itself be approached in a calculating fashion. By its very nature, language's grant or promise is distinguished by uncertainty, indeed, as should now be obvious, by an essential uncertainty. The grant, the promise, the address can never be suspected, anticipated as a sure thing. They are owed to and owned by the Other; they are the Other itself. As such they can only be assumed, supposed, conjectured. The guide word, although beckoning us away from current notions of language, lets us "only suspect [*vermuten*] at first the memorable thing [*Denkwüdiges*] toward which it beckons us," Heidegger remarks (p. 96). Supposition is, therefore, the adequate mode in which thinking can and must relate to what in essence is not in the power of the subject but belongs instead to the Other, that is, the promise or grant of language.

The guide word is an imposition because it demands to attend to what can only be supposed, the grant or address of and by language as Other. Let me recall that the imposition in question occurs within the framework of a thinking experience with language that not only proceeds in the uncertain mode of conjecturing but also starts out with the assumption that "the neighborhood [of poetry and thinking] . . . is the place that gives us room to experience how matters stand with language"

(p. 92). The guide word is to indicate how to arrive at the assumed nearness of poetry and thinking. For Heidegger, "it is not merely an expedient that our attempt to prepare for a thinking experience with language seeks out the neighborhood of poetry; for the attempt rests upon the supposition that poetry and thinking belong within one neighborhood. Perhaps this supposition corresponds to the imposition [*vielleicht entspricht diese Vermutung der Zumutung*] which we hear only vaguely so far: the being of language—the language of being" (p. 80). The supposition that both poetry and thinking share a region, and that their determination is always suspended from the relation to their respective other, is thus, perhaps, what the imposition of the guide word demands that we think and endure. The guide word requests that we suppose, and that the supposition in question correspond to what is imposed on us. Vice versa, what strikes thinking as a flagrant imposition is also something that thinking has presumed or conjectured. Heidegger remarks, "we conjecture what it is that might be imposed upon thinking [*Wir vermuten, was dem Denken zugemutet sein könnte*]" (p. 85, translation modified). On the one hand, supposition is a tending toward what our thinking has to endure as an imposition; on the other hand, the imposition is an imposition only if it comes from a source that thinking can entertain only in the mode of a supposition. Moreover, as is quite obvious from all the passages quoted, the relations of correspondence between supposition and imposition lack any certainty. They may or may not be the case. Indeed, the thinking that experiences the imposition and that conjectures what it is that is imposed on it is not a thinking that seeks to gain knowledge but a thinking experience with language, more precisely with what in language is other, language's address or grant. It is a thinking that "knows" that nothing can guarantee this experience, and hence all it seeks are the conditions that enable thinking to possibly make such an experience.[12] "'Possibility' so understood, as what enables, means something else and something more than mere opportunity [*mehr als die blosse Chance*]," Heidegger notes (p. 93). The guide word, as we have seen, hints at how to arrive at the assumed "place that gives us room to experience how matters stand with language" (p. 92). But to enter that place effectively is a matter of luck (*Glück*). Heidegger writes: "If we were to succeed for once [*wenn es einmal glückte*] in reaching the place to which the guide-word beckons us, we would arrive where we have a possibility of undergoing an experience with language, the language known to us" (p. 95).[13] Although only a *perhaps* prevails in this thinking that seeks the enabling conditions for an experience with the grant of language, a chance exists that the request will be granted. It is a chance that is not a mere chance because it is owed to what in the imposition addresses itself to us in expectation of a response. Having recourse to the meaning of the archaic verb *muten, seinen Sinn worauf richten, begehren*, that is, to direct one's mind upon something, to desire, one could say that it is a chance in the sense of *Glück* since it is, perhaps, suspended from what in the imposition *mutet uns zu*, directs itself upon us. Whether or not thinking finds the place where the possibility exists to make an experience with language as address or grant is not calculable. It is absolutely unnecessary from the perspective of calculating thought. If it is a question of chance, not of mere chance (*blosse Chance*) but perhaps, in Mallarmé's and Blanchot's words, of "pure chance," this is because the advent of an experience with language as address or grant is a gift of the Other, of what in language may or may not claim us.

Yet the complex play that we have laid out so far, the play of supposition and imposition, of *Vermutung* and *Zumutung*, does not yet exhaust Heidegger's meditation on the enabling possibilities for an experience with language. At the beginning of "The Way to Language," he remarks that if "we experience the way to language in the light of what happens with the way itself as we go on, then an intimation [*Vermutung*] may come to us in virtue of which language will henceforth strike us as strange [*uns . . . befremdend anmutet*]" (p. 111). Although the verb *anmuten*, rooted in the Middle High German *anemuoten*, is quite similar to *vermuten* and means to demand or expect something from someone, it means as well to appear, to seem, to strike as. The supposition, then, one that is perhaps imposed on thinking and that moreover might correspond to such an imposition, may result in language's striking us henceforth as strange. Language no longer appears the same as it did when we set off on our way to language. But *befremdend* does not simply mean "strange" here. In the imposed supposition, language directs itself upon us in such a way that we, or our thinking, become *befremded*: not alienated or estranged (*entfremded*) but, to create a neologism, *bestranged*. By virtue of the supposition we become stricken by bestrangement. The supposition ultimately concerns, as we have seen, language as grant, language as Other. As a result of such a supposition, language not only becomes strange, other to us, but also "affects" us by its strangeness and no longer lets us be what we were before. A language that addresses us as address and grant is a language that avows itself to us and claims us, rather than the other way around. It is through this demand that we undergo a strangeness, which is to be recognized as the strangeness of a thinking that, rather than a questioning, is a listening, always already facing the Other, *here*, the grant or promise of language.[14]

For Heidegger a thinking experience is such only if one becomes struck, overwhelmed, transformed. Experience is thus not to be understood as having its origin and initiative in the subject. It takes place only as letting oneself be addressed by what comes toward us, what arrives, and by receiving what thus strikes us (*das uns Treffende empfangen*), letting oneself be expropriated from the start in a bestrangement by an Other. *Vermutung*, *Zumutung*, and *Anmutung* are nothing less than the constituting gestures (*Gebärden*) of a thinking that is, or rather seeks, experience in this sense. They are the gestures of a thinking that seeks to settle in the place where thinking has always already been, in other words, where it assumes its primary characteristic as a listening. However, such a thinking experience, with language for instance, is something, Heidegger suggests, that "could be [*vielleicht*] . . . too much for us moderns" (pp. 57–58). In addition, and more fundamentally, it is a question of luck whether the attempt to bring us face to face with the possibility of such an experience will succeed. The reason for such uncertainty is not only that we moderns have become deaf to the call of what now is merely an object for a subject's representations. The uncertainty in question lies deeper. It is, first, linked to the conjectural nature of a thinking that seeks a thinking experience. Yet if such thinking must be conjectural, this is not, as should be obvious by now, because it is loose but because such conjecturing is the mode imposed on thinking by what it seeks to encounter. What conjectural thinking corresponds to is language as address, as grant, as promise, and such language strikes thinking with bestrangement. Rather than being rooted in the *cogito* and having thus a secure self-certain ground, thinking becomes suspended, in this case from what addresses itself to it, from the Other's granted address, from the address as an Other. The uncertainty here, then, signaled by all the *perhapses* (and modal auxiliaries, such as "could," "may," etc.), which condition all of this thinking's gestures, is bound up with the *responsive* nature of this thinking. A thinking that, prior to all questioning (of the nature of language, for instance), is a listening to what directs itself toward it (Saying, for instance)—in short, a thinking that attends to the Other (language as address or grant, for example)—unfolds only within the limits of the *perhaps*. It owes (itself) to the Other.[15] In "The Nature of Language," *perhaps* registers this suspension of all thinking certitude about language from the *Zusage* or *Zuspruch* of language. *Perhaps* is the mark of thinking's bestrangement by the Other as address. Yet even a thinking successfully modalized by a *perhaps* is not a sure confirmation of its responsive character. *Perhaps* is, as it were, modalized by itself. Indeed, it is up to the Other whether, perhaps, a response to its address has taken place. The thinking experience is, therefore, in essence always a singular event, indeed, a question of luck, more precisely of happy luck, of *Glück*.

In conclusion, the modalizer *perhaps* is not necessarily a characteristic of everyday discourse. It is not necessarily the sign that assertions are put in suspension. In a discourse of a thinking experience, which Heidegger clearly demarcates from the philosophical inquiry into the essence of language, *perhaps* modalizes thinking's gesturing toward an Other. But as we have seen, such an attempt to seek the enabling conditions for an experience with an Other no longer proceeds in a sequence of statements. The various stages of the way to language—"way" understood as what lets arrive (*Gelangenlassen*) (p. 92)—cannot be scientifically verified or falsified. Yet, for the same reasons, *perhaps* is no longer a grammatical-logical category in such a meditation. Since it no longer characterizes propositions or statements, it is no longer a modality. Perhaps *perhaps* is here successfully removed from its customary usage. However, no certainty allows us to state that this is the case. *Perhaps* is the mark of a response, but as a response to the Other, it remains infinitely suspended from it.

(1992)

PART IV

RHYTHM AND ZIGZAG

On the Nonadequate Trait

Any discussion of the relation between Heidegger and Derrida requires that we first gain an appropriate understanding of the notion of "relation" itself. In our context, Heidegger's elaborations on this notion offer themselves as the most likely starting point. The analysis of Heidegger's notion of relation must precede not only the interrogation of the proximity of Derrida's work to Heidegger's enterprise but also the interrogation of what might fundamentally separate these two types of investigation. Since the levels at which one could analyze these relations pertinently are hardly obvious, the issue here is only to discover one such problematic level, through which one could perhaps begin to ask the question of the relation between Heidegger and Derrida in a way that is no longer impressionistic.

But why precisely would one want to interrogate the relation between Heidegger and Derrida within the frame of a problematic concerning the relation as such? First and foremost because this question is, if we can say it, at the very "center" of Heidegger's thought. By critically pursuing the intentional analyses of correlation that Husserl opened up—an investigation that according to Hans-Georg Gadamer represents the very heart of phenomenology—Heidegger is led to pose the problem of the relation as such. If there is a relation between Heidegger and Derrida, then it must necessarily be connected to what is involved in this question.

I

When Heidegger evokes, at the end of the 1956 Addendum to "The Origin of the Work of Art," the overwhelming difficulty that defines the thought of the relation between Being and the being of man, he is evoking what was his major concern from *Being and Time* to all the later texts of the so-called *Kehre*. From the Dasein analytic to "The Letter on Humanism," Heidegger stressed that this relation is not an anthropological relation (based on a definition of man either as *animal rationale* or as *ens finitum* created in God's image). In fact, we are already conceiving it inappropriately if we state it in the form of a relation between Being and man. The Dasein analytic in which Heidegger first asks the question of the relation between Being and man is neither an anthropology nor even the outline of an ontological foundation for a possible anthropology. "Yet the analytic of Dasein," Heidegger writes in *Being and Time*, "is not aimed at laying an ontological basis for anthropology; its purpose is one of fundamental ontology."[1] According to this aim, the issue in *Being and Time* is only to interrogate the meaning of Being, that is, of Being as Being, "insofar as Being enters into the intelligibility of Dasein" (*BT*, p. 193). Contrary to all (metaphysical) investigations that attempt to discover a "beyond" of Being, fundamental ontology posits a "necessary connection between Being and understanding" so that "Being 'is' only in the understanding of those entities to whose Being something like an understanding of Being belongs" (*BT*, p. 228). Those entities are Dasein. Consequently, if it is the case that "only as long as Dasein *is* (that is, only as long as an understanding of Being is ontically possible) 'is there' Being," then fundamental ontology must be constituted in the first place as the existential analytic of this Dasein (*BT*, p. 255).

Exactly because this fundamental ontology is an analytic of Dasein, it is essentially a philosophy of finitude (a philosophy of finitude, however, that does not fall into some sort of relativism or perspectivism). The most universal and general question, the question therefore of Being, is inseparable from Dasein, which is characterized each time by an irreducible "mineness." Thus the question of Being has the possibility of its own precise individualization for any particular Dasein (*die Möglichkeit ihrer eigenen schärfsten Vereinzelung auf das jeweilige Dasein*) (*BT*, p. 63). Heidegger will not abandon this "finitistic" conception of Being even when he eventually replaces the Dasein analytic with the interrogation of the history of Being. "There is Being only," he writes in *Identity and Difference*, "in this or that particular historic character [*in dieser und jener geschichtlichen Prägung*]."[2] What I want to emphasize here—and this is my first thesis—is that the finitude of Being does not lie in the fact that Being appears only by means of the exemplary being that is Dasein or only in the diverse historical "sendings" of Being, but rather lies in what *Being and Time*, for example, calls the *equiprimordiality* of Being *and* the truth of Dasein (*BT*, p. 272). In other words, the finitistic conception of Being depends entirely on the nature of its relation. What must hold our interest here is the *constellation* (a term Heidegger uses in *Identity and Difference*), the *belonging-together* that characterizes the relation of Being and Dasein, their *Zugehörigkeit*, on whose basis alone we will be able to conceive the terms that are related here. The question of finitude must be conceived as a question of relation, a question of the relation of what, considered apart from that relation, arises out of the metaphysical order: Being and finite man in their presence.

What therefore is relation (*Bezug*)? We can certainly begin to answer this question by citing the following negative definition Heidegger gives in "What Are Poets For?" when he discusses the use of this word in Rilke's authentic poetry:

We only half understand Rilke's word *Bezug*—and in a case such as this that means not at all—if we understand it in the sense of reference or relation. We compound our misunderstanding if we conceive of this relation as the human ego's referring or relating itself to the object. This meaning, "referring to," is a later one in the history of language. Rilke's word *Bezug* is used in this sense as well, of course; but it does not intend it primarily, but only on the basis of its original meaning. Indeed, the expression "the whole *Bezug*" is completely unthinkable if *Bezug* is represented as mere relation.[3]

The *belonging*-together of Being and man does not resemble a relation of a subject to an object, or a relation of an effect to a cause. It should not be understood as either an "attachment" (*Zuordnung*) or a "coordination" (*Zusammenordnung*), as a relation therefore constituted or explicated on the basis of either man or Being.

We stubbornly misunderstand this prevailing *belonging* together of man and Being as long as we represent everything only in categories and mediations, be it with or without dialectic. Then we always find only connections [*Verknüpfungen*] that are established either in terms of Being or in terms of man, and that present the belonging together of man and Being as an intertwining [*Verflechtung*]. (*ID*, p. 32)

Beziehung and relation are, indeed, only the formal determinations uncovered "directly by way of 'formalization' from any kind of context, whatever its subject-matter or its way of Being" (*BT*, p. 108). Just as the system of reference that constitutes the significance of Dasein's worldhood is allowed to be understood as a network of relations only at the price of a leveling down that empties all these relations of their own content, the relation between Being and the being of man can be amenable to a functional analysis only by sacrificing the very specificity of this relation.

As *Being and Time* attempts to demonstrate, such a relational and functional analysis is rigorously applicable only to the present-at-hand (*Vorhandenes*), to the beings, therefore, whose Being has the nature of pure substantiality. In contrast to the ready-to-hand, which is ontologically prior and in whose opening our daily encounter with beings occurs, *Vorhandenheit* designates a mode of Being that depends on the function of an epistemological relationship between an (abstract and mundane) subject and the world represented as an object. In *Being and Time*, Heidegger insists upon the fact that "a '*commercium*' of the subject with a world does not get *created* for the first time by knowing, nor does it *arise* from some way in which the world acts upon a subject." Moreover, knowing, for Heidegger, "is a mode of Dasein founded upon Being-in-the-world" (*BT*, p. 90). The assumption of relations between a subject and an object is possible "only *because* Dasein, as Being-in-the-world, is as it is" (*BT*, p. 84). Thus, in *Being and Time*, Heidegger will attempt to ground ontologically the subject-object relation (and *a fortiori* the establishment of formal relations between objects) in a mode of Dasein, in this being that has for its Being a relation of Being to its Being (*Seinsverhältnis*). In other words, he is forced to establish that all subject-object relations are opened ontologically only in the interior of the relation (*Bezug*) of Dasein and Being.

Heidegger will pursue his "striving" against *Vorhandenheit* and against epistemology, particularly in the writings concerning technology, in the form of a "striving" against objectifying representation (*vergegen-ständlichende Vorstellung*). According to the historical conception of Being that characterizes Heidegger's thought after *Being and Time*, objectifying representation as well as the relations of production that modern man maintains with the world and with himself unfold from a historical alien-ation of man's essence. Heidegger writes in "The Letter on Humanism," "But then the essence of man is too little heeded and not thought in its origin, the essential provenance that is always the essential future for his-torical mankind."[4] Whatever Heidegger is intending with such an essence (an essence that is neither simply a past present nor a future present but rather that from which temporality as a modification of the present is de-rived), he is not trying to do away with the subject-object relation. The is-sue for Heidegger, on the contrary, is to inscribe the subject-object rela-tion as a constellation of Being into what it dissimulates. In "The Letter on Humanism" again, Heidegger says:

Man is never first and foremost man on the hither side of the world, as a "sub-ject," whether this is taken as "I" or "We." Nor is he ever simply a mere subject which always simultaneously is related to objects, so that his essence lies in the subject-object relation. Rather, before all this, man in his essence is ek-sistent into the openness of Being, into the open region that lights the "between" within which a "relation" of subject to object can "be." (*BW*, p. 229)

The relations between man and Being, the relations that found the rela-tions confining the human to a subject conversing with an object, appear here as a "between," as a clearing (*Lichtung*) between. In what follows, I am going to try to highlight this intermediary nature of the relation—the *Zwischen* of the *Bezug*—within which alone something like a relation of a subject to an object can take place. I will begin, therefore, by explicating the major features that, according to Heidegger, characterize the relation between man and Being. I will extract these features from Heidegger's own discussion of the Dasein analytic in "The Letter on Humanism."

The Dasein analytic asserts that man must *first* be thought as Da-sein determined by its being-in-the-world and as a being relating itself to itself through the Being that is to be. Paradoxically (although this might not be a paradox) Dasein, which exists in the clearing of Being, is itself this clearing: "Man occurs essentially in such a way that he is the 'there' [*das 'Da'*], that is, the lighting of Being. The 'Being' of the *Da*, and only it, has the fundamental character of ek-sistence, that is, of an ecstatic inherence in the truth of Being" (*BW*, p. 205). Man as Dasein therefore is the same clearing in which he ek-sists. Or again, man is himself the "between" of the relation that opens the possibility of a subject-object relation. He is himself this "between" insofar as it enters into the Being of his Being. As a result, the problem of the "between" (and of the relation) appears inseparable from the relationship that Being possesses with itself within the clearing of its own "there." Nothing could be easier than to confuse the unity of these two aspects of the problem with an identity and to misunderstand Dasein's self-relation as a specular relation. To fall prey to such confusions would amount to missing entirely what Heidegger is trying to do in *Being and Time*; it would amount to a rejection of what one can think here in regard to the question of the relation. The relation as an "entre-deux" that clarifies every subject-object relation by itself appearing in the clearing of Dasein is an intermediary that is necessarily "out of joint," dis-placed, nonadequate in relation to itself. It is a milieu that is dislocated in its own taking place. Thus, for example, man, even though he is himself the clearing in which he ek-sists, does not occupy the center. The reason for this is that what is at issue in his existence is not him but Being: "the essence of man is essential for the truth of Being, specifically in such a way that the word does not pertain to man simply as such" (*BW*, p. 224). The privilege that Heidegger gives to Being here does not imply that he is now starting to think the relation of Being and man on the basis of Being. On the contrary, as we shall see more clearly in the argumentation that follows, what will always be at issue is to think the relation *as* Being.

As we just saw, man is in his essence, he is the clearing of Being in which he ek-sists only insofar as he has been called there by Being. "Only so long as the lighting of Being comes to pass does Being convey itself to man. But the fact that the *Da*, the lighting as the truth of Being itself, comes to pass is the dispensation of Being itself" (*BW*, p. 216). Already determined as the median openness thrown off-center by relating to itself, thrown off-center to the extent that the relation of Dasein and Being is a function of Dasein's openness, the relation taken as the relation of man and Being must further be understood as a reply (*Gegenwurf*, literally, a counterthrow). According to this determination, not only do Dasein and Being face one another in order to be called reciprocally, but the very relation is, as we say, a "decentered" reply. First, let us go into how Dasein and Being are related by a reply. As a reply to Being, man, for Heidegger, is the guardian of Being. Man has been destined by Being as a reply to itself.

What throws in projection is not man but Being itself, which sends man into the ek-sistence of Da-sein that is his essence. This destiny comes to pass as the lighting of Being, as which it is (*BW*, p. 217).

But how should we think the double nature of the relation, a duplicity according to which, first, man comes into his essence only by means of Being, which nevertheless he is himself, a Dasein always particularized, and a duplicity according to which, second, Being destines man to be Dasein in order to be able to appear in Dasein as the "there" guarded by man? In "The Letter on Humanism," Heidegger poses the question in the following terms: "But how—provided we really ought to ask such a question at all—how does Being relate to ek-sistence? Being itself is the relation to the extent that It, as the location of the truth of Being amid beings, gathers to itself and embraces ek-sistence in its existential, that is, ecstatic, essence" (*BW*, p. 211). Being itself is the relation (*Verhältnis*), says Heidegger. This relationship is to be explicated neither on the basis of man nor on the basis of Being to which man relates in the relation of Being to ek-sistence. The "between," qualified here by Heidegger as the relation (the *Verhältnis* of what comes face to face in the *Gegenwurf*), is not uniquely the place where the subject-object relation emerges, but is, more fundamentally still, the very relation of Being and Dasein. Man can be in a relation to Being only within the openness of the relation "that Being destines for itself" (*BW*, p. 211). The relation is, therefore, to be thought not on the basis of that to which it gives birth (Being and man) but on the basis of Being *as* relation.

By thinking the relation from itself, we do not, however, escape from the apparent paradoxes that I raised in regard to the nature of the duplicity of the relation. To think the relation as such is to think its dislocation, or rather, to think the dislocation solely in terms of itself. Only

202 RHYTHM AND ZIGZAG

on this condition can what Heidegger calls *Bezug* or *Verhältnis* be understood as that from which "man and Being have first received those determinations of essence by which man and Being are grasped metaphysically in philosophy" (*ID*, p. 32). But this is not all. The relation (or Being as relation) is still the a priori of the ontological a priori (of Dasein and the Being of Dasein) that *Being and Time* investigated. It is an a priori that precedes all (metaphysical) representations of man and of Being. Consequently, Heidegger, with this determination of Being as relation, thinks a *before* prior to all fundamental ontology, a relation therefore that precedes the relation of Dasein and Being, which itself had to have, as we have seen, the subject-object relation inscribed into its openness.

In a note bearing on the notion of *Verhältnis* as it was used in "The Letter on Humanism," Heidegger says, "Plato's Doctrine of Truth: Relation on the basis of fundamental comportment (with-drawal) of the denial (of the with-drawn)."[5] Continuing the excavation of the relation as *Verhältnis*, I shall follow from this note another trail, which leads to "On the Essence of Truth." Analyzing the intrinsic possibility of the concept of truth as adequation, Heidegger notes here that the difference between thing and proposition (the difference between the thing appearing in its stability and moving at the same time toward and into the proposition) presupposes an open domain, an opening "the openness of which is not first created by the presenting but rather is only entered into and taken over as a domain of relatedness [*Bezugsbereich*]." Heidegger continues, "The relation of the presentative statement to the thing is the accomplishment [*Vollzug*] of that *bearing* [*Verhältnis*] which originally and always comes to prevail as a comportment [*ein Verhalten zum Schwingen bringt*]" (*BW*, pp. 123–24). In 1954, Heidegger wrote in the margin of the third edition of "On the Essence of Truth" precisely on the subject of this notion of *Verhalten*: "Comportment—to linger in the lighting (standing earnestly in the lighting) of the presencing of what presences."[6] The openness or the clearing, therefore, represents here the place of the manifestation of everything that is joined, of the *Zueinander-Anwesen* of what lingers awhile (cf. Heidegger's "Anaximander Fragment"), or again, the manifestation of what Heidegger calls *Gezüge* in "The Origin of the Work of Art." But the openness, of course, is also the domain open for a being's self-relating comportment. The comportment, the subject-object relation, and the *Gezüge* (the whole of what is in relation), all of which presuppose the openness of the relation or the openness of the *Verhältnis*, are, however, because of the nature of the openness of *Verhältnis*, its originary *and* at each time particular actualization.

How then are we to understand the relation between *Verhältnis* (relation) and *Verhalten* (comportment)? In "On the Essence of Truth," Heidegger conceives *Verhältnis* as the "fundamental comportment of letting be [*Verhaltenheit des Sein-lassens*]," that is, as freedom (*BW*, p. 129; my translation). Opening itself in the openness of this *Verhaltenheit*, all comportment (*Verhalten*) appears then as "being attuned in a way that discloses beings as a whole" (*BW*, p. 131). All comportment presupposes and simultaneously reveals the openness of the relation. As *Vorenthalt* (withdrawal or concealment, or privation), the *Verhaltenheit* (fundamental comportment) of *Verhältnis* also entails its own concealment because of the *Verhalten* (comportment and restraint) that actualizes it.

As letting beings be, freedom is intrinsically the resolutely open bearing [*Verhältnis*] that does not close up in itself. All comportment is grounded in this bearing and receives from it directedness toward beings and disclosure of them. Nevertheless, this bearing toward concealing conceals itself in the process, letting a forgottenness of the mystery take precedence and disappearing in it. (*BW*, pp. 133–34)

We should therefore note, as a sort of conclusion to this first examination of Heidegger's notion of the relation, that because of its displaced and decentered self-relation, the relation as *Verhältnis* or *Bezug* not only is a double relation of an ontologically stratified duplicity but also is marked by undecidability. As we were able to see, this undecidability always springs from the re-mark of the unconcealed by the concealed. In fact, the *Verhaltenheit* of the *Verhältnis* results in the fact that the letting-be of fundamental comportment is especially and always first the concealment of what happens to be revealed. Before attempting the impossible and inadmissible task of formalizing the movement that characterizes the relation, that is, Being itself, I am going to take up again the whole preceding problematic of the relationship between Being and Dasein in terms of the way Heidegger discusses it when he explores the relations between mortal man and the Earth.[7]

II

According to Heidegger in *Erläuterungen zu Hölderlins Dichtung* (Commentaries on Hölderlin's poetry), man is the one who must bear witness to his belonging-to (*Zugehörigkeit*) the Earth. This testimony "occurs through the creation of a world and its ascent, and likewise through the destruction of a world and its decline."[8] What then is this belonging-to and how does Heidegger conceive it?

The most originary conception of the essence of man, more fundamental than the rational or theological definition, is, according to Heidegger, a conception claimed by Being (illuminating itself in beings) during the morning of Western destiny: "[the 'Greek' essence of man] unfolds historically as something fateful, preserved in Being and dispensed by Being, without ever being separated from Being."[9] According to this destiny, man, joined to Being, belongs in a remarkable way to the totality of what is: it is precisely *man* who, by "illuminating, apprehending, and thus gathering, lets what is present as such become present in unconcealment" (*EGT*, p. 38). As Heidegger says in "Aletheia," the relation of humans to the clearing of Being lies in the fact that "they are luminous in their essence" (*EGT*, p. 120).

In particular, man realizes this relation to Being by allowing the Earth to be disclosed in a world. By means of this revelation, man is the inheritor of all things and belongs to the Earth. Man testifies to this belonging to the Earth by being capable of death. But what does being mortal mean? In "Building, Dwelling, Thinking," Heidegger says: "The mortals are the human beings. They are called mortals because they can die. To die means to be capable of death *as* death" (*PLT*, p. 150). And what does being capable of death *as* death mean? In "The Thing," Heidegger makes the following response:

To die means to be capable of death as death. Only man dies. The animal perishes. It has death neither ahead of itself nor behind it. Death is the shrine of Nothing [*Schrein des Nichts*], that is, of that which in every respect is never something that merely exists, but which nevertheless presences, even as the mystery of Being itself. As the shrine of Nothing, death harbors within itself the presencing of Being. As the shrine of Nothing, death is the shelter of Being. We now call mortals mortals—not because their earthly life comes to an end, but because they are capable of death as death. Mortals are who they are, as mortals, present in the shelter of Being [*Gebirg des Seins*]. They are the presencing relation to Being as Being [*Sie sind das wesende Verhältnis zum Sein als Sein*]. (*PLT*, pp. 178–79)

The belonging of humans to the Earth lies not only in their allowing the Earth to be illuminated in a world but also in their furnishing of a shelter for the revealed Earth. This shelter is precisely death. By dying, man offers a crypt to the Earth unconcealed in the openness of a world. Thereby, he remains faithful to the Earth, which is nothing other than its own withdrawal into unconcealment. Man's finitude, namely, his being capable of death as death, is destined by the Earth. His finitude becomes then the *Gebirg des Seins*, its own shelter, its own withdrawal.

When Heidegger, however, writes in "Building, Dwelling, Thinking" that man dies "continually, as long as he remains on earth, under the sky, before the divinities," man's death is still being thought as a function of the Earth revealed as the fourfold (*Geviert*) (*PLT*, p. 150). The fourfold is the pre*sent* articulation of the world, the world that itself represents the Earth's illumination. Heidegger says in "The Thing," "When we say mortals, we are then thinking of the other three along with them by way of the simple oneness of the four" (*PLT*, p. 179). These other three are the earth, the sky, the divinities; with them, man participates in the fourfold of the world. In other words, as Dasein determined by its being-in-the-world, man dies continuously. The world of the fourfold is, as I mentioned, the clearing and illumination of the Earth. In this world, the Earth appears as the fourfold of the earth and sky, of the humans and divinities. And the Earth's appearance as the fourfold will become folded back again into itself, into this same Earth, in order to be sheltered there. (On this subject we should consult "The Origin of the Work of Art.")

This double movement affecting the earth-world relation holds as well for the relations between the four parts of the fourfold. Before demonstrating this, we must note first that Heidegger conceives the belonging-together of the four parts of the fourfold in terms of reflection.

Earth and sky, divinities and mortals—being at one with one another of their own accord—belong together by way of simpleness of the united fourfold. Each of the four mirrors in its own way the presence of the others. Each therewith reflects itself in its own way into its own, within the simpleness of the four. This mirroring does not portray a likeness. The mirroring, lighting each of the four, appropriates their own presencing into the simple belonging to one another [*Das Spiegeln ereignet, jedes der Vier lichtend, deren eigenes Wesen in die einfältige Vereinigung zueinander*]. (*PLT*, p. 179)

How does the continuous death of man take place in the reflecting play of the fourfold? By re-*flecting* the presence of the other three parts: the immortals, the sky, and the earth. Death therefore is the specifically human way that enables the other three to reach what is proper to them, while man discovers what is proper to him by dying in the re-flection of the other three. Thus the fact of being able to die as death is an essence that is sent back to man by way of the other three. This mirror-play of the fourfold, instead of elevating man to the status of an autonomous subject reflecting itself in a homogeneous reflection, can enter into its own essence only by means of his own self-effacement in the letting-be of the others. This self-effacing movement, which characterizes the relation of man to the other three parts, holds as well for each part. Each of them has a particular manner of self-effacement by means of letting the others be, and therefore by means of being re-flected, by the others, into what is its own.

How are we to understand, then, the whole play of the fourfold? Heidegger writes:

Mirroring in this appropriating-lighting way, each of the four plays to each of the others. The appropriative mirroring sets each of the four free into its own, but it binds these free ones into the simplicity of their essential being towards one another.

The mirroring that binds into freedom is the play that betroths each of the four to each through the enfolding clasp of their mutual appropriation [*aus dem faltenden Halt der Vereignung*]. None of the four insists on its own separate particularity. Rather, each is expropriated, within their mutual appropriation, into what is proper to it, its own [*zu einem Eigenen enteignet*]. This expropriative appropriation [*enteignende Vereignen*] is the mirror-play [*das Spiegel-Spiel*] of the fourfold. Out of the fourfold, the simple onefold of the four is ventured. (*PLT*, p. 179; translation modified)

The reflecting play of the fourfold's four parts is identical to the movement that characterizes the relation of Being as a relation to its appearance in its own openness, that is, as appearing as comportment and as the whole of what is joined. Thus this play must be understood as a expropriative mutual appropriation. Through this play, as we have seen, each of the four parts acquires what is its own by a reflection that lets the others be. Through self-effacement, by becoming the mirror for the other, the self is sent back, by this other, to what is properly its own. The proper (or what is one's own) therefore is never constituted by speculative reflection; there is propriety in the fourfold only insofar as there is always already expropriation. Instead of reflecting the parts into themselves, the mirror-play of the fourfold dislocates them.

This mirror-play, a play of expropriative mutual appropriation, is a play that every process of propriety presupposes. Something can become "properly" proper only by abstracting from this originary play. Thus, the play of fourfold, which is the Earth revealed and concealed as world (and nevertheless refolded again back into the Earth), is not only a play of relations decentered in their very structure but also and especially a play preceding every reflective and speculative movement. This mirror-play of the relation (of *Bezug* or *Verhältnis*), appearing here as the openness of the world, is nothing less than what Heidegger attempts to think as the complex simplicity of thought as this relation itself. In order to demonstrate this, it is necessary first to re-legate, re-flect, re-fold, the play of the world, the mirror-play, into what it brings to appearance, into the Earth, therefore, into Being.

III

We turn therefore to " ... Poetically Man Dwells ... ," to the "between," to the *Zwischen* or *entre-deux*, of the earth and sky. From this "between" as *dimension*, man lifts his gaze to the heavens. This span, this diametrical measure of dimension, opens what we traditionally call the space where the sky and the earth come to be opposed. "Man does not undertake this spanning," says Heidegger, "just now and then; rather, man is man at all only in such spanning" (*PLT*, p. 221). By dwelling between the sky and the earth, man actualizes his very relation to Being. Because of this, we are now going to have to interrogate how "relation" and "between" communicate. Man actualizes the relation to Being (to the Being of the relation) by remaining in between the sky and the earth, or again, by participating in the double "between" of the fourfold. We must try then to conceive this "communication" in its greatest generality. The relation and the "between" can each in turn, however, be thought only in a singular way. Will it be necessary then to proceed by generalizing on the basis of the whole of all the particular manifestations of the relation and the "between"? Certainly not. This procedure would amount to reducing the relation and the "between" to their most empty concepts. Before sketching an answer to these questions, I shall begin by analyzing a particular case of communication between the relation and the "between," the *logos*.

In the section of *Being and Time* entitled "The Concept of Logos," Heidegger determines this primary mode of being-in-the-world as an essentially aphonic *apophansis* (a letting something be seen, a making manifest). The *logos* is also said to let "something be seen in its *togetherness* with something—letting it be seen *as* something" (*BT*, p. 56). Consequently, the apophantic function is doubled by a synthetic function. This double function of the *logos*, simultaneously apophantic and synthetic, according to Heidegger, positively binds together all the equivocal significations of this term. In the later essay "Logos," where Heidegger continues to penetrate the double nature of the original meaning of the *logos*, the primordial relation of man and being appears as a speaking, a discourse, a recounting—all terms that translate the Greek term *legein*. In "On the Being and Conception of *Physis* in Aristotle's *Physics* B, 1," Heidegger translates the word "legein" with the German "lesen": gathering or collecting.[10] In fact, the literal usage of "legein" denoted leading the scattered and its multiplicity back into a unity and thus making manifest what was previously in withdrawal. It denoted letting something be seen in its entry into presence. Heidegger writes:

In the Greek definition of the essence of the human being, *legein* and *logos* mean the relation on the basis of which what is present gathers itself for the first time as such around and for human beings. And only because human beings *are* insofar as they relate to beings as beings, unconcealing and concealing them, can they and must they have the "word," i.e., speak of the being of beings. But the words that language uses are only fragments that have precipitated out of the word, and from them humans can never find their way to beings or find the path back to them, unless it be on the basis of *legein*. Of itself *legein* has nothing to do with saying and with language. Nonetheless, *if* the Greeks conceive of saying as *legein*, then this implies an interpretation of the essence of word and of saying so unique that no later "philosophy of language" can ever begin to imagine its as yet unplumbed depths.[11]

This gathering at work in *legein* is to be understood as a "letting-lie-together-before" that aims at a "letting-lay-out-together-before." On the basis of the novel translation of *legein* by the German *legen*, to lay, Heidegger notes in "Logos": "Laying, as *legein*, simply tries to let what of itself lies together here before us, *as* what lies before, into its protection, a protection in which it remains laid down" (*EGT*, pp. 62–63). As *lesendes Legen*, as a laying that simultaneously gathers, *legein* genuinely conforms to its essence only on the condition of not being reduced to a subjective and arbitrary act of man. There is true *legein* only as authentic listening to the *logos*. "If there is to be proper hearing, mortals must have already heard the *logos* with an attention [*Gehör*] which implies nothing less than their belonging [*gehören*] to the *logos*" (*EGT*, p. 67).

   Legein can always be only a "letting-lie-together-before" of what the *logos* has always already gathered. Because of this prior gathering in the *logos*, the *legein* of the mortals cannot be reduced to simple understanding; it consists in a comportment (*Verhalten*), itself constituted by the relation (*Verhältnis*) of mortals and Being. *Legein*, says Heidegger, is a comportment that adheres in the sojourn of the mortals (*das sich im Aufenthalt der Sterblichen hält*), who are authentic only on the condition of their having been destined by Being. Only then can man discover a stay (*Halt*) by which he "is brought into a firm relation [*Bezug*] and given a basis."[12]

   In "On the Being and Conception of *Physis* in Aristotle's *Physics* B, 1," does not Heidegger recall the original signification of *logos* (insofar as it depends upon the root *legein*) as *Verhältnis*, as the relation as such? "What does *logos* mean? In the language of Greek mathematics the word '*logos*' means the same as 'relation' and 'proportion.' Or we say 'analogy,' taken as 'correspondence,' and by this we mean a definite kind of relation, a relation of relations; but with the word 'correspondence' we do not think of language and speech."[13] Thus, the *legein* of the mortals, which distinguishes their relation to Being on the condition of having its stay (*Halt*) in a comportment (*Verhalten*) destined by Being, is literally a relation to the relation that is the *logos*. This relation of *legein* to *logos*, the relation of the relation to the relation, is not one of imitation. Insofar as the *legein* of humans is appropriated to *homologein*, it remains sheltered in and by the *logos. Ereignis* mutually appropriates: the mortals' *legein* is sheltered in the *logos*, while the *legein* itself is the illumination of the *logos*. Even though every (human) relation to the relation of relation (therefore, to the *logos*) is thus also a function of the *legein* of the mortals, this dependence does not transform the *logos* into an imitation of human *legein*. This dependence, furthermore, hardly implies that the *legein* represents a mere imitation of the *logos*. Therefore Heidegger can conclude: "If this is so, then neither can *logos* be the overcoming of mortal *legein*, nor can *legein* be simply a copying of the definitive *logos*. Then whatever essentially occurs in the *legein* of *homologein* and in the *legein* of the *logos* has a more primordial origin—and this in the simple milieu between both" (*EGT*, p. 75).

Let us recapitulate before proceeding to the analysis of this simple milieu. By trying to formalize the "logic" of the relation, I have extricated the mirror-play of the expropriative mutual appropriation constitutive either of the fourfold or of the relation of man to the Earth. Characterizing the relation, this mirror-play, in which I have also emphasized the dissymmetrical doubling, can be read in the following ways. First, the action of relating to the *legein* (as the relation of *homoiosis* to Being) is the dissimulating clearing of the relation to relations that is the *logos*. Second, the *logos* as a relation of relations is the shelter that the mortal *legein* relinquished in order to return to it. By a sort of unfortunate conceptual coincidence the preceding statements can easily be understood with a speculary if not speculative content. To do so, however, would be to misunderstand them. For the *logos* is nothing like an abstract universal; it manifests itself always (*es gibt*) and only in an extreme singularity (*in schärfster Vereinzelung*). It must never be confused with the *legein* as such or in the dialectical form of a concrete universal. Just like the relations between the *logos* and the human *legein*, the relations between the two stated propositions regarding the formal "logic" of the relation, instead of overlapping each other, differ. Consequently, it will be necessary to pay attention to what distinguishes them in their mutual referral and to attempt to think the fundamental dissymmetry that they articulate. This, then, leads me to the "simple milieu" between *legein* as *Verhalten* and the *logos* as *Verhältnis*.

We recall that Heidegger, in particular in the later work *Identity and Difference*, emphasizes the necessity of thinking the relation between Being and man as such, but not on the basis of either Being or man. Earlier, in *Being and Time*, when defining the nature of being-in (*In-Sein*), Heidegger stresses that this mode of the Being of Dasein must not be confused with a property "that is effected, or even just elicited, in a present-at-hand subject by the 'world's' Being-present-at-hand." Heidegger continues:

> But in that case, what else is presented with this phenomenon than the *commercium* which is present-at-hand *between* a subject present-at-hand and an Object present-at-hand? Such an interpretation would come closer to the phenomenal content if we were to say that *Dasein is the Being* of this "between." Yet to take our orientation from this "between" would still be misleading. For with such an orientation we would also be covertly assuming the entities between which this "between," as such, "is," and we would be doing so in a way which is ontologically vague. The "between" is already conceived as the result of the *convenientia* of two things that are present-at-hand. (*BT*, p. 170)

The notion of the "between" therefore can be contested since it cannot be thought without implicitly referring to the things between which this "between" establishes itself. This line of reasoning is confirmed by Heidegger's rejection of all generalizing thought. The "between" as such therefore does not allow itself to be conceived. But do these valuable objections concerning the task of thinking the mode of Being of the being-in remain pertinent here, where the issue is one of determining the relation between Being and man as such, where the issue is one of thinking the "simple milieu" between *legein* as *homologein* and the *legein* of the *logos*? Can we still oppose the same argument of an ontologically indeterminate presupposition to the attempt to clarify the relation as such? By thinking the relation as such, are we not already moving well within the whole analytic of Dasein and its aim of a fundamental ontology?

　　In fact, the task of conceiving the "simple milieu" between the mortal *homologein* and the relation of relations of the *logos* is susceptible to the preceding objections only up to a certain point. Certainly, as the "between," the relation as such always remains relative to that between which it takes place. The poles of this "between," however, would be no longer beings. The "between" as such, the very matter of thought, is a "between" between the relation of mortals to Being and the relation of relations of the *logos*. The "between" therefore is relative only to what is of the same nature as it, to the "between." This relativity is not misleading; it only testifies to the finite nature of the relation considered in its greatest generality. The "simple milieu," then, is what differs essentially, insofar as it is the "more primordial origin," from what it produces, while existing as a finite origin consisting of the same nature as that between which it "is." This "simple milieu" as the relation between the *legein* of the mortals and the *legein* of the *logos* is the *logos* (itself) as the relation of relations, precisely because of this finitude. The *logos* as the "between" is the *différant*, the other of/in the same (*Selbe*). This milieu, Heidegger says, is the "more primordial origin" of the *legein* as comportment (*Verhalten*) and of the *logos* as relation (*Verhältnis*). But it is this origin only insofar as the *legein* and the *logos*, to which it gives way, are the very dissimulation of this "simple milieu." Once more, the "logic" of the mirror-play, such as the discussions of the fourfold and of the relations between man and Being made clear, turns out to constitute as well the thought of the "simple milieu," the thought of the *logos* as such. Because the issue here is to think Being as the "between," we are going to see that Heidegger will soon "simplify" this logic of the mirror (which must not be confused with a specular reflection) in order to unify it with what he calls the "trait."

Before demonstrating this, however, we shall pause for a moment and try to think the *milieu* as such. Immediately, the milieu must be distinguished from what it is not, and here we shall make use of "What Are Poets For?" Heidegger's "simple milieu" must not be confused with Rilke's "unheard-of Open." Insofar as it is Being thought within the horizon of the forgetfulness of Being, Rilke's "unheard-of Open" abstracts from the whole of beings in order to represent the milieu of attraction that Being has for beings, the milieu that puts beings in equilibrium and that mediates them within the draft of the "whole *Bezug*" (*PLT*, p. 105). Despite its invisibility, this milieu or Open is still a milieu belonging to the order of the heart, to the order of interiority where the things of the world come to lose what opposes this order in order to be elevated into the undivided presence of the *Erinnerung* of all exteriority; it is therefore not the openness that the "simple milieu" represents for Heidegger. Instead of being openness in the sense of *Unverborgenheit*, Rilke's "unheard-of Open" is therefore "what is closed up, unlightened, which draws on in boundlessness" (*PLT*, p. 106). Contrary to the "unheard-of Open," in which Rilke turns subjective experience into a reversal of consciousness, the "simple milieu" cannot be the object of any sort of immediate encounter. Since it is an origin that always reveals itself only in its dissimulating effects, the "simple milieu" lets itself neither be felt right on the body nor be apprehended intellectually; the experience of the simple milieu, according to Heidegger, is possible only in the *Dichtung* of thought.

Thus, for example, in "'Wenn wie am Feiertage'" ("As on a holiday . . . "), Heidegger describes the extremely mediated relations that the poet (the intermediary between the people and the heavens) maintains with the immediate, with the "simple milieu" from which all mediation flows: "Since neither the humans nor the divinities ever happen to fulfill by themselves the immediate relation to the Sacred, the humans are in need of the divinities and the heavens are in need of the mortals."[14] By means of the love that mediates the humans and the divinities, the latter "do not precisely belong to themselves but to the sacred, which is for them the rigorous essence of mediation, the law" (*EHD*, p. 69). Thereby expropriated, the divinities send to the poetic mediator "den losgebundenen Blitz," the liberating lightning bolt that enables the immediate to be said by letting it be in its fundamental inaccessibility (*EHD*, p. 70). By means of "the sweetness of the mediate and mediating speech," the poets "must leave to the immediate its immediacy and however at the same time assume its mediation as the Unique" (*EHD*, p. 71). Such is the task incumbent upon the poets: to remain in relation "to the highest mediators."

That the Sacred would be then confined to a mediation by god and the poets, and gives birth therefore to the hymn, this precisely threatens to pervert the very Being of the Sacred. The immediate becomes thereby mediate. Because the hymn awakens only with the awakening of the Sacred, the mediate comes from the immediate itself. (*EHD*, pp. 72–73)

Let us return then to Rilke's "unheard-of Open": it appears now that this Open is an immediate transformed into the mediate, the very contrary of the immediate, the very contrary of all mediation. However, in the speech of an authentic poet like Hölderlin, as Heidegger says, mediation lets the immediate be. It lets the "the terror of immediacy be" without turning it into its contrary (*EHD*, p. 71). Based on the model of authentic poetry, the *dichtendes Denken* that is called to think the "simple milieu" (the "between" or the relation as such) has the purpose of letting these be and not transmuting them into their contrary: to think them in a way that does not confuse them with what they mediate, with what in them and by them appears in order to obfuscate them as the origin, to think them in such a way that they are not changed into empty and abstract universals, to think them, instead, in their essential finitude.

IV

Defined by Heidegger as "the richest and most prodigious event: in it the history of the Western world comes to be bourne out," metaphysics is not dashed into nullity by the phenomenological *destruction* of the history of philosophy (*EGT*, p. 51). Just as the extreme forgetfulness of Being signals toward *Ereignis*, Heidegger's thought can only wish to refold the truth of metaphysics into the truth of Being. The issue, indeed, is to reinscribe the discourse of metaphysics by refolding it into what Heidegger, in "The Anaximander Fragment," calls the thought of Being as the most original mode of *Dichten*. The thought of the "simple milieu," of the "between," of the relation as such, is precisely the thought that must poetize on the riddle of Being (*am Rätsel des Seins dichtet*) (*EGT*, p. 58). The saying more essential than the saying of metaphysics applies itself, from *Being and Time* up to *On Time and Being*, to the task of weaving a discourse upon Being *as* Being, that is, a discourse that refuses to think what is proper to Being on the basis of being. To cite "The Anaximander Fragment," this discourse would return from the modern determination of Being as presence (*Präsenz*) in representation (*Repräsentation*), from Being as the presence of representational thinking (*Vorstellen*), to a more primordial determination of Being as *Anwesen*, as *Gegenwart* (*EGT*, pp. 56–57). Thus neither *Anwesen* nor *Gegenwart* should be translated by "presence." But worse still would be a confusion of *Anwesen* with an immediate *Gegenwart*. As Heidegger notes in *On Time and Being*:

The present in the sense of presence [*Anwesen*] differs so vastly from the present in the sense of the now that the present as presence can in no way be determined in terms of the present as the now. The reverse would rather seem possible. . . . But we have so far omitted showing more clearly what the present [*Gegenwart*] in the sense of presence means. Presence determines Being in a unified way as presencing and allowing-to-presence, that is, as unconcealing. What matter are we thinking when we say presencing? To presence [*Anwesen*] means to last [*Wahren*]. But we are too quickly content to conceive lasting as mere duration [*Anwahren*], and to conceive duration in terms of the customary representation of time as a span of time from one now to a subsequent now. To talk of presencing, however, requires that we perceive biding and abiding in lasting as lasting in present being. What is present concerns us, the present [*Gegenwart*], that is: what, lasting, comes towards us, us human beings.[15]

This determination of Being as *Anwesen* still speaks the language of philosophy, because *Anwesen* is a more primordial determination of presence thought traditionally on the basis of a now, and because man, when he encounters what Being brings forward in *Anwesen*, is also determined from the perspective of a humanism more fundamental than metaphysical humanism. This determination of Being as such, as *Anwesen*, also already speaks the *other* language that, as Heidegger says in a 1949 note to "The Letter on Humanism," remains always in the background.[16] By thinking Being as *Anwesen*, on the basis of what Being is *not*, Heidegger weaves the background language that represents thoughtful *Dichtung* about the enigma of Being.

If we look at Heidegger's "Anaximander Fragment," we can make one or two features of the notion of *Anwesen* clear. There Heidegger says, "Presencing [*Anwesen*], in relation to what is present [*Anwesende*], is always that in accordance with which what is present comes to presence" (*EGT*, p. 48). There is no doubt that the relation in question here does not designate the foundation of what is pre*sent* (*Anwesende*) in a greater and more primordial presence. In relation to the pre*sent* that comes forth, presencing (*Anwesen*) is not to be confused with a full or living presence. Likewise, what is pre*sent* (*Anwesende*) is not therefore already present. The relation between pre*sent* and pre*sence* is a relation of unconcealment, the manifestation into the unhidden. Presencing, however, unveiling itself as what is present, is not unveiled as such. Presencing absents itself in its unconcealment. It is its own absenting in the very act of revealing. "What is for the time being present, what presently is, comes to presence out of absence [*Abwesen*]," Heidegger says (*EGT*, p. 37). In short, *there is* presence only on the basis of ab*sence*, a pre*sence* unconcealing and concealing itself in what is pre*sent* and in what is ab*sent* (*Abwesendes*).

Yet presencing is not unveiled only under the form of the opposition pre*sent*-ab*sent*. It is as well the very clearing where this appearing takes place. "*Presencing brings unconcealment along with itself.* Unconcealment itself is presencing. Both are the Same, though they are not identical" (*EGT*, p. 55). And that is not all: as unconcealment and the openness of all appearing, presencing is also its own dissimulation, the closing of its opening. Pre*sence* is thus also the absence of unconcealment, an absence that is not "simply absentness; rather, it is a *presencing*, namely, that kind in which the *absencing* (but not the absent thing) is present."[17]

Presencing is double (*zwei* or *zweifach*) in a double sense. First, it is double by relating to what the absent and the present bring to light, thereby obfuscating presencing itself. Second, it is double in that it is then again the openness and the closure of its own appearing in the dyad of the present and the absent. Although two times double, presencing is only one (*einfältig*). Revealing itself according to this double trace (*Spur*), presencing is the unitary fold (*Einfalt*). Presencing, manifesting itself according to the double trace as the unitary fold, comes to language as the self-relation to what is present. This relation (*Beziehung*), says Heidegger, is unique (*eine Einzige*). It remains "altogether incomparable to any other relation. It belongs to the uniqueness of Being itself" (*EGT*, p. 52). This relation is presencing itself. Illuminating itself according to the double trace, the relation, nevertheless, does not appear as such. It implies in no way, Heidegger says, that "difference appears as difference" (*EGT*, p. 51). The relation, difference as such that never appears as such, remains yet to be thought.

Let us begin by considering the relation of presencing to itself in the double trace by which it is manifested in self-reservation. The double way in which presencing appears, either as the present and the absent, or as the very clearing of this manifestation, is the same. The question of the relation, then, is stated as follows: How is the same related to itself?

The same, we note immediately, is clarified by what Heidegger designates under equiprimordiality (*Gleichursprünglichkeit*). This equiprimordiality defines the *plural* ontological characteristics of an original irreducible phenomenon. In *Being and Time*, we see that the multiplicity of these characteristics must not be derived from a simple primal ground. This multiplicity is constitutive (*BT*, p. 170). How are we to think the relation that governs the plural traits of an original irreducible phenomenon, if these traits are equiprimordial with each other?

Heidegger conceives the relation as a relation of correlation (*Wechselbezug*). After *Being and Time*, he still specifies this relation as a being "mutually inclined toward each other" (*EGT*, p. 114). Being mutually inclined toward each other in a relation of *Gegenwendigkeit*, the traits of the same constitute no circular reciprocity. Since it is an always undecidable relation (and, consequently, always susceptible to neutralization or even to sublation), this same, characterized by *Gegenwendigkeit*, accommodates itself to each side of the indecision. It leans toward the side of the *Zuneigung* (*philia*), to inclination, as in "Aletheia," or else to the side of *Gegenwendigkeit* in the strict sense, to the striving against the other (*neikos*), as can be seen in "The Origin of the Work of Art." These two possibilities, which distinguish the correlating relation of the traits of the same, are the same as each other only on the condition of being dissymmetrical. This principle is valid all the more for the relation of the double trace to itself in the unitary fold of presencing. The dissymmetry of this duplicity explains why exactly presencing can be revealed by a trace that simultaneously dissimulates it. Is not presencing as relation *and* difference, then, a duplicity governed by this law of dissymmetry? What are we to conclude when we take account of the *zuneigende Gegenwendigkeit* or the *gegenwendige Zuneigung* that characterizes the dissymmetrical self-relation of the doubly articulated presencing, or yet the self-relation of the same or of the trace always double? According to Heidegger, from taking this into account "the simplicity of this essence [*die Einfalt ihres Wesens*]" necessarily follows.[18] But how are we to understand the simplicity of the fold of the double trace or of the twice-folded presencing? How are we to think this *Einfalt*, preserving its essential dissymmetry and not reducing it to a unity of reciprocity and circular exchange? To answer these questions, it will be necessary to outline briefly the problem of truth in Heidegger.

In fact, the double articulation of presencing as what is simultaneously present and absent in the clearing of Being, *and* as this clearing dissimulating itself, is nothing other than the actualization of *aletheia*. According to its "logic," presencing is marked by what Heidegger calls the *Grundzug*, the fundamental trait. This trait is the trait of unconcealment-concealment. In "Aletheia," Heidegger writes about the word *a-letheia*:

"By the manner of its saying, the Greek announces that concealing—and therefore at the same time remaining unconcealed—exercises a commanding preeminence over every other way in which what is present comes to presence. The fundamental trait of presencing itself is determined by remaining concealed and unconcealed" (*EGT*, pp. 106–7).

Aletheia designates nothing other than the fundamental trait. This fundamental trait is, as Heidegger notes in "The Anaximander Fragment," the trait pure and simple, the *Zug* of the early illumination of Being. The aletheic trait is the most primordial unconcealment-reconcealment, *Ereignis* in its greatest simplicity. According to the "logic" of the fundamental trait, however, its unconcealment as Being, as presencing, is of such a sort "that thinking simply does *not* pursue it" (*EGT*, p. 26). Between two "veilings," between the primordial hiddenness and the hiddenness that follows the unhiddenness, the unveiled trait not only is double but also is folded unequally. Because the trait in its self-relation does not overlap with itself, because it is not adequate to itself, the unveiled trait is folded back into what is veiled. What prevails in the trait is its *re-trait*, its withdrawal.

Heidegger, in "The Anaximander Fragment," refers to the trait as a sign: "As it reveals itself in beings, Being withdraws. Being thereby holds to its truth and keeps to itself. This keeping to itself is the way it reveals itself early on. Its early sign is *A-letheia*. As it provides the unconcealment of beings it founds the concealment of Being" (*EGT*, p. 26). The aletheic trait is dominated by this "keeping to itself," by the reconcealment, the veiling, forgetfulness, and so on. The trait is no longer simple; it is unitary only on the condition of being thereby unequally refolded. Revealed in the "early hours" of Western destiny as Being in order immediately to go back into forgetfulness, this trait is presencing as relation *and* difference, and is therefore the relation as such, the difference as such. At its deepest level, this trait is *only* the "as" as such.

Are there any means left by which to excavate the fold of the trait and its unequal overlapping in the retrait? *Fuge*, the fault that joins, the jointure that differs, is another name for the trait. In "Aletheia" Heidegger notes "that the jointure [*Fuge*] thanks to which revealing and concealing are mutually joined [*ineinanderfügen*] must remain the invisible of all invisibles, since it bestows shining on whatever appears" (*EGT*, p. 115). Joined by being turned toward itself, the fold of the *Fuge*, without any appearance at all, produces all appearing. In "The Anaximander Fragment," Heidegger submits this notion to its greatest development. In this context, the *Fuge*, a word Heidegger uses to render *adikia*, designates the fundamental trait that characterizes all *eonta* (all *Jeweiliges*), that is, Being taken between its becoming "present" and its disappearance, which necessarily follows: "Between this twofold absence the presencing of all that lingers occurs. In this 'between' whatever lingers awhile is joined. This 'between' is the jointure. . . . [Likewise] presencing is conjointly disposed towards absence" (*EGT*, p. 41). Heidegger concludes: "Everything that lingers awhile stands in disjunction. To the presencing of what is present, to the *eon* of *eonta*, *adikia* belongs. Thus, standing in disjunction would be the essence of all that is present" (*EGT*, p. 42).

Does this development of the *Fuge* bring anything new to the thought of the trait and its re-trait? Perhaps it permits me to reinforce the nonappearance of the traced trait. These passages demand that we think the provenance of the presencing of the present from (and on the basis of) the *Fuge*. Presencing, doubly folded, is *of* the fold(s). It originates in the *Fuge* between two absentings. *Of* the fold(s), twice folded presencing is refolded, re-folded into the fold of a double absenting. This re-folded fold, or this trait in re-treat, "is" Being itself, Being as presencing such as it was unveiled in order to withdraw itself at the very "daybreak" of Western destiny.

What, therefore, is Being in its relation to man? In these terms the question is inadequate. For Being is precisely this relation, what Heidegger, in *Identity and Difference*, calls difference *as* difference, the *Unter-Schied*. Being is the "Es" of "Es gibt," as Heidegger puts it in *Being and Time*. Difference *as* difference, the "as" as such, "alone grants and holds apart the 'between,' in which the overcoming and the arrival are held toward one another, are borne away from and toward each other" (*ID*, p. 65). Difference *as* difference, the "as" as such, is the "between" of the advent of the difference between Being and beings, the advent of the difference between the present and the absent, only insofar as it is of the re-fold, only insofar as it is dissymmetrically impressed upon itself. Are not these unequal proportions that we have been considering, difference *as* difference, fundamentally also *rhythmos*? Like *Ereignis*, rhythm is the self-vibrating domain (*der in sich schwingende Bereich*) (*ID*, p. 38), the pulsing domain, that is, the relation "which originally and always comes to vibrate [*Schwingen*] as a comportment [*Verhalten*]" (*BW*, p. 124; translation modified). The most original comportment, however, is none other than language: "the most delicate and fragile vibration" (*ID*, p. 38; translation modified).

(1980)

Translated by Leonard Lawlor

11

Joining the Text

> But because the word is shown in a different, higher rule, the relation to
> the word must also undergo a transformation. *Saying* attains to
> a different articulation, a different *melos*, a different tone.
> —Martin Heidegger

In an article entitled "The *Retrait* of Metaphor," Jacques Derrida argues that within a certain context (but only in the limits of this context), the French word *retrait* is "the most proper to capture the greatest quantity of energy and information in the Heideggerian text." *Retrait*, having a variety of meanings in French, such as retrace, withdrawal, recess, retraction, and retreat, translates (without translating) Heidegger's notion of a withdrawal of Being (*Entziehung, Entzug*).[1] If this word became indispensable to Derrida when trying to account for Martin Heidegger's statements on metaphor, it becomes indispensable to me as well when trying to assess, as economically as possible, the nature of the relation between Heidegger and Derrida. Considering that the very nature of this relation is far from obvious, and that even the discursive levels of such a comparison of these two philosophers have still to be determined, the Heideggerian notions of trait (*Zug*) and retrait (*Entzug*) promise the most effective treatment of this relation. Let us then attempt to understand how the word *retrait* (*Zug-Entzug*) structures Heidegger's text, as well as the text of Derrida's exchange with Heidegger.

In the first place, what is a trait or a *retrait*? The trait is *retrait*, the trait is withdrawn, writes Derrida: It signifies an "essential and in itself double, equivocal movement."[2] But what are the different moments that characterize this essentially plural word? Let us try to account for these moments in a stepwise fashion so that the reasoning will be quite clear.

First of all, the word trait (*Zug*) refers to the tracing of a way or a rift (*Riss*) that, as an in-between (*Zwischen*), opens a first relation (*Bezug*). The trait accomplishes the differential mark that allows language to name and to put into relation what it names. Yet the trait is nothing before the tracing it achieves or before what it subsequently brings into relation. The trait is not independent of what it permits to come into its own.

Second, the trait withdraws, retreats, in the very act of its tracing an in-between for a relation. However, being nothing except what it gives rise to, the trait is not to be mistaken for what it brings forth. Indeed, "the trait is, *a priori*, withdrawal, unappearance, and effacement of its mark in its incision." The trait comes forth only by being blotted out. It *"succeeds only in being effaced (n'arrive qu'à s'effacer)."* "The *re-* of *retrait* is not an accident occurring to the trait."[3] On the contrary, this self-eclipsing of the forthcoming trait characterizes its double and equivocal movement.

Third, the trait cannot simply be identified with this seemingly alternating movement of forthcoming and subsequent extinction, because the retreat of the trait is also what allows the trait to come forward from under its obliteration as *retrait*. Without a retreat of the *retrait*, without a *retrait* of the *retrait*, the trait would not be capable of tracing its self-eclipsing way or of opening in the first place. Derrida writes, "The trait of the incision is . . . veiled, withdrawn, but it is also the trait that brings together and separates [*écarte*] at once the veiling *and* the unveiling, the *withdrawal* and the *withdrawal of the withdrawal*."[4] The trait is always *retrait*, withdrawal. But this withdrawal of the trait does not operate according to a simple structure of ambiguity in a well-equilibrated exchange of opposing meanings; rather it takes place in an essentially dissymmetrical manner. The *re-* of the *retrait* is double since it accounts for both the veiling and the unveiling of the trait. Because the *re-* of the trait as *retrait* dominates its structure, its movements are fundamentally dissymmetrical. Derrida emphasizes this dissymmetry when ascertaining that the trait "withdraws *itself* [*se retire*] but the ipseity of the pronominal *se* (itself) by which it would be related to itself with a trait or line does not precede it and already supposes a supplementary trait in order to be traced, signed, withdrawn, retraced in its turn."[5] The trait does not affect or reflect itself into an identity. Because such a reflection presupposes the supplementary trait that is being brought forth by the trait's withdrawal, the trait is barred forever from itself.

But to what does the word "trait" (and the movements that characterize it) refer in Heidegger's work? As I argued in the previous chapter, the word "trait" gathers Heidegger's most radical developments on Being *as* Being. The question of Being is a question that concerns Being *as such*, the meaning or the truth of Being as never explicitly reflected upon in the history of Western metaphysics. Indeed, Western philosophy, as onto-theo-logy, has always determined Being in terms of what is (*Seiendes*), that is, as just another, although higher, being in the chain of beings. It has thus eluded the question of the ontico-ontological difference, the difference between Being and beings, of Being *as* Being. Contrary to what one may be inclined to think, the question of Being is not just one more philosophical question in a process of escalating abstraction. As a question concerning the ontico-ontological difference itself, it is, rather in a strange way, the last possible *question*.[6] With the insight that metaphysics presupposes the difference between Being and beings without, however, being able to think Being other than just another, although higher, being (as God, the Spirit, etc.), the ontico-ontological difference becomes thematized as such. As the question of the meaning of Being, of Being as Being, this thematization of the difference between Being and beings becomes an interrogation of the very opposition and hierarchy of what constitutes the traditional dyad. Thus the effort to think the meaning of Being as the ontico-ontological difference itself is to think on an altogether different level than the onto-theo-logical determination of Being as an infinite being reigning over all finite beings. With the question of Being as a question of difference as such, notions like opposition and hierarchy cease to be leading categories. The same is true of such dyads as the abstract and the concrete, the universal and the particular, infinity and finitude. As an inquiry into the difference between Being and beings, the question of Being demonstrates the essential finitude of infinity (God as always another, only higher, being) and thus questions its hierarchical status as well as the nature of its difference from finite beings. The question of Being is thus the question of finitude *par excellence*, precisely because it is an investigation into the ontico-ontological difference. Heidegger's subsequent determination of Being in terms of temporality and historicity (*Geschichtlichkeit*), that is, in terms of finitude, is only a consequence of this inquiry into the difference itself.[7] As difference, as *Unter-Schied* (as Heidegger will later spell this word), the meaning of Being or Being *as such* is, then, radically different from a romantic chiasm as an endlessly engendering and procreating gap, as well as from any constituting transcendental in either a Kantian or a Husserlian fashion. The rift of Being (*Fuge des Seins*), instead of *engendering*, finitizes everything that is to be referred to it as to the locus of the thing's coming forth.[8]

This being established, it becomes possible to indicate how Heidegger's most penetrating meditations on Being *as* Being culminate in the idea of the trait. Instead of representing a mere weakness of Western thought, says Heidegger, the obliteration of the question of Being is inscribed in the original event (*Ereignis*), at the dawn of Western metaphysics itself. This event is characterized by the fact that Being originally revealed itself only to withdraw again instantly. The forgetting of Being is, consequently, the very destiny of Being (*Geschick des Seins*). However, this forgetting of Being, which is characteristic of Western man, brings about the danger of a growing alienation from that destiny itself. Hence the necessity of a *step back* in a gesture comparable to Nietzsche's *active forgetfulness*, so that this withdrawal may lift again the original retreat of Being at the moment of its revelation. Such a stepping back, such a withdrawal of withdrawal, is no reflection, as if the original event were something that could be objectified by a subject. It is what Heidegger calls a *Besinnung* or an *Andenken* that allows for the return of the forgotten. Consequently, the question of Being yields to the "double, equivocal movement," or more precisely, to the threefold movement that distinguishes the "logic" of the trait.

But since the forgetting of Being is decreed by Being itself, and since the step back coincides with a listening to Being (*hören auf*), to think the history of the forgetting of Being, as well as to inaugurate a *destruction* of the tradition of this forgetting by Western philosophy, is to think Being as such. And Being as such appears to be "nothing" but this

essentially double movement of its dissimulating disclosure and of its return through a step back.

After this all-too-succinct presentation of Heidegger's question of
Being as the question of the trait, let us linger for a moment upon "The
Anaximander Fragment." In this text, which commonly has been misun-
derstood as a return to a very traditional notion of beginning (since this
fragment is considered to be the oldest of Western thinking), Heidegger,
with an increasing acuteness of vision, risks the statement that Being revealed itself at the origin of Western thought as, precisely, this trait of Being.[9] If Being disclosed itself in a gesture that was simultaneously dissimulating, it is only because Being is the same as the trait as *retrait*. Indeed,
in its greatest simplicity, Being coincides with the trait of a-*letheia*
(truth), wherein the movement of *retrait* is greatest in the very disclosure
of Being. But since Being is "nothing" but this trait itself, Being is, then,
the trait folded back in the very moment of its coming forth, a folding
back that simultaneously lifts the veil of the initial concealment. Being-
as-trait—Being-*as-retrait*. For being what lifts concealment by concealment and what is simultaneously revealed in concealment, Being-*as*-trait
is a trait dissimilar to itself, in which the thrust to disclose never equals
the pulling back into retreat.

Because of this fundamental dissymmetry one may want to call the
trait nonreflexive. Indeed, it will never coincide with itself, for the *re-* of the
trait as *retrait* is always in excess over any possible identity. But to talk here
of reflexivity is shortsighted insofar as reflexivity is a function of a subject-
object relation constitutive of self-consciousness.[10] The "logic" of the trait,
however, precedes and governs all reduction of Being to objectivity and its
subjection to a nonmundane subject of cognition. The trait is in excess
over all self-affection, which itself is the condition of possibility for self-
reflection. For reasons of strategy, however, and within the limits of this
context, I will call this lack of self-coincidence of the trait nonreflexiveness.

By determining the meaning of truth as Being as the trait of Being,
Heidegger's question concerning Being *as* Being (*ens tanquam verum*) appears to be an inquiry into the very structure of thinking and understanding. In his Marburg lectures of winter 1925/26, published as *Logik:
Die Frage nach der Wahrheit* (Logic: The question of truth), Heidegger, attempting to approach the essence of language, determined the primary

structure of understanding as the as-structure (*Als-Struktur*).[11] Yet the question of Being, as a question concerning Being *as such*—the *tanquam* of the *ens tanquam verum*—is "nothing else" but an inquiry into the structure of the *as* as such. In other words, the structure of Being as trait is the *same* as the structure of primary understanding. Thus, the question of Being as the question of the trait coinciding with the structure of thinking leads to a determination of the as-structure as the differential and nonreflexive instance of language. The question of Being and the question of analogy are the same.[12]

However, with the question of Being turning into a question of the *tanquam*, into a question of the smallest philosophical operator, it becomes possible to ascertain that Heidegger's notion of Being and Derrida's notion of text are akin. If the structure of Being is understood according to the "logic" of the trait, Being and text appear to be words that can be exchanged and substituted for one another. The Derridean word *text* is a translation (without translation) of the Heideggerian word *Being*.[13]

By affirming the similarity of Heidegger's notion of Being and Derrida's notion of text, one immediately excludes a variety of definitions of textuality. No doubt, Derrida's notion of text does not refer to the colloquial understanding of the text as a sensible and palpable corpus to be encountered in empirical experience. There is also little doubt that Derrida's notion of text cannot be equated with either an intelligible or an ideal definition (the text as the sum of all the connections between the differential features of the linguistic signs that form a text) or with a dialectical concept according to which the text as "form" would sublate both its sensible and intelligible components. On the contrary, like the notion of Being, the notion of text, as it is employed by Derrida, is rather the result of a transcendental experience of sorts, following the systematic bracketing of all the regions of natural (and even eidetic) experience. Not having been obtained through a factual or regional experience, and thus not having much in common with the object of linguistic or literary studies, the notion of text in Derrida is a *sort* of transcendental concept. Vincent Descombes rightly remarks that Derrida refers to "a *general* experience," "the experience of the *general text*," that is, not to a particular and thus empirical experience. Yet precisely because this general experience is the experience of a nonphilosophical (because nonpresent) thought, the thinking of this experience does escape not only empiricism but "'philosophical empiricism'" as well, as Descombes notes.[14] But then it becomes, strictly speaking, impossible to call such an experience a general, universal, or transcendental experience. And, as a corollary, the object of such an experience cannot claim any universality either. The transcendental experience of the text is, indeed, neither the experience of a universal and eidetic *object* nor simply a repetition of a *transcendental experience* in either a Kantian or a Husserlian sense. The transcendental gesture in Derrida simultaneously escapes the danger of naive objectivism and the value of transcendentality itself. In *Of Grammatology*, Derrida has clearly stated that the thought of the trace, and consequently of the text, can no more "break with a transcendental phenomenology than be reduced to it."[15] The Derridean notion of text, as in the earlier Heideggerian notion of Being, literally "occupies" the locus of the transcendental concept, which is to say that the former is not identical with the latter. The text, like the trace, is to be understood as a pathway (*parcours*) through that locality. Thus, the notion of text corresponds to a transformation of the transcendental concept and of the very locus that it represents. The text is certainly no eidetic object. It has no constitutive function. It is not an a priori condition of possibility for, let us say, signification and meaning. (Nor is it, let us add, a chiasm of engenderment and destruction, precisely because of its structure as a chiastic *invagination*.)[16] Thus, it needs to be emphasized that the notion of text in Derrida can be understood only if one is aware of its function and effects with regard to the transcendental.[17]

Only with this background will it be possible to outline the concrete resemblances of Being and text and to evaluating the specific philosophical problems both notions are addressing. One will certainly not be surprised to learn that this demonstration hinges on Derrida's reading of Mallarmé's textual practice. But before unfolding Derrida's notion of text and textuality, let us briefly question the reasons that make it possible to introduce Mallarmé and his writings in this particular context. The point I will try to make is that the notion of text developed by Mallarmé is a nonempirical concept and operates in the realm of what one calls the transcendental. Moreover, Mallarmé anticipated some of Heidegger's major insights. Instead of giving a detailed demonstration, let us consider only the last paragraphs of Mallarmé's "Notes sur le théatre" (Notes on the theater). Toward the end of this essay, Mallarmé ascertains that for him, who has meditated about men and about himself, there is nothing else in the mind but "an exact account of purely rhythmical motives of being which are the signs by which it can be recognized [*un compte rendu de purs motifs rythmiques de l'être, qui en sont les reconnaissables signes*]."[18] For Mallarmé then, as for Heidegger, Being is neither substance nor form in the sense of *eidos*. It is rhythm. Mallarmé evokes the purely rhythmical motives of Being; Heidegger speaks of "the domain pulsating in itself [*in sich schwingender Bereich*]," of "the moving wave [*bewegende Woge*]," of language as "the all-containing undulation [*alles verhaltende Schwingung*]," and so on.[19] Both mean by "rhythm" an ordered and recurrent alternation. Both evoke what had been considered, until Émile Benveniste's essay "La notion de 'rythme' dans son expression linguistique" (The notion of rhythm in its linguistic expression), its etymological root: *rein* (the regular flow of waves). But both Mallarmé and Heidegger also refer to the genuinely Greek meaning of "rhythm" as the well-proportioned arrangements of parts in a whole. Heidegger writes: "Rhythm, *rhusmos*, does not mean flux and flowing, but rather form [*Fügung*]. Rhythm is what is at rest, what forms [*fügt*] the movement of dance and song, and thus lets it rest within itself. Rhythm bestows rest."[20]

This meaning of *rhuthmos* or *rhusmos*—which, as Benveniste has argued, dates back to the inventors of atomism, Democritus and Leucippus—is equivalent to *schema* and approximately signifies something like form, configuration, disposition. Just as Mallarmé claims to have discovered purely rhythmical motives of Being by meditating on himself and others, so the Greeks employed *rhuthmos* to designate the individually distinctive form of the human character.[21] As Heidegger stressed in his seminar on Heraclitus (1966), this meaning of rhythm as "form" implies a determination of "form" as imprint, seal, and character.[22] Yet, precisely this meaning of rhythm is to be found in what Mallarmé calls *sceau*, *moule*, *coupe*, and so on. Let us quote one example of Being as a mold, drawn from "Solennité" (Solemnity):

Sign! at the central abyss of a spiritual impossibility that nothing is exclusively to all, the divine numerator of our apotheosis, some supreme mold that does not take place insofar as that of any existing object: but, in order to animate a seal in it, it borrows all the scattered, unknown, and richly floating veins, then to forge them.[23]

(Signe! au gouffre central d'une spirituelle impossibilité que rien soit exclusive-
ment tout, le numérateur divin de notre apothéose, quelque suprême moule qui
n'ayant pas lieu en tant que d'aucun objet qui existe: mais il emprunte, pour y
aviver un sceau tous gisements épars, ignorés et flottants selon quelque richesse,
et les forger.)

Because the supreme mold to which Mallarmé refers does not take place
in the guise of an existing object—because this mold does not exist in the
same way as the existing objects (it does *not take place* altogether)—it is
then, like the essence, the truth or meaning of Being, no longer of the order of what is present, that is, just another being. Like Being, the
supreme mold withholds itself in what springs forth from it.

Mallarmé likes to decipher the visible signs of Being as rhythm (*il
me plaît de les partout déchiffrer*). These signs of Being as rhythm are to be
discovered in what Mallarmé designates as "great traits." At the end of
"Notes sur le théatre," we read:

Note that beyond the narration created to imitate life in its confusion and vast-
ness, there are no means by which to theatrically reproduce an action, except to
rediscover by instinct and through elimination one of these great traits, here not
the least pathetic; it is the eternal return of the exile, his heart filled with hope, to
the earth which was forsaken by him but changed into an ungrateful one, now
someone at the point where he must leave it voluntarily this time, where! with a
glance he surveys the illusions suggested to his youth by the beckoning of the na-
tive land.[24]

(Tenez que hors du récit fait à l'imitation de la vie confuse et vaste, il n'y pas de
moyen de poser scéniquement une action, sauf à retrouver d'instinct et par élim-
ination un de ces grands traits, ici non le moins pathétique, c'est l'éternel retour
de l'exilé, coeur gonflé d'espoir, au sol par lui quitté mais changé ingrat, main-
tenant quelconque au point qu'il en doive partir cette fois volontairement, où!
en enveloppant d'un coup d'oeil les illusions suggérés à sa jeunesse par le salut
du lieu natal.)

What then is a "great trait," which, as a sign of Being as rhythm, makes it
possible to stage an action that does not coincide with any mimetic representation of the turmoils of life? As the quoted passage suggests, Mallarmé detects such a non- or pre-mimetic trait in the (rhythmic) motive
of the eternal return of the exiled to a homeland that has become so un-
accommodating that he will, this time, leave it voluntarily. The return to

the homeland, following an exile and preceding another, characterizes this sequence of events as yielding to the double or threefold "logic" of the trait as *retrait*. As a sign of Being, Mallarmé's great trait corresponds to Heidegger's notion of Being as *Zug* and *Entzug*.

In short, then, both Mallarmé and Heidegger understand Being as no longer to be predicated in terms of being (and beings).[25] Both attempt to determine the nature of Being as *don* or *Gabe*, as gift, as an allowing to come forth of what, according to the repetitive and temporal structure of the *rhuthmos*, is folded back in the very moment of its coming forth into presence. With this information at hand, it is possible to infer the concrete similarities between Heidegger's question of Being and Derrida's notion of text. To make my point, I will limit myself to a most concise analysis of Derrida's "The Double Session."

In this essay, Derrida establishes that a text like Mallarmé's "Mimique" deconstructs the Platonic values of truth and reference of mimesis as subject to these values. If "Mimique" does not simply invert the Platonic hierarchy between the original and the copy, mimetic art and the discourse of truth, but undertakes a genuine deconstruction of these values as well as of the very idea of hierarchy, it is not because "Mimique" would be characterized by what has been called literariness since the Russian formalists, but because it is a text in a very particular way. In what follows, I will try to determine as precisely as possible this particular notion of textuality—what I will from now on call the textual instance. According to Derrida, the subjection of mimesis to a horizon of truth is radically displaced at the moment when writing marks and doubles in a certain syntactical operation the marks of the text by means of an undecidable trait. "This double mark escapes the pertinence or authority of truth: it does not overturn it but rather inscribes it within its play as one of its functions or parts."[26] In the context of "The Double Session," the textual mark is determined as a double mark or *re-mark*. But what is a re-mark?

Because "Mimique" does not abolish the differential structure of mimesis in spite of its deconstruction of the Platonic distinctions, it is a simulacrum of Platonism. "Mimique" achieves such a simulacrum not only by means of an extraordinary formal and syntactical *tour de force* but by thematic means as well. The event narrated by the mime of "Mimique" is a hymen, the marriage of Pierrot and Columbine. This marriage culminates in Pierrot's assassination of his wife by tickling her to death (that is to say, by means of a perfect crime, which leaves no traces) and in Pierrot's death in front of the laughing portrait of his victim (a death that will not show any traces either). The two deaths, resulting from an orgastic spasm, represent Pierrot and Columbine's consummation of their marriage. The miming of this event in which nothing has taken place exhibits the textual structure of Mallarmé's "Mimique." As Derrida states, "It is a dramatization which illustrates nothing, which illustrates *the nothing*, lights up a space, re-marks a spacing as a nothing, a blank: white as a yet unwritten page, blank as a difference between two lines" (p. 208). Yet this dramatization is nothing but a staging of the theatrical space itself. What remains when the stage comes to double the stage, when the mimed hymen is nothing but an illustration of the theatrical space itself, that is, a miming of miming, without referent, a miming that mimes only reference, is what Mallarmé calls "the pure medium, of fiction," a "*perpetual allusion without breaking the mirror* (pp. 210–11).

A hymen, at first, names the fusion of two during the consummation of marriage. It signifies the abolition of difference between desire and satisfaction. Moreover, it leads to the suppression of the difference between image and thing, empty signifier and the signified, imitation and the imitated. It leads to a complete confusion of exteriority and interiority. The hymen in Mallarmé's writing produces, according to Derrida, "the effect of a medium. . . . It is an operation that *both* sows confusion *between* opposites *and* stands *between* the opposites 'at once.' What counts here is the *between*, the in-between-ness of the hymen" (p. 212).

But second, for Mallarmé, "the hymen, the consummation of differends, the continuity and confusion of the coitus, merges with what it seems to be derived from: the hymen as protective screen, the jewel box of virginity, the vaginal partition, the fine, invisible veil which, in front of the hystera, stands *between* the inside and the outside of the woman, and consequently between desire and fulfillment" (pp. 212–13). Derrida can thus conclude that "with all the undecidability of its meaning, the hymen only takes place when it doesn't take place, when nothing *really* happens, when there is an all-consuming consummation without violence, or a violence without blows, or a blow without marks, a mark without a mark (a margin), etc., when the veil is, *without being*, torn, for example when one is made to die or come laughing" (p. 213). The manner in which the double structure of the hymen relates to itself is that of a reflection without penetration: "The *entre* of the hymen is reflected in the screen without penetrating it" (p. 215). This reflection without penetration, this doubling without overlaying or overlapping of the hymen, this is what constitutes, as the fictional milieu of Mallarmé's "Mimique," the textual mark as a remark.

If the mime of "Mimique" only imitates imitation, if he copies only copying, all he produces is a copy of a copy. In the same manner, the hymen that comes to illustrate the theatrical space reduplicates nothing but the miming of the mime. Miming only reference, but not a particular referent, Mallarmé keeps the Platonic differential structure of mimesis intact while radically displacing it. Instead of imitating, of referring to a referent within the horizon of truth, the mime mimes only other signs and their referring function. Signs in the text of "Mimique" are made to refer to what according to metaphysics is only derived, unreal, unpresent, that is, to other signs. Such a doubling of the sign, of a sign referring to another sign and to its function of referring, is what Derrida calls re-marking.

"A copy of a copy, a simulacrum that simulates the Platonic simulacrum—the Platonic copy of a copy . . . have all lost here the lure of the present referent and thus find themselves lost for dialectics and ontology, lost for absolute knowledge" (p. 219). This double sign, a sign referring to another sign, reflecting itself in it without penetrating it and without overlaying it, is *the* textual instance. The operation and re-marking that constitutes it is an operation by which what traditionally was conceived of as a mark for a present referent becomes duplicated and refers not to itself but to something similar to it, another mark. This re-marking of the Platonic simulacrum—a scandal in the horizon of truth—gives rise to a *tertium quid*. "*Tertium datur*, without synthesis," writes Derrida (p. 219). It is the textual instance, to be conceived of no longer as yielding to the Platonic opposition of copy and original but as a genuinely third entity.

The textual instance as illustrated by the hymen as a re-mark, as a reflection without penetration, as a duplication without identity, escapes and precedes all ontology of the text. All ontologies of the text, whether they determine text in terms of the sensible, the intelligible, or dialectically as form, remain within the horizon of metaphysics and its Platonic notion of a mimesis subject to truth. The textual instance, on the contrary, as a mimesis of mimesis, as a hymen between mimesis and mimesis, appears as no longer contained in the process of truth. Instead, it is the horizon of truth that is inscribed in textual mimesis. Only an act of violence, either arbitrary or conventional, can make the textual mark signify a referent.

The reason why only violence can transform the textual instance into a Platonic sign or simulacrum, into a sign signifying a referent, lies in the particular nature of the re-mark's undecidability. Note that what Derrida calls the undecidable is called so only "provisionally, analogically" (p. 211). He writes:

"Undecidability" is not caused here by some enigmatic equivocality, some inexhaustible ambivalence of a word in a "natural" language, and still less by some *"Gegensinn der Urworte"* (Abel). In dealing here with *hymen*, it is not a matter of repeating what Hegel undertook to do with German words . . . marveling over that lucky accident that installs a natural language within the element of speculative dialectics. What counts here is not the lexical richness, the semantic infiniteness of a word or concept, its depth or breadth, the sedimentation that has produced inside it two contradictory layers of signification. . . . What counts here is the formal or syntactical *praxis* that composes and decomposes it. . . . [A word like "hymen"] produces its effect first and foremost through the syntax, which disposes the *"entre"* in such a way that the suspense is due only to the placement and not to the content of the words. Through the "hymen" one can remark only what the place of the word *entre* already marks and would mark even if the word "hymen" were not there. (p. 220)

As Aristotle demonstrated, semantic ambiguity can always be sublated or dissolved in a polysemic unity of meaning. Yet the undecidability of the textual instance springs not from any semantic richness but from "the irreducible excess of the syntactic over the semantic." The syntactic in question can be either "'internal,' articulating and combining under the same yoke . . . two incompatible meanings, or 'external,' dependent on the code in which the word is made to function. But the syntactical composition and decomposition of a sign renders this alternative between internal and external inoperative" (p. 221). From everything discussed up to this point, it is obvious that a word like "hymen" has a very specific relation to writing and the text. However, if it doubles the text in Mallarmé's

"Mimique," if it re-marks its textuality, this is not because it would be a totalizing emblem that would, like the romantic image, assume the eschatological function of subduing a text to having its meaning in reflecting itself. If a word like "hymen" can have this specific relation to a text, this is, on the contrary, because it is a textual instance itself. It possesses a structure of re-marking and a syntactically determined undecidability. Thanks to this structure, the textual instance appears folded, as does the text itself when re-marked by such words: "Insofar as the text depends on them, *bends* to them [*s'y plie*], it thus plays a *double scene* upon a double stage. It operates in two absolutely different places at once, even if these are only separated by a veil, which is both traversed and not traversed, *inter*sected [*entr'ouvert*]" (p. 221). To determine with greater precision the textual instance that now appears as a re-mark of syntactical undecidability, let us investigate the nature of the fold of the two heterogeneous marks (the simulacrum and the simulacrum of the simulacrum) that reflect each other without ever penetrating, without ever coinciding with each other.

The double mark that constitutes the textual instance not only no longer refers to any referent, escaping in that manner the Platonic determination of model and copy, but also no longer belongs to the order of the sign, to the order of the signifier and the signified. "In folding it back upon itself, the text thus *parts* (with) reference," writes Derrida (p. 239). In folding itself back upon itself, the textual mark discards at the same time all semiotic function. Yet this does not mean that the textual instance would refer to *itself* (a reflexive pronoun). Precisely because the re-mark maintains the Platonic differential structure of mimesis, it marks not itself but another mark. The re-mark, as well as the folding back of reference upon the text itself, undermines the text's reference to itself as to an ultimate referent. Indeed, if the text became its own referent, as is the case in romantic poetry, the text would remain within a simple inversion of Platonism. Such an inversion, by the way, would be as conventional, say, as the valorization of empiricism. The doubly folded mark of the text is, as I said already, a *tertium quid*.

The textuality of a text is remarked in the fold and in the blank of a re-mark like the word "hymen" only under the condition that the angle and the intersection of the "re-mark that folds the text back upon itself, [does so] without any possibility of its fitting back over or into itself, without any reduction of its spacing" (p. 251). But if the re-mark represents a sort of doubling where the two sides of the fold do not coincide with each other although they mirror each other, the textual instance is not reflexive. It is precisely the excess of reflexivity, the supplement that exceeds what is reflected in the folded mark, that raises it to the status of a textual instance. "The fold is not a form of reflexivity. If by reflexivity one means the motion of consciousness or self-presence that plays such a determining role in Hegel's speculative logic and dialectic, in the movement of sublation (*Aufhebung*) and negativity (the essence is reflection, says the greater *Logic*), then reflexivity is but an effect of the fold as text" (p. 270). The re-mark is a dissymmetrical instance. It is constituted by a supplement that exceeds any self-mirroring of the two sides of the fold. Dissemination, writes Derrida in "Outwork," "is written on the reverse side—the tinfoil—of this mirror" of specular reflection (p. 33).

To get a better understanding of the dissymmetrical and supplementary nature of the nonreflexive folding of the textual instance, it may be useful to circle back to the figure of the hymen, which may have appeared as nothing but a theme in Derrida's reading of Mallarmé. The hymen, as a theme, becomes a sort of totalizing emblem that is thus made to refer back upon itself in a gesture of closure. Indeed, as a supplementary mark the hymen comes to represent metaphorically and metonymically the whole series of double marks that constitute the text of "Mimique." But at the same time, this mark is also only one among the many marks that form the text. The mark of the hymen, consequently, names the whole series of the double marks of the text by tropologically supplementing it while remaining inscribed in it. Yet of the fan (*éventail*), another Mallarméan image, Derrida writes:

This surplus mark, this margin of meaning, is not one valence among others in the series, even though it is *inserted* in there, too. It has to be inserted there to the extent that it does not exist outside the text and has no transcendental privilege; this is why it is always *represented* by a metaphor and a metonymy (page, plume, pleat). But while belonging in the series of valences, it always occupies the position of a supplementary valence, or rather, it marks the structurally necessary position of a supplementary inscription that could always be added to or subtracted from the series. (pp. 251–52)

236 RHYTHM AND ZIGZAG

The supplementary mark, instead of closing the text upon itself, instead of reflecting it into its own as a totalizing image is supposed to do, illustrates nothing but what Derrida calls "the general law of textual supplementarity" (p. 254). The surplus mark re-marks the whole series of the double marks of the text by illustrating what always exceeds a possible closure of the text folded, reflected upon itself. In excess of the text *as a whole* is the text "itself."

Any double mark can, in this manner, represent the exceeding supplement of textuality. Any double mark can represent what makes the totality of all textual instances possible. In other words, any textual instance can assume the function of naming the whole series of the marks of a text insofar as it occupies the position of a supplement to that totality, a supplement that (as the text itself) is the locus of the "engendering" of the whole series. Suffice it to say that this "engenderment" of the whole series by its exceeding supplement is neither that of an emanation or creation of any sort nor a constitution by means of a transcendental instance.

The double mark is folded upon itself in such a manner that what exceeds its reflection becomes the locus of its coming forth; the double mark is abysmally dissymmetrical. In the context of "The Double Session" this may be the most concise determination of a textual instance. Rigorously speaking, only when understanding the notion of text in this manner can the text be said to have any deconstructive properties. If one neglects the fact that *text* is the dissymmetrical excess of the folded mark, one will fall prey to textual fetishism, and one will mistake its operation of deconstruction either for the romantic notion of a chiastic engendering (and destruction, or rather ironization) of the self-reflexive text, or for the dialectic sublation of opposite terms in the reflexive and speculative gesture of the philosophy of identity.

Because the textual instance is determined in terms of supplementarity, of an excess to itself, it will never be able to come into appearance as such. Because of what always exceeds the text as its supplementary scene of "engendering," the text as such necessarily remains concealed. When revealing itself as a whole, as a series of double marks, the text folds itself at once back into what, as a supplementary mark of comprehension, represents tropologically the whence of the whole series. For this very reason, there cannot be a phenomenology of the text. Especially not in the vulgar meaning of "phenomenon." And as little according to the meaning of the Kantian formal concept of phenomenon. But can there be a phenomenology of the text in terms of the phenomenological concept of the phenomenon as "that which shows itself in itself [*das Sich-an-ihm-selbst-Zeigende*]"?[27] To decide upon this extremely delicate question, one would first have to elaborate upon what distinguishes the Heideggerian disclosure of Being in beings from Derrida's determination of the relation of the supplement to the whole that it exceeds. Since I cannot broach here an analysis of the specific similarities and differences between Heidegger's and Derrida's approaches to the problem of transcendental derivation, I limit myself to the recognition that there cannot be a phenomenology of the text, as Derrida states (p. 265), because as a supplement to itself, the text or the re-mark is in constant withdrawal, in constant retreat from itself. It does not exist, or more precisely, it is not. Yet if the text is not, it is precisely because *there is* text. *Il y a* text, *es gibt* text. Derrida notes: "If there were no fold, or if the fold had a limit somewhere—a limit other than itself as a mark . . . —there would be no text. But if the text does not, to the letter, exist, then *there is* perhaps a text. A text one must make tracks with" (p. 270). The textual instance that is never present, but that donates the text, "has no proper, literal meaning; it no longer originates in meaning as such, that is, as the meaning of being" (p. 229). "No present in truth presents itself there, not even in the form of self-concealment" (p. 230). The textual instance, by casting aside reference, is *being aside*, aside of being (*être à l'écart*) (p. 242). The textual instance occupies the margin of Being. "At the edge of being, the medium of the hymen never becomes a mere mediation of work of the negative; it outwits and undoes all ontologies, all philosophemes, all manner of dialectics. It outwits them and—as a cloth, a tissue, a medium again—it envelops them, turns them over, and inscribes them" (p. 215). At this point of our development of Derrida's notion of text, the continuity between the question of Being and the question of the text cannot be overlooked anymore. The question of the text repeats, in at least a formal manner, all the movements that characterize Heidegger's elaborations on Being. This similarity, however, should not have made us blind to the (particularly in the last quotes) slight yet all the more persistent displacements that positively hint at the impossibility of phenomenologizing the textual trace in even a Heideggerian fashion. Let us, indeed, not forget that, of all things, the phenomenon *par excellence* is Being. But before attempting to face what distinguishes the question of the text from the question of Being, the similarities of the two questions must first occupy us. In sum, the logic of the trait as *retrait* that subtends the Heideggerian notion of Being, and the particular locus (*Ortschaft*) that Heidegger attributes to Being—its place at once inside and outside all the conceptual dyads that it allows to come forth or as which it shows itself—are the major formal similarities between the Heideggerian and the Derridean questioning. If these findings correctly indicate the level of philosophical reflection on which Derrida elaborates his notion of text, a level that indeed excludes all pragmatic, empirical, rationalistic, and dialectical approaches, and if they also hint at the nature of the problems that Derrida tries to solve by the question of the text, do they also allow us to conclude, as Gérard Granel does with regard to the Derridean notion of writing, that the question of Being and the question of the text are one and the same? Were they identical, why would Derrida shrink from admitting this identity? Granel suggests that Derrida may hesitate to confess the essential similarity of the two questions because of a *"remaining kinship . . .* between the [Heideggerian] Difference which crosses out the origin, the ground, self-proximity, in short all the modalities of presence, *and* what it crosses out in this manner."[28] Although involved in the same philosophical enterprise of questioning Western metaphysics, Heidegger and Derrida would differ in their perception of the other of metaphysics. Granel adds: "Is the breeze of Danger that blows 'on the other side'—once one has climbed, followed and left the ridge of metaphysics—simply not the same, or is it not sustained and recognized by Heidegger and Derrida in the same way?"[29] When in *Writing and Difference* Derrida agrees with Emmanuel Levinas on the necessity of leaving the climate of Heidegger's philosophy, this statement may serve to support Granel's argument. The difference between the two philosophers may well be presented as one of tone, of accent, of style, and so on, if one recalls certain of Derrida's remarks: On one hand, toward the end of "Violence and Metaphysics," Derrida wonders whether Heidegger's question of Being is not essentially a theological question and whether what Heidegger calls the historicity of Being can be thought without invoking an eschatology. On the other hand, in an essay entitled "On a Newly Arisen Apocalyptic Tone in Philosophy," Derrida raises the apocalypse to a sort of transcendental condition of all writing (and *a fortiori* of all thought).[30] Basically, this difference would amount to the not-unimportant one between, on the one hand, the comforting tone of the Black Forest philosopher who, dwelling near the origins, calls upon Hölderlin to assure us that where there is danger there grows also what saves, and on the other hand what Derrida evokes as "the generalizing catastrophe."[31] No doubt, such a difference can easily be made out in the work of the two thinkers. Yet to reduce their difference to a question of tone or style would imply that from Heidegger to Derrida little conceptual discovery has taken place, unless one were to demonstrate that the question of tone and style does not remain exterior to the effort of conceptualization. As we have seen, the questions of Being and of the text are indeed, conceptually speaking, the same. In terms of conceptual refinement there seems to be no great difference between the Heideggerian notion of trait and Derrida's notion of archetrace.

However, at this point, one can no longer avoid asking the question whether the relation of Heidegger and Derrida can still be examined in terms of concepts and of questions. It also becomes impossible to further shun the topic of the possible effects that a repetition of Heidegger by Derrida may have on the Heideggerian problematics itself. Does not the question of tone and style, then, point rather toward a radical rupture in regard to the philosophical problems with which Heidegger coped? And, finally, would one not have to acknowledge that though it formally repeats Heidegger's concept of Being, the text as a re-mark of Being may well be an entirely new concept?

Undoubtedly, Heidegger's repeated attempt to elaborate Being independently of being and beings, his inquiry into the ontological difference itself as what donates all particular differences, is an approach to a meaning of Being that escapes all metaphysical determination made hitherto. As Granel has emphasized, "meaning is understood here precisely as a *totally different* meaning compared to its understanding in the whole of Western metaphysics."[32] Yet, despite these insights into a meaning of Being that is no longer a meaning and does not refer to being(s) anymore—insights constituting that "other language" that already haunts Heidegger's admittedly still-metaphysical discourse—Heidegger's philosophy remains within the horizon and the themes of Western philosophy. One of these themes, the major one, has always concerned being. The question of Being in all its *radicality*, and perhaps precisely because of its radicality, continues this problematic. Despite Heidegger's extraordinary use of language, his philosophy remains subjected to the traditional ways in which these problems were expected to be solved. Moreover, in conceiving of the quest for the meaning of Being in terms of a history of the fates of Being, Heidegger bends to the traditional canon of problems that constitutes philosophy, saving, in addition, the pretension of classical philosophy to universality. If these all-too-hasty remarks contain a grain of truth, then the question of the difference between Heidegger and Derrida cannot be reduced simply to one of climate or tone.

Derrida has made it clear that the word "text" can be substituted for the word "Being." "Text" is a translation for "Being." It is a word, the use of which became indispensable to him in a very specific historical situation. For this very reason its importance is only strategic, and there is no intrinsic value to it. Thus while naming Being, the text is also something very different, if not without any relation at all to Being.

To conclude, let us try to assess as succinctly as possible the difference at issue. To begin with, one has to realize that Derrida's determination of metaphysics in terms of *ethico-theoretical decisions* opens up an entirely different level of debate than Heidegger's conception of metaphysics as a forgetting of Being. Consequently, with this passage to the order of discourse of philosophy, to its textual organization and rhetorics, the Heideggerian notions of trait, between, fissure, and so forth, become displaced in such a way as to form, together with the specifically Derridean notions of supplementarity, *différance*, re-mark, text, and so on, "tools" that serve to account for the "deep structures" organizing the conceptual, reflexive, and speculative discourse of philosophy. In other words, though the notion of text in Derrida is formally the same as the notion of Being-as-trait in Heidegger, it assumes a very different function in Derrida's enterprise.

But the break between Heidegger's question of Being and Derrida's investigations of what is only provisionally termed "text"—an inquiry that, by the way, may no longer yield to the order of the question in Heidegger's sense—is even more thorough. It is almost indiscernible, but nonetheless all the more piercing.

Heidegger's turning away from Husserlian phenomenology was motivated by the need to ground phenomenology more originally. As an investigation into Being as Being, the question of Being crowns the attempt of the fundamental ontology to account for the coming into presence of the phenomena—Being being the phenomenon *par excellence*. Heidegger's philosophy, then, because it continues the problematics of being, but in particular because it inquires into the very meaning of Being, remains as such within the realm of metaphysics, as Derrida has argued.[33] But Derrida also locates—besides Heidegger's preoccupation with the meaning of Being, which almost entirely constitutes his enterprise—another gesture in Heidegger's thinking.[34] This is a gesture that, contrary to the question of Being, risks as much as the very name, the very word "Being." By emphasizing this aspect of Heidegger's later philosophy, Derrida comes to drive a wedge into Heidegger's enterprise insofar as it still remains indebted to its initial orientation toward a fundamental ontology. The word "text," the donation of the text, for re-marking the word "Being," is precisely what is no longer answerable to the meaning of Being. With the word "text," Derrida names an instance that, crossing out all the modalities of presence, at once *intersects* with the instance whence the presencing of the presence comes to be, Being as the phenomenon *par excellence*. There is (*es gibt*) text, at the margin of Being. With the word "text," with the elaboration of the law of supplementarity of the re-mark, Derrida unfolds a discourse that, although it repeats the question of Being, inscribes it, and thus remains altogether extraneous to this still-philosophical question.

(1980)

12

On Re-Presentation

A reading that moves *across* a text, traversing it from one end to the other, going over the whole of its surface, is a reading intent on covering it, exhausting it. The endless iterations of this movement would be limited by the boundaries of the text alone. Husserl could have described this manner of proceeding through a text as reading in "zigzag fashion." Indeed, despite what this term connotes of drunkenness and erratic motion, it enjoys a quite special status in Husserl's methodological reflections. In *Logical Investigations*, for instance, Husserl notes that although "systematic clarification, whether in pure logic or any other discipline, would in itself seem to require a stepwise following out of the ordering of things, of the systematic interconnection in the science to be clarified," such smooth and continuous development is unsuited to lay down the phenomenological foundation of logic. He adds: "Our investigation can . . . only proceed securely, if it repeatedly breaks with such systematic sequence, if it removes conceptual obscurities which threaten the course of investigation *before* the natural sequence of subject-matters can lead up to such concepts. We search, as it were, in zig-zag fashion." As the two distinct vowels of the term suggest, to zigzag is to move in two different directions, to take sharp turns at alternate angles. The zigzag breaks with the direct line, straying from its progressive continuity. But, as Husserl contends, this break with systematic exposition does not sacrifice clarity.

On the contrary, to defer that goal by swerving from the direct road only serves to better secure its initial concerns. Commenting on his use of the term "zigzag" to describe the mode of exposition in phenomenological investigations, he notes that it is "a metaphor all the more apt since the close interdependence of our various epistemological concepts leads us back again and again to our original analyses, where the new confirms the old, and the old the new."[1] From *Logical Investigations*, but also from *The Crisis of European Sciences*, it is evident that zigzagging follows necessarily from a certain circularity proper to the phenomenological concern with meaning and its systematic clarification. Husserl writes in *The Crisis*:

> We find ourselves in a sort of circle. The understanding of the beginnings is to be gained fully only by starting with science as given in its present-day form, looking back at its development. But in the absence of an understanding of the *beginnings* the development is mute as a *development of meaning*. Thus we have no other choice than to proceed forward and backward in a zigzag pattern; the one must help the other in an interplay.[2]

Zigzag, as understood by Husserl, is thus the movement of turns at alternate angles required by the hermeneutic circle that makes the understanding of the end, or whole, dependent on a prior understanding of the beginning, or part, and vice versa. The zigzag line to which such a mode of movement gives rise circles back into itself, creating a starlike pattern. One leaves the straight line alternately to return to it, all the while going back and forth from a center, covering and encircling, weaving, so to speak, the whole.

Going through a text can also mean moving out of, ahead of, and beyond the text. The zigzag movement here, rather than serving the constitution of sense, leads one to distance oneself from the text and its meaning. But to traverse a text in this manner is not to simply desert it. On the contrary, in such a reading, the text itself with all its insoluble difficulties, contradictions, and aporias can provide an opportunity for an unheard-of approach and problematic. Distinct from a reading whose aim is to produce continuity, and which lays stress only—as Walter Benjamin remarked in a discussion of the genre of "'appreciation,' or apology"—"on those elements of the work which already have become part of its influence," the passage through a text intent on going beyond such continuity finds its hold on the text's "crags and jagged prongs [*die Schroffen und Zacken*]" that escape a reading concerned with continuity.[3] Grasping these cliffs and jags for support, reading displays a zigzag movement. But the zigzag is also elicited by the fact that the movement beyond must constantly negotiate with the text to be left behind. To the extent that the transition to a beyond is the effect of a traversal of the text, the passage in question commences an unending commerce between the text left behind and its beyond, which is all the more intimate since the possibility of the new text cannot causally be derived from the first. Indeed, the function words "through" and "across" also suggest a means, agency, or intermediary. Going beyond the text can only be achieved by way of the text, by going through it and remaining indebted to what has been left behind. Zigzagging is thus no longer limited to a subservient procedure in the establishment of sense; rather it exceeds meaning, and becomes the rule of such establishment. Since nothing escapes this rule, neither the text at the beginning nor the beyond for which it has been left, the movement of zigzag ultimately turns into what a reading that goes through texts has to center in on and what it conceptualizes as such.

Zigzag circulation in this sense, without "circularity or linearity," without "a regulative horizon of totalization," is precisely, as Leonard Lawlor has shown in *Imagination and Chance: The Difference Between the Thought of Ricoeur and Derrida* and elsewhere, a distinctive trait of Derrida's writings on Husserl, one that sets his approach apart from Ricoeur's appraisal of Husserl's work, and from the dialectical hermeneutics it seeks to develop.[4] In his account of Derrida's analysis of Husserl's "The Origin of Geometry," Lawlor shows how Derrida illuminates all of Husserl's zigzag movements—"between the genetic and the structural project, between the specificity of the geometrical science as a cultural product and culture in general, between a posteriori and a priori, between finally origin and end."[5] If Derrida characterizes this zigzag course as "a detour and a surprising turnabout,"[6] this is because, as Lawlor notes, Husserl's *Rückfrage* ("questioning back") for the origin of geometry and for its genesis, never seem to arrive at the sought destination. For Lawlor, steering this zigzag course results less from dodging the possibly disquieting consequences of a radically genetic approach than from a positive recognition on Husserl's part of "the reciprocal implication of end and origin."[7] Holding Derrida to follow Husserl in such ultimate zigzag, Lawlor thematizes "zigzag" in Derrida in particular with respect to the concept of tradition and history. "*Zigzagging* defines the way Derrida reinscribes and perverts certain terms against the tradition's system," Lawlor remarks. And he notes in conclusion that this reinscription proceeds by reinterpreting all the classical oppositions according to "the irreducible unity of essence and fact."[8] In the following, I wish to continue to develop this "motive" of the zigzag highlighted by Lawlor, and in particular its pertinence for a reading of Husserl that understands itself as going *through* the latter's writings.

"*Through* [*à travers*] Husserl's text" is indeed the way Derrida has characterized his reading of the First Logical Investigation in *Speech and Phenomena*.[9] This is a reading that cuts across the text in order to go beyond it. Needless to say, in the eyes of certain Husserl scholars, a reading intent on going through the text in this sense reveals a total lack of respect for the work. When they are not simply frightened away from Derrida's writings on Husserl by this approach, they find such a reading to take inexcusable liberties with the text, and in the worst case simply to have gotten it wrong. Derrida himself expressed discomfort on the occasion of the publication of his *Le problème de la genèse dans la philosophie de Husserl* (The problem of genesis in the philosophy of Husserl), a study written between 1953 and 1954 but not published until 1990, which covers almost the entirety of Husserl's writings. These demurs notwithstanding, this early study has the virtue of being a much more traditionally conceived piece of scholarly work, one that ought to allay these scholars' suspicions that Derrida has not done his homework. But this patient, cautious, and even benevolent reading of Husserl's thought is also significant in that it shows, perhaps in a more accessible way than *Speech and Phenomena*, what kind of overall interpretation of Husserl's writings and, more generally, of Husserlian phenomenology motivates Derrida's singular way of going through Husserl's texts. As *Le problème de la genèse* suggests, "phenomenology must end, in a certain way, in a genetic turn [*devenir génétique*]. This is how phenomenology must complete itself."[10] Undoubtedly, Husserl himself recognized the necessity of such further development and, after *Ideas I*, increasingly turned to genetic analyses.

But the questions raised by the genetic problematic, and in particular by its implications for the phenomenological project itself, remain without response, according to Derrida. Indeed, Derrida asks (*PG*, p. 215), is it possible to develop a philosophy of genesis and to remain faithful to the principles of phenomenology in their purity? These principles and their conceptual premises, as put forth in *Logical Investigations* and left unchanged despite the multiple revisions in the later work of other aspects of his thought, concern the necessity of eidetic and phenomenological reduction and rest on the essentialism that phenomenology shares with philosophy in general. Having invoked the law that the absolute beginning of philosophy must be essentialist, Derrida remarks: "To the extent that this law is 'methodological'; and to the extent that it is not grounded on the effective movement of the constituting genesis anterior to the essences, thus governing all philosophical elucidation, it [this law] makes formalism and idealism, or if you prefer, eidetism, the inaugural moment of all actual or possible philosophy" (*PG*, p. 226). Husserl's unshakable faithfulness to "the absolute necessity of eidetic reduction" in phenomenology, and hence to the premises of philosophical thinking in general, make it rigorously impossible for him to achieve the goal of laying bare an ultimate genetic source (*PG*, p. 226). The principles of phenomenology dictate that he encounter on his search for this source only moments that are already constituted moments and that therefore presuppose the originary temporal stratum that is in question. Without exception, Husserl misses the description of an authentic transcendental genesis, Derrida contends. What is supposed to be the constituting source, reduced and essentialized in eidetic reflection, turns out to be something constituted as well. Husserl, according to Derrida, has tried to escape from the dilemma in question, from what at times takes the form of a true aporia (*PG*, p. 129), by continuously promising and announcing the thematization of transcendental temporality but simultaneously deferring its radical solution. The only way to truly overcome what Derrida terms "the profound uneasiness" of Husserl's philosophy (*PG*, p. 216) would have been to understand the dilemma in its foundation. "Such a thematization, however, if total, would have overthrown the initial givens of phenomenology," Derrida writes (*PG*, p. 214). In submitting genesis, as well as history, to a reduction, even at the moment when the latter becomes the main concern of his thought, Husserl reveals "to what point [he felt that] all true genesis would run the risk of jeopardizing the phenomenological and philosophical purpose in general, and even entirely doom it to failure" (*PG*, p. 206). Thus if Derrida concludes, in *Le problème de la genèse*, that the overcoming that Husserl's philosophy calls for can consist in either an overcoming that merely prolongs his philosophy with all its inherited difficulties, or "a radical reformulation that amounts to a complete conversion" (*PG*, p. 41), several things become clear about the professed need for a reading of Husserl that moves across his text.

First, the necessity of such a reading derives from an insight into the limits not of Husserl's philosophy in the first instance but of philosophy in general—into an inevitable insufficiency that is a function of the essentialist exigencies on which philosophy necessarily rests and without which no philosophy with its required rigor could come into its own. What is remarkable about Husserl's thought, however,—and this helps to explain the unquestionable privilege that his thought enjoys throughout Derrida's work—is that all the while that he faithfully sticks to the elementary exigency of eidetic reduction, he also recognizes the need for a transcendental inquiry into temporality as constitutive of essences. Such an inquiry, however, is not without potentially unsettling consequences. Indeed, with such an emphasis on constitution, genesis, and history, a tension arises in Husserl's phenomenology that undoubtedly culminates in paradox, contradiction, aporia, and even sheer confusion, but that also harbors the possibility of explicitly bringing to light the limits of philosophy in its classical form. To read across the text, then, follows from the need to "resolve," so to speak, the Husserlian dilemma by working out the contradictory demands of philosophy in what Derrida at one point had called "a theory of philosophical discourse."[11]

Second, the overcoming sought by a reading that moves across the Husserlian text remains indebted to Husserlian phenomenology. For it is phenomenology itself that "seems, continuously and incessantly, to have prepared a vast methodological access to a sphere that is not very accessible to phenomenological elucidation," as is the sphere of genesis (*PG*, p. 206). Furthermore, the radical conversion of phenomenology at which *Le problème de la genèse* aims (and which consists in thinking the contradictory demands of Husserl's thought together in and as an infinite zigzag) follows from the *de facto* shape of Husserlian philosophy. Reading through the text of phenomenology is therefore also a matter of accounting for what Husserl *does* in his texts, in contradistinction to what he *says*.[12]

Third, since the radical philosophical conversion sought in *Le problème de la genèse*—which, at the time, was called a "dialectic . . . that is one with the idea of philosophy itself" (*PG*, p. 217)—consists in "a simultaneous or *a priori* synthetic awareness of the necessary insufficiency [of Husserlian philosophy] and of possible rigor" (*PG*, p. 226), passing through Husserl's text compels a thematization of the infinite oscillation, or zigzag for that matter, that contaminates and complicates all phenomenological purity. If, indeed, phenomenological purity appears to itself as such only insofar as it is a genetic composite, all such purity combines with an alterity in "*a priori* ambiguity." Derrida discusses this infinite referral and zigzag under the title "*A Priori* Synthesis." Within the parameters of his early work, he understands such a referral as an "originary dialectic," a dialectic distinct from the one of which Tran Duc Thao and indeed Hegel speak (*PG*, p. 257). As the term "dialectic" indicates, the radical conversion of phenomenology aimed at in *Le problème de la genèse* is to be understood as a more comprehensive philosophy, one that goes to the roots of the phenomenological dilemma and is capable of "resolving" it in a certain way. Unlike Husserl, who "would not admit that all beginning of philosophy and meaning is an *a priori* synthesis whose absolute evidence points to an irreducible indefinite" (*PG*, p. 41), Derrida, in this early work, shows that this conclusion follows necessarily from Husserl's work itself, even though "in all likelihood . . . [Husserl] would have contested the right to such an interpretation" (*PG*, p. 32). This conclusion gives rise to a new philosophy, both beyond and tributary to phenomenology, a philosophy that makes differential contamination its central theme. Yet if in the *Avertissement* to *Le problème de la genèse* Derrida has distanced himself from that early work, he has done so, I hold, not only because of terms such as "dialectic" but primarily because the discovery and investigation of the a priori synthesis of the pure principles of phenomenology, though unquestionably of philosophical nature, undercut the possibility of continuing to simply thematize such synthesis in the form of and as a singular philosophy. But, circling back to *Speech and Phenomena*, we shall see that the concern with "differential contamination," and hence with "*a priori* synthesis," have remained the thrust of Derrida's reading through Husserl.

I understand the following developments as a long footnote to an already quite long footnote by Derrida himself in the chapter of *Speech and Phenomena* titled "Meaning as Soliloquy." This footnote is of special interest to me since Derrida closes it by saying that in it he has indicated "the prime intention—and the ultimate scope—of the present essay," that is, of *Speech and Phenomena* as a whole (*SP*, pp. 45–46). If I linger on this footnote, it is in order to further clarify the implications of a reading that moves across the Husserlian text, this time in a book that, unlike the early genesis book, is "more than a simple interpretation of Husserl," to quote Rudolf Bernet.[13] Describing his reading as going *through* Husserl's text, Derrida specifies this as meaning that it "can be neither simple commentary nor simple interpretation" (*SP*, p. 88).

The context in which the footnote in question occurs needs to be briefly outlined. In the First Logical Investigation, characterized by "Foreword II" as having a "merely preparatory character," Husserl engages nonetheless in an analysis of "essential distinctions" on whose possibility and purity rests, in principle, the entire phenomenological enterprise (*LI*, p. 48). Although "expressions were originally framed to fulfill a communicative function," they "also play a great part in uncommunicated, interior mental life," Husserl contends in the First Logical Investigation (*LI*, pp. 276, 278). Despite the brevity of the analysis devoted to expression in solitary mental life, this particular analysis is absolutely crucial to the whole of the *Logical Investigations* in that it demonstrates not only that living in the understanding of expressions is possible, whether they are addressed to anyone or not, but that such an experience of the meaning of expressions is in truth the more essential experience. In the course of his analysis, Husserl remarks that all intimation (*Kundgabe*), hence also all indication, or sign function, is absent from silent soliloquy. Meaningful expression in solitary mental life is still linked to words, but unlike words in communicative discourse, those in the intimately unified experience of sense-filled expression in silent mental life do not serve as indications, not even "as indications, of one's own inner experiences" to oneself (*LI*, p. 279). No self-intimation takes place here. In soliloquy one does not communicate something to one self (as an Other). Moreover, in silent monologue, to quote Husserl, "we are in general content with imagined [*vorgestellten*] rather than with actual words." Lacking reality, imagined words are in themselves "intrinsically indifferent, whereas the sense seems the thing aimed at by the verbal sign and meant by its means: the expression seems to direct interest away from itself towards its sense, and to point to the latter. But this pointing [*Hinzeigen*] is not an indication [*Anzeigen*]" (*LI*, p. 279). Having no existence and no longer calling any attention to themselves, words are no longer signs in a strict sense. As words fade away before the meaning they point at, meaning in solitary life can be experienced or lived fully in and for itself in absolute distinctness from signs, that is, from indication and intimation. With this Husserl believes he has established the existence of an experience of meaning in which meaning can be intuited and evidenced in purity and in which it can be present as such without outside contamination, fully present and self-present, without the intervention of the sign. This demonstration is crucial because phenomenology depends upon the possibility of such a distinct experience of meaning, which ultimately also represents phenomenology's proper domain.

To establish an experience in which meaning can give itself purely and simply thus hinges on the possibility of bracketing the sign character of words by merely representing words. In the imaginary representation of words, for instance, the word's existence, whether that existence is empirical or imaginary, becomes neutralized. As Derrida recalls,

the imagination of the word, the imagined, the word's being-imagined, its "image," is not the (imagined) word. In the same way as, in the perception of the word, the word (perceived or appearing) which is "in the world" belongs to a radically different order from that of the perception or appearing of the word, the word's being-perceived, so the (imagined) word is of a radically heterogeneous order from that of the imagination of the word." (*SP*, p. 44)

However, according to Derrida, in determining the merely representational character of words in soliloquy, Husserl does not content himself with understanding the represented words in terms of the critical phenomenological category of the being-imagined, or phenomenon, of the word. The rationale for not conceiving of the imagination of the word in terms of a being-imagined of the word is that reference to the existence of the word does not occur in imaginative representation, as it does in the perception of the word. In chapter 8 of "Investigation I," Husserl writes with unmistakable clarity:

> We should not . . . confuse imaginative presentations, and the image-contents they rest on, with their imagined objects. The imagined verbal sound, or the imagined printed word, does not exist, only its imaginative presentation does so. The difference is the difference between imagined centaurs and the imagination of such beings. The word's non-existence neither disturbs nor interests us, since it leaves the word's expressive function unaffected." (LI, p. 279)

And Derrida concludes: "In imagination the existence of the word is not implied, even by virtue of intentional sense. There *exists* only the imagination of the word, which is absolutely certain and self-present insofar as it is lived" (*SP*, p. 44). Now what has Husserl achieved by eliminating phenomenality, and with it reference to the existence of the word, from the presentative imagination of words in solitary mental life? He has, Derrida contends, succeeded in isolating "the subjective experience [*le vécu subjectif*] as the sphere of absolute certainty and absolute existence" (*SP*, p. 44). Yet in reflecting on the argumentation itself by means of which Husserl arrives at this result, he notes that it "would be fragile indeed if it merely appealed to a classical psychology of the imagination" (*SP*, p. 45). After recalling Husserl's critique of the psychological conception of the image, according to which it is a picture-sign whose *reality* indicates the imagined object, Derrida stresses that the argument by which imagined words are stripped of reference to existing words rests on an understanding of imagination as a phenomenal experience that does not belong to reality—whose status is that of a *reell* component of consciousness—and of the image as intentional or noematic, in other words, as even less real than the act of imagination in that it is a non-*reell* component of consciousness. In short then, Husserl's contention that it is possible to isolate an experience of meaning in which meaning can be intuited and evidenced as such presupposes the possibility of construing inner discourse as an irreality through and through.

The footnote in question thus occurs in the context of an assessment of Husserl's conception of imagination and the image as nonreal components of consciousness. Having quoted Husserl from *Ideas I* on the necessity of conceiving experiences as differences that concern consciousness (rather than as being constituted by material characters), Derrida writes:

The original phenomenological data that Husserl thus wants to respect lead him to posit an absolute heterogeneity between perception or primordial presentation (*Gegenwärtigung, Präsentation*) and re-presentation or representative reproduction, also translated as presentification (*Vergegenwärtigung*). Memory, images, and signs are re-presentations in this sense. Properly speaking, Husserl is not *led* to recognize this heterogeneity, for it is this which constitutes the very possibility of phenomenology. For phenomenology can only make sense if a pure and primordial presentation is possible and given in the original. This distinction (to which we must add that between positional [*setzende*] re-presentation, which posits the having-been-present in memory, and the imaginary re-presentation [*Phantasie-Vergegenwärtigung*], which is neutral in that respect), part of a fundamental and complex system, which we cannot directly investigate here, is the indispensable instrument for a critique of classical psychology, and in particular, the classical psychology of the imagination and the sign. (*SP*, p. 45)

In his inquiry into what sanctions the essential distinctions that are to be brought to logical clarity in the First Logical Investigation, Derrida highlights one particular distinction. Although it is not the final one, against whose foil all the other distinctions are to be situated—indeed, it is said to be part of a complex system of similar distinctions—this particular one enjoys a special privilege in that its conception of a radical irreality and self-sufficiency of phenomenological experience is a clear expression of phenomenology's attempt to secure an autonomous domain for itself free of all the objective references in which psychology remains entangled. The distinction in question stipulates the possibility and the existence of a "lived experience [that] is immediately self-present in the mode of certitude and absolute necessity" (*SP*, p. 58), hence, of a pure perception, or originary presentation, in which the given gives itself in simple and unadulterated presence. Distinct from re-presentation, presentation, or more precisely, primordial presentation is free from the delegating or representative function of indicative signs. Indeed, the indivisibility of the presence to self of what is given in the mode of immediate presence assures the irreducibility of re-presentation (*Vergegenwärtigung, Repräsentation*) to presentative perception. As a modification of presentation, representation is then something that happens to presentation from the outside. Yet as Derrida will show throughout *Speech and Phenomena*, the distinction between presentation and re-presentation, however essential and necessary it might be, cannot be upheld in the purity required by the phenomenological project as envisaged by Husserl. In no way, however, does this impossibility imply that the project must be abandoned. On the contrary, what Derrida attempts to do in *Speech and Phenomena* is to link up the possibility of presentation, and with it that of originary truth in the phenomenological sense, with what ultimately necessitates its impossibility. This interlinkage of possibility and impossibility takes shape as a zigzag movement. It should already be obvious that zigzagging is not limited to Derrida's style of reading Husserl. Undoubtedly, Derrida faithfully zigzags along all of Husserl's voluntary and involuntary zigzags. But zigzagging in Derrida extends as well to the relation that obtains between presentation and its enabling and disabling condition. A transcendental or, rather, quasi-transcendental "status" of the zigzag thus begins to emerge. However, before further elaborating on this movement and its difference from the zigzag pattern that Husserl has said is required for phenomenological investigation and exposition, let me first return to the footnote. I quote again:

> But can't one assume the necessity for this critique of naïve psychology only up to a certain point? What if we were to show, finally, that the theme or import of "pure presentation," pure and primordial perception, full and simple presence, etc., makes of phenomenology an accomplice of classical psychology—indeed constitutes their common metaphysical presupposition? In affirming that *perception does not exist* or that what is called perception is not primordial, that somehow everything "begins" by "re-presentation" (a proposition which can only be maintained by the elimination of these last two concepts: it means that there is no "beginning" and that the "re-presentation" we were talking about is not the modification of a "re-" that has *befallen* a primordial presentation) and by reintroducing the difference involved in "signs" at the core of what is "primordial," we do not retreat from the level of transcendental phenomenology toward either an "empiricism" or a "Kantian" critique of the claim of having primordial intuition; we are here indicating the prime intention—and the ultimate scope—of the present essay. (*SP*, pp. 45–46)

On what grounds can Derrida affirm that perception in the phenomenological sense, that is, as a primordial presentation, does not exist? To understand this claim, it is imperative to recall two points. First, the presentation in question obtains in the looked-for purity only within the limited case of the presence to consciousness of ideal, purely intelligible, and nonreal objects. Second, in *Speech and Phenomena*, Derrida determines "the ultimate form of ideality, the ideality of ideality . . . [as] the *living present*, the self-presence of transcendental life" (*SP*, p. 6). Now, according to Husserl, an authentic ideality, that is, an ideality that *is*, must be one that can be infinitely repeated in the identity of its presence. Yet for Husserl, an "ideality is not an existent that has fallen from the sky." Consequently, its origin has likewise to be "the possible repetition of a productive act" (*SP*, p. 6). Given, further, that the "metaphysical form of ideality" (*SP*, p. 7) has been shown to be the presence of the *living present*, it follows that Derrida's analyses in *Speech and Phenomena*—analyses of what breaches originary presentation, or perception, from within—would center in privileged fashion on this repetition constitutive of ideality in terms of the re-presenting modalities of presentation. But the possibility of such repetition, without which ideality in the form of the present could not come about, is precisely, as Derrida will show throughout *Speech and Phenomena*, what serves to establish an "irreducible nonpresence . . . an ineradicable nonprimordiality" in the living present as well, and hence, in nonworldly ideal objects (*SP*, pp. 6–7). The crux of Derrida's argument consists, then, in demonstrating that Husserl's own descriptions of the movement of temporality and the constitution of intersubjectivity unmistakably establish repetition—and with it everything that ought to derive from presence—to be required by presence and all ideal objectivity in general. Considering the space at my disposal, I cannot reconstruct in detail the various steps of Derrida's complex analysis. Let me only say that the titles under which repetition assumes the constituting role in question are all of the order of modifications of presentation, primarily, re-presentation and appresentation. In Derrida's own words:

it is a question of (1) the necessary transition from retention to *re-presentation* (*Vergegenwärtigung*) in the constitution of the presence of a temporal object (*Gegenstand*) whose identity may be repeated; and (2) the necessary transition by way of *appresentation* in relation to the *alter ego*, that is, in relation to what also makes possible an ideal objectivity in general; for intersubjectivity is the condition for objectivity, which is absolute only in the case of ideal objects. (*SP*, p. 7)

Although retention and re-presentation must remain separated for Husserl by an abyss, Derrida argues that Husserl's conception of retention, which is to say, of the necessary presentation of a past present, that is, of a nonpresence, for a present now to come about, implies that it must harbor repetition in the mode of a re-presentation of what once was but no longer is present. Moreover, since ideality cannot be constituted except in relation with an Other, a repetition of the originary presentation in the form of analogical appresentation must inhabit originary presentation from the start. As Derrida maintains, such repetitive representation or appresentation within ideality and its form of presence "does not impugn the apodicticity of the phenomenological-transcendental description, nor does it diminish the founding value of presence" (*SP*, p. 7). The reason for this is that the nonpresence in question is not just any nonpresence. The most singular status of such re-presentation and appresentation follows from their being not derivative upon or secondary to a prior presence but necessarily implied by all presence or ideality. Derrida writes: "What in the two cases is called a modification of presentation (*re*-presentation, *ap*-presentation) (*Vergegenwärtigung* or *Appräsentation*) is not something that happens to presentation but rather conditions it by bifurcating it [*en la fissurant*] *a priori*" (*SP*, p. 7). Limiting myself to the question of re-presentation, I note only that Derrida speaks of it as a "primordial representation" (*SP*, p. 57), that is, as an originary *Vergegenwärtigung* upon which presentation in the form of *Vorstellung* itself, and as such, is shown to depend. It is thus certainly not a question of criticizing or doing away with Husserl's essential distinctions, among them the distinction between presentation and re-presentation. On the contrary, Derrida's intention is to show that what these essential distinctions seek to isolate in purity can only be (successfully) achieved if, say, originary presentation is made to presuppose a prior re-presentation, that is, the constituting movement of a representation that lacks as yet a constituted presence to relate to.

In the course of investigating the distinctive criteria with which Husserl demarcates a domain proper to phenomenology and radically separate from psychology, Derrida focuses in particular upon the isolation of an experience of originary presentation, of presentation in the shape of *Vorstellung*, which Husserl in general asserts to be irreducibly different from all modes of re-presentation. Derrida illuminates a limitation of this isolated sphere that is also—paradoxically—a condition of possibility for demarcating the sphere in question and thus securing (within these limits) the possibility of a pure experience of meaning in the Husserlian sense.

In the context here under examination, and only in this context at first, the limit takes the form of generalized or originary re-presentation.

In his essay "Derrida et la voix de son maître" (Derrida and the voice of his master), Rudolf Bernet asks whether "in his crusade against the philosophy of presence, Derrida does not gather too fast under one banner these different forms of representation that are imagination, repetition, the concrete occurring of a generality, and representation by means of a sign."[14] Needless to say, only an extremely detailed and careful analysis of Derrida's discussion of all these modes of representation could provide an answer to Bernet's question. For the moment, therefore, the following remark must suffice. Undoubtedly, all of the following (and I name only a few) are taken as different aspects of representation: presence (*Gegenwart*); presentation (*Gegenwärtigung* or *Präsentation*); representation in the general sense of *Vorstellung*, that is, as the locus of ideality in general; representation as repetition or reproduction, that is, as a modifying *Vergegenwärtigung* including imaginary representation; and representation in the sense of what occupies the place of another *Vorstellung*, that is, what Husserl calls *Repräsentation*, *Repräsentant*, or *Stellvertreter*. But rather than being lumped together or rendered identical, all these different senses of the term "representation" are shown to be distinct elements of what Derrida refers to as a "representative structure" (*SP*, p. 50), which itself has a repeatable formal identity. According to this structure, *Vorstellung* as the locus of ideality in which expression in the Husserlian sense partakes necessarily implies all the other possible modifications of representation that Husserl, for his part, had confined to the sign-function and to communicative manifestation. And the reverse also holds. This notion of a representative structure is that the sign and language in general necessarily include the possibility of a representation in the sense of *Vorstellung*. This representative structure in which presentation and the modifications of representation are tied together with necessity is, for Derrida, "signification [*Bedeutung*] itself." From the start, this structure causes actual inner or outer discourse to be "involved in unlimited representation [*représentativité indéfinie*]" (*SP*, p. 50). At all moments, therefore, signification itself must be characterized by re-presentation in general, or "originary" re-presentation.[15] To put the matter in terms of the footnote that I am commenting upon, everything begins by re-presentation.

The primordiality of such re-presentation not only restricts the purity and radicality with which the distinction between originary presentation, or idealizing *Vorstellung*, and iterating re-presentation can be drawn, but also establishes a definite limit insofar as the distinction between classical psychology and phenomenology is concerned. However necessary it may be to demarcate phenomenology from psychology critically, such critique fails in the end not only because the phenomena described by both are possible only on the basis of assuming an originary re-presentation but also, as the footnote suggests, because the two share the same metaphysical presupposition of a pure perception, or presentation, and hence of pure and simple presence. Indeed, classical psychology's understanding of the sign as a representation that stands in for something else shows it to presuppose that primal impression of a being given without mediation which phenomenology has made its main object of concern.

To emphasize this complicity between classical psychology and phenomenology, a complicity beyond all their essential and legitimate differences, also means to emphasize that the notion of an originary re-presentation cannot simply be a generalized extension of the empirical concept of representation. The claim that everything "begins" with "re-presentation" can, indeed, be upheld only if the concepts both of beginning and of representation are recast. Obviously enough, "the *re-* of this re-presentation does not signify the simple—repetitive or reflexive—reduplication that *befalls* a simple presence (which is what the word *representation* has always *meant*)." Therefore, to call this primordial re-presentation is thus to name it only provisionally and, as Derrida says, "within the closure whose limits we are here seeking to transgress" (*SP*, p. 57). On its last pages, *Speech and Phenomena* goes so far as to deny completely the possibility of *knowing* "whether what was always presented as a derived and modified re-presentation of simple presentation" bears any determinable relation (such as being "older" than presence) to originary re-presentation. And he adds:

We therefore no longer know whether what has always been reduced and abased as an accident, modification, and re-turn, under the old names of "sign" and "re-presentation," has not repressed that which related truth to its own death as it related it to its origin. We no longer know whether the force of the *Vergegenwärtigung*, in which the *Gegenwärtigung* is de-presented so as to be re-presented as such, whether the repetitive force of the living present, which is re-presented in a *supplement*, because it has never been present to itself, or whether what we call with the old names of force and *différance* is not more "ancient" than what is "primordial." (*SP*, p. 103)

For all these reasons, one must conclude that in order to conceive of the representative structure, or the originary re-presentation, one "will have to have other names than those of sign or representation" (*SP*, p. 103). From this inevitable need to approach the relationship between presence and representation in terms other than those of re-presentation and sign-function, one must conclude that no word or concept can ever hope to represent it adequately. For structural or, say, representative reasons, the term "re-presentation" must open itself and make room for other terms, such as "force" and *différance*, to name only those explicitly mentioned by Derrida. Although the term "re-presentation" had imposed itself in the context of a discussion of Husserl's efforts to radically distinguish phenomenology from psychology and had been a meaningful term in that context alone, this term must hence be repeated, substituted, and supplemented with a difference by other terms. The same reasons that call for the replacement of the term "re-presentation" also make possible the extension of that term to other contexts, in which case, however, the explicatory achievements of the term change as well.

To conclude, let me circle back to the question of re-presentation's primordiality with respect to presentative perception, and hence also to the living present itself. If it is true that all presentation, or perception in the Husserlian sense, presupposes the possibility of a repetition in the shape of a re-presentation that is constitutive, and which thus does not double something already constituted, then "the presence of the perceived present can appear as such only inasmuch as it is *continuously compounded* [*composé continûment*] with a nonpresence and nonperception, with primary memory and expectation (retention and protention)" (*SP*, p. 64). What follows from this is, as Derrida recalls in the final paragraphs of *Speech and Phenomena*, that "there never was any 'perception'; and [that] 'presentation' is a representation of the representation that yearns for itself therein as for its own birth or its death" (*SP*, p. 103). But even though presentative perception never existed and never will exist in the purity and self-identity sought by Husserl, it exists as the desire of itself, as fissured by a re-presentation that holds out its birth, or that in-scribes within it the mark of finitude that is the possibility of death. The question to be asked therefore concerns the relation between, on the one hand, presentation and the perceived living present, and on the other hand, re-presentation, nonperception, and nonpresence. Although Der-rida also speaks of this relation as a being rooted (*enracinée*) in finitude (*SP*, p. 67), his characterization of it as a relation in which presentation continuously *compounds* with re-presentation, or in which the possibility of presence and primordial truth in the phenomenological sense depends on a compromise with nonpresence, needs here to be especially empha-sized. If the present of self-presence, and presentation, for that matter, are not simple but, as Derrida writes, "constituted in a primordial and irre-ducible synthesis" (*SP*, p. 61), in which they compound and incessantly compromise with a primordial re-presentation and nonpresence, then this relation of synthesis has, indeed, the "form" of a zigzag, or more pre-cisely, of a movement of infinite referral of one term to "its" dissymmet-rical Other. Zigzagging thus describes the consequent movement of the genesis, or constitution, of presence and of its presentation—of a consti-tution that does not fall back on something already constituted. In draw-ing out a zigzag of this kind, by repeatedly breaking with its systematic exposition, Derrida no longer follows Husserl's prescription to proceed securely in the search for truth in the phenomenological sense. He also goes much further than exhibiting the numerous zigzag movements to which, according to *Le problème de la genèse*, Husserl more or less unwill-ingly seems to have had recourse in order to delay the always-promised description of authentic transcendental genesis. Neither a methodologi-cal device on the way to and within the horizon of truth nor a necessary but unfortunate detour, the constituting movement of zigzag that I have sketched out here makes good on Husserl's demand for a genuine tran-scendental genesis. But in doing so, this zigzag shows that making good on this demand implies jeopardizing the phenomenological principles themselves. Conversely, only by interminably putting their purity at risk can they be maintained as philosophically effective principles—inter-minably, in the movement of a zigzag.

(1993)

PART V

RELATION AT THE CROSSROADS

13

Reading Chiasms

Coming to a text (or, for that matter, a collection of texts), the reader-critic normally expects that its constellation will yield to the unity of a configuration of thought. Yet if a work deliberately situates itself between figures, themes, or motifs that could and normally would authoritatively confer unity, what, then, is its status? Indeed, what sort of unity does an in-between establish, particularly if the work does not occupy the precise middle of that interspace, if, on the contrary, it is at once in-between and to the side? If the figures of thought at the crisscross of which the work places itself are neither identical to one another nor in a relation of otherness, the difficulty of the work increases considerably. This is definitely true when those figures are themselves inquiries into the intricacies of the in-between. The work we are speaking of, then, sides with an irreducibly endless series of interfaces. Lacking a determining negation by the other, these figures of thought cannot reflect themselves into mere identity; rather, the work in question remains suspended betwixt and between, to the side of, by right, only a virtual middle between nonidentical interfaces. It follows that the question of the (literal and figural) unity of such work must take a different turn.

Although Andrzej Warminski's *Readings in Interpretation* invites its reader to think about such a turn, this work must also be regarded as a book on Hölderlin, Hegel, and Heidegger.[1] It is, no doubt, a major contribution to the history of German idealism and romanticism, since it re-assesses the differences between some of the outstanding exponents of that tradition—the singular place of Hölderlin in that history, for instance—differences that, in the wake of romanticism, have become nearly imperceptible. *Readings in Interpretation*, however, is far more than the arduous attempt to correct a significant imbalance in the history of philosophy. It is a study concerned with the concept of history itself, the relation between philosophy and literature, hermeneutical and dialectical interpretation, the inscription of the reader in the philosophical text, as well as the status of representation and exemplarity. Yet within this array of questions, and through the specific nature of his strategies of questioning, Warminski shows that he is primarily concerned with a problematic whose objectivity is thoroughly different from that of the traditional disciplines and their objects of study. Indeed, Warminski has undertaken the difficult exploration of what constitutes that very space of the in-between (of interpretations, figures of thought, opposing motifs and themes), its relational and differential nature, as well as the crossroads and turning points that divide its fragile unity.

Were it not for the fact that the term is used at random—"à tous les biais et à toutes mesures," as Montaigne would have said—we could have called this work in a certain sense "deconstructive." Because of its micrological analyses, its sometimes vertiginous and seemingly abyssal argumentation, or simply because it does not make for easy reading, the reader may have already classified Warminski's work in this manner. If not, he will hardly be able to resist that temptation when encountering certain so-called key terms that are believed to characterize the perverse critical activity labeled "deconstruction." Undoubtedly, one of these terms is *always already*. But would the reader's irritation at the repeated use of that expression lessen if he knew what the term stands for and if he were thus in a position to consider its appropriateness within a given context?

Always already is an expression that may have found its first systematic use in Heidegger's thinking, where it denotes both the temporal mode of the fore-understanding in which the meaning of Being is available to Dasein and the specific mode of anteriority in which Being claims man. *Always already* names something prior to, and it thus seems to correspond to the formal determination of the a priori. To speak of *always already* rather than of a priori becomes a necessary move, however, when, as in Heidegger, the temporal character of Being itself is at stake. The a priori, which in the ontological tradition serves to denote the determinations of Being, contains the idea of a temporal succession in a very pallid way at best. In Heidegger's thinking, therefore, the *always already* stands for a temporal priority, which, as that of Being, has nothing to do with time as it is known according to its vulgar concept.

Always already is put to a similar use in Derrida's philosophy, where it designates the temporal mode of a certain accidentality, contingency, and supplementarity shown to be "constitutive" of presence and essence. Presence and essence within the metaphysical tradition, as Husserl has demonstrated, presuppose the fundamental form of idealization that is the "always again [*immer wieder*]." Whereas this structure accords a privileged position to the retentional dimension of intentionality, Derrida's use of the *always already* focuses on an anteriority that is, rather, of the order of the retentional dimension of intentionality. But if the *always already* in Derrida stands for a past and a passivity older than presence and essence, this does not mean that Derrida simply privileges retention. In the same manner that Heidegger's *always already* names a temporality that is radically different from the vulgar concept of time, Derrida's *always already* points at a radical past, at an absolute past and passivity that can never be fully reactivated and awakened to presence. Yet if the absolute past of the *always already* effaces itself and is from the outset in retreat, it nonetheless leaves a mark, a signature that is retraced in the very thing from which it is withdrawn, indicating that the essence or the presence that it constitutes is this past's belated reconstitution. What is *always already* has never and can never be present itself. The very possibility of essence and presence hinges on such a past, according to Derrida.

The *always already* is thus not mere wordplay or the result of linguistic infatuation. It is an expression that implies an anteriority to essence and presence, that not only would no longer be a determination of Being, as is the a priori, but would also take priority over Being: if, as Derrida contends, Heidegger's radical temporality of Being is still caught in the vulgar concepts of time that it was supposed to displace, the radical past to Being could no longer be altogether of the order of Being. The specific nature of the time of the quiddity of the past hinted at by Derrida understands Being itself from the past (and not only beings, as in the case of Heidegger). Discussing supplementary substitution at one point in *Of Grammatology*, Derrida asks, "How *was it to be* [*était-elle à être*]— for such is the time of its *quiddity*—what it necessarily is?"[2] Throughout *Of Grammatology*, this temporal structure of *was to be* appears as the structure of an imperfect tense that makes it possible for what *ought to have been* (*aura* or *aurait dû être*)—namely, presence and, in the last instance, Being itself—to come into being. Yet since the absolute past in question can never become present, since it is not the trace of an already constituted and bygone present, it is also, as that which withdraws from what it lets come to the fore, that which ultimately makes presence and Being impossible. Contrary to the a priori, therefore, the *always already* is not only a condition of possibility but a condition of impossibility as well.

Having named the time of the quiddity of the *always already* as the time of what *had to be* in order for something *to be*, Derrida has shown that the *always already* is another expression for the concept of essence, or more precisely—and this explains the substitution of *always already* for essence—for a certain temporality at the origin of essence. The time of the quiddity of the *always already* is, indeed, the time of quiddity. Let us recall here that *quidditas* is the consecrated translation not of *ti esti* but of the Aristotelian expression *to ti en einai*. This strange formula—strange because of its double use of the verb *to be* and the unexpected use of the imperfect tense—answers the question of what a thing's essence and essential attributes are. It states that the essence of a thing is *what it has been*. The Scholastics translated this formula *quod quid erat esse*, and one will certainly remember Hegel's famous coining of the same formula: *Wesen ist was gewesen ist*. Accordingly, what a thing is in and by itself (*kath'auto*) is determined retrospectively. It is revealed as a past, as what it was to be. Now one may interpret this anteriority of essence either in a Scholastic fashion as what something existent already was before its actualization or realization or, with Pierre Aubenque, in a probably more Greek fashion as pertaining to the essence of things of the sublunar world only and as a reflection of the fact that here in the sublunar world essential accidents may, *ex post*, have contributed to determining what a thing or a man will, in the end, have turned out to be.[3] In either case, this anteriority is still understood in terms of an already constituted time. Yet the past that Heidegger and in particular Derrida refer to with the *always already*—the time of quiddity, the time of the essence of Being—is a temporalizing passive synthesis that allows the temporal differences of past, present, and future to appear in the first place. *Always already* before constituted time, this absolute past or passivity, to which no intramundane concept or metaphor corresponds, accounts for the fact that the anteriority of essence, and the permanence of its presence, have been dependent not so much on a particular passage of a given time sequence as on a structure of temporal referral in general. It is this very structure of temporal referral that Derrida calls absolute past or absolute passivity and that he refers to with the expression *always already*. In short, then, the term *always already* articulates the "quiddity" of quiddity, and is, according to its nature as a past that was never a past-present and that consequently can never become fully present, at once the condition of possibility and impossibility and impossibility of essence. The temporality of the *always already*, although it reveals what makes essence possible, is at the same time the a priori of a counteressence that prevents it from ever coming into its own, from ever being absolutely itself. An irreducible part of chance and probability is thus shown to enter into the constitution of an essence, yet such contingency and accidentality are not graspable through the Aristotelian distinction of inessential accidents and essential accidents (*symbebekota kath'auta*), in which the latter forms a constitutive part of what *has been* the essence of a thing or human being. Deconstruction, in a Derridean sense, is the double affirmation of essence and counteressence, and the expression *always already* is nothing other than this affirmation.

This lengthy (yet, obviously, all too brief) elaboration on the expression *always already* should not only clarify what is meant by this notion but also give an inkling of the leading hypotheses that organize Warminski's exploration of the relational and differential space of the in-between. His formula "*always already* and *always not yet*" is a clear echo of Derrida's double affirmation as well as of the latter's search for a priori infrastructures or undecidables that function as conditions of possibility, conditions that, at the same time, limit what they constitute. In what follows, it remains for us to examine the terms in which Warminski thematizes in-between structures, as well as the manner in which these structures differ from the results yielded by grammatological and rhetorical or tropological readings. To understand the sort of linguistic "inauthenticity" Warminski aims at—a linguistic "property" perhaps less tangible than Derridean infrastructures and ostensibly less scandalous than Paul de Man's interruptive tropes but nonetheless equally constitutive (undialectically and untranscendentally)—we cannot avoid lingering for a moment on what is called *reading* in *Readings in Interpretation*.

Warminski's work, as I have already intimated, is an analysis of the reading implied in interpretation, wherein certain techniques of inversion built into the structure of texts produce discrepancies, and through which, as Wolfgang Iser has shown, the integrating achievement of the *Gestalten* of interpretations is constantly disrupted.[4] By transposing such an analysis into the history of philosophy, Warminski not only understands history as "textual history"—that is, as a history in which thinkers are related to one another in a bipolar fashion—but is also in a position to dispute the integrating achievement of the interpretations of one philosopher by another. In his work, Warminski argues that the act of interpretation consists in neither less nor more than the interpreter's systematic reduction—systematic, and not accidental, nor owing to the interpreter's human finitude—of one or several diametrically organized oppositions of either concepts or images in the text to be interpreted. *Readings in Interpretation* is, thus, concerned with the stress that interpretative reading places on only one of the poles of the oppositions, or on one of two possible readings. Warminski's work exhibits all sorts of "arbitrary, unverifiable decisions" that lead to such one-sided privileging. In chapter 5, "Pre-positional By-play," it becomes evident that it is the interpreter's competence in, and justification of, differentiating between sides that is particularly under investigation. Apart from the possibility of such recognition of difference, Warminski questions the collapsing of sides insofar as the collapsing of two diametrically opposed elements renders a text's meaning simplified and decidable. Subjecting the art of division, of distinguishing *specific* differences (i.e., the operation of *diaeresis*), to a radical doubt is as decisive as questioning the art of synthesis, because it is in this art that the philosophical claim to totality is grounded. Examining the art of distinguishing differences within and with respect to generic forms, Warminski aims here at fundamental presuppositions of the claim to totality, presuppositions that are necessary to the possibility of interpretation as such.

As Warminski's examples reveal, these decisions constitutive of interpretation are motivated by the history of philosophical exegesis, by what has become sedimented as the substrate of acquired and binding knowledge. Because philosophical interpretation obeys a canon of sanctioned philosophical problems, because it yields to the tradition that decides what philosophical discourse can achieve and what it cannot, interpretation does not *read* what it interprets. It is, according to Warminski, not concerned with the text. Interpretation unreads. In contrast, *reading* would presuppose a certain bracketing of the inherited criteria involved in the process of interpretative decision-making. Yet, just as the Husserlian *epoche* by no means represents a negation or annihilation of what is put into parentheses, so *reading* hardly excludes the interpretative achievements of the tradition, as Warminski's overwhelming references to secondary literature on the authors he deals with demonstrates. For the same reason, *reading* does not imply nostalgia for an unadulterated and uncontaminated *Urtext* beyond the blemish of interpretation and history. As understood by Warminski, *reading* precludes the very possibility of a text in and for itself. A text is possible only because it has no self of its own.

A more precise understanding of what happens in interpretation is thus required if we want to get a further hold on *reading*. The interpreter, by determining the difference between possible meaning in terms of philosophically sanctioned pairs of oppositions, or by collapsing different textual elements into one, flattens out the difference and suppresses what Warminski calls the two-way narrative, the history between things that are different. Yet owing to this two-way history between textual facets, all interpretative readings of a text, precisely because they are reductive, are *read* and undone by the text under interpretation. Thus, Warminski will demonstrate that what remains unthought in Heidegger's interpretation of Hegel submits Heidegger's text, in turn, to a reading by Hegel's text. To suppress this two-way history between textual poles, a history that involves all interpretation in a fundamental double bind and that ensures that what it interprets will interpret it in turn, is to suppress the text. If Warminski's theory of reading did not, in the end, exclude the idea of an *Ur-text*, one would inevitably come to suspect that *reading* is an operation that aspires to total adequation with the text. Yet this faithfulness that seems to characterize *reading* is pushed here to such a point that, paradoxically, it reveals the constitutive lack of all ultimate textual propriety. To suppress the twofold narrative between the bipolar agencies of a text by deciding, say, on either its literal or its figurative meaning is to erase the literary qualification of the text. The *literary reading* that is faithful to the text insofar as it accepts, in Warminski's own words, "the text as it appears, and presents itself, to us: that is, as a written text to be read" (p. 113) "independently" of its history of reception and response—without, however, pretending to any immediate access to it—is a reading that focuses on the play of relations constituting the two-way narrative of the interface between dyadic images, concepts, or principles in a text. According to Warminski, such a literary reading is what "always comes *before* the text of the interpretation (*Auslegung, Erläuterung*) as its condition of possibility, but . . . also always goes *after* the text of the interpretation as its condition of impossibility" (p. 150). Indeed, if every movement of thought and its interpretation are vulnerable to being seen, taken, or read literarily, this is because these movements and interpretations can never hope to master or subsume the simulation and mimicry of literary reading. Literary reading, or *reading* in short, is thus that reading which, by being faithful to the play of relations that forms the in-between space of dyadic textual items, demonstrates the impossibility of reading in the sense of interpreting. And the text that is being *read* in this manner appears, then, as a narrative of the impossibility of reading, that is, as the impossibility of mastering except in always limited readings that are being reread (i.e., undone by the text's neglected and opposite possibilities of interpretation). Contrary to interpretation, which represents an operation of decision making in a totalizing perspective, *reading* is the reading of the text's unreadability, that is, of its structural incapacity to lend itself to unequivocal and unproblematic totalizations. By centering on the relational intertwining that characterizes textual bipolar organization, *reading* aims at what Philippe Lacoue-Labarthe once called a certain "active neutrality of the interval between [*entre-deux*]."[5] This space of neutrality is not the space of what the New Critics called ambiguity. It lends itself neither to mediating semantic sublation nor to the pathos of undecidability. Sharply distinguishing between ambiguity and undecidability,

Warminski conceives of the latter as the space of a truly and *radically* undecidable difference, that is, of an undecidability that undermines all possibility of pathos by putting the reading subject into question.

As should be evident by now, Warminski's interrogation of the integrating achievements of interpretation is not governed by a totalizing perspective. He certainly does not conceive of the double bind of interpretation in either a reflexive or a speculative manner. On the contrary, Warminski's work is deconstructive precisely insofar as it attempts to synthesize the interplay of mutually self-limiting interpretations in a nondialectical way. Given Warminski's conception of the history of interpretation and of the structure of texts as a web of essentially bipolar and dyadic elements, the structure or figure that will account for the set of relations that characterizes the space between poles will be primarily that of chiastic reversal. It is in the figure of the chiasm that all the threads of Warminski's analyses initially seem to converge.

Although we are cautioned not to take terms of this kind for master words or slogans, it may well be appropriate to clarify what is meant by the term *chiasm* before discussing how the chiasm may offer a nondialectical "solution" to the problem of the interplay of textual elements and to the relation between text and interpretation. Since both de Man and Derrida have systematically referred to this figure, Warminski's use of the term—at the crossroads between the two thinkers—may indeed interweave various determinations of *chiasm* from different sources into a unique combination.

Chiasm or *chiasmus* is an anglicization of the Greek *chiasma*, which designates an arrangement of two lines crossed like the letter X (*chi*) and refers in particular to cross-shaped sticks, to a diagonally arranged bandage, or to a cruciform incision. As a grammatical and rhetorical device, the figure of chiasm corresponds, basically, to inverted parallelism. In chiasm, the order of words in one of two balancing clauses or phrases is inverted in the other so as to produce the well-known crisscross effect. It is not without interest to note that this figure has received rather negative valorization from the early scholiasts on to the more recent standard handbooks of rhetoric. It is usually considered deliberately contrived and artificial, no more than a practical device. Such negative judgment still resonates in the *Dictionnaire de poétique et de rhétorique*, where Henri

Morier writes, "The chiasm would only be a sort of silly affectation were it not motivated by a superior reason, the desire for variation, the need for euphony and expressive harmony."[6] But chiasm, which occurs in great abundance in ancient writing, especially in Near Eastern literature, but in Greek and Latin literature as well, is a decisive ordering principle employed on all levels of complexity, that is, with respect not only to sounds but to thoughts as well. As John W. Welch notes, it "may give structure to the thought pattern and development of entire literary units, as well as to shorter sections whose composition is more dependent on immediate tones and rhythms."[7] Certainly, where chiasm is predominantly grammatical and rhetorical, its function may be merely ornamental and may amount to an unpretentious play on crossover effects of words and sounds. But in Hebrew and other Oriental literatures, and, as Welch has shown, in the Greek and Latin literary arena as well, chiastic inversion also rises to much more elaborate levels when it assumes the function of a constructive principle, or structural principle of form. When used as an ordering device of thoughts, the chiastic reversal is also called *hysteron proteron* (i.e., the latter first). The grammarians and rhetoricians think in particular of Homer's fondness for having his characters answer plural questions in a reverse order. Welch remarks, "*hysteron proteron* describes passages which are constructed so that their first thought refers to some latter thought of a preceding passage, and their latter thought, to some preceding passage's former thought."[8] Although the *hysteron proteron* is formally equivalent to the chiasm of formal rhetoric, it is functionally different insofar as it gives order to ideas and not merely to words or sounds. As distinct from chiasm—a distinction largely responsible for the relegation of chiasm to a secondary and merely ornamental role—the *hysteron proteron* is said to serve as a principle for creating continuity without the use of transitory particles between multitermed and contrasting passages.[9] The careful ligaturing undertaken by the *hysteron proteron* in order to achieve unbroken and continuous succession in a narrative, as Samuel E. Bassett has shown, is basically a psychological device, a function of the relation of the (Homeric) poet to his listener, "which assists the narrator to hold the attention of his listener with a minimum of effort on the part of the latter."[10] But grammatical, rhetorical, or psychological explanations cannot exhaust the role of chiasm. Indeed, when employed in order to draw together and connect juxtaposed and emphasized terms in opposition, this ordering form exceeds rhetoric and psychology, or *lexis*, especially where, as in Heraclitus, it becomes dependent on content. Chiasm, then, no longer is a merely ornamental or psychological device but instead reveals itself as an originary form of thought, of *dianoia*. Originarily, as a form, as *the* form of thought, chiasm is what allows oppositions to be bound into unity in the first place. It is a form that makes it possible to determine differences with respect to an underlying totality. The chiasm, so to speak, cross-bandages the crosswise incision by which it divided a whole into its proper differences. Emmanuel Levinas, therefore, may rightly speak of "a pleasure of contact at the heart of the chiasm."[11]

It is in this sense that the chiasm is one of the earliest forms of thought: it allows the drawing apart and bringing together of opposite functions or terms and entwines them within an identity of movements. In Heraclitus, in particular, the chiasm acquires this role of establishing the unity of opposites. Thanks to the form of chiasm, "that which is in opposition is in concert, and from things that differ comes the most beautiful harmony."[12] Nothing opposite is left standing in an isolated manner; rather, through the chiasm, opposites are linked into pairs of parallel and inverted oppositions on the ground of an underlying unity, a *tauto*, which manifests itself through what is separated. Whether this unity is that of the totality of the universe or that of the singular does not concern us here. On the contrary, what concerns us is the idea that chiastic reversals secure, by the very movement of the inversion of the link that exists between opposite poles (i.e., through a back-stretched connection), the agreement of a thing at variance with itself. Heraclitus's fragment 51 (according to Hermann Diels), to which we are referring here, and which Plato paraphrased in the *Symposium* as "the one in conflict with itself is held together [*hen diapheron eauto*]," implies that by linking everything to its opposite (i.e., the terms of a relation, as well as the relation itself when turned back upon itself), not only does one reveal a fundamental and pristine unity underlying the terms, which have in this manner acquired the status of differences, but one also yields to the demands of reason as *logos*.[13] By connecting isolated terms and relations into one whole, the chiasm is a true form of thinking. Its movements have been analyzed by Plato and Aristotle in terms of analogy, the importance of which cannot be overestimated as a form of thought in philosophy. In short, then, the chiasm is a form through which differences are installed, preserved, and overcome in one grounding unity of totality. It is in this sense that the chiasm can be viewed as the primitive matrix of dialectics in its Hegelian form. No one recognized this filiation better than Hegel himself, who claimed to have incorporated all of Heraclitus's propositions into his *Science of Logic*.

One must keep in mind the chiasm's initial function as a form or figure of unity of thought if one wishes to evaluate the significance of the recent recourses to that figure by Derrida and de Man. In view of de Man's frequent and quite systematic use of *chiasm*, in *Allegories of Reading*, for a rhetorical structure based on substitutive reversals, aligning it with metaphor, metonymy, metalepsis, hypallage, and so forth, he may seem to have borrowed the term from the discipline of rhetoric.[14] Yet it becomes clear, throughout the book, that chiasm functions not as mere figure of elocution but indeed as a structure of texts as texts. In addition, and even more important, the chiasm is not a figure of closure for de Man. To determine it in this negative manner is already sufficient indication of the philosophical provenance of de Man's notion of chiasm and the nature of his debate.

For de Man, the inversion brought about by the cross-shaped figure is not, interestingly enough, simply chiastic; it is fundamentally asymmetric. Indeed, contrary to the philosophical notion of the chiasm in which unity is achieved through an attunement turned back upon itself (i.e., through an all-inclusive totalization of all oppositions), de Man's notion of chiasm understands the reversal of polarities as a failing attempt to invert a "first" textual displacement. Instead of harmoniously linking parallel clauses or terms to their inverted order and thus creating unity, the chiasm in de Man's work fails to bring about unity because the inversion does not succeed in neutralizing the rhetorical character of the text. Only such neutralization, according to de Man, could restore the literal, the proper, or the true (i.e., that which could truly confer unity). All the chiasm achieves, however, is a substitution of a substitution, by which it prolongs the rhetorical delusions of the text as such. The figure of the chiasm, instead of allowing a final concluding exchange, a final reflection into self of the text, consequently becomes a figure, or rather a nonfigure, for the rhetorical dimension of the text, a dimension that makes it an infinitely self-deferring and self-exceeding totality. It thus appears that the structure of the chiasm as thematized by de Man, although originating in the tradition of rhetoric, is also a debate with the chiasm as a form of thought. In short, the chiasm, as a rhetorical structure, suspends the totalizing functions of the literal and the figural in a text and, as a figure, endlessly defers (temporalizes, historicizes, allegorizes) the closure of a text—by either its content or its form—through the infinite substitutability implied by its asymmetry. Understood in this manner, the figure of chiasm is one among several figures analyzed by de Man in a similar perspective.

In *Positions*, Derrida states that all writing is caught in and practices chiastic reversals. "The form of the chiasm, of the X, interests me a great deal, not as a symbol of the unknown, but because there is in it . . . a kind of fork . . . that is, moreover, unequal, one of the points extending its range further than the other," he writes.[15] But this asymmetry becomes visible, according to Derrida, only if one understands the chiasm's making of cross-connections—and the double participation that it implies—no longer as the mixing of previously separate elements into the punctual identity and simplicity of a *coincidentia oppositorum* but rather as a *referral back* (*renvoi*) "to a *same* that is not the identical, to the common element or medium of any possible dissociation."[16] As Derrida points out in *Archaeology of the Frivolous*, instead of simply folding opposites into one unity, "the chiasm folds itself with a supplementary flexion."[17] This supplementary fold makes the chiasm a structure that refers all mediation of opposites—whether reflexive or speculative, whether by analogy or dialectically—to "the medium in which opposites are opposed, the movement and the play that links them among themselves, reverses them or makes one side cross over into the other."[18] It is the very reference to this reserve that makes the chiasm an unequal fork. Hence, it is neither simply constitutive nor simply disruptive of totality; rather it is the figure by which a totality constitutes itself in such a manner that the reference to the reserve or the medium of dissociation inseparably inscribed into the figure clearly marks the scope and limits of totality. No unity engendered chiastically includes within itself the play of difference to which it must refer in order to constitute itself.

Derrida has further developed this chiastic structure in two essays on Maurice Blanchot: "The Law of the Genre" and "Living On: *Border Lines*." This development is intimately linked to a close reading of Blanchot's *La folie du jour* (The madness of the day). In these two essays Derrida ties the chiastic reversal to a movement of invagination, thus demonstrating his continued concern with the unthought of "totality." Chiastic invagination is a movement that constitutes and deconstitutes the border, the limit of a closure. As Derrida has pointed out in "The *Retrait* of Metaphor," a border and a limit are understood in metaphysics as a circular limit bordering a homogeneous field. Regarding the representation of metaphysics as *one* metaphysics, he writes that the "representation of a linear and circular closure surrounding a homogeneous space is, precisely . . . an auto-representation of philosophy in its onto-encyclopedic logic."[19] Because of the twisted figure of the chiastic invagination, the apparently outer edge of an enclosure "makes no sign beyond itself, toward what is utterly *other*, without becoming double or dual, without making itself be 'represented,' refolded, superposed, *re-marked* within the enclosure, at least in what the structure produces as an effect of interiority."[20] In short, it is the structure according to which a border, which is always seemingly the limit of an interiority set off against an exteriority, cannot but re-mark and reapply that reference to the outer within its interiority, between its center and its circumference.

What is an invagination? It is, writes Derrida, "the inward refolding of *la gaine* [sheath, girdle], the inverted reapplication of the outer edge to the inside of a form where the outside then opens a pocket."[21] Where such invagination occurs, it is impossible to settle upon the limits of the border. As a result, the edge *of* a form turns outs to be a fold *within* the form. Constantly in excess of the form, the part (the border) is then necessarily greater than the form itself. As "Living On" and "The Law of the Genre" have attempted to argue, using the example of Blanchot's *La folie du jour*, such an invagination of the borders of a form (corpus or any other enclosed totality) is in principle double and chiastically inverted. In Blanchot's text, this structure of double crisscross invagination is confirmed by the fact that the upper edge of the outer face (the supposed beginning of *La folie du jour*), which is folded back inside to form a pocket and an inner edge, extends beyond the invagination of the lower edge (the supposed end of *La folie du jour*), which is equally folded back inside to form a pocket and an outer edge while extending itself to the upper edge. What consequently becomes clear is the following: since a border encloses an interiority only if this border refers to its outer other, and since this reference to the other cannot but be inscribed within the interiority, not only do borders acquire an extremely twisted structure, but the interiority, the very space where the relationship of the form to itself takes place, appears to be at the same time the gathering space of the double invagination that crosses out the identity of the form.[22]

It is important to note that in "Living On," Derrida's analysis of a text's relation to its limits does not broach this problem in general terms. Not only does "Living On" deal with this question solely insofar as the text *as a narrative* is concerned, but its scope is even more restricted to the extent that it is narrowed down to a narrative narrating a demand for a narrative. Double invagination, as a structure of the borders of a text, thus pertains, at first, only to a text determined in such a manner; it does not represent a truth of all texts. It would, therefore, be foolish to look for it in all texts, totalities, envelopes, or enclosures. The borders of texts are not always *de facto* doubly invaginated. Yet it is a possibility that *can* come about in any kind of ensemble. Although the structure of double invagination has been developed only with respect to a very determined sort of text, it could potentially affect all texts since texts are made up of traces. Traces are not only referential but also iterable. "The chiasma of this *double invagination* is always possible, because of what I have elsewhere called the iterability of the mark," writes Derrida.[23] Indeed, this possibility of iteration is that of duplication, and where one has duplication one also has the possibility of crisscross invagination. Yet if double chiastic invagination is the result of the iterability of the trace, it is always possible, and hence a *necessary possibility* that has to be accounted for when determining the nature and the status of an ensemble. If this possibility, however, delimits ensembles, if it makes determining their edges structurally impossible, then it points to an essential *unfinishedness* of all ensembles. This unfinishedness "cannot be reduced to an incompleteness or an inadequacy" since these latter are only the negatives of completion and adequacy; unfinishedness constitutes ensembles into texts.[24] By illimiting ensembles, unfinishedness *generalizes* the text.

At this point, where double invagination appears as an accident that by right *can* befall all texts as ensembles, which consequently must be conceived as *essentially* unfinished, it becomes necessary to distinguish, however briefly, Derrida's discoveries about the chiasm from those of Maurice Merleau-Ponty. In *The Visible and the Invisible*, in a famous chapter entitled "The Intertwining—The Chiasm," Merleau-Ponty refers to the figure of the chiasm in order to conceptualize it in terms of "a new type of intelligibility," leading in principle to "a complete reconstruction of philosophy," to the locus where reflection (coincidence) and world, subject and other are not yet distinguishable, instead coexisting all at once, pell-mell.[25] This "general thing" beyond the body and the world, the reflexivity of the subject and the object, the visible and invisible (the ideas), is for Merleau-Ponty a "sort of incarnate principle" that he calls "flesh," or the "generality of the Sensible in itself."[26] In other words, it is an opening toward the world, whose generality and transcendentality is a function of what is intertwined, and which is, thus, marked by an essential *finitude*. This general opening—"that is not the shadow of the actual but is its principle, that is not the proper contribution of a 'thought' but is its condition"—is characterized "by a sort of folding back, invagination, or padding."[27] In it the dehiscence of consciousness and object occurs, yet in such a manner that both are mediated through a reversal or chiasm (a double chiasm, in fact), with the result that, in reality, no bifurcation or positing of isolated and opposite entities takes place. It is imperative to realize that, for Merleau-Ponty, this prereflexive and preobjective mediating reversal does not imply a union of contradictories: "it is a reversibility always imminent and never realized in fact."[28] No coincidence between its poles ever takes place. Its chiastic folding upon itself does not produce a totality. The reason for this impossibility of closure—an impossibility that is not a failure—lies for Merleau-Ponty with the finitude of the human being, with the limitations specific to his or her experience. And yet, of this reversibility characteristic of prereflexive experience, he states that it is "the ultimate truth," the element, or "the concrete emblem of a general manner of being."[29]

For Merleau-Ponty, then, the cosmic reversal that constitutes all prereflexive experience warrants an essential finitude of the opening of the truth of consciousness toward the world. Although it secures the generality of that opening, it prevents it from being absolute. As such a figure of finitude, Merleau-Ponty's concept of chiasm remains, however, linked to the problematic of consciousness, to man's experience of himself or herself and the world.[30] Derrida's notion of the chiasm as the possibility of an essential *unfinishedness* of totalities must be clearly set apart from those reasons of *finitude* for which Merleau-Ponty holds that the chiasm prevents totalities from ever coinciding with themselves. The unfinishedness in question does not follow from man's limitations as a human and experiencing being. It is, on the contrary, a *structural* possibility affecting in principle all totalities precisely because their borders refer to an outer, to another, and hence because iterability characterizes them as traces. It is therefore not by chance that Derrida speaks not of the finitude of texts but rather of their generalizing unfinishedness.

The form of the chiasm, according to Derrida, is the outline of a movement that, by taking note of a totality's irreducible reference to other in the very process of its self-constitution, becomes a counterlaw to the same constitution. Since the reference to other, or the totality's out-gate, remains re-marked and reapplied within the totality (i.e., in a non-inclusive mode), the structure of the chiasm "is itself related so remotely to a dialectical structure that it even inscribes dialectics."[31] Indeed, the chiasm in Derrida is to be understood as the form of that exceedingly strange space within which the philosophical form of chiasm makes its incision, in order to cross-bandage, by analogy and dialectics, the same wound. In other words, the doubly invaginated chiasm is what both makes possible and deconstitutes dialectics. It is an a priori counterlaw to the unifying role of the chiasm, a counterchiasm, so to speak, within which the totalizing function of dialectics is rooted. This counterchiasm does not annihilate dialectics; it does not destroy it but "merely" shows it to its "proper" place.

To conclude this exposition of the form of chiasm in Derrida's philosophy, let us emphasize that the chiasm is only *one* of the possible and manifold consequences of the infrastructure of the trace (i.e., iterability or repeatability and structural referral to otherness). In itself, the chiastic form has no special privilege in Derrida.[32] Nor is it a necessary empirical characteristic of texts, corpuses, ensembles, or wholes of whatever sort. It is, on the contrary, a necessary possibility of such ensembles. The struc-

ture of chiastic and invaginated reversal corresponds, therefore, to an axiom of nonclosure, to a principle establishing a fundamental law of in-
completion with regard to all possible totalities.

Having in this manner distinguished de Man's, Merleau-Ponty's,
and Derrida's notions of the chiasm with regard to its philosophical determination as a unifying form of thought, let us now consider its function in Warminski's work, where it seems, as we have suggested, to assume a dominant role.[33] The reader of *Readings in Interpretation* will be
struck by the virtuosity with which Warminski handles this figure. In
view of the extreme audacity with which positions become inverted in
sometimes apparently vertiginous ways, one may suspect Warminski not
only of being a dialectician of formidable refinement but even of enacting
the orginary agonistic nature of dialectics. Indeed, considering the specific
style of Warminski's argumentation, one might be tempted to compare
his procedure to that of the inventor of dialectics—Zeno of Elea—who,
according to his prevailing representation in the history of philosophy,
used dialectical reasoning to demonstrate that an adverse thesis contains
the radical opposite of what it affirms. Used in this way, dialectics becomes a sometimes invincible tool of refutation and destruction, which
seems to be at the service of the most extreme nihilism. But it must be re-
marked that Zeno's polemical use of dialectics is not simply destructive. It
is destructive only of adverse theses that oppose plurality and movement
to the Parmenidean One. In other words, it is a negativity that presupposes and promotes the idea of unity and Oneness. But can Warminski's
theoretical enterprise be thought of in these terms at all? Is the dialectics
in which he seems to excel merely negative or secretly positive? Is his mas-
terly manipulation of chiastic reversals simply agonistic and polemical, or
is it at the service of a hidden harmony? Is his systematic demonstration
of the illusionary character of all interpretation a function, in fact, of a
certain enigmatic unity of the texts?

Before trying to answer these questions, let us recall that there is
reason to believe that dialectics, as a philosophical method of argumentation, is rooted in the sacred games and fierce riddle contests of ancient
Greece. All these ritual riddles are said to have been concerned with describing the unfathomable One, and philosophical thought may indeed
have surged from such cultic competitions. Defined by Aristotle as an im-

possible combination of words, as a juxtaposition of irreconcilable terms, as a joining of adverse notions, the riddle appears to be the basic structure of Heraclitus's chiastic propositions.[34] The solution of these notoriously obscure statements is, according to the same structure, the invisible attunement by which what is separated becomes united. The One that is divided in itself is the answer to the Heraclitean enigmas.

Rather than manipulating dialectical thought for either negative or positive purposes, Warminski wrestles with the *enigmatic character of dialectics*, or more precisely, with the enigma of its enigma. He is, indeed, concerned with it in a manner profoundly critical of the negative by which dialectics brings about the riddle's positive solution. As we will see, Warminski aims at a sort of negativity that is not dialectically recuperable and that cuts to the very heart of the enigma of the One. *Readings in Interpretation* is about this negativity, which does not yield to the traditional opposition of part and whole but goes to the kernel of the chiastic relations by which parts are bound into one embracing whole.

If the figure of the chiasm seems to take on a predominant role in Warminski's thinking, this is also because "as a simulacrum of the transcendental" it is a direct function of his "rhetorization" of textual schemes, an operation that he borrows from de Man's later work and that serves to "read only what was always 'there'—but not in a Hegelian (dialectical) sense or a Heideggerian (hermeneutic) sense" (p. 208). The a priori made readable by "rhetorization" is, for Warminski, primarily the structure of chiastic reversal, an a priori structure distinct from similar structures in Heidegger and Hegel, in that it is intended to tackle the problem of unity and totality, particularly insofar as they are both the result of dialectical sublation. Thus, the chiasm's rhetorical provenance does not prevent it from interrogating the philosophical problems of the One and of primary division. Warminski's "rhetorization" of the texts represents an attempt at "an other possible (and necessary) rereading of the all-important *hen diapheron eauto*" (p. 55), of the One differentiated in itself. If this differentiation and unification is chiastic, as we have seen, Warminski's "rhetorization" will consist in bringing another chiasm to bear, in which the differentiation would not be that of an identical One, and in which what is different is not in a relation of determinate negation.

Although this chiasm that will be located within its philosophical counterpart corresponds to de Man's notion of chiasm, as a movement of endlessly repeated failure to neutralize textual displacements, the questioning of the relation of the chiasm's attuned elements in terms of nondeterminate negation pursues Derridean motifs.

Warminski understands dialectics as an operation taking place according to chiastic reversals. It is important to remark that the essential moments of dialectical conversion are conceived as both symmetrical and asymmetrical. What makes the dialectical chiasm at once symmetrical and asymmetrical is that one of its poles is in a position of determinate negation with respect to the other. Contrary to what Hegel terms "abstract negation" (i.e., a negation that altogether negates the singularity of a thing), determinate negation is the negation of a determined thing. Since determining a thing consists in defining it as the other of a self-same, determinate negation serves to enrich one of the poles of a dialectical contradiction. Thanks to this fundamental asymmetry, the whole in which the poles are situated is not irrevocably divided against itself but open to processwise movement and thus ultimately capable of sublation. Dialectical contradiction, therefore, is a tempered and regulated contradiction in which the exchange or passage into the other leads to the production of unity on a higher level. The nondialectical properties of the chiasm that Warminski attempts to thematize would, on the contrary, be to the side of, or asymmetrical to, the already dialectical asymmetry. To come to grips with this other figure of the chiasm, *Readings in Interpretation* centers on the analysis of what de Man has pointed out as the void or lack in which the rotating motion of the chiasm is grounded.[35] Warminski is interested not only in the turning points of texts but in what makes them truly vertiginous, or in other words, with a certain opacity in dual relations, in the pivot of the reversal (i.e., in a negativity that renders the chiasm asymmetrical and that differs from recuperable and sublatable determinate negation without simply being of the order of abstract negation). The negativity pursued in Warminski's work—a negativity of unsettling, because unsublatable, asymmetry—is made visible either in mutually exclusive (abstract, in Hegel's terms) and one-sided oppositions or else in oppositions in which the terms are contaminated to the point of *indifference*. Warminski shows these oppositions to be situated laterally to the oppositions within which dialectical and hermeneutical interpretation take place. The two sides of such slanting oppositions cannot be reconciled or mediated because they are either not symmetrical at all or symmetrical to such a degree that they become indistinguishable; therefore, the two sides of such oppositions cannot enter into a relation of negative determination. They cannot be in a relation of otherness to one another, and hence they remain radically undecidable. Like a cleft at the heart, and to the side, of the chiasm, they prohibit all conclusive exchange. These bipolar agencies become recuperable only after the philosophical art of division, differentiation, and difference establishes a contact, and thus a unity, between them. In themselves, however, they remain in a transverse position to such chiastic or dialectical appropriation, irrevocably divided against themselves, or radically indistinguishable.

Contrary to appearances, Warminski's work is thus less concerned with the chiasm *per se* and its effects than with the chasm in the chiasm. Unlike de Man, for whom the figure of the chiasm describes the endless deferral of the closure of the text, and Derrida, for whom the chiasm is a structure of referral that always divides a totality by what it believes is left at its borders, Warminski seems to consider the chiasm as the fatal figure or structure of interpretative discourse. In this figure, each interpretative discourse, as a discourse of mastery, becomes reversed by its complementary other. For Warminski, it is the figure of the logic of the unreading of each particular interpretation of a text, a logic that ensures it will be itself undone by the text it decides upon. It is also the movement by which one interpreter's thought is turned upside down by his counterpart. The chiasm, then, not only is the form of thought (of interpretation and philosophy) that makes totalizations possible, but is also the form that makes these totalizations undo each other—endlessly, or *always again*. As a function of unreading, and of the millenary constraint of interpretation by the frameworks of the tradition, the chiasm is also an operator of idealization, and of the substitution of one ideal construct for another. The gap that, for *reading*, becomes tangible at the heart of the chiasm is both what ultimately makes chiastic mastery of thought possible and what makes it forever a mock mastery. At the core of the chiasm one sees either an absence of contact between infinitely distant terms or terms contaminated by each other to such an extent that all attempt to distinguish between them corresponds to an arbitrary decision or an act of violence. This excessive gap or excessive opacity allows the chiastic reversals of interpretation to take place, insofar as they provide the space for interpretative (mis)reading. To *read* that gap at the heart of the chiasm is to suspend the appropriating and totalizing act of interpretation. To bring that radical undecidability into view is also to hold the chiasm in suspension, and with it the possibility of dialectical or analogical unification. The other negativity represented by the chasm therefore appears to suspend the formulation of the enigma, not to speak of its answer. As the pivot around which the differentiation and subsequent chiastic crossings of bipolar terms occur, this other negativity—other than dialectically determined negation—subverts the presupposed, as well as the final, attunement.

Because of this void's opacity, because of this ultimately radical undecidability, all interpretations are, in the end, delusive or illusionary. Interpretations are fundamentally accidental and inessential, although not in the terms of what would normally be considered the essence or truth of the text. Interpretations have the status of examples. In essence they are of the order of the particular and are caught in the logic of *Vorstellung*. *Reading*, for Warminski, is therefore necessarily *exemplary reading*. Examples are traditionally understood as representations of particular cases, which render a universal proposition or a universal concept intuitable. Examples are also conceived as particular cases illustrating a particular rule and are supposed to induce imitation. *Exemplary readings*, however, are not exemplary or typical of either a universal or a generic whole or rule. It is thus exemplarity that is at stake in these readings, for if exemplarity is the enigma that attunes the examples, an *exemplary reading* is nothing less than a literal unraveling of that enigma.

(1986)

"A Relation Called 'Literary'"

Deconstruction has undoubtedly been an invitation to rethink the relation between philosophy and literature as it has been understood by philosophers and, in their wake, by literary critics. But are we truly prepared to meet this challenge? The work of literary critics favorable to deconstruction suggests that we are not. In the first place, the claim either that philosophy is literature, or that literature is philosophy, falls short of meeting the challenge that deconstruction presents, for such neutralization of the difference in question effectively closes off any consideration of the relation between these two disciplines. In the second place, the claim that literature is the more primordial genre and that philosophy occupies a mere province within the wider domain of the literary merely inverts the traditional view on the relation between philosophy and literature. Finally, in the third place, attempts to argue that literature is the Other of philosophy likewise miss the opportunity to rethink the relation insofar as such gestures tend to fill in the blank space of the Other with either a highly conventional and unquestioned conception of literature or an obscurantist mystification of it. The thought of the relation of philosophy to an Other such as literature thus does not even begin to address that relation according to the terms that come with the notion of Otherness.

But if the deconstructive literary critics have missed the opportunity, so have certain philosophical appraisals critical of Derrida. Take Jürgen

Habermas, for instance. Following essentially the same interpretation of deconstruction prevalent among many literary theorists, the difference being only in his affixing negative signs to what the latter valorize, Habermas understands the treatment of the relation in question "by the influential school of deconstructionism as putting into question the usual difference of genres." According to Habermas, this "liquidation" and "leveling of the generic difference" between literature and philosophy, as well as between literature and the sciences, comes from the radical expulsion, if not exorcism, of all remnants of the philosophy of consciousness from philosophical conceptuality that marks the turn to the philosophy of language. As a consequence of such extirpation of

all connotations of self-consciousness, self-determination and self-realization . . . language (instead of subjectivity) can become autonomous to such a degree that it turns into the epochal destiny of Being, the frenzy of the signifier, the competitive repression of the discourses. With this the limits between literal and metaphorical meaning, logic and rhetoric, serious and fictive discourse, become blurred in the stream of a general happening of the text (indiscriminately administered by both thinkers and poets).[1]

The "radical contextualism" that springs from such a hypostatization of language "reckons on a liquefied language, a language that exists only in the mode of its streaming." "All intramundane movements," and with them "the system of relations to the world, speaker perspectives and validity claims inherent in linguistic communication," are "pulled into the whirl of this nonorientated stream of language," from which they spring forth to begin with.[2] Language is here conceived of as "a universal happening of the text in which the difference between fiction and reality is leveled, and all intraworldliness is overcome."[3] Needless to say, if language is thus made the dominant "force," all differences are liquefied and liquidated, first and foremost those between levels of reality and, in their wake, between kinds of texts and text genres. The evidence for such a conception of language is "primarily based on aesthetic experiences, more precisely, on evidences that originate in the domain of literature and theory of literature," Habermas claims.[4] Perhaps. In any case, I will not take issue with this assessment of deconstructionism insofar as it represents certain contemporary trends in literary criticism. However, I would hold

that this assessment misses the thrust of Derrida's thought and in particular evades a debate with the way in which the relation between literature
and philosophy is approached in Derrida's work. For Habermas's massive,
if not clumsy, conceptuality and binary schematic reductionism itself
leads to a leveling of differences between Derrida's thought and the deconstructionism in literary theory and, perhaps, in literature itself. In the
chapter from Habermas's *Nachmetaphysisches Denken* (Postmetaphysical
thought) from which I have been quoting, entitled "Philosophie und
Wissenschaft als Literatur" (Philosophy and science as literature), Italo
Calvino's conception of language personified by the character Marana,
who is in search of "the truth *about* literature," is said "to coincide, and
not fortuitously so, with Derrida's theory." Habermas even speaks of
"Marana / Derrida." In this exercise of neutralizing distinctions by pulling
them into the stream of monotonous indifference, Habermas, however,
admits that Calvino, in elaborating the theory of language in question, is
much more consistent and consequential than Derrida.[5] But could it not
be that this inconsistency imputed to Derrida's approach to language, literature, and the difference between genres of texts derives more from its
difference from what Habermas thinks it to be?[6]

For a number of reasons, Derrida has not made it easy for us to address the relation between literature and philosophy either without ambiguity or without immediately falling prey to an understanding determined
by the already constituted poles of the difference. If one believes that philosophy and literature are positive, known entities, then one can think of
their relation only in terms of the differents themselves. In this case, one
must see philosophy or literature as dominating, embracing, or subser-
viently yielding to its Other, or alternatively as involved in a more or less
harmonious and reciprocal exchange, unrelenting struggle, or dialectical
interplay of sublation. But if deconstruction presents an invitation to rethink the relation between philosophy and literature, it does so by calling
our attention to the relation itself as a relation of constitution, to use classical terms. The question with deconstruction is no longer whether one or
the other is primordial, more essential, or broader, whether one is made to
tremble by its richer, more plentiful or more abyssal Other, and the like,
but how philosophy and literature become, or more precisely, begin to become what they are in their respective difference. A deconstructive focus

on the relation between philosophy and literature requires not only that both be taken seriously in their irreducible difference but also that difference be seen to rest on an infinite bringing forth of itself and its respective differents. For deconstruction, the difference between philosophy and literature is not an established, positive given. On the contrary, what makes philosophy philosophy and literature literature takes place in a constituting "process," in which philosophy calls upon literature as *an* (rather than *its*) Other so as to be able to demarcate itself and be what it is in difference from something like literature. Neither is literature, for its part, without such address to an Other on whose response depends the possibility for literature to be what it is.[7] However, despite the constitutive role that literature plays with respect to philosophy, and vice versa, it does not follow that literature is in a privileged position. As we shall see, literature is not poetry, or *Dichtung*. Literature is only one of philosophy's possible Others.

But there are other reasons for the difficulties of assessing within deconstruction the relation between philosophy and literature. The first is that, to date, Derrida has given not one but several answers to the question of how philosophy and literature relate. Since what might be called Derrida's "performative turn," such plurality appears to be inevitable. The answers provided to that question are not only context-bound but also always necessarily singular, especially insofar as they have the structure of answers. Intimately combining categorial statement and idiomatic singularity, Derrida's elaborations on the relation in question afford no easy generalization, and hence defy application. Indeed, what follows from deconstruction's concern with accounting in a radically "genetic" mode for the surge of philosophy in difference from literature and vice versa is that a response to that demand must be invented each time anew.

From what I have said so far it should be clear that a deconstructive treatment of the relation between philosophy and literature is of necessity an investigation into what philosophy calls "conditions of possibility." Classically, the inquiry into conditions of possibility is a transcendental inquiry, in that with it human reason, rather than remaining in its own sphere of the experience and cognition of objects, transgresses its cognitive achievements by inquiring into how reason can have objects to begin with, that is, into reason's object-constituting achievements. Within the context of Kant's thought, it is the noumenal and phenomenal divide that instigates such an inquiry. Since the noumenon is beyond the reach of human reason, is a transcendence that transcends it, the question arises as to what makes human knowledge or moral behavior possible, what are its transcendental conditions of possibility, and what, in fact, such cognition or morality amounts to.[8] But I wish to claim that what is so provocative and, if you will, philosophically decisive about Derrida's elaborations on the commerce between philosophy and literature is that they put to work the traditional concept of a "condition of possibility" in an entirely different way: "condition of possibility" no longer names the a priori conditions of cognition but concerns the possibility and the limits (hence, in a strict sense, the impossibility) of distinction, division, difference. To understand deconstruction as suggesting the priority of the literary over the philosophical, or the identity of the literary and the philosophical, is to miss irrecoverably the chance of encountering this philosophical debate with the notion of the condition of possibility.

Hereafter I wish to discuss Derrida's treatment of the relation between literature and philosophy from such an angle, and will do so on the basis of an analysis of Derrida's text entitled "Before the Law." Within the limits of the present chapter, my analysis must be quite brief and schematic and cannot hope to take up in depth any of that text's numerous hints at possible further contextualizations, for instance, Derrida's repeated reference to Kant's Second Critique. "Before the Law" is a text on Kafka's parable of the same name. One of the several issues discussed by Derrida in this text is whether Kafka's story belongs to literature and what such belonging implies and means. Derrida's essay starts out by invoking the conventions that predetermine our understanding of Kafka's text as belonging to the genre of literature. But the discussion of the relation of literature and philosophy that follows brackets, as it were, all prejudgment about the nature of either. However, this is not to say that Derrida's intention is to discover a more essential nature of the relation in question, one that would give the lie to all the prejudgment and axiomatic beliefs about the respective natures of literature and philosophy. As we shall have to see, there are no distinctive essences from which either literature or philosophy could be defined. Rather, the question raised in "Before the Law" concerns the constituting and differentiating function of the axiomatic beliefs about literature and philosophy and the law to which they yield in that respect.

The relation to be investigated is not one between two already constituted and known entities—literature and philosophy. I will discuss not only what makes these entities possible and distinct from one another, but also why this relation of constitution as it is thought makes it impossible ever to start off from the constituted as a simple given, as a fact. However, before proceeding to argue the latter point, which is clearly what Derrida intends to show in "Before the Law," I must address a possible objection. Does not Derrida, after mentioning in his concluding remarks the peculiar relation between Kafka's insular parable and *The Trial*, of which the parable is also a part, raise the possibility that everything he has developed about the parable might well be included *en abyme* by the novel and hence have to be relativized? Indeed he does. Yet I shall leave this threatening possibility out of consideration in the following. For not only has Derrida suggested that "Before the Law" might do "the same thing through a more powerful ellipsis which itself would engulf *The Trial*, and us along with it" (p. 217), but what Derrida says in this reading of the parable about the relation between literature and the law, literature and philosophy, and so on, contains already *in nuce*, structurally as it were, the possibility of such a *mise en abyme*.

Derrida's essay is an inquiry into "what and who" "decides that *Before the Law* belongs to what we think we understand under the name of literature" (p. 187). Even though this inquiry is framed by repeated allusions to a seminar on the moral law and the notion of respect in Kant, Heidegger, and Freud, in which Kafka's story was first discussed, its thrust is not philosophical in a general or technical sense. This is so first because the philosophical is primarily invoked under the title of the philosophy of the (moral) law, the philosophy of law. Second, as Derrida says, even if "it would be tempting, beyond the limits of this reading, to reconstitute this story without story within the elliptic envelope of Kant's *Critique of Practical Reason* or Freud's *Totem and Taboo*, . . . we could never explain the parable of a relation called 'literary' with the help of semantic contents originating in philosophy or psychoanalysis, or drawing on some other source of knowledge" (p. 209). What and who decides whether Kafka's story belongs to literature is not to be answered in a philosophical and epistemological fashion, and this is so for essential reasons. To become aware of these reasons, let me circle back to the above-mentioned seminar on the Second Critique, in which Derrida reports having been interested in the status of the example, the symbol, and what Kant calls, in distinction to schematism, the typic of pure practical reason, as well as the role of the "as if" in the second formulation of the categorical imperative. Derrida evokes the seminar in the following passage:

I tried to show how it [the "as if"] almost [*virtuellement*] introduces narrativity and fiction into the very core of legal thought, at the moment when the latter begins to speak and to question the moral subject. Though the authority of the law seems to exclude all historicity and empirical narrativity, and this at the moment when its rationality seems alien to all fiction and imagination—even the transcendental imagination—it still seems *a priori* to shelter these parasites. (p. 190)

What is at stake here is certainly not that the philosophy of law would be literature, and even less that its claim to authority and autonomy would be undermined or canceled out by the presence in its core of narrativity and fiction. First of all, with the "as if," narrativity and fiction are said to be only *almost*, or more precisely, *virtually* present in the pure and in principle unrepresentable law. In other words, they are present as possibilities, not as actualities. In addition, if Derrida can say that the thought of the pure law seems a priori to shelter narrativity and fiction, it is because he understands these possibilities to be conditions, rules, laws under which alone the thought of pure law becomes possible. In short, then, there is an a priori structural necessity for the pure moral law, or legal thought in general, to be inhabited not by actual narrativity, fiction, or literature but by their virtual possibility. The philosophical, in the shape of moral thought, must combine with the possibility in its core of an Other—that is, here, with the literary—if it is to be possible at all.[9] Apart from the fact that we here encounter a novel concept of an a priori condition of possibility, a concept that is novel as well with regard to how philosophy and literature relate, the dependence of the law upon the possibility of fiction and narration also points to a recast conception of the universal and the singular. That this is the case should become clear below when I turn to Derrida's elaborations on the literary status of "Before the Law."

First, however, I recall that Derrida begins his text by listing a number of axiomatic beliefs regarding identity, unity, singularity, authorship, completion or noncompletion, generic belonging, and so on, which, in our Western culture, predetermine our approach and hence prejudge the work in question. Present from the start in the way we think about works, the system of these conventions explains why we take it to be self-evident and "a priori, inviolable" (p. 184) that a work is characterized by identity, unity, and unicity, for instance.[10] Yet even though all these conventions are now guaranteed by positive law, "by a set of legal acts which have their own history" (p. 185) and their "lot of 'guardians,' critics, academics, literary theorists, writers, and philosophers" (p. 215), the conditions of what is thus presupposed of works actually remain enigmatic (pp. 184–85). The attribution of a work to the realm of literature is a case in point. Indeed, as Derrida notes, the criteria to which we resort in defining a work as a literary phenomenon—narrativity or, more narrowly, "fictional, allegorical, mythical, symbolic, parabolic narrative, and so on" (p. 186)—are not sufficient to establish a rigorous distinction, since narrativity does not belong exclusively to literature and since "there are fictions, allegories, myths, symbols, or parables that are not specifically [*proprement*] literary" (pp. 186–87). Yet the law guarantees a work's literariness, its distinction from nonliterary works, just as it "requires and guarantees that . . . the *presumed* reality of the author . . . [is] one thing, while the fictitious characters within the story [are] another," even though the distinction in question is "as fragile as an artifice" (p. 185). Given, on the one hand, the flagrant lack of truly specific and hence rigorous marks of distinction to explain the literariness of a work, its belonging to the realm of the literary, and on the other hand, the consensus that there must be a proper difference between the literary and the nonliterary, a consensus moreover codified by positive law, the question as to how the distinction is made, on *what* basis and by *whom* becomes important. Regarding the determination that a work is literature, Derrida asks: "Who decides, who judges, and with what entitlement . . . ?" Put this way, however, this question is that of a subject who would claim to understand a work (Kafka's "Before the Law," for instance) as literary, "and [who] would classify it conventionally as literature; s/he would believe that s/he knew what literature was and would merely wonder, being so well armed: what authorizes me to determine this relation as a literary phenomenon? Or to judge it under the category of 'literature'?" (p. 188). But the subject's presumption to know in advance what literature is, together with his question about what authorizes him to judge a work as literary, is precisely what is in question in "Before the Law." Although, strictly speaking, no specific criteria are available, the law requires that there be a difference between philosophy and literature. Although no specific, that is, essential difference can be discerned between them, the law requires that they be distinct. There must be a difference, and this difference is instigated by the axiomatic beliefs and conventions alluded to above. Yet if they permit the (pre-)judgment that something is literary (and hence distinct), it is in the name of a law that requires that there be difference where there is, in principle, none. It is before this law that Derrida, in this essay, will summon the utterance of the double question, the claim it makes, as well as the subject of its enunciation.

Before I continue, let me summon up the stakes. "Before the Law" is an inquiry into how difference is achieved in the absence of all natural or simply conventional criteria. It is an investigation into the necessity to differentiate in advance of all such criteria, before the discursive distinction natural/conventional arises, which serves only after the fact to justify the differences incurred by the need for there to be difference. In the case of what distinguishes literature, it should be obvious that such distinction is a function of a juridical performative. But Derrida's prime interest in the essay is with the law that requires that there be difference in the first place. If the difference between the two realms of literature and philosophy is ultimately rooted in a juridical performative, the questions regarding their relation, their difference, and the condition of possibility of their respective identity necessarily take a very particular shape. What we will have to face in this case is a conception of identity according to which propriety requires disappropriation. The propriety, specificity, and identity of what *must* be different, in the absence of any natural or arbitrary foundation for that difference, obtains only on condition that it not be entirely itself and with itself. The conditions of possibility for such differents must thus imply impossibility as well. Inevitably, each condition of this kind has its own particular status. The same applies to what the differents have in common. In anticipation of what I hope to show, let me say that rather than belonging to truth, they are of the order of (and this does not mean they are identical to) the nontruth that Heidegger claims is the truth of truth (see p. 206). More precisely, these conditions of possibility for difference and identity where no generic or specific differentiation already exists (if it ever does) must have something to do with fiction, not in the sense, however, of a work of fiction, of something imaginary, the narrative of an imaginary event, but in the sense of a quasi-transcendental (legal) fiction, not to say schematism, of a fictionating though not fictitious legislation.

From what has been established so far, it should come as no surprise that Derrida shall offer no answer to the double question about *what* and *who* judges: "I shall say without further delay that I cannot give nor am I withholding an answer to such a question" (p. 187). Instead of answering it, he will "only focus [*aiguiser*, to point or sharpen], at the risk of deforming [it], this double question (who decides, who judges, and with what entitlement, what belongs to literature?) and, above all, . . . summon before the law the utterance itself of this double question" (p. 188). If the (double) question is not to be answered, this is because it is not the right question, this right question being one that concerns the law that permits prejudgment and guarantees distinction where no proper distinction can be made. To pose the right question, that is, the question regarding the differential law that makes distinction possible, is first of all to transform the nature of the question itself, its questioning form. But this question knows no answer either. Its answer avoids the question by essentializing the law that permits prejudgment, that is, by establishing in advance something about the law that is the law in advance of all knowledge and distinction. Hence answering the question not only evades the challenge of the question but leads to an infinite regress.[11]

Let me reemphasize that the axioms presupposed in judging a literary text—its self-identity, uniqueness, completion, and so forth—concern the work's distinctness not only in respect to things that are not works, but also in respect to other works and other genres of work. The axioms in question consist in setting and settling on distinctions, divisions, separations. To make appear before the law the question of who decides whether a work belongs to literature and according to what criteria is thus to conjure the right to distinguish before the law that makes such distinction possible. Before the law, the question in question can no longer remain the question it initially was. It has been sharpened but also deformed to the point of losing the form of the question, its questioning-form. This sharpening of the double question, in the process of which the question loses its form as a question, derives from the very law that the question addresses. In other words, any "adequate" response to this law forbids the law to be the object of an address that has the form of an answer-seeking question, a question that according to its form must inquire into the being or the essence of the law. Undoubtedly, what this means is that the law in question cannot be known. It can certainly not be the object of what Habermas calls "competitive cognition." According to Habermas, surrendering such cognition is the price that philosophy pays in order to secure its propriety and its relation to totality, a price, moreover, that marks "its turn into the irrational."[12] Unfortunately, the law that is here thought is no totality, not even in the negative shape of the totality with which, according to Habermas, postmodern irrationality begins. Nor does it follow from this impossibility of providing an answer to the question about the law that the law (itself) would be irrational, and that the only response possible to such a law would have to be of that same irrational order. Absence of competitive cognition, in Habermas's sense, does not exclude competitive intelligibility altogether. Is not the transformation of the question—the sharpening and simultaneous bracketing of its answer-seeking form—a response, precisely, in the strictest sense possible, to the law in that such transformation is "adequate" to it? Is this transformation, by which the question responds to something that lacks the distinctness of a self-identical essence and that responds to it by stripping itself of the distinctness specific of the questioning-form thus enacting the law, not a mode of acknowledging the law? But such a mode of response, despite its noncognitive shape, is not, on that account, the symmetrical Other of cognition, that is, mystical intuition. Beyond the distinction of cognition and mystical intuition, in advance of this distinction, the transformation of the question is an "adequate" relation of acknowledgment that has the form of performance. The sharpening transformation of the question enacts the law, and does so in a singular way. The transformed question is a singular happening of the law in question. The very nature of what is being investigated here—a law in advance of all distinctions, a law that distinguishes—thus calls for a transition from the cognitive mode of address and what Blanchot calls "unreason, or a secret way of seeing, or elusive thought," all of which are "still traps that reason intends for the part of itself that escapes it, and where it takes itself at its true beginnings,"[13] to what I have previously termed Derrida's performative turn. To evaluate this turn, it is important to recall what Derrida says about the possibility (not actuality), implicit not only in Kafka's story but in any text, of laying down the law—and laying it down in the first place for itself. The performative turn in Derrida is to be characterized by the passage from a merely argumentative mode to doing *and* saying, by "saying what it does by doing what it says" (p. 212). More precisely, in the performative turn (the act of) saying does not simply produce a said, it produces a said that, before it applies to anything else, first applies to itself. Speaking of the identity of Kafka's text, Derrida notes that it is "the effect of a juridical performative. This (and it is no doubt what we call the writing, the act and signature of the 'writer') *poses before* us, preposes or proposes a text that lays down the law, and in the first place with respect to itself. In its very act, the text produces and pronounces the law that protects it and renders it intangible" (p. 212). The text respects what it says. It is first to yield to the claims it makes. A saying that thus expects its own propositions to respect what they advance—a saying, consequently, in which handed-down distinctions such as form and content, discourse and argument, saying and the said, writing and the written, and so forth, become foregrounded—such a saying is performative in the Derridean sense. This performative—which is not to be understood from its opposite, the constative—is the adequate mode of relating to what precedes all divisions, distinctions, and separations as their law.

To the question of what and who decides whether Kafka's parable belongs to literature Derrida shall thus give no direct answer. Nor will he answer the transformed, sharpened question, not, however, because of some incompetence or belief "that when it comes to literature we cannot speak of a work belonging to a field or class, that there is no such thing as a literary essence" (p. 187). Rather, essential reasons prohibit the question from being answered in the first place, and especially from being answered in general, universal terms, by establishing or invoking a universal law. Derrida admits that in the position of being before "Before the Law" (before the text of Kafka's parable, first of all), he is "less interested in the generality of these laws or these problematical conclusions than in the singularity of a proceeding which, in the course of a unique drama, summons them before an irreplaceable corpus, before this very text, before *Before the Law*" (p. 187). I note that the inquiry into the question that a knowing subject poses to him- or herself about his or her rights to judge a work to be literary, summons it "'before the law,' before *Before the Law*" (p. 188). The essay, then, is concerned with how such general laws fare before the tribunal of a singular text, in particular before a text about the law; and being before the law, it is, more precisely, concerned with how general laws about the essence of literature—that literature has no essence, that it is not rigorously identifiable, that no specific criterion exists for it to be demarcated absolutely, that there is no proper name for it, and so forth—are in their very generality tied up with a certain singularity. The laws in question that are to establish the truth about literature— that, for instance, there is no truth to, of, or about literature—even those claims are thus summoned before a unique, irreplaceable singular (text) in a proceeding (*procès*) that itself is singular, since the mode of the relating of universality to the singular is, each time, marked by singularity as well. Derrida writes: "There is a singularity about relationship to the law, a law of singularity which must come into contact with the general or universal essence of the law without ever being able to do so" (p. 187). As should thus be obvious, the emphasis on the inevitably singular relation to the law does not mean that there would be no universal thrust to it but means instead that singularity is the condition under which there can be something like a law at all, a law that is pure, nonrepresentable, and as such, in purity, inaccessible. In "Before the Law," we thus see Derrida inquiring into "a law of singularity" that makes the encounter between the order of the universal and the order of the singular at once possible and impossible, where the impossible is not to be understood as the simple negative modality of the possible. It is a law for the "conflict without encounter between law and singularity, [for] this *paradox* or *enigma* of being-before-the-law" (p. 187). It is a law that the law must be pure, nonrepresentable, untouchable, inaccessible, and that it must be possible to stand before its universality as a singular human being as well. In short, it is a law that the law must be both a universal and a singular law, that the universal law must be a singular law, the law for a singularity. As Derrida's invocation of the Greek term *ainigma* reveals, the conflict between universal law and singularity, rather than making itself amenable to a purely conceptual treatment and hence to a universally articulable truth, has a narrative, storylike quality. There is, then, something irremediably singular about the conflictual nature of this relation in general.

Derrida dealt with Kafka's story "Before the Law" in his seminar on morality not because it is a philosophical text but because its narrative "proposes a powerful, philosophic ellipsis" of pure practical reason—in other words, because it contains the virtual possibility of the philosophical thought of the moral law. Whereas the philosophical text of the Second Critique was shown to "contain an element of the fantastic or of narrative fiction," the literary text "Before the Law" contains something of the order of legal thought. The distinction between the literary and the philosophical remains intact, but what transpires is that the so-called literary text by Kafka contains encrypted within itself the possibility of an Other (of itself), the possibility, but not actuality, of the philosophical-legal discourse. And this encrypted possibility of philosophical-legal thought is what makes it a "literary" text as distinct from philosophy. It is *from* that encrypted possibility of the philosophical that the literarity of "Before the Law" is engendered, or becomes intelligible. Kafka's text is thus a literary text on condition that it does not entirely belong to literature but also refers, by means of the virtual "presence" within it of the possibility of a philosophy of the moral law, to an Other (of itself).

Let me reiterate: the distinction between the philosophical and the literary remains intact even though, or precisely because, each one a priori shelters the possibility of the other.[14] Indeed, this unbreached and unconditional difference not only is required for the "logic" of contamination of one by the other to make sense, but is precisely what such contamination "engenders." Let me, therefore, try to bring the undiminished difference between the literary and the philosophical into greater relief. The thrust of Derrida's essay on Kafka is to make the question of who judges the literariness of a work and according to which criteria appear before the law, singularly, before "Before the Law." It is a question about the borders between the literary and the philosophical. But as the whole of Derrida's analysis of Kafka's text demonstrates, to make something appear before the law is not to make something appear before the law itself, since the law itself does not manifest itself. Speaking of the way "the story [of Kafka's parable], as a certain type of *relation*, is linked to the law that it relates, appearing, in so doing, before that law, which appears before it," Derrida remarks that "nothing really presents itself in this appearance" (p. 191). "Here, we know neither *who* nor *what* is the law, *das Gesetz*" (p. 207). The invisibility of the law, its hiddenness—one does not know what sort of law it is (natural, moral, judicial, political?) or whether it is a thing, a person, a place, or something else—is a function of the transcendence of the law qua law. Its unconditionality and universality require that it remain unrepresentable. As such, the law cannot be known; it escapes phenomenality. For it to become visible, and hence accessible, would mean for the law to stop being the law: "the very universality of the law exceeds all finite boundaries" (p. 196). But, paradoxically, by this same necessity, the law becomes divided and separated from itself. "Itself" is prohibited, it prohibits "itself," since all relation to itself, all exhibition of and to itself *in propria persona* would amount to an impermissible phenomenologization. Yet such discontinuity with itself is unavoidable. "This silence and discontinuity constitute the phenomenon of the law" (p. 192), Derrida writes. He adds: "Originary division of the law. The law is prohibited" (p. 204). In short, then the law exists only as a divided law, a law that divides (first of all, itself). Yet since the law is nothing in itself—no presence that could be entered—the paradox of submitting to the law is that one can only be before the law. The law also instigates a dividing line that runs between itself and what is before it and is, as Derrida suggests, ultimately nothing but this power of topological division and separation. Between the law and its subject an absolute difference prevails by virtue of which the subject's position is that of being before the law in a topological or spatial sense of the word "before." But this law also causes the subject to be an "outlaw," to always be, in a temporal sense, before the law, and hence this law is also the law of temporalization, or temporalizing division. From this follows the singular nature of all relating to the law in that all singular subjects "must come into contact with the general or universal essence of the law without ever being able to do so [*doit se mettre en rapport sans jamais pouvoir le faire*]" (p. 187). The division between the order of the law and that of the singular subject is radical to such a degree that the conflict between the two is a "conflict without encounter" (p. 187). However, this is not yet the end of the divisions and differences that the law instigates. As Derrida's analysis of Kafka's story demonstrates, being-before-the-law divides as well, and separates itself from itself. Indeed, before the law, the man of the country stands before the doorkeeper, the guardian of the law, who himself is also before the law. Summing up his analysis of the respective places that the two occupy, Derrida writes: "Neither is in the presence of the law. The only two characters in the story are blind and separated from one another, and from the law. Such is the modality of this rapport, of this relation, of this narration: blindness and separation, a kind of non-rapport" (pp. 201–2). Being before the law prescribes "two inverse and adverse positions, the antagonisms of two characters equally concerned with it" (p. 201). It is a division and a difference that arises only insofar as both characters are before the law, in relation to a law that qua law does not manifest itself.

Derrida's essay summons both literature and philosophy before the law, "Before the Law." Not unlike the doorkeeper and the man of the country, they stand in adverse positions. They are separated and blind to one another. And yet, from what we have seen, they are different only to the extent that they imply one another. Moreover, their difference is precisely a function of their relating to the prohibited law. It now should be clear that this law can be nothing but the law that assigns their respective places, not on the basis of any essential or specific criteria intrinsically proper to each one of them—their truth, as it were—but in order that there be difference in the first place. It is thus a law that they share despite their uncompromising difference and that they share insofar as they are what they are only on the basis of their inscription within themselves of the possibility of the Other. They have this law in common even after their respective differences have a posteriori been justified on the basis that they have been rooted in essential difference. If, however, this is how literature and philosophy acquire their respective identities, then it also follows that there are no such things that one could unequivocally call and *know* as literature or philosophy. Indeed, there are no such things as literature or philosophy in the sense of self-identical substances or essences. As far as literature is concerned (but in principle the same ought to be the case with philosophy), there is "only" "a relation called 'literary.'" The literary, rather than being of the order of a substance or essence, is of the order of a relation. Yet what does "relation" mean here? Of the several senses of relation at play in Derrida's essay, I retain the following: on the one hand, the idiomatic (French) sense of relation as account, report, narrative, statement; on the other, the, as it were, categorial sense of close connection, in particular, of reference. As "Before the Law" argues, the literary is a mode of reference to the law, but in a fictional mode (as opposed to the cognitive or practical mode of philosophy). Now, if both philosophy and literature are constituted by the inscription of the possibility of their respective Other, in other words, by a relation to an Other, then literature and philosophy are never present to any theoretical gaze, never established once and for all. Their identity is owed to the Other and consequently admits no essentializing arrest. Rather, they are marked by temporality, by the temporality of a future, and a futural time, a time that is not of the present. They will always have been in the future—*à venir*.[15]

There is no way that I could even come close to doing justice to Derrida's reading of Kafka's parable and his multilayered analysis of the modes in which the story narrates a story whose content has all the allure of a philosophical topos. In order to conclude, I must nonetheless briefly speak of it. One way of doing this is to tease out Derrida's explicit statements about the law, to "systematize" them and to reformulate the questions I have been asking in terms of and with respect to this issue about the law. At the beginning of the essay he raised a question that may be rendered more clearly now that we know he was concerned with understanding the specificity of the philosophical and the literary from the possibility of the Other encrypted in each of them. He writes: "What if the law, without being itself transfixed by literature, shared the conditions of its possibility with the literary object" (p. 191). What, finally, are these shared conditions? How is one to conceive of them? What is their ontological status, if they have any?

From what we have seen, the specificity of the literary, and likewise the philosophical, depends on the inscription within its core, not of a positive Other, and certainly not of *its* Other, but merely of the possibility of an Other. With this elaboration of the virtual "presence" of the possibility of literature in philosophy and of the possibility of philosophy in literature, Derrida invokes what Heidegger had called the neighborhood of poetry and thinking, intent on recasting the thought of a common ground for both. This recasting happens in several ways: first, by consid-

ering as the Other of philosophy neither "belles-lettres, poetry [nor] discursive art in general" (p. 187) but, very prosaically, simply literature; second, by disjoining *Dichten* and *Denken* as a relation in which thinking
has a rapport to a privileged Other, ultimately, to the poetry of just one
single poet (Hölderlin); third, by conceptually refining the way in which
the encrypted relation to an Other can be thought. From everything that
has been shown, the recasting of the idea of a common ground for the literary and the philosophical can take place not in general terms but only
via singular nonliterary and literary texts, in an intimate conjunction of
the categorial and the idiomatic.

Before addressing the question of the shared conditions of possibility—obviously of the order of the inscription of a merely virtual "presence"—let me first sketch in broad strokes a few things about the law, the
law of the law, what it is that appears before the law, and the relation to
the law. The law, in order to be endowed with categorial authority, must
be underivable and inaccessible. "That would be *the law of the law*," Derrida insists (p. 191). This law of the law is to be distinguished from all particular laws, say from the moral, the natural, the juridical, and the political law. It is what makes these particular laws laws to begin with, what
confers upon them their being-law. Within them, the law of these laws
remains invisible. In conformity with what the concept of the law qua
law implies, "what remains concealed and invisible in each law is . . . the
law, that which makes laws of these laws, the being-law of these laws"
(p. 192). For the law of the law, as distinct from particular laws, "it is
never a question of trial or judgment, nor of verdict or sentence" (p. 205).
Indeed, insofar as the law of the law must be invisible, it prohibits, defers,
all relation to it. "One can never reach it, and it never reaches the depths
of its original and proper taking-place [*au fond de son avoir-lieu originel et
propre, elle n'arrive jamais*]" (p. 205). Even though the law of the law is
what makes the law a law, it is not therefore an essence. Its essence is to
have no essence.

Before such a law, whose judgment never arrives, one is thus always
in the position of having been prejudged, in a double sense. The paradox
of the law is that although, by virtue of prohibiting all access, it is such
a categorial law, it is so only on condition that it is the law for something
or someone. Hence, whatever or whoever is before and outside the law

is prejudged by the law. But it, or she or he, "is also, in both an infinite and a finite way, the prejudged . . . as a subject before a judgment which is always in preparation and always being deferred. Prejudged as having to be judged, arriving in advance of the law which only signifies 'later'" (pp. 205–6).

The unpresentable and inaccessible law is such a law only if it is the law for something or someone. Hence, the law calls, and demands a response, a responsible response. Since I am interested here in figuring out the shared conditions of possibility of the literary object and the law, which are made to appear before one another in "Before the Law," I need to ask what literature must be in order to be able to appear before the law in the first place, and what it could mean for it to respond responsibly to the law's call. At this point we must briefly digress to consider the status of the "literary," as opposed to poetry, belles lettres, verbal arts in general, not to mention Heidegger's *Dichtung*. Why does Derrida inquire into the relation between philosophy and literature rather than into the one between philosophy and poetry? Undoubtedly there are several reasons. One of these is that literature has indeed a relation to the law in several senses. As we have already seen, literature, in the absence of any intrinsic determinative criteria, is the object of a legal jurisdiction, a juridical performative. Indeed, a number of axiomatic beliefs sanctioned by law tell us what literature is. Since the history of these conventions and presuppositions, as well as the law that guarantees them, "is very recent" (p. 185)— the law in question became established between the late seventeenth and early nineteenth centuries in Europe—the literary object is a thoroughly historical and hence singular object (unlike poetry, seemingly less historical, rooted in natural law and as old as mankind). Because it is constituted by a law or set of laws, literature, rather than poetry, belles lettres, and so forth, is summoned in Derrida's essay before the law. Derrida writes: "If I speak of 'literature' rather than of poetry or belles-lettres, it is to emphasize the hypothesis that the relatively modern specificity of literature as such retains a close and essential rapport to a period in legal history" (p. 214).

But literature has a relation to the law in still another sense. First, I note that in the position before the law, the man of the country decides not to enter the law. "This contradictory self-prohibition allows man the freedom of self-determination, even though this freedom cancels itself through the self-prohibition of entering the law. Before the law, the man [of the country] is a subject of the law in appearing before it" (p. 204). Before the law that prohibits all access to it, the man of the country thus gives himself the law, and thus becomes a subject of the law. This is what the law, from beyond being, presence, and essence, incites him to do. It is his responsible response to the absolutely inaccessible law. Literature relates to the law in a similar fashion.

Literature has specificity and identity only insofar as it appears before the law that says what it is, that guards and guarantees it. This, however, is not to say that literature's specificity and identity is simply constituted by (and derived from) a positive law in the legal history of Europe. For the specificity of the literary text, according to Derrida, also derives from its "power to *make the law*, beginning with its own" (p. 214). This "subversive juridicity" presupposes

a power to produce performatively the statements of the law, of the law that literature can be, and not just of the law to which literature submits. Thus literature itself makes the law, emerging in that place where the law is made. Therefore, under certain determined conditions, it can exercise the legislative power of linguistic performativity to sidestep existing laws from which, however, it derives protection and receives its conditions of emergence. (p. 216)

In short, then, before the law, literature makes the law and gives it to itself. This is how it acquires an identity and specificity, which, however, obtain only to the extent that they are sanctioned by the law that they subvert.

Yet at the very moment that literature *plays the law* and gives the law to itself, thus acquiring a specificity of its own, literature also, paradoxically, runs the risk of jeopardizing its own identity. Indeed, what are the "certain determined conditions" under which "literature can *play the law*, repeating it while diverting or circumventing it" (p. 216)? At this juncture, Derrida invokes "the referential equivocation of certain linguistic structures" (p. 216). What seems to remain *at work* in a literary text, after all that does not necessarily belong to literature has been cast off, is something that has

an essential rapport with the play of framing and the paradoxical logic of boundaries, which introduces a kind of perturbation in the "normal" system of reference, while simultaneously *revealing* an essential structure of referentiality. It is an obscure revelation of referentiality which does not make reference, which does not refer, any more than the eventness of the event is itself an event. That this nevertheless makes up a work is perhaps a gesture toward literature. An insufficient gesture, perhaps, but a necessary one: there is no literature without a work, without an absolutely singular performance. (p. 213)

In the final analysis, then, literature is—perhaps—the revelation of the "essential structure" of referring, of referentiality (*référentialité*), that is, a categorial, universal law (in purity, since it does not refer). But this revelation makes up a work (*fait oeuvre*), and that is why it is an "obscure revelation." It is revealed in a singular performance, in an irreplaceable, unique work that as such "engages the idiomatic, as literature always must" (p. 213). But if, ultimately, literature is the singular revelation of a universal law, is it still literature? Derrida remarks:

In the fleeting moment when it plays the law, a literature passes literature. It is on both sides of the line that separates law from the outlaw, it splits the being-before-the-law, it is at once, like the man from the country, "before the law" and "prior to the law." Prior to the being-before-the-law which is also that of the doorkeeper. But within so unlikely a site, would it have taken place? Would it have been appropriate to name literature? (p. 216)

Thus far, we have sketched a rough outline of the different statements about the law and the relation to it that appear throughout Derrida's essay. Literature and the law, literature (as a noncognitive rapport with the law) and philosophy (as having a cognitive rapport), rather than standing in a relation of exclusion, appear to be profoundly imbricated, to share the rapport with the law. They are both "modalities" of the law, as it were. Or rather, they appear to display and to interconnect different, perhaps even nonhomogeneous kinds of laws. "Before the Law" could thus be understood as a (performative) meditation on these different laws, on their rapports and nonrapports. It could be understood as aiming at exhibiting, in the shape of this singular essay, the (infrastructural) law of all those laws.

In "Before the Law," Derrida poses the question of the shared conditions of possibility of literature and the law. As should have become clear by now, this question concerns how the law instigates difference. It is a question that arises about the mode in which the making of difference is to be thought in the absence either of any "true," specific difference, or any consensual difference. What are these conditions, what must they be, what "only" can they be, if we take into account that the law here is a "force of law," a law of "forced" difference?

As Derrida recalls, for the law to be the law, for it to have categorial authority, it "must be without history, genesis, or any possible derivation" (p. 191). To intervene as an absolutely emergent order, the law "cannot be constituted by some history that might give rise to any story" (p. 194). And yet, as Freud's *Totem and Taboo* demonstrates, "the inaccessible incites from its place of hiding. One cannot be concerned with the law, or with the law of laws, either at close range or at a distance, without asking where it has its place and whence it comes" (p. 191). Incited by the purely categorial thought of a law without origin, Freud invents the event of the murder of the father to explain the origin of the moral law. As Derrida shows, it is the story of an event in which nothing happens (especially since what originates from it, the law, already presupposes the moral law); it is a pure story, one that is only narration, because it narrates nothing. "If there were any history [of the moral law], it would be neither presentable nor relatable: the history of that which never took place," Derrida claims (p. 194). Freud's idiomatization of the moral law through the fiction of the murder of the father is precisely this, a fiction called upon, incited by the moral law, but a fiction that annuls itself, the pure fiction of a nonevent. This idiomatization and narrativity at the core of categorial thought—mind you, not a narrative or positive fiction but the "fiction *of* narration as well as fiction as narration: fictive narration as the simulacrum of narration and not only as the narration of an imaginary history"—is not only the origin of law but, as Derrida underlines, the origin of literature as well (p. 199). With this notion of a pure fiction of a quasi-event, of a fiction in which nothing is narrated but which the purely categorial calls upon and thus harbors in its core, Derrida, within the singularizing parameters of the texts discussed, puts his finger on the general condition of possibility shared by both the philosophical thought of the law and literature. To share this condition of possibility does not imply that the law would be "itself transfixed [*transie*] by literature" or vice versa. For on the one hand, this condition of possibility is not yet literature but only its possibility. On the other hand, literature in the proper sense can only stage this pure fiction by simultaneously gesturing in its core toward the law. Rather than being itself this pure fiction in purity, literature, while enacting this fiction, must compromise with the possible thought of something categorially without origin.

I return to Kafka's parable. According to Derrida, "Before the Law" tells of a law of which we know neither *who* nor *what* it is. Kafka's text is not a text of philosophy, science, or history. "Here one does not know the law, one has no cognitive rapport with it; it is neither a subject nor an object *before* which one could take a position." Knowledge of neither *who* nor *what* the law is: "this, perhaps, is where literature begins," Derrida remarks (p. 207). But the story in question, in which nothing happens, indeed in which the threshold of the law is never crossed and which thus seems to recount a nonevent, also relates the origin of the law in the man's decision to adjourn his entrance into the law. In forbidding himself to cross the threshold, he not only makes the inaccessible law accessible but also makes the law the law and becomes a subject of the law. As a result, this apparently pure story, relating an event in which nothing takes place, is pregnant with the germ of the philosophical thought of the law. In literature, then, the pure fiction that it shares as a condition of possibility with philosophy cannot not turn into, say, a call for something like the Second Critique.

A pure story, or the fiction of narration, is the condition of possibility that literature and philosophy (philosophy as moral philosophy, more precisely) share. To quote Derrida: "the fictitious nature of this ultimate story which robs us of every event, of this pure story, or story without story, has as much to do with philosophy, science, or psychoanalysis as with literature" (p. 209). In classical terms, one could, if this were indeed possible, call it a transcendental narrativity. It is pure in that it relates nothing, but as narrativity it is also the condition for the idiomatization of what, in principle, is cut off from singularity, namely, the categorial. But a note of caution is required here. One cannot simply proceed to generalize what has been set forth in "Before the Law." The pure story, we have been told, cannot be simply cut off from the texts through which it became elaborated. The question itself from which Derrida started, a question with a transcendental thrust, namely, whether literature and philosophy, or the thought of the law, share the same condition of possibility, is itself marked by singularity. In conclusion, one final quote from the very beginning of the text: "In order to formulate this question [*aujourd'hui*, today] in the briefest manner, I will speak of an *appearance*, in the legal sense, of the story and the law, which appear together and find themselves summoned one before the other: the story, as a certain type of *relation*, is linked to the law that it relates, appearing, in so doing, before that law, which appears before it" (p. 191).

(1994)

The Felicities of Paradox

At the beginning of "Literature and the Right to Death" Maurice Blanchot remarks that all answers to the question "What is literature?" have proved to be meaningless. Further, to the astonishment of all whose approach to literature has been guided by this very question, its answers have underrated and disparaged literature. Even more, the "what is" question, whose form ("the form of the question") assumes an essence or substratum for its object, becomes spurious when applied to literature. The question "What is literature?" is a reflective and cognitive question.[1] Such a question and the reflective attitude that it presupposes immediately disintegrate in the face of poetry or the novel, Blanchot holds. However, thus failing to understand literature does not mean that understanding would be altogether out of the question. Quite the contrary. The lack of essence that the meaningless and belittling answers to the "what is" question with its essentializing thrust imply, as well as the tendency of the reflective approach to consume itself in the presence of literature, or rather in the presence of literature's lack of an essence present to itself, might well provide auspicious conditions for an understanding of literature whose questioning form would be distinct both from the cognitive question addressed by the philosopher about the nature of literature and from the writer's self-questioning, his own doubts and scruples.

The denigration of literature that springs from the question's concern with the essence of literature is, of course, not accidental. It results not from the narrowness of the questioner but rather from "the form of the question" itself. Thus arises the necessity of understanding why the reflective approach comes to grips with literature only by disparaging it. But such an inquiry may well locate this failure in the insufficient degree to which literature has become disparaged. Might it not be that literature offers itself to understanding only where it is radically put into question, only where it is seen as a nullity? Certainly, in "Literature and the Right to Death," Blanchot suggests that reflection, with its gravity and serious- ness, with the importance that it attributes to itself and its object, must withdraw in the face of literature. The retreat of the reflective and essen- tializing attitude signals that "literature once again becomes something important, essential, more important than the philosophy, the religion or the life of the world which it embraces," he writes (p. 302). Throughout, his essay, Blanchot seeks to hold the philosophical question, and hence philosophy as a whole, at bay so that literature can make itself manifest in all its force and importance. When it comes to literature, although one cannot avoid asking the philosophical question, it is, to cite Roger La- porte, "la question de trop" ("the uncalled-for question").[2] But oddly enough, the distancing of the philosophical gesture in hopes of doing jus- tice to literature also belittles literature. Literature reveals itself as some- thing vain, vague, and impure. Refusing the essentializing approach, lit- erature becomes its own self-negation. It denounces itself as deceitful, as illegitimate. But this movement of self-negation does not stop here: "lit- erature is not only illegitimate, it is also null," Blanchot adds (p. 301). It is hard to imagine what could be more devastating to literature, yet this is the radical consequence of Blanchot's concern with literature itself, of his attempt to understand it by holding "the form of the question" in check.

Putting aside the question so that literature can manifest itself from itself thus means that literature presents itself as a nullity, or more pre- cisely, as its own absence. To state the matter differently, as soon as the question regarding the essence of literature is put on hold, literature reemerges as the question itself, and of itself. The nullity of literature has in fact allowed literature to appear, to manifest itself, as the question of its own possibility. This is a question entirely different from that of Jean- Paul Sartre, for example. Indeed, it is a question that the nullity of literature addresses to itself and with which it itself coincides. It is nothing *but* that question, a "pure" question as it were, one whose subject is as much a nullity as its object, a question that presumes no self-present essence of what it questions.

"Let us suppose that literature begins at the moment when litera-ture becomes a question," Blanchot writes (p. 300). The question, to be rigorously demarcated from the writer's self-questioning, with which lit-erature is said to begin is literature's own question about "the possibility of writing" (p. 300). Literature becomes a question in the act of writing in which the writer's pen, without asking why it writes, will always have passively performed that question. "Now you have done what you did not do; what you did not write has been written: you are condemned to be indelible," a writer tells his pen (p. 300). This question is "present on the page" once writing has taken place. It is not asked by the writer; and perhaps even without his knowledge, it incessantly addresses itself to him as he writes. And once the writing is done, it speaks to the reader. But this quasi-objective question addresses itself questioningly not primarily to the writer and the reader but "to language, behind the person who is writing and the person who is reading, by language which has become lit-erature" (p. 301). From this it follows that this question that is the begin-ning of literature is not a self-reflexive question. For at the beginning there is nothing yet to reflect upon in the hope of achieving self-identity. The question is addressed to Others—the writer, the reader, common language. Moreover, since literature begins only as literature becomes a question, the question on the page asks questioningly about the possibil-ity of becoming a question as well. Addressed to Others, the question is in question as well.

Left to itself, free from the impositions of the reflective and essen-tializing question, literature comes into being as being nothing but the question of its own possibility, begins where it becomes such a question. It reveals itself in its beginning, beginning to exist as the question, and continuing to exist only as its incessant beginning. If literature, then, is constituted by the question of its possibility, is this question perhaps a transcendental question in a philosophical sense? Since the question is all that literature is, it would seem not to be so. If the question that is litera-ture were in a position to enable anything, it would only be itself, or what amounts to the same, namely literature, "this concern that literature has with itself" (p. 301). What is more, remaining suspended from the response of the Other to whom it is addressed, this question, rather than constituting literature in a technical sense, voids it. The question about the possibility of writing or literature coincides with literature's own self-negation. It is the latter's "own negation" (p. 301). If literature begins with the question concerning its possibility, then literature is not, has not yet been, and has no essence as yet. It exists as this absence of itself, as the question of its possibility. In the absence of the reflective gesture and "the form of the question," literature presents itself as a mere nullity.

The question, to quote Blanchot, is "the secrecy of works and loath to emerge into broad daylight [*au sein de l'oeuvre . . . repose silencieusement la même interrogation*]." Moreover, "the meaning of this question is . . . difficult to discover." It tends to disguise itself under all the appearances it takes, especially by turning into art's self-indictment, into the "prosecution of art and art's capacities and goals" (p. 301). Since it concerns the possibility of literature, the work, or writing, we will have to ask whether this silent question at the heart of literature does not derive from what Blanchot establishes about the involvement of literature with the whole. In *The Work of Fire*, he notes that "this All in which poetry now finds itself involved also involves it in an extreme intensity of mysteries, questionings, and oppositions" (p. 116). Is it because of literature's ambition to be the whole that it cannot but begin and take shape as a question? As will become clear hereafter, this concern with the whole is a concern with meaning, with meaning itself, and as such. Although I will put off a discussion of literature's claim to totality until later, the following remark on Kafka's thinking already provides a clue. It is, says Blanchot, "a style of thinking that plays at generalization but is thought only when caught up in the density of a world reduced to the unique instance." Kafka's thought concerns the general; more precisely, it plays at thinking the general, but at the same time, "it is singular, that is to say, it rightly belongs to a single person; in vain does it use abstract terms . . . it resembles a strictly individual story." Because of this embedment of the thought of generality in the thickness of the world or in an individual history, Kafka's thinking "is not completely thinking [*n'est pas non plus tout à fait une penseé*]." It is *not quite* thinking since it is unable to "rest easy in the general" with which thought is intrinsically tied up. And yet, while this thinking occurs only as a singular shape, it remains thinking, for it is not confined to incommunicable absolute solitude (pp. 3–4). Not quite thinking, but thinking nevertheless, literature and poetry make the "general depend on what is unique," as Blanchot notes in his essay on René Char. But such dependence and its lack of rest causes literary thinking to amount to essentially nothing but the "anxiety of a movement without beginning or end." To understand that in a poem the general depends on what is unique "is also to understand why the poem is division, vexation, torment" (p. 101). In other words, if the generality constitutive of thinking in literature is intrinsically dependent on uniqueness and singularity, this thinking, unable to ground itself in a higher truth, is tortured by a dependence on something that stands in a relation of contradiction to it. It is a thinking that, put into question by singularity, is tormented by the question of what underwrites it. It puts itself into question and becomes the question of itself. In literary thinking, thinking then is reduced to "nothing" but a question concerning itself. The shape that thinking takes when its entirety has shrunk to an interrogation about itself is nothing other than the question concerning its possibility.

When thus allowed to negate itself, become a nullity, and be reduced to the condition of its possibility, literature works a marvel. Alluding to the surrealists, Blanchot remarks, "if literature coincides with nothing for just an instant, it is immediately everything, and this everything begins to exist: what a miracle [*grande merveille*]" (pp. 301–2). Sheltered from the reflective question, left free to be a nullity, literature reveals, in lieu of an essence, the opposite pulls of paradox. Its *existence* coincides with the marvelous movement by which an absence, emptiness, or nullity turns into everything, the existing totality of the whole. Pushed to its extreme in a literature that assumes the nullity in question—where literature becomes "the exposure of this emptiness inside, . . . open[ed] up completely to its nothingness, realiz[ing] its own unreality" (p. 301)—this nullity becomes an extraordinary force, the force of everything, of the whole (*le tout*). Blanchot writes, "as long as this nullity is isolated in a state of purity, it may constitute an extraordinary force, a marvelous force" (p. 301). The aim of what follows—an analysis of Blanchot's essay in light of this marvel—is to argue not that Blanchot delights or even revels in paradox but rather that paradox is the necessary although insufficient condition for the happening of the chance of literature. If paradox plays such a role in his understanding of literature, if he celebrates it as a marvelous force, it is because Blanchot, against the prevailing opinion of paradox as logical antinomy and hence as having been fully accounted for, takes such antinomy to be the fortunate condition for a possible (yet not for that matter necessary) happening of literature.

Given the dominating presence of Hegel's *Phenomenology of Spirit* in "Literature and the Right to Death"—a presence visible not only in the numerous themes borrowed from Hegel but especially in the order in which Blanchot develops his arguments—one could be tempted to classify the movement from nullity to everything as a Hegelian dialectical inversion, and paradox as merely a speculative proposition and leap (*Satz*). Undoubtedly, this temptation is neither fortuitous nor entirely unjustified. It would even seem to impose itself, for does not Blanchot's own mode of exposition and argumentation in the essay have all the earmarks of a dialectical proceeding? Certainly Blanchot has recourse to *this* man who lived some 150 years before to substantiate his contention that the "volatizing and volatile force which literature seems to have become" (p. 302) today is not the result of passing historical conditions but is coextensive with literature itself, once philosophical reflection and its essentializing question have been put at a remove. Nonetheless, it would be difficult to reduce Blanchot's subsequent description and analysis of all the contradictions faced by the writer, the work, and literary language to a display of the contradictory moments of literature's dialectical self-manifestation.[3] Are not precisely all these Hegelian references, whether thematic or formal, part of the movement by which literature, after philosophical reflection has retreated, "once again becomes something important, essential, more important than . . . philosophy" (p. 302)? Of Mallarmé, Blanchot holds in *The Space of Literature* that "his Hegelian vocabulary would merit no attention, were it not animated by an authentic experience."[4] The same is true of Blanchot's own borrowings from Hegel. Right from the start, he acknowledges that his remarks on Hegel "are quite remote from the text of the *Phenomenology* and make no attempt to illuminate it" (p. 302). These remarks serve nonphilosophical, nonreflective purposes.[5]

Blanchot sketches out the main features of his conception of paradox and its "constitutive" role in a series of developments that call on a number of (often consecutive) passages in Hegel's *Phenomenology*. The first passages to be invoked are from the section "Individuality Which Takes Itself to Be Real in and for Itself," more precisely from its first chapter, "The Spiritual Animal Kingdom and Deceit or the 'Matter in Hand' Itself," an analysis, according to Blanchot, of "human work in general" in which Hegel is also said to describe the contradictions "in which someone who has chosen to be a man of letters" becomes entangled (p. 302). The writer, he notes, from "his very first step . . . [is] stopped by a contradiction": to write, a writer needs talent, but he has no talent until he has proven it by writing. In this first account of what Blanchot terms the "anomaly" constitutive of "the essence of literary activity" (p. 303), Blanchot seems faithfully to reproduce the Hegelian dialectic between the individual and his effective reality as work, including the final solution of this contradiction by means of the individual's advance consciousness of his work "as *entirely his* own, i.e. as an *End*" (p. 303). Yet Blanchot concludes the rendering of this contradiction with the remark that "the same [contradictory situation] is true for each new work, because everything begins again from nothing" (p. 303). In short, now that the contradiction in question has been sublated, Blanchot, rather than following Hegel to another and higher contradiction, hangs on to what Hegel leaves behind. Blanchot continues to insist on the necessity that the writer go endlessly through the same contradictory motion without respite. What is more, he complicates the initial dilemma of the writer, deepening it, making it ever more hopeless, first by asking why the writer who has his future work present as an End should still translate it into words; and second by remarking that if the writer is aware that his work has value only as a realized work, "he will begin to write, but starting from nothing and with nothing in mind—like a nothingness working in nothingness" (p. 304). The requisites considered by Hegel for the dialectical solution of the writer's contradiction are thus shown only to aggravate his situation. As should already be evident, Blanchot's emphasis in these descriptions is the insolubility of the contradiction. He notes that the problem of talent and work "could never be overcome if the person writing expected its solution to give him the right to begin writing" (p. 304). The contradiction we are dealing with is thus not to be solved, dialectically or otherwise. "The writer both must and must not overcome" it, we are told (p. 303). Or again, to overcome it he must not overcome it. To be a writer and to bring forth a work, he must hold out the contradiction in all its insolubility. While Blanchot appeals to Hegel's authority to claim that the writer must "start immediately, and, whatever the circumstances, without further scruples about beginning, means, or End, proceed to action" (p. 304), the immediacy of the act of writing Blanchot has in mind is indicative of the insolubility of the problem, not of the beginning of the solution of the contradiction itself in the actual work. For, indeed, the work in which the contradiction is overcome is logically, or dialectically, underivable from the contradiction. For a work to arise from it, a work that merits that name, the contradiction must be unsolvable. The unsolvability of the contradiction and its "immediacy," that is, the irreducibility of what springs from it, are thus the first traits of paradox that we need to refine further.

Let us now suppose with Blanchot that the work has taken shape and that with it the writer has been born. This situation exhibits a new set of contradictions, which Blanchot couches again in Hegelian language, drawing on the dialectics of exteriorization as developed in the second half of the chapter "The Spiritual Animal Kingdom." Still, one must not lose sight of what has been established so far about the work. The work, supposed to have come into existence ("let us suppose"), can only be a work that stands in no causal or dialectical relation to the contradictory conditions of its production. In addition, the new set of contradictions that arises once the writer has shown his talent in producing a work is incommensurate with the first set. It is not derived from the first set, nor is it made up of higher contradictions. It is just one more set. What then do these additional contradictions amount to? Although the work makes the writer a writer, it does so only to the extent that it is not exclusively his work but "belongs to other people, people who can read it." But the interest other people have in his work differs from his own interest in it and "transforms it into something different, something in which he does not recognize the original perfection" (p. 306). None of the possible solutions to this "disconcerting ordeal [*épreuve déconcertante*]" (p. 306)—that the writer suppress the work as a public institution by insisting on individual authorship, or that he suppress himself as a writer by letting the reader be the true author of the work—have any chance in succeeding. Valéry's answer to this dilemma, based on a reflection on the technique involved in the creation of an art work, fails as well, Blanchot argues. But what of the claim that this disconcerting ordeal reveals something objective about the work, something of the order of "the truth of the work, where the individual who writes—a force of creative negation—seems to join with the work in motion through which this force of negation and surpassing asserts itself" (p. 308)? This idea of a synthesis of work and individual, in Hegel's terms, the "Thing itself" ("the matter in hand itself," A. V. Miller translates), plays, Blanchot admits, "a vital role in the literary undertaking" (p. 308). Yet what Hegel understood to be a (still abstract) Concept gained by self-consciousness in the process of its self-realization through the work, and hence a (first) solution to the contradictions in question, is immediately shown to engender yet another set of contradictions.

It is necessary already, but particularly in anticipation of what Blanchot will establish about the new set of contradictions, to broach the question about the notion of contradiction itself as used in "Literature and the Right to Death." Are the exigencies between which the writer and his work find themselves contradictions in a strict sense? First, what is one to make of the fact that while elaborating upon the conflict a writer encounters when attempting to write, Blanchot describes as contradictions moments that for Hegel call upon one another? Although Hegel speaks of contradiction when he begins his discussion of the dialectical relations between work and individual (*der Grundwiderspruch des Werks*), the analysis of the moments of talent and action serves only to show that the individual, eager to bring about a work, is caught in a (nonvicious) circle. Hegel writes: "The individual who is going to act seems, therefore, to find himself in a circle in which each moment already presupposes the other, and thus he seems unable to find a beginning, because he only gets to know his original nature, which must be his End, *from the deed*, while, in order to act, he must have that End beforehand." Hegel emphasizes that the individual "is beginning, means, and End, all in one." Talent, action, and end, being intimately interconnected (*verknüpft*) as his own moments, are sublated contradictions from the start. The contradictions between them are only contradictions on the face of it. Hegel even speaks in this context of the "illusory appearance of an antithesis."[6] It is thus apparent that Blanchot's understanding of contradiction is not identical to Hegel's. Hence, a satisfactory answer as to how one is to take "contradiction" in Blanchot's text will depend on a deeper understanding of the conflictual nature of the positions outlined. But this much should already be clear: they are not contradictions in the formal logical sense. Indeed, as Blanchot remarks, they do not represent a "problem [that] could never be overcome" (p. 304); they are not "an insurmountable problem, [that is] nothing more than the impossibility of writing" (p. 305). But despite the pervasive references to Hegel, neither are they dialectical contradictions capable of reconciliation. Blanchot writes, "There is no reconciliation of opposites: oppositions, contradictions do not get to rest in some higher synthesis, but hold themselves together by an increasing tension, by a choice that is at once an exclusive choice and a choice of contradiction" (p. 290). Like logical contradictions, they are absolutely unsolvable, but unlike logical contradictions, they give rise to a hopeless situation that can be overcome, as what has been shown about the "work" illustrates. The opposite pulls between which writer and work find themselves do not lend themselves to a reconciliation. No causal, mechanical, logical, or dialectical solution can be conceived. And yet the work *is*, in its very underivability from the insurmountable ordeal, in its *impossible solution* of that conflictual situation.

If Hegel's "Thing itself" plays a capital role in the literary undertaking, it is because through all the variegated meanings it may take, it stands for "everything which, above the work that is constantly dissolved in things, maintains the model, the essence, and the spiritual truth of that work just as the writer's freedom wanted to manifest it and can recognize it as its own." As the idea of the work (in distinction from the actual worldly work), the "Thing itself" is at the origin of "a perpetual enticement, an extraordinary game of hide-and-seek." Blanchot distinguishes two such games in which the writer takes both himself and his reader in and which make up opposite sides of a divide. In the first, recourse to the ideal of the work allows the writer to claim that "what he has in mind is not the ephemeral work but the spirit of that work and of every work" (p. 308), and thus to fool not only others about the nature of his work but himself as well. Every failed work can be declared a success since failure must be the essence of the work that can never be adequate to its ideal. But should the writer opt for the second game, and relinquish this claim, pretending to write for the reader alone, he again fools himself and the reader as well. "Were [he] not concerned with literature as his own action, he could not even write" (p. 309). Blanchot offers the politically engaged writer as an illustration of the mechanics of the second game. The example, neither arbitrary nor a veiled reference to Blanchot's political involvement with the far right, comes from the same chapter of the *Phenomenology* that Blanchot has been following through its consecutive moves.[7] Although the engaged writer claims to be on the side of a Cause, as soon as the Cause claims him, he shows himself to be "only on his own side" (p. 309). The analysis of the politically engaged writer allows Blanchot to indicate yet another "equivocation," as he now calls it. If the writer disengages himself from worldly causes, turning himself rather to the wall, he transforms that wall into the world, not a solitary universe but a space that "contains within itself a point of view which concerns everyone" (p. 310). The writer who withdraws into pure self-intimacy fools himself and his readers in the same way as the engaged writer. Playing off Hegel's ruminations in "The Spiritual Animal Kingdom" regarding the honest consciousness—the consciousness whose truth is the "Thing itself" or "the true work"—in which he concludes that the honest consciousness owes its honesty to its own thoughtlessness and thus is caught up in a number of deceptions of both self and others, Blanchot draws the much less dialectical conclusion that, paradoxically, deceit is the necessary condition of the writer's honesty. Blanchot writes: "What is striking is that in literature, deceit and mystification not only are inevitable but constitute the writer's honesty, whatever hope and truth are in him" (p. 310). There is no escaping the contradictions that the writer faces when he approaches the task of writing, nor, when the work is complete, is there any escape from the equivocations just mentioned. Self-deception and the deception of others are the writer's inescapable condition. But this mystification and deceit are not simply negative, for they represent the condition under which a writer can be a writer, that is, honest and truthful. Without the equivocations in question, the writer would be absolutely unable to realize the truth that is in him.

To throw this "logic" of contradiction and equivocation more clearly into relief, Blanchot opens a discussion of the so-called sickness of works, only to conclude that "this sickness is also the words' health. They may be torn apart by equivocation, but this equivocation is a good thing [*heureuse équivoque*]—without it there would be no dialogue. They may be falsified by misunderstanding—but this misunderstanding is the possibility of our understanding. They may be imbued with emptiness—but this emptiness is their very meaning" (p. 310). Like contradiction, equivocation is good and felicitous, provided that the tear, here, within words themselves, is absolute. In Blanchot's own terms, the contradiction, the equivocation, the paradox, must be "rigorously contradictory" (p. 128).[8] Only where there is no possible solution, no way out, that is, where "each aspect [of the contradiction] asks to be seen fully" and where "each [aspect] asks to be given meaning, strengthened, [and] made visible to the extreme" (p. 53), can the equivocation of words become the possibility of dialogue, understanding, and meaning. More generally, the positive insolubility of contradictions or equivocations, the impossibility of their reconciliation, can turn into the very condition under which a "solution" of sorts becomes possible. Contradiction, equivocation, paradox, are forces "at once friendly and hostile" (p. 343), that if completely hopeless, offer a chance for their solution. Speaking of rigorously contradictory attempts that cannot lead anywhere, Blanchot remarks: "And all the same, it [the contradictory attempt] is valuable only in its impossibility, it is possible only as impossible effort" (p. 80). But, this solution would not attain if the contradictions and equivocations were immanently to lend *themselves* to their resolution. A solution to a rigorous contradiction, or a positively unsolvable paradox, must be "made possible by that which makes it impossible" (p. 72). The condition for any solution worth the name must be the condition that makes it rigorously impossible. A felicitous equivocation may not contain within itself the means of its possible overcoming. For Blanchot, a "solution" is only a solution where it is neither preprogrammed by nor anticipatable from the contradictory elements.

Literature, writing, the work, *are* solutions to the positively irreconcilable contradictions and equivocations. Poetry, Blanchot writes is "the realization of a complete irrealization, such that when achieved, the primal absence would be asserted in it . . . on which all our deeds, our acts, and the very possibility of our words rise up" (p. 72). Now, although literature *is* the solution to unresolvable paradoxes, it cannot be a logical or dialectical solution. It must remain a solution that even though it occurs is impossible. Blanchot, after evoking the hopeless challenge of poetry, writes: "At first sight, such an attempt appears to be contradictory, unrealizable, and, as Mallarmé says, only a delusion. But it must be noted that real poetry is an effort toward this unrealizable, that . . . it has as its foundation this impossibility and this contradiction that it tries vainly to realize" (p. 64). Literature or poetry, then, are positively this solution to the extent that they are the effort and aspiration to carry through the unrealizable attempt. Yet even though such a solution perpetuates its impossibility, it is irreducible to the impossibility that makes it possible in the first place. With literature and poetry irreducible to and underivable from the felicitous conditions from which they have sprung forth, the question of their possibility becomes pressing. It is indeed the silent question that lies at the core of all works of literature. If literature is a marvel, a wonder (*une merveille*), as Blanchot holds, it is so precisely because its origin is a mystery. It occurs in ways that are not predictable. It happens as if it had no antecedents, each time new and singular. The contradictory conditions that give rise to literature are felicitous, precisely because it remains mysterious how literature depends on them. The wonder of literature is nothing but the silent wonder about its existence.

Before further exploring the felicity of equivocation and contradiction, it is imperative to follow Blanchot's analysis step by step. Imposture is an inevitable characteristic of the writer, first, because "literature is made up of different stages [*moments*] which are distinct from one another and in opposition to one another." Since the writer is "the action [*mouvement*] that brings them together and unifies them," another series of contradictions arises. Given that he is the gathering movement of the different moments in question, when "challenged under one of his aspects," the writer cannot but "present himself as someone else" (p. 311). He constantly shifts or glides between all the aspects of the writerly activity and the work. "This shifting [*glissement*] on the part of the writer makes him into someone who is perpetually absent, an irresponsible character without a conscience, but this shifting also forms the extent of his presence, of his risks and responsibility" (pp. 311–12). Asserting one aspect when approached about another, he always eludes being pinned down, avoiding any responsible response to the demand to identify him-self. But this irresponsibility that derives inevitably from the status of the writer as the gathering movement of all the contradictory aspects is also the sole condition under which he can be truly present and responsible. How is one to understand this? The difficulty that the writer faces is not only that he is "several people in one, but [that] each stage [*moment*] of himself denies all the others, demands everything for itself alone, and does not tolerate any conciliation or compromise. The writer must re-spond to several absolute and absolutely different commands at once, and his morality is made up of the confrontation and opposition of implaca-bly hostile rules" (p. 312). However, what would seem the tragic situation *par excellence* is in fact not tragic. The rules that face the writer are ab-solutely incompatible—they are not merely the moments of an underly-ing substance that would embrace them—and hence tolerate no media-tion or reconciliation. Consequently, as the writer takes (momentary) refuge in one rule as he escapes the immobilizing identificatory power of another, never does the writer identify himself with a whole substance through a single one of its moments. The exit open to the tragic hero is thus not open to the writer, nor does he call upon himself the wrath of the excluded rule. Even though at one point Blanchot will use the term "tragic" to describe the conflictual nature of literature, the conflict of the writer is not tragic in a strict sense. Indeed, it is even more difficult. Whereas the tragic hero must respond to one rule, and through it to the whole that has divided into opposite rules, the writer must respond to several "implacably hostile rules" at once. His is an impossible task, yet his work *is* and is only a response to these uncompromisingly conflictual demands to the extent that it responds to this impossible challenge. Through his work, the writer will have succeeded in providing an answer, one that, because of the impossibility of the task, is inevitably singular and unique. There is no general rule for the "solution" that such a work provides to the insurmountable conflict. The rule that presides over an answer to the "implacably hostile rules" can only be an irreducibly singu-lar rule, which hence cannot serve as a model for future responses. Such a response on the part of the writer and his work thus always runs the risk of failing. Without this danger, however, there would be no chance of re-sponsibly succeeding. A responsible response to contradictory commandments, that is, to an impossible task, literature's response pivots upon itself and becomes the questioning of its own possibility.

Yet although the hostile rules' demands on the writer are such that one might think of literature as merely the dream of a response, literature is not nothing. Literature is not a passive manifestation on the surface of the world; it is a concrete intervention in the world, Blanchot claims. Closely following Alexandre Kojève's rendering of the master/slave chapter in the *Phenomenology*, in which work is defined "as the force of history, the force that transforms man while it transforms the world" (p. 313), Blanchot ascertains that "a writer's activity must be recognized as the highest form of work" (p. 313), and that his work is one "to an outstanding degree" (p. 313). However, in spite of these new references to Hegel, a concept of work emerges from these developments concerning the book as a work that does not easily square with the Hegelian concept. Blanchot states:

> For me, the written volume is an extraordinary, unforeseeable innovation—such that it is impossible for me to conceive what it is capable of being without writing it. This is why it seems to me to be an experiment whose effects I cannot grasp, no matter how consciously they were produced, and in the face of which I shall be unable to remain the same, for this reason: in the presence of something other, I become other: But there is an even more decisive reason: this other thing—the book—of which I had only an idea and which I could not possibly have known in advance, is precisely myself become other. (p. 314)

According to Blanchot, the work as a response to a positively insoluble contradiction must be absolutely unpredictable. With work that meets an impossible challenge, something entirely new comes into existence. Although Hegel might admit that to the finite consciousness of the writer, his book may appear as "an extraordinary, unforeseeable innovation," this is an illusion to be overcome in the dialectical process. For Blanchot, in contrast, the quality of unpredictability and extraordinary novelty is an objective aspect of a work. Strictly speaking, it is a work—"a work in the highest sense of the word" (p. 314)—only if it has been unforeseeable and if, in addition, its effects also escape the writer. The work is an Other in that it is unpredictable, unmasterable in its effect, and escapes reappropriation. It is not an Other in the Hegelian sense of being the Other of self. Its Otherness is that not of the alienated self but of something that refuses derivation from self and hence remains irrecoverable. The book, indeed, is "this *other* thing" (emphasis mine). If it changes the writer, it is a change in a radical sense. It others its creator. Rather than triggering a self-consciousness through the dialectical reappropriation of one's alienated self, the work that represents "myself become other," that is, myself become unpredictable to myself, hence no longer assimilable to myself, turns the author of the work into an Other as well, into someone strange, foreign to himself, unable to master himself dialectically.

But let us return to the question of the history-making writer. Undoubtedly, the writer is free to negate all there is and to transform the existing world into a world of freedom. "In this sense, his work is a prodigious act, the greatest and most important there is" (p. 315). But however incomparable, this world-transforming feat of the work must instantly be put into question by its opposite determination. Indeed, since the writer achieves such a transformation of the world in immediate fashion, that is, through an abstract negation of the real and of all limits, his action discredits all action and remains merely in the margins of history. Literature thus represents a danger to any possible active intervention in the world, yet not so much because it distracts us from the problems of real life by luring us into an *imaginary* world as because it puts the *world* as a *whole* at our disposal. The writer "makes *all* of reality available to us. Unreality begins with the whole. The realm of the imaginary is not a strange region situated beyond the world, it is the world itself, but the world as entire, manifold, the world as a whole," Blanchot remarks (p. 316). What kind of world or whole is it that literature puts at our disposal? It is a whole in the sense that all its particular realities are negated. The whole that literature offers us through a global negation is the world itself as the absence of everything that is in the world, from which absence everything in the world is to be re-created. Literary creation, Blanchot specifies, begins "by the realization of that absence itself . . . when literary creation goes back over each thing and each being . . . [in] the illusion that it is creating them, because now it is seeing and naming them from the starting point of *everything*, from the starting point of the *absence* of everything, that is, from nothing" (p. 316). These diametrically opposite and mutually exclusive determinations of the literary—as action *par excellence* in or as escape from the world—explain the three temptations faced by the writer which Blanchot develops in conformity with the three ways in which self-consciousness shapes itself before being sublated by Reason. In the chapter immediately following the one on the master/slave dialectic, Hegel distinguishes these shapes as stoicism, skepticism, and unhappy consciousness.[9] But there is a fourth temptation, a temptation unlike the previous three, to which Blanchot devotes a lengthier analysis. This additional temptation arises from the "movement which proceeds without pause, and almost without transition, from nothing to everything," a movement seen at work in the two determinations of the literary (p. 318). The immediate cause for considering this fourth temptation is once again Blanchot's reading of the *Phenomenology*, specifically of Hegel's account of Jacobinism in the French Revolution in the section "On Spirit," the chapter "Absolute Freedom and Terror."[10] The fourth temptation consists in the wish to realize *in practice*, rather than merely through the unreality of words, the whole abstracted from all there is and from which the writer as writer could re-create everything in the form of the literary work. It is thus a wish that conflicts both with what the work qua *literary* work achieves and with the status of its creator. For, indeed, the fourth temptation is the wish to re-create the concrete world in the name of the whole and to make the writer a public, historical person. The temptation of "the writer [to] see himself in the Revolution" is not just any temptation. It is an unavoidable temptation, coextensive with writing itself. "Any writer who is not induced by the very fact of writing to think, 'I am the revolution, only freedom allows me to write,' is not really writing," Blanchot asserts (p. 321). But if Blanchot lingers on this fourth temptation, he does so not only because it is coextensive with writing but because it comprises the maximum of contradictions. Of Sade, who exemplifies this temptation, Blanchot contends: "Sade is the writer par excellence, he combines all the writer's contradictions" (p. 321). Whereas the stoic, the nihilistic writer, and the writer of unhappy consciousness are caught in a limited number of contradictions, the writer of the fourth temptation enacts them all. His literature is hence also literature in a paradigmatic fashion. It is the mirror image of the Revolution. Evoking a famous passage from the preface of the *Phenomenology*, Blanchot comments: "Literature contemplates itself in revolution, it finds its justification in revolution, and if it has been called the Reign of Terror, this is because its ideal is indeed that moment in history, that moment when 'life endures death and maintains itself in it' in order to gain from death the possibility of speaking and the truth of speech."[11] He concludes, "This is the 'question' that seeks to pose itself [*à s'accomplir*] in literature, the 'question' that is its essence [*être*]" (pp. 321–22). As we have seen already, the question of the possibility of literature is the silent question at the heart of literature. But in what sense can we identify as a *question* the fact that the Revolution is that historical moment in which "life endures death and maintains itself in it" in order to gain (for whom? life or literature?) "from death the possibility of speaking and the truth of speech"? Blanchot himself puts "question" between inverted commas. The "question" that makes up the heart of literature is not simply a question. It is not an essence; it only seeks to pose itself, or rather, to carry itself out, to formulate itself as a question. This "question" seeks to become the question, to cross the threshold of silence and to articulate itself as literature. But what is the question that literature, after speaking to the writer, reader, and common language, addresses to the Revolution in which it mirrors itself? Undoubtedly, it is a question concerning its possibility as well. The question is addressed to the Revolution in the first place because "revolutionary action is in every respect analogous to action as embodied in literature: the passage from nothing to everything, the affirmation of the absolute as event and of every event as absolute" (p. 319). Undoubtedly, the question concerns the paradox that there is only life in death, and that speech and its truth are rooted in the human being's mortality. In these decisive moments of history "when everything seems put in question" (p. 318), the question is, first, active negation: it creates an emptiness. But, second, this emptiness is the immediate realization that "*everything* is possible" (p. 318). As Blanchot's account of the Reign of Terror demonstrates, the passage from nothing to everything is achieved in the Revolution by holding out a maximum of contradictions. For our purposes let us only point out that in the Reign of the Terror, the first act, the act of negation, is also the final act; that the individual is universal freedom itself; that to be alive is to be dead; that to die is to be alive and to achieve absolute freedom; that death has no importance but is also "the richest moment of meaning" (p. 320); that there is nothing more to be done since all has been done, and so on. The task of literature is to emulate this infinite power to endure contradiction, and thus to allow the "question" to manifest itself. In literature such emulation takes the form of the question—the question of how it is that it can be everything; in short, the question of its own possibility. From the Revolution it also seeks to learn something about the "question" itself that is its most intimate being. From the Revolution it desires to learn not only how to realize the question but also what this "question" *is*. Addressing itself to the Revolution, literature inquires into how "to gain from death the possibility of speaking and the truth of speech." In general terms, this silent question concerns the possibility of possibility, of how possibility arises from impossibility. In the final analysis, it is a question about the possibility of the "question."

Blanchot sets out to describe the fourth temptation as follows: "Let us acknowledge that in a writer there is a movement which proceeds without pause, and almost without transition [*presque sans intermédiaire*], from nothing to everything" (p. 318). In the pages that follow his discussion of this last temptation—pages that deal with language in general and the language of literature in particular—we now must seek further as to how to read the passage in question. These pages discuss the object of literature's manifold inquiries and addresses. How is negation, first and foremost, to be understood here? This is, of course, a question about how the silent question at the heart of literature marvels at the wonder that literature *is*.

Claiming that "all . . . poets whose theme is the essence of poetry" have felt that "the act of naming is disquieting and marvelous [*une merveille inquiétante*]" (p. 322)—he mentions Hölderlin and Mallarmé—Blanchot begins his reflections on language by elaborating upon naming. Understood from the perspective of naming, language is "life's ease and security" (p. 322) because names put things into our possession and allow us to control and manipulate them. But such naming presupposes a prior, profoundly disquieting annihilation and suppression of what is named, Blanchot holds. What naming annihilates is the particularity of things, their status as uniquely real things, or as *existants*, as Blanchot also writes, thus gesturing toward the Levinasian distinction between *existence* and *existant*. But this approach to language in terms of appropriation and annihilation is Hegelian in origin. After citing a text by Hegel on Adam's naming of the animals, Blanchot remarks, "The meaning of speech . . .

requires that before any word is spoken, there must be a sort of immense hecatomb, a preliminary flood plunging all creation into a total sea" (p. 323). Things only enter language as universal and ideal things, deprived of the singularity of their being, without their "flesh-and-blood reality" (p. 322). Language is the medium of universality, Hegel says at the beginning of the *Phenomenology*. In the daylight of language, in its never-ending light, to use Blanchot's words, beings dissolve in their here and now, to resuscitate in the universal signification that is Being.

For Blanchot, the annihilation through which signification comes about in language is in the end a function of the human being's mortality. It announces real death: "my language means that this person, who is right here now, can be detached from herself, removed from her existence and her presence, and suddenly plunged into a nothingness in which there is no existence or presence" (p. 323). But more important is the fact that real death, the inevitable possibility of real destruction, makes language possible as an idealizing and universal medium of signification. More precisely, language is the mode in which the factuality of death has acquired universality and the ontological status of ideality. Language is the thought of death, death as thought. According to "Literature and the Right to Death": "My language does not kill anyone. But if this woman were not really capable of dying, if she were not threatened by death at every moment of her life, bound and joined to death by an essential bond, I would not be able to carry out that ideal negation, that deferred assassination which is what my language is" (p. 323). In other words, mortality is the condition under which language can proceed to that idealizing destruction of a singular reality in the flesh, thus making it ideal and, by the same token, the object of a possible address. Without the prior annihilation of immediate existence by means of which the latter is separated from itself, made other than itself in its singular and unique existence, it could not possibly become an Other for me to address.[12] But for me to speak, I too must be a universal subject, that is, I must be distanced from myself. "The power to speak is alone linked to my absence from being," Blanchot explains (p. 324). As soon as I say "I," "it is as though I were chanting my own dirge" (p. 324). It is not as a full, dominating, and self-certain presence that I achieve the ideal destruction through which the Other becomes not only the Other of a possible address but an Other in the first place. "No fullness, no certainty can ever speak; something essential is lacking in anyone who expresses himself," Blanchot notes (p. 324). Death thus appears to be intrinsically linked to the possibility of language. Without negation of the singular being in the name, no Other would arise, nor would I be in a position to be a possible speaker. Moreover, not only does negation separate the other being from the uniqueness of its existence, or myself from myself, but it also opens the space between me and an Other, thus providing the essential condition for all possible communication and understanding. "My speech is a warning that at this very moment death is loose in the world, that it has suddenly appeared between me, as I speak, and the being I address: it is there between us as the distance that separates us, but this distance is also what prevents us from being separated, because it contains the condition for all understanding." Blanchot can therefore conclude that "without death, everything would sink into absurdity" (pp. 323–24).

Several consequences follow: if the one who speaks must negate his existence, and negate the existence of what he speaks about, "if true language is to begin," "language can begin only with the void" (p. 324). Language at its most fundamental, prior to any linguistic act, be it even that of naming, is the voice of mortality. "When I first begin [to speak], I do not speak in order to say something; rather, a nothing demands to speak, nothing speaks, nothing finds its being in speech, and the being of speech is nothing" (p. 324). At its most primordial, language is death as the opening of signification, death itself become meaningful. It is the emptiness of death separated and detached from itself, the void turned to ideality, real death metamorphosed into universality. What speaks at the beginning, before I say anything, is nothing but signification, meaning pure and simple, language itself. We must now ask the question regarding the status of negativity in language. Undoubtedly, Blanchot is much indebted to Hegel's concepts of negation and negativity. But his emphasis on death as the condition for the ideality of language, for the constitution of the Other, and more generally for communication, shows negation to enjoy a status unlike that which it occupies in Hegel. Take, for example, the negation incurred in a linguistic relation with a human being who is at first a singular and unique existence. By annihilating that existence in the immediacy of its being, by making it "other than his being" (p. 324), negation in language does not transform immediacy into an Other that would simply be the Other of self, but allows the Other to emerge as the possibility of address. Such an Other is an absolutely dissymmetrical Other whose address is unpredictable, and which is the place that must have been opened in advance for an Other who is the Other of a self to present itself. Unlike negation in its Hegelian conception, negation in Blanchot allows a place for the unforeseeable.

Given that language begins with negation and that its meaning derives not from what exists but rather "from its own retreat before existence," different approaches to language become possible. The first, which corresponds to the ideal of literature, is the temptation "to proceed no further than this retreat, to try to attain negation in itself and to make everything of nothing" (p. 324). The second approach is the one taken by ordinary language, for which negation of beings only serves to resuscitate beings, now more alive than ever, in the shape of their ideas and meanings. Whereas ordinary language is made by this last approach a reliable source of certitude, "literary language is made of uneasiness; it is also made of contradictions. Its position is not very stable," Blanchot notes (p. 325). The analysis of the contradictions in question will help to explain why the ideal of literature cannot but divide into two conflicting forms. Literary language seeks to attain the absence of the thing, that is, its meaning, "absolutely in itself and for itself, to grasp in its entirety the infinite movement of comprehension" (p. 325). Words here are nothing but the transparency of the absence of things and of "the savage freedom of the negative essence" (p. 326). But since words are also "a nonexistence made *word*, that is, a completely determined and objective reality" (p. 325) in which the negativity in question finds itself imprisoned, this conflict, Blanchot maintains, forces literature into a struggle with ordinary language's deceptive assumption that the negating power of language can be stabilized by the limited presence of the word. As a result, literature, in defiance of the word, takes the shape of a liberation, of the wild freedom of negation, or of a mandate that the whole of language do justice "to the uneasy demands of one single thing that has been deprived of being and that, after having wavered between each word, tries to lay hold of them all again in order to negate them all at once, so that they will designate the void as they sink down into it—this void which they can neither fill nor represent" (p. 326). But with this the conflictual tasks of literary language are not yet exhausted. Indeed, since the negation constitutive of language, and thus of the life of the spirit and of the light of the day, "cannot be created out of anything but the reality of what it is negating" (pp. 326–27), a question arises for literary language: what it is that was lost in the beginning? Literature thus becomes haunted by the thought of what had to be put to death for language to come to life. It turns into a search for what preceded it. But this inquiry into the moment anterior to the "wonderful power" of speech puts literature into contradiction with itself (p. 327). "How can I recover it," Blanchot asks, "how can I turn around and look at what exists *before*, if all my power consists of making it into what exists after" (p. 327). Indeed, the double bind in which literature finds itself caught is that the search for what had to be excluded from language for language to arise in the first place is inevitably linguistic. Literature can devote itself only to this search because it has already proceeded to the annihilation of the something in question. "The torment of language is what it lacks because of the necessity that it be the lack of precisely this [*ce qu'il manque par la nécessité où il est d'en être le manque*]. It cannot even name it," Blanchot concludes (p. 327).

Literature begins where literature becomes a question. This question, which is now addressed to language itself, shows itself to be a question that for structural reasons arises with necessity. By virtue of being "the terrible force that draws beings into the world and illuminates them" (p. 326), language must seek the "something" that had to be excluded. But the very reasons that prompt this quest also render impossible any satisfactory answer to this question. Indeed, a definite answer to this question would amount to nothing less than a collapse of language.

In its (impossible) quest for what precedes language, literature discovers the materiality of language. This materiality—the reality, physicality, opacity of the word—no longer the obstacle that it was to a literature that sought to attain absence absolutely in and for itself, now becomes the writer's "only chance," Blanchot ascertains (p. 327). The happy fact that language is physical—"Yes, happily, language is a thing" (p. 327)— becomes the chance of acceding to the senseless, the anonymous, and the obscure that precedes it. But such a literature is not the world itself, a "negation asserting itself," but rather "the presence of things before the *world* exists" (p. 328). As Blanchot notes, literary language's attempt "to become the revelation of what revelation destroys . . . is a tragic endeavor" (p. 328). Indeed, in this inevitable quest for the moment anterior to language, literature experiences its inability to escape universality. Undoubtedly, literary language may succeed in destroying the meaning of the word as the word becomes itself an obscure thing, but this meaninglessness is itself meaningful in that it represents what had to disappear for language to become meaningful. Blanchot writes:

> When literature refuses to name anything, when it turns a name into something obscure and meaningless, witness to the primordial obscurity, what has disappeared in this case—the meaning of the name—is really destroyed, but signification in general has appeared in its place, the meaning of the meaninglessness embedded in the word as expression of the obscurity of existence, so that although the precise meaning of the terms has faded, what asserts itself now is the very possibility of signifying, the empty power of bestowing meaning—a strange impersonal light. (p. 329)

In its quest for what language excludes, literature discovers signification in general, not, however, as a transcendental in the strict sense of language's capacity to make something appear, but as an inescapable degree zero of meaning to which even the meaningless must bend. Literature thus experiences the condemnation of language to signify, its inability to disappear and stop making sense. As it seeks to disclose the secret of the day (of meaning, universality, ideality), literature discovers (only) the fatality of light: "day in the form of fatality is the being of what is prior to the day, the existence we must turn away from in order to speak and comprehend" (p. 330).

　　But the other ideal of literary language, that of reaching absence absolutely in and for itself, is no less tragic. It too encounters contradiction. Seeking to achieve meaning in its fullest extent by destroying the totality of particular things, this language cannot avoid resurrecting this particularity in the being of the words. According to Blanchot, literary language in this sense "is the movement through which whatever disappears keeps appearing. When it names something, whatever it designates is abolished; but whatever is abolished is also sustained, and the thing has found a refuge (in the being which is the word) rather than a threat" (p. 329).

　　Literature, thus divided between two slopes, each divided in itself, is "made of uneasiness," "made of contradictions," "not very stable or secure" (p. 325). But this contradictory condition is the chance of literature. Were it possible to resolve any of its contradictions, not only would the variegated manifestations of the language of literature disappear, but literary language itself would cease to exist. Literary language can be viable at all, can show its infinite possibilities or riches, only because it is structurally deficient—having to perform negation absolutely, yet being capable of doing so only by providing a refuge for the things that have been abolished in the form of the word, on the one hand, and on the other, having to inquire into the moment that precedes language while coming up against signification in general. Everything that Blanchot advances about the two internally divided slopes of literature demonstrates that limitation is the sole condition under which the respective quests can be successful. Were it not for the inner obstacles that prevent the two kinds of literature from realizing themselves in purity, literature would have no chance.

A literature that composes with the movement of negation "by which things are separated from themselves and destroyed in order to be known, subjugated, communicated" cannot content itself with partial or fragmentary results. "It wants to grasp the movement itself" in its totality, that is, the "unreal whole" of the world to which all real things refer back (p. 330). Nonrealism is thus necessarily inscribed in the realism characteristic of the first slope. Literature, on this slope, "looks at things from the point of view of this still *imaginary* whole which they would *really* constitute if negation could be achieved. Hence its non-realism— the shadow which is its prey. Hence its distrust of words, its need to apply the movement of negation to language itself and to exhaust it by realizing it as that totality on the basis of which each term would be nothing" (p. 330). In short, if the literature of realism strives to make things known, it must grasp the movement of negation required to achieve this task as such. But in so doing, this kind of literature applies the movement of negation to its own language, disembodying its own words, making them nothing, but thereby running the risk of losing its capacity to communicate. In other words, the realism of literature on the first slope is a viable possibility only on the condition that its intrinsic nonrealism threatens its very possibility. If, by contrast, literature shows a concern for the reality of things before they acquire linguistic meaning,

334 RELATION AT THE CROSSROADS

it must ally itself "with the reality of language," now "a matter without contour," in which words have become opaque and hence meaningless (p. 330). But there are also limits to this latter drift. Blanchot remarks:

Beyond the change that has solidified, petrified, and stupefied words two things reappear in its metamorphosis: the meaning of this metamorphosis, which illuminates the words, and the meaning the words contain by virtue of their apparition as things. . . . Literature has certainly triumphed over the meaning of words, but what it has found in words considered apart from their meaning is meaning that has become thing: and thus it is meaning detached from its conditions . . . wandering like an empty power . . . the simple inability to cease to be, but which, because of that, appear[s] to be the proper determination of indeterminate and meaningless existence. (p. 331)

In sum then, on this second slope of literature on which meaning was to be left at the threshold, meaning reappears as the impossibility of leaving meaning behind. Its success at making things reveal their prelinguistic reality by turning language itself into an opaque thing obtains only where this reality and its opaqueness *signify the absence of meaning*, hence where the project of this kind of literature fails and meaning returns as the meaningful absence of meaning. Thus success on either slope depends on an exigency that, although intimately associated with each slope, ultimately limits such success. However, without this uneasy condition, without the intrinsic impossibility that inhabits each slope, there would be no slope to begin with, and hence no literature. What Blanchot says about the impossibility of succeeding on each one of the two seemingly incompatible slopes in purity and in "distinctly different works or goals" (p. 332) further emphasizes the constitutive power of the unresolvable contradictions.

"An art which purports to follow one slope is already on the other," Blanchot writes (p. 332). In an absolute sense, this contamination of one slope by the other undercuts the possibility of "distinctly different works or goals" (p. 332). But the lack of incompatibility that such contamination implies entails neither the loss of the slopes' distinctiveness from each other nor their annihilation; rather it serves to guarantee a certain specificity to each slope. The lapse into its opposite, its lack of purity, allows the distinction and difference of one slope from the other. How is this point made in "Literature and the Right to Death"? As we have seen, on the first slope is a literature of realism, like that of Flaubert, which seeks its realization through *meaningful prose*, that is, by means of a language that expresses things according to their meaning. Yet Flaubert's realism demonstrates that such a language, insofar as it corresponds to everyday speech, is not sufficiently meaningful. Meaningful prose must therefore correct this situation by seeking a language able to recapture the movement of negation itself without which there is no meaning. Meaningful prose discovers this language, and its corresponding art form, in the language and art of Mallarmé. Unlike ordinary prose, Mallarmé's language, which "represents the world for us, . . . teaches us to discover the total being of the world," safeguards the movement of negativity by which meaning becomes truth (p. 333). On the second slope is *poetical language*, that side of Mallarmé's poetry, for example, concerned not with negation and meaning but with the materiality of language. Poetical language is interested "in what things and beings would be if there were no world," Blanchot states. Francis Ponge, who "has gone over to the side of objects, sometimes he is water, sometimes a pebble, sometimes a tree" (p. 334), is exemplary of the literature of this slope. But as Blanchot points out, though none of the works characteristic of the second slope can be called works of prose, their attempt to describe things as they would describe themselves cannot but have recourse to meaningful prose if they are to give expression to the muteness of things or to the senseless. While it is true that those prose descriptions of poetical language do not belong to the world in the same way as Flaubert's realism, but rather belong "to the underside of the world," they remain "perfectly meaningful prose" (p. 335), harboring a language of negativity and meaning in poetical language itself.

Each slope veers away from itself to the other. But as the discussion of poetical language in "Literature and the Right to Death" demonstrates, being always already on the opposite slope is the sole condition under which literature can hope to be truthful. One cannot choose one's spot in literature "because literature has already insidiously caused you to pass from one slope to the other and changed you into something you were not before. This is its treachery," Blanchot writes. But "this is also its cunning version of the truth [*Là est sa traîtrise, là aussi sa vérité retorse*]" (p. 333). Blanchot's discussion of how both meaningful prose and poetical language supplement, correct, or fulfill each other heightens the possibilizing or enabling function of literature's treachery by demonstrating that the other is always other in a specific way. Indeed, the Mallarmé who creeps into Flaubert is not the same as the Mallarmé who has recourse to Flaubert. No cancellation of one slope by the other occurs here. If the two slopes stand against one another, they are not, for that matter, reversible. No neutralization takes place here. Rather, the insidious passage of one slope into the other is always a passage to a distinct Other that helps accomplish the truth of the first slope. This truth is, no doubt, a twisted truth, but a truth nonetheless. Although the two slopes, like affirmation and negation in Kafka's writings, are subject to a "continuous threat of reciprocity" (p. 83), the fact that the other slope is present in the first in a particular shape eliminates the danger of their mutual annihilation. I recall here that the division of literature into two slopes derives only from a certain point of view. "If one looks at it in a certain way, literature has two slopes," Blanchot writes (p. 330). Further, he notes that they are only "apparently incompatible" (p. 332). Indeed, the division in question does not establish that literature is duplicitous, that is, made up of parts standing in binary opposition. The slopes are not symmetrically opposed. Rather, the attempt to recapture the movement of negation itself on the first slope endows this slope with a privilege unlike any that poetical language might claim for itself. And, as we have seen, the second slope arises of necessity from the destruction of particular things on the first slope, a destruction that allows these things to be known and communicated. This second slope does not therefore escape the light of day brought forth by the first.

Because the treacherous conversion of one slope into the other that insidiously undercuts all wishful identity on the part of either slope also enables the first slope to achieve a certain distinctness, there is also no end to the conversion in question. As little as the two slopes cancel each other out in reciprocity, does the recourse that each slope must have to its other in order to be what it is know a fulfillment? Having wondered at which exact point Lautréamont's transparent prose turns poetically opaque and meaningless, or at which point in de Sade's clearest prose one hears "an impersonal, inhuman sound" (p. 336), that is, the muteness of things before the world occurred, Blanchot asks: "Where is the end? Where is that death which is the hope of language? But language is *the life that endures*

death and maintains itself in it" (p. 336). The passage from one slope to
the other never ceases. It does not die. Indeed, death, to the extent that it
might be the hope of language, is not simply an end but the negative to
be held out for language to achieve truth. I now return to the question of
the contradictions, equivocalities, and paradoxes that constitute literary
language on all its levels and in all its manifestations. Is there a matrix for
all of literature's ambiguities? More precisely, where does this ambiguity
originate, and what is its ultimate and most economical structure? It has
been observed that "a fundamental ambiguity seems to inhabit all of
Blanchot's thinking."[13] My question is whether this ambiguity can be described in such a way that the manifold paradoxes, contradictions, and
equivocalities can be derived from it. Yet what would a "fundamental ambiguity" have to be for it to have a grounding or explicatory value? What
"fundamental ambiguity" could, beyond indistinctness, uncertainty, and
obscurity, have a constituting function? The last pages of "Literature and
the Right to Death" perhaps harbor an answer to these questions.

"If we want to restore literature to the movement which allows all
its ambiguities to be grasped, that movement is here: literature, like ordinary speech, *begins* with the *end*, which is the only thing that allows us to
understand," Blanchot remarks (p. 336). In the final analysis, then, all the
ambiguities that make up literature and its language stem from this fundamental ambiguity that it must begin with the end, in other words, with
death, with death's intrinsic ambiguity.

If we are to speak, we must see death, we must see it behind us. When we speak,
we are leaning on a tomb, and the void of that tomb is what makes language
true, but at the same time [this] void is reality and death becomes being. There
is being—that is to say, a logical and expressible truth—and there is a world, because we can destroy things and suspend existence. This is why we can say that
there is being because there is nothingness: death is man's possibility, his chance,
it is through death that the future of a finished world is still there for us [*c'est par
elle que nous reste l'avenir d'un monde achevé*]; death is man's greatest hope, his
only hope of being man. (pp. 336–37)

The argument of this passage, which also illuminates the title of Blanchot's piece, is familiar by now. Without the real possibility of death, no
idealizing detachment of beings from themselves and hence no universally shareable meaning is possible.[14] Man's humanity depends on his

eventual death, to which man as man must thus claim to have a right. If he could no longer die, he could no longer be human. But as this passage also underscores, although death is a necessary condition, a right, it is not a sufficient reason for ideality, universality, and communality to occur. Death entails no guarantee whatsoever that being, man, or literature will be. No cause or mechanical relation exists between death and what it can render possible. Death is merely the possibility, chance, or hope for being, man, the world, literature to come into being. Death is ambiguous in more than one respect, but first and foremost in the following: on the one hand, its negation can be final, without any effect; on the other hand, it is a possibility for something to occur, come, arrive—for the world to be a world, to have a future, for a future finished world. This fundamental ambiguity is communicated to everything for which the end becomes the chance for a beginning. This ambiguity that structures death, death's structural ambiguity, needs further illumination.

In Blanchot's discussion of Kafka's belief that literature might be a way out of the ambiguity of the human condition, in which he shows such a quest merely to transform death as the impossibility of dying into the mockery of immortality, he raises the question of the power of literature. Why, he asks, could "a man like Kafka decide that if he had to fall short of his destiny, being a writer was the only way to fall short of it truthfully?" (p. 341). This question, posed against all the contradictions, equivocalities, and paradoxes of literature that have been staged up to this point, seems unanswerable. The reason for its being unanswerable is not contingent, but, as will become clear hereafter, it is unanswerable by right if answering means "to clear it up" (p. 341). "Perhaps this is an unintelligible enigma," Blanchot holds, "but if it is, the source of the mystery is literature's right to affix a negative or positive sign indiscriminately to each of its moments and each of its results" (p. 341). This "strange right," he claims, is "linked to the question of ambiguity in general" (p. 341). This right, in which the power of literature is rooted, is thus not one more characteristic of literature added to its contradictory, equivocal, paradoxical nature. For not only does this right give rise to the contradictory nature of literature, but it will also help us to understand both ambiguity in general and the particular reason, or rather the minimal ambiguity, on which all of literature's ambiguity hinges.

"Why is there ambiguity in the world?" Blanchot asks. "Ambiguity is its own answer. We cannot answer it except by rediscovering it in the ambiguity of our answer, and an ambiguous answer is a question about ambiguity. One of the ways it seduces us is by making us want to clear it up," he tells us (p. 341). The question regarding ambiguity is thus structurally unanswerable. It is a question whose answer invariably turns into a question again. "Literature is language turning into ambiguity [*qui se fait ambiguïté*]," Blanchot writes (p. 341). Earlier in *The Work of Fire*, he had said: "Literary art is ambiguous. That means that none of its demands can exclude the opposite demand; on the contrary, the more they oppose each other, the more they evoke each other" (p. 193). Whereas ordinary language seeks to remove ambiguity and to limit equivocality by putting a term to understanding, in literary language ambiguity is set free and held out. In contrast to ambiguity in ordinary language, ambiguity in literary language is "in some sense abandoned to its excesses by the opportunities it finds and exhausted by the extent of the abuses it can commit" (p. 341). But literature is not only a place were this ambiguity is met; in a final ambiguity, literature renders it inoffensive. Blanchot continues:

It is as though there were a hidden trap here to force ambiguity to reveal its own traps, and as though in surrendering unreservedly to ambiguity, literature were attempting to keep it—out of sight of the world and of the thought of the world—in a place where it fulfills itself without endangering anything. Here ambiguity struggles with itself [*l'ambiguïté est là aux prises avec elle-même*]. (p. 341)

But precisely because in literary language ambiguity becomes ambiguous itself—as the event in which ambiguity is faced in and for itself, literature also immediately becomes a neutralizing event—the struggle, in literature, of ambiguity with itself perhaps reveals something essential about ambiguity itself. In literary language, "each moment of language can become ambiguous and say something different from what it is saying, but . . . the general meaning of language is unclear: we do not know if it is expressing or representing, if it is a thing or means that thing" (pp. 341–42). The struggle of ambiguity with itself not only concerns the possibility of determining the singular moments of language but concerns literary language itself and ultimately the ambiguity itself that is its most es-

sential characteristic. The possibility—constitutive of literature—of affixing indiscriminately opposite, contradictory, equivocal values to any
moment of language, to literature as a whole, and to ambiguity itself,
shows literature to be the event of a proliferation of ambiguity. It is an
ambiguous event itself in that it remains undecidable whether this proliferation is of the order of a generalization or a *mise en abyme* of ambiguity.
Literature *is this* ambiguity.

If Blanchot could claim that ambiguity is its own answer, this is because ambiguity is fundamentally a question. It is a question to such an
extent that it even returns in the answers that it solicits. But if "ambiguity . . . is the essential movement of poetic activity," then literature is also
all question, a silent question identical with the structure of literature itself. Ambiguous through and through, including its determination as being ambiguous, literature's ambiguity is indicative of what Blanchot terms
"an ultimate ambiguity," to which all of its contradictions, divisions, and
oppositions refer back (p. 342). "These reversals from *pro* to *contra* . . .
have very different causes" and differ in "kind, and meaning" (p. 342).
They are not modifications of a homogeneous realm of contradictions;
rather they are heterogeneous in nature. Yet in their very disparity, they
"refer back to an ultimate ambiguity whose strange effect is to attract literature to an unstable point where it can indiscriminately change both its
meaning and its sign" (p. 342). Because literature refers to this ultimate
ambiguity that is the reason for the ambiguity affecting its own characterization can literature be the place where and in which contradictions,
divisions, opposites of incompatible nature and status can meet. One ultimate ambiguity, then, is to be construed as the reason for all the diver-
gent reversals that we have seen, and rather than homogenizing them, it
explains why they can cohere in literature in spite of their disparity. What
is this final ambiguity responsible for literature's essential instability,
which manifests itself in the vicissitude, inherent in every work, of choosing between the "daylight of affirmations or the backlight of negations"
(p. 342)? What is this last ambiguity that "is always in the process of
changing the work from ground up," but does so "deep within" the literary work and in silence, for neither "the content of the words nor their
form is involved here" (pp. 342–43)? It is, says Blanchot, the ambiguity of
"that life which supports death and maintains itself in it—death, the amaz-

ing power of the negative, or freedom, through whose work existence is detached from itself and made significant" (p. 343). The question then is: what *is* death, for it to play this invisible yet pivotal role? In what sense can it be the ultimate ambiguity, with which consequently everything *begins* and which communicates its ambiguity to everything, with the result that what begins has also already reached its end?

Death is this last point of instability in the life that maintains itself in it—the life of daylight, language, universally communicable meaning, and so forth—hence the last point of the possibility of the indifferent reversals of negative and positive values. For at the very moment it makes meaning possible, death continues "to assert itself [*s'affirme encore*] as continually differing possibility [*comme une possibilité toujours autre*]" (p. 343). Within the meaning that it renders possible, death remains as the affirmation of its negation and as the possibility of an always other possibility. Death is the power of an always other or alternate possibility (*alternative*) and hence the "cause" of ambiguity, because even though it allows ideality, universality, and meaning to come about, it continues to perpetuate "an irreducible *double meaning*, a choice whose terms are covered over with the ambiguity that makes them identical to one another as it makes them opposite" (p. 344). Indeed, death is the inevitable power of the additional possibility of a foundering of meaning, a lack of meaning, and a loss of the chance of its occurrence. Ideality and universality are always in jeopardy. There is always the possibility that they may not occur. This means also that all relation to an Other and all possible address could possibly be missing. Needless to say, the possibility of such infelicity is not the simple symmetrical opposite of meaning. All the reversals discussed up to this point have their matrix in this dissymmetrical, always-other possibility that death be what one perhaps too lightly terms "real death." If, for Blanchot, death is the ultimate ambiguity, it is because, as an always other possibility, it is the minimal ambiguity presupposed by any other ambiguity. "The nothingness of death" (p. 344) to which death as the chance of meaning continues to refer as a possibility, that is, the possibility that death "becomes the disappearance of every way out" (p. 344), but the disappearance of every issue as well—this is what makes all meaning ultimately ambiguous.

Blanchot ends "Literature and the Right to Death" as follows:

This original double meaning, which lies deep inside every word like a condemnation that is still unknown and a happiness [*bonheur*] that is still invisible, is the source of literature, because literature is the form in which this double meaning has chosen to show itself behind the meaning and the value of words, and the question it asks is the question asked by literature. (p. 344)

Literature, it now appears to us, becomes a question—the question asked by literature—when it becomes the form in which the original ambiguity manifests itself. Literature silently poses the question posed by the original double meaning. To conclude, then, let me question one more time the irreducible double meaning deep within literature and its language. I recall that for Blanchot death is the power of detachment from which meaning arises. But once everything—the whole, totality, the world—begins in detachment, the power of the other possibility is already at work. Detachment is not only the origin of ideality, universality, and meaning. It is not only the condition under which a relation to an Other can arise. Detachment is also a laceration, a tearing, or ripping apart. "Death ends in being: this is man's laceration [*déchirure*], the source of his unhappy fate, since by man death comes to being and by man meaning rests on nothingness," Blanchot writes (p. 344). Detachment, consequently, is always already the power of alternatives. Without this possibility of the always other possibility, death could not inaugurate the idealizing process of language in detachment. Without this possibility no Other could possibly emerge, and no address take place. Death is thus first and foremost this minimal ambiguity of an always other possibility. It is the prodigious power of the negative only because it is first of all the opening for the occurrence of another possibility. As we have seen, this possibility is that of the arrival of an unpredictable (non-Hegelian) Other. It is a structural trait inscribed everywhere. As I have discussed, this trait is the mark in everything that it also might not have come forth, the mark of the possibility that rather than something, nothingness could have prevailed. But this trait's minimal ambiguity does not stop here. Indeed, this mark is also positively the mark of something that has become meaningful through the detachment of death. It also points to the possibility that meaning can spring forth from negation and destruction. It affirms that there is a chance for meaning to occur, that an Other can present itself in an address, and that it/he/she is a possible addressee for us.

The "always other possibility" is thus ambiguous as well—nothingness / the chance of everything. This compels me to define death, beyond the negative and positive valorizations that it can affix to just anything, as affirmation—affirmation of the possibility of nothingness, of the chance for being to be. But death as such a *yes* manifests itself in that it asks. Its beginning in affirmation ends in a question. Death as the affirmation of an always other possibility begins in that it asks. It is in literature that death asks this question, the silent question of the possibility of literature.

(1993)

REFERENCE MATTER

Notes

INTRODUCTION

1. Marcus Fabius Quintilianus, *Institutionis Oratoriae* (Darmstadt: Wissenschaftliche Buchgesellschaft, 1975), 2: 196 (8,4,21). Quintilian speaks here of a "relatione ad aliquid," in which the term, deriving from *referre*, "to carry back," is used in a distinct, and technically logical, way.

2. Aristotle, *The Complete Works*, ed. J. Barnes (Princeton, N.J.: Princeton University Press, 1985), 2: 1612 and 1719. Here Aristotle writes, "the relative is least of all things a real thing or substance."

3. Mark G. Henninger, SJ, *Relations: Medieval Theories 1250–1325* (Oxford: Clarendon, 1989), pp. 95, 65.

4. Constantine Cavarnos, *The Classical Theory of Relations: A Study in the Metaphysics of Plato, Aristotle and Thomism* (Belmont, Mass.: The Institute for Byzantine and Modern Greek Studies, 1975), pp. 75, 83.

5. See Armand Maurer, "*Ens Diminutum*: A Note on Its Origin and Meaning," *Medieval Studies* 12 (1959): 216–22.

6. Thomas Aquinas, quoted from Cavarnos, p. 83.

7. The expression is that of Durandus De S. Porciano. See *Historisches Wörterbuch der Philosophie*, ed. J. Ritter and K. Gründer (Darmstadt: Wissenschaftliche Buchgesellschaft, 1992), 8: 590.

8. Rorty, speaking of the debate about the assumption that relations are internal (although his point obtains as well when relations are said to have external reality), stresses "how intimately the issues about internal relations are bound up with a whole range of other philosophical problems—problems about the notions of substance, of essence, and of 'bare particulars,' about 'real' versus 'nominal' definitions, about nominalism versus realism, about the way in which we refer to and identify particulars, and about the nature of necessary truth. It is perhaps not too much to say that a philosopher's views on internal relations are themselves internally related to all his other philosophical views." Richard Rorty, "Relations, Internal and External,' in *The Encyclopedia of Philosophy* (New York: Macmillan and The Free Press, 1972), vol. 7/8, p. 126.

9. Julius Jakob Schaaf, "Beziehung und Beziehungsloses (Absolutes)," in *Subjektivität und Metaphysik: Festschrift für Wolfgang Cramer*, ed. D. Henrich and H. Wagner (Frankfurt am Main: Klostermann, 1966), p. 278.

10. In this context Christopher Fynsk has convincingly argued that if language is thought from relationality, it "relates" to a relationality that, in distinction from Heidegger's contention that all relation opens with language, is "beyond" language, and thus is of the order of something that is not linguistic. See Christopher Fynsk, *Language and Relation ... that there is language* (Stanford, Calif.: Stanford University Press, 1996).

11. Schaaf, p. 288–89.

12. Aside from minor stylistic corrections, the essays are for the most part reproduced here without changes. The only exception is Chapter 2. As one of the first that I wrote in English, it needed some rewriting, but only to make its original points and argumentation more accessible. Several of the essays have been renamed for the purposes of this volume.

CHAPTER I

1. "The fact that a thing is itself is the single reason and the single cause to be given in answer to all such questions as 'why the man is man, or the musician musical,' unless one were to answer 'because each thing is inseparable from itself, and its being one just meant this.'" And again: "In the case of all things which have several parts and in which the totality is not, as it were, a mere heap, but the whole is something beside the parts, there is a cause; for even in bodies contact is the cause of unity in some cases, and in others viscosity or some other such quality. And a definition is a set of words which is one not by being connected together like the *Iliad*, but by dealing with one object. What, then, is it that makes man one; why is he one and not many?" Aristotle, *Metaphysica*, in *The Works of Aristotle*, vol. 8, trans. W. D. Ross (Oxford: Clarendon, 1928), 1041a 15–20 and 1045a 5–15.

2. Gaston Bachelard, *The Psychoanalysis of Fire*, trans. Alan C. M. Ross (London: Routledge and Kegan Paul, 1964), p. 80.

3. All quotations from *Ecce Homo* are from Friedrich Nietzsche, *"On the Genealogy of Morals" and "Ecce Homo,"* ed. Walter Kaufmann (New York: Random House, 1967), p. 290. All page references in the text of this chapter are to this edition.

4. Jean-Jacques Rousseau, *Dictionnaire de Musique,* in his *Oeuvres complètes* (Paris: Furne, 1835), 3: 744.

5. See, for instance, Pliny, *Natural History*, bk. 34, chap. 70.

6. The whole meaning of *recurrence* in Nietzsche depends, in fact, on the determination of that nature of the recurring which is the *moment*.

7. Indeed, *Stein*, in German, means "stone."

8. For the problem of type, of typography, and of the relationship of this to autobiography, see the remarkable essay by Philippe Lacoue-Labarthe, "Typography," in *Typography*, trans. C. Fynsk (Stanford, Calif.: Stanford University Press, 1998), pp. 43–138.

9. See, for instance, *Die Philosophie im tragischen Zeitalter der Griechen*, in Friedrich Nietzsche, *Werke in drei Bänden* (Munich: Carl Hanser, 1954), 3: 349–413.

10. Friedrich Nietzsche, *The Gay Science*, trans. Walter Kaufmann (New York: Vintage, 1974), p. 346.

CHAPTER 2

1. On October 30, 1888, Nietzsche wrote to Peter Gast: "On my birthday, I began again with something that seems to be going well and has already made considerable progress. It is called *Ecce Homo*, or *How One Becomes What One Is*. It concerns, with great audacity, myself and my writings" (Friedrich Nietzsche, *Selected Letters*, ed. and trans. C. Middleton [Chicago: University of Chicago Press, 1969], p. 319). See also the letter of November 14, 1888, to Meta von Salis: "This *Homo*, you will understand, is myself, including the *Ecce*" (p. 324).

Jacques Derrida is one of the very few to have attempted a reading different from the standard philosophical (and that includes literary) readings of *Ecce Homo*. See his "Otobiographies," in *The Ear of the Other*, ed. C. McDonald (Lincoln: University of Nebraska Press, 1985).

2. Martin Heidegger, *Nietzsche*, vol. 3, *The Will to Power as Knowledge and as Metaphysics*, trans. J. Stambaugh et al. (New York: Harper and Row, 1987), pp. 3–4.

3. Martin Heidegger, *Nietzsche*, vol. 2, *The Eternal Recurrence of the Same*, trans. D. F. Krell (New York: Harper and Row, 1984), p. 9.

4. Philippe Lacoue-Labarthe, "Obliteration," in *The Subject of Philosophy*, trans. T. Trezise et al. (Minneapolis: University of Minnesota Press, 1993), pp. 57–98.

5. Eugen Fink, *Nietzsches Philosophie* (Stuttgart: Kohlhammer, 1973), p. 43.

6. "One thing will live, the sign-manual [*Monogramm*] of their inmost being, the rare flash of light, the deed, the creation." Friedrich Nietzsche, *The Use and Abuse of History*, in *The Complete Works of Friedrich Nietzsche*, ed. O. Levy (New York: Russel, 1964), 5: 18–19.

7. G. W. F. Hegel, *Phenomenology of Spirit*, trans. A. V. Miller (Oxford: Oxford University Press, 1977), p. 160. On Hegel's use of the notion of *Gestalt* see also Martin Heidegger, *Hegel's Concept of Experience*, trans. J. Glenn Gray (New York: Harper and Row, 1970).

8. Martin Heidegger, "The Origin of the Work of Art," in *Poetry, Language, Thought*, trans. A. Hofstadter (New York: Harper and Row, 1971), pp. 64, 77, 84.

9. Martin Heidegger, "What Are Poets For?" in *Poetry, Language, Thought*, pp. 100–101.

10. Martin Heidegger, *The Question of Being*, trans. W. Kluback and J. T. Wilde (New Haven, Conn.: Twayne, 1958), p. 90.

11. For a more elaborate account of Heidegger's conception of *Gestalt*, see the essay by Philippe Lacoue-Labarthe, "Typography," in *Typography*, trans. C. Fynsk (Stanford, Calif.: Stanford University Press, 1998), pp. 43–138.

12. René Descartes, *"Discourse on Method" and the "Meditations,"* trans. F. E. Sutcliffe (New York: Penguin Books, 1968), pp. 35–36.

13. To Lou Salome, Nietzsche wrote on June 10, 1882: "Pindar says somewhere, 'Become the being you are.'" Nietzsche, *Selected Letters*, p. 183.

14. For the *fictitious* nature of the notions of becoming and being in Nietzsche, see Paul de Man, *Allegories of Reading: Figural Language in Rousseau, Nietzsche, Rilke and Proust* (New Haven, Conn.: Yale University Press, 1979), pp. 126–27.

15. "It smells offensively Hegelian," Nietzsche wrote, referring in *Ecce Homo* to *The Birth of Tragedy*. Friedrich Nietzsche, *"On the Genealogy of Morals" and "Ecce Homo,"* trans. Walter Kaufmann (New York: Vintage Books, 1967), p. 270. All page references in the text of this chapter are to this edition.

16. Ibid., p. 221. See also the following passage from a letter of November 20, 1888, to Georg Brandes: "I have told my own story with a cynicism that will make history." Nietzsche, *Selected Letters*, p. 326.

17. Descartes writes: "But I, who am certain that I am, do not yet clearly know enough what I am; so that henceforth I must take great care not imprudently to take some other object for myself, and thus avoid going astray in this knowledge which I maintain to be more certain and evident than all I have had hitherto." Descartes, *"Discourse on Method" and the "Meditations,"* p. 103.

18. Nietzsche writes here: "On this perfect day, when everything is ripening and not only the grape turns brown, the eye of the sun just fell upon my life: I looked back, I looked forward, and never saw so many and such things at once. It was not for nothing that I buried my forty-fourth year today; I had the *right* to bury it; whatever was life in it has been saved, is immortal. The first book of the *Revaluation of All Values*, the *Songs of Zarathustra*, the *Twilight of the Idols*, my attempt to philosophize with a hammer—all presents of this year, indeed of its last quarter! *How could I fail to be grateful to my whole life?*—and so I tell my life to myself" (*"On the Genealogy of Morals" and "Ecce Homo,"* p. 221). This intermediary space in the text of *Ecce Homo*, which is the object of Derrida's study "Otobiographies," is a space that, according to Heidegger, exemplifies the poet himself insofar as he or she is born from the bridal encounter (*Brautfest, Brauttag*) of men and gods as the one who "stands between men and gods and endures this

'in-between'." Martin Heidegger, *Erläuterungen zu Hölderlins Dichtung* (Frankfurt am Main: Klostermann, 1971), p. 100.

19. Friedrich Nietzsche, *Beyond Good and Evil*, trans. H. Zimmern, in *The Philosophy of Nietzsche*, ed. W. H. Wright (New York: Modern Library, 1954), p. 601.

20. "A thing that is explained ceases to concern us.—What did the God mean who gave the advice, 'Know thyself!' Did it perhaps imply: 'Cease to be concerned about thyself! Become objective!'—And Socrates?—And the 'scientific man'?" Nietzsche, *Beyond Good and Evil*, p. 454.

21. This subversion of all individuality for the benefit of *what one is* considerably limits the scope of Gilles Deleuze's reevaluation of the question of *who one is*. See Gilles Deleuze, *Nietzsche and Philosophy*, trans. H. Tomlinson (New York: Columbia University Press, 1983), pp. 75–78.

22. Derrida writes: "It is out of the unfolding of this 'same' as differance that the sameness of difference and of repetition is presented in the eternal return." Jacques Derrida, "Differance," in *"Speech and Phenomena" and Other Essays on Husserl's Theory of Signs*, trans. D. B. Allison (Evanston, Ill.: Northwestern University Press, 1973), p. 149.

23. See in particular Bernard Pautrat, "Nietzsche Medused," in *Looking After Nietzsche*, ed. L. A. Rickels (Albany: SUNY Press, 1990), pp. 159–74.

24. Deleuze, *Nietzsche and Philosophy*, pp. 25–29. As to the image of the die, see, for example, *Use and Abuse of History*, p. 20, where Nietzsche speaks of the real historical nexus of cause and effect, which, rightly understood, would only prove that nothing quite similar could ever be cast again from the dice-box of fate and future.

25. Friedrich Nietzsche, *The Gay Science*, trans. Walter Kaufmann (New York: Vintage, 1974), p. 224.

26. On December 29, 1888, Nietzsche wrote to Meta von Salis: "thank heaven that in all my instincts I am a Pole and nothing else." Nietzsche, *Selected Letters*, p. 343.

27. Klossowski concludes his analysis of the passage concerning Nietzsche's double origin as follows: "Hence, Nietzsche was never the father of himself because *he was dead as his father*." Pierre Klossowski, *Nietzsche and the Vicious Circle*, trans. D. W. Smith (Chicago: University of Chicago Press, 1997), p. 189.

28. Nietzsche seems here to elaborate on a fragment by Heraclitus in which birth is seen to be an adversity. The fragment reads as follows: "When they are born, they are willing to live and accept their fate (*death*); and they leave behind children to become victims of fate." Kathleen Freeman, *Ancilla to the Pre-Socratic Philosophers* (Cambridge, Mass.: Harvard University Press, 1983), p. 26.

29. "THE THIRD EYE.—What! You are still in need of the theatre! are you still so young? Be wise, and seek tragedy and comedy where they are better acted, and

where the incidents are more interesting, and the actors more eager. It is indeed by no means easy to be merely a spectator in these cases—but learn! And then, amid all difficult or painful situations, you will have a little gate leading to joy and refuge, even when your passions attack you. Open your stage eye, that big third eye of yours, which looks out into the world through the other two." Friedrich Nietzsche, *The Day of Dawn*, in *Complete Works of Nietzsche*, ed. Levy, 1964), 9: 353.

30. "For an individual to posit his own ideal and to derive from it his own law, joys, and rights—that may well have been considered hitherto as the most outrageous human aberration and as idolatry itself. The few who dared as much always felt the need to apologize to themselves, usually by saying: 'It wasn't I.' Not I! But *a god* through me." Nietzsche, *The Gay Science*, p. 191.

31. Fink, pp. 65, 82, 114, 118.

32. Nor does it coincide with the Heideggerian notion of the "unmediated character of a [genuine] beginning." Heidegger defines this as follows: "A genuine beginning, as a leap, is always a head start, in which everything to come is already leaped over, even if as something disguised. The beginning already contains the end latent within itself." Heidegger, "Origin of the Work of Art," p. 76.

33. Ibid., p. 14. See also Heidegger, *Nietzsche*, 2: 9, where Heidegger understands Nietzsche's self-reflection (*Selbstbesinnung*) as precisely the opposite of idle self-mirroring (*Selbstbespiegelung*).

CHAPTER 3

1. For the Lutheran connection, see Julian Roberts, *Walter Benjamin* (London: Macmillan, 1982), pp. 126–27.

2. Gershom Scholem, *Walter Benjamin und sein Engel* (Frankfurt am Main: Suhrkamp, 1983), pp. 14–15.

3. Bernd Witte, *Walter Benjamin: Der Intellektuelle als Kritiker, Untersuchungen zu seinem Frühwerk* (Stuttgart: Metzler, 1976).

4. Walter Benjamin, *Briefe*, ed. G. Scholem and T. W. Adorno (Frankfurt am Main: Suhrkamp, 1966), 1: 372.

5. Walter Benjamin, *Selected Writings*, vol. 1 (covering 1913–26), ed. M. Bullock and M. W. Jennings (Cambridge, Mass.: Harvard University Press, 1996), p. 202. All page references in the text of this chapter are to this edition.

6. Winfried Menninghaus, *Walter Benjamins Theorie der Sprachmagie* (Frankfurt am Main: Suhrkamp, 1980), p. 16.

7. Richard Wolin, *Walter Benjamin: An Aesthetic of Redemption* (New York: Columbia University Press, 1982), p. 40.

8. Jacques Derrida, "Des Tours de Babel," trans. J. F. Graham, in *Difference in Translation*, ed. J. F. Graham (Ithaca, N.Y.: Cornell University Press, 1985), p. 180.

9. See the "Epistemo-Critical Prologue," in Walter Benjamin, *The Origin of German Tragic Drama*, trans. J. Osborne (London: NLB, 1977).

10. Benjamin, *Origin of German Tragic Drama*, p. 165.

11. For the German original, see Walter Benjamin, *Gesammelte Schriften*, vol. 4, pt. 1 (Frankfurt am Main: Suhrkamp, 1974), p. 16.

12. Harry Zohn's translation of *Art des Meinens* as *mode of intention* is not altogether wrong, contrary to what Paul de Man contends in "'Conclusions' on Walter Benjamin's 'The Task of the Translator'" (in Paul de Man, *The Resistance to Theory* [Minneapolis: University of Minnesota Press, 1986], pp. 86–87), since it is precisely in the way in which language is meant to mean that it realizes its intention toward pure, or divine, language.

13. For the religious connotations of "Lehre," or doctrine, see Gershom Scholem, *Walter Benjamin—Die Geschichte einer Freundschaft* (Frankfurt am Main: Suhrkamp, 1975), pp. 73–74.

14. Benjamin, *Origin of German Tragic Drama*, pp. 35–36.

15. Ibid., p. 28.   16. Ibid., p. 29.

17. Ibid., p. 216.   18. Ibid., p. 179.

19. Scholem, *Walter Benjamin und sein Engel*, p. 54. For a discussion of the saturnine in Benjamin, see also Susan Sontag, *Under the Sign of Saturn* (New York: Farrar, Straus, Giroux, 1972), pp. 109–34.

20. Benjamin, *Origin of German Tragic Drama*, p. 33.

CHAPTER 4

1. Benjamin's borrowing of some conceptions from Kant does not preclude his rejecting of other, major aspects of Kant's doctrine. Thus, in the essay "Program of the Coming Philosophy" (trans. M. Ritter, in *Benjamin: Philosophy, Aesthetics, History*, ed. G. Smith [Chicago: The University of Chicago Press, 1989], pp. 1–12), Benjamin, although positioning Kant as the starting point for a new philosophy, severely criticizes him for maintaining distinctions such as intuition/intellect, subject/object, and epistemology/metaphysics. Indeed Benjamin relinquishes all the major distinctions constitutive of Kant's critical enterprise in the First Critique. He does so in order to overcome what he calls the remnants in Kant of the religious and historical blindness of the Enlightenment, and to establish a higher concept of experience—higher than "naked, primitive, and self-evident [empirical] experience"—in which experience is "reduced to nadir, to a minimum of significance," in which "something absolute" is encountered, namely God, and which would characterize the coming philosophy as a theology or as a metaphysics. But Benjamin disagrees with Kant's doctrine of aesthetic judgment as well, and dismisses the phenomenology of experience on which it is based. As Claude Imbert has argued, Benjamin objects to Kant's aesthetics be-

cause of the reflective judgment's suspension of the phenomenology of the object, and because in this case there simply is no object to suspend. Yet, as I shall argue, Benjamin hereafter has recourse to Kant's aesthetics at the precise moment he needs to dispel the magic of the aura, and the auratic object as well. Imbert's contention that Benjamin objected to the unifying gesture of transcendental deduction—to what he called Kant's despotism, in other words, to his transcendentalism—is highly suggestive of what sort of Kant is operative in Benjamin's own work: a Kant folded back into the empirical, "a criticist economy without transcendentalism." See Claude Imbert, "Le présent et l'histoire," in *Walter Benjamin et Paris*, ed. H. Wismann (Paris: Cerf, 1986), pp. 747, 769.

2. Susan Buck-Morss, *The Origin of Negative Dialectics* (New York: MIT Press, 1977), pp. 160–61.

3. In a superb essay entitled "Zeit zur Darstellung: Walter Benjamin's Das Kunstwerk im Zeitalter seiner technischen Reproduzierbarkeit" (*MLN*, German Issue, 107, no 3 [1992]), Eva Geulen attempts to determine the epistemological point of view from which Benjamin wrote the essay in question as that of a yet undecided future in whose perspective the present appears as past. She then accounts for the double nature of the loss of the aura—a doubleness at which so many interpreters have pointed—on the basis of what she analyzes as the simultaneity of method and object, that is, on the basis of the performative dimension of Benjamin's criticism. She writes:

> The theory of aura is the attempt to describe history not only in practical terms, but theoretically as well from a position for which no factual ground exists as yet. In other words, the concept of aura must mark out and localize itself in the essay itself. Aura belongs to the vocabulary of a possible, futural historiography. As anticipation of the future, the aura achieves intervention in history, stating, in this manner, what is now. That the specificity of traditional art consisted of its aura, can show itself only, when, and in so far as it has lost this character. The perception of aura arises from its loss." (p. 598)

In passing I note that Geulen's interpretation of history in Benjamin as constructed, that is, as represented, hence as disfigured history, lays to rest objections such as those formulated by Peter Bürger, *Theorie der Avantgarde* (Frankfurt am Main: Suhrkamp, 1974), according to which Benjamin's periodizations of art would be historically erroneous, and rooted in pseudomaterialist theorems (pp. 36–40).

4. Walter Benjamin, *Illuminations*, trans. H. Zohn (New York: Schocken, 1969), p. 221; the corresponding German page is Walter Benjamin, *Gesammelte Schriften*, vol. 1, pt. 2 (Frankfurt am Main: Suhrkamp, 1974), p. 478. All paired page references in the text of this chapter refer to these two editions, with the English page number preceding the German.

5. In a letter of October 28, 1935, to Werner Kraft, Benjamin describes the philosophical and historical viewpoint from which he approached the theory of art in the essay "The Work of Art," a first, programatic version of which had been sketched out in September or October of that same year. He writes: "As far as I am concerned, I try to direct my telescope through the bloody fog upon a mirage of the nineteenth century, which I seek to depict according to those features that it will show in a future state of the world liberated from magic." Walter Benjamin, *Briefe* (Frankfurt am Main: Suhrkamp, 1966), 2: 698.

6. For a detailed and extremely suggestive analysis of the notion of tradition, see Alexander Garcia Düttmann, "Tradition and Destruction: Benjamin's Politics of Language," *MLN*, 106 (1991).

7. Benjamin, *Gesammelte Schriften*, vol. 1, pt. 1, pp. 174, 179.

8. Walter Benjamin, *"One Way Street" and Other Writings*, trans. E. Jephcott and K. Shorter (London: Harcourt Brace Jovanovich, 1978), p. 243.

9. Ibid., p. 250.

10. In "The Work of Art" Benjamin also conceives of the destruction of the aura in terms of a tearing or prying of an object from its shell, that is, in terms that not only seem to be at odds with everything else said about the loss of the aura but are used elsewhere, in the Goethe essay for instance, to warn against philosophical barbarism, of art criticism that would seek to account for the beautiful by lifting its veil. Thus it is necessary to interpret the simile in question in the context of what he establishes in the essay of 1935. Benjamin writes: "To pry an object from its shell [*die Entschälung des Gegenstandes aus seiner Hülle*], to destroy its aura, is the mark [*Signatur*] of a perception whose 'sense of the universal equality of things' has increased to such a degree that it extracts it even from a unique object by means of reproduction" (pp. 223; 479–80). According to this definition, the shell is what makes an object auratic. To pry it from its shell is to destroy the aura. Hence, the shell must correspond to the object's appearing in a phenomenal, that is, singular and unique, actualization. To tear the object from its shell, therefore, is to rob the object of its appearance, with the result that it can no longer manifest itself as the unique appearance of a distance. An object deprived of its shell, of the phenomenal actualization that renders it distant, brings the object into proximity with those objects that in everyday life are too close to us to warrant any particular attention. Only when sheltered behind its appearing can an object be distant and endowed with auratic magic, something like a thing-in-itself!

11. Benjamin, *One Way Street*, pp. 250, 249, 250, 251.

12. Ibid., p. 247.

13. Ibid., pp. 244, 245.

14. Ibid., p. 247.

15. Benjamin, *Gesammelte Schriften*, vol. 1, pt. 1, p. 138.

16. The concept of the aura can be a positive instrument of analysis only if entirely recast. This is what Andrew Benjamin has set out to do in "The Decline of Art: Benjamin's Aura," in Andrew Benjamin, *Art, Mimesis and the Avant-Garde* (London: Routledge, 1991), pp. 143–54.

17. Walter Benjamin, "Critique of Violence," in *Selected Writings*, vol. 1 (covering 1913–26), ed. M. Bullock and M. W. Jennings (Cambridge, Mass.: Harvard University Press, 1996), p. 249.

18. Benjamin, *One Way Street*, p. 251.

19. Ibid., p. 252.

20. Benjamin's analysis of dadaism ought to be read in conjunction with his parallel developments on the shock experience in the great nineteenth-century metropoles, particularly in his "On Some Motifs in Baudelaire," in Benjamin, *Illuminations*, pp. 155–200.

21. Shock is thus not to be understood as merely the "denial of sense," as Bürger construes it in *Theorie der Avantgarde* (p. 108). With this, the meaning of shock is restricted to what Benjamin had called "the moral shock effect."

22. "Some of the players whom we meet in Russian films are not actors in our sense but people who portray *themselves*—and primarily in their own work process. In Western Europe the capitalistic exploitation of the film denies consideration to modern man's legitimate claim to being reproduced" (pp. 232; 494).

23. Benjamin, *One Way Street*, p. 256.

24. A careful reading of section 3 of "On Some Motifs in Baudelaire" would be required here.

25. Immanuel Kant, *Critique of Pure Reason*, trans. N. Kemp Smith (New York: St. Martin's Press, 1965), p. 153.

26. Immanuel Kant, *Anthropology from a Pragmatic Point of View*, trans. V. L. Dowdell (Carbondale and Edwardsville: Southern Illinois Press, 1978), p. 102.

27. Ibid., p. 104.

28. Everything, indeed, that Benjamin advances about the genre of the novel in "The Concept of Criticism in German Romanticism" (in Benjamin, *Selected Writings*, 1: 116–200)—its prosaic, sober nature—suggests that the film is the novel's legitimate heir.

29. Kant, *Anthropology*, p. 77. For the important role of *absentmindedness* in the flaneur, see Benjamin, "On Some Motifs in Baudelaire."

CHAPTER 5

1. Martin Heidegger, *Basic Writings*, ed. D. F. Krell (New York: Harper and Row, 1977), p. 365.

2. Martin Heidegger, *The Basic Problems of Phenomenology*, trans. A. Hofstadter (Bloomington: Indiana University Press, 1982), p. 35.

3. Ibid., p. 126.

4. Martin Heidegger, *Being and Time*, trans. J. Macquarrie and E. Robinson (New York: Harper and Row, 1962), p. 88. All page references in the text of this chapter are to this edition.

5. Martin Heidegger, *Logik: Die Frage nach der Wahrheit*, vol. 21 of *Gesamtausgabe* (Frankfurt am Main: Klostermann, 1976), p. 158.

6. Ibid., p. 156.

7. Ibid., pp. 159–60.

8. Ibid., p. 157.

9. Heidegger, *Being and Time*, pp. 40, 25, and 44. *An Introduction to Metaphysics* refers even to Being as "determinate, wholly indeterminate Being (*Sein als das bestimmte völlig Unbestimmte*)." Martin Heidegger, *An Introduction to Metaphysics*, trans. R. Manheim (New Haven, Conn.: Yale University Press, 1959), p. 78.

10. Heidegger, *Logik*, p. 160.

11. Heidegger, *Basic Writings*, p. 366.

12. Certain developments in "On the Essence of Truth" (in Heidegger, *Basic Writings*) and also the hyphenation of *Be-stimmung* in *What Is Philosophy?* suggest that there is perhaps a proper meaning of that word, a meaning upon which the technical (and current) meaning of the term depends.

13. In a handwritten comment in the margins of his own copy of *Being and Time*, Heidegger notes with respect to the quoted passage, "dass es zu seyn hat: Bestimmung!" (*Sein und Zeit*, vol. 2 of *Gesamtausgabe* [Frankfurt am Main: Klostermann, 1977], p. 56). I translate: "that is has to be: destination!" Being attuned to, disclosedness, and destination are thus intimately interlinked. It is a fine example of how the temporal meaning of determination becomes tied into Heidegger's attempt to foreground the question of determination in that of state-of-mind, in moods.

14. Heidegger, *Logik*, p. 308.

15. Ibid., p. 294.

16. Ibid., p. 322.

17. See in this context Michel Haar, *Le Chant de la Terre* (Paris: L'Herne, 1985), pp. 88–102.

18. See, for instance, the reference work *Der Grosse Duden*.

CHAPTER 6

1. Martin Heidegger, "On the Essence of Truth," in *Basic Writings*, ed. D. F. Krell (New York: Harper and Row, 1977), p. 121. All page references in the text of this chapter are to this edition.

2. For how justice, as universal egalitarian leveling, is revealed at the end of

metaphysics as the essence of truth, see Reiner Schürmann, *Heidegger on Being and Acting: From Principles to Anarchy*, trans. C.-M. Gros (Bloomington: Indiana University Press, 1987), pp. 192–93.

3. Martin Heidegger, *Nietzsche*, vol. 3, *The Will to Power as Knowledge and as Metaphysics*, trans. F. A. Capuzzi et al. (New York: Harper and Row, 1987), p. 219.

4. Henri Birault, *Heidegger et l'expérience de la pensée* (Paris: Gallimard, 1978), p. 467.

5. It must be noted here that in "The Essence of Truth," the chain of *stimmen* (*Übereinstimmen, einstimmen, bestimmen*, etc.) intersects with a chain of *weisen* (*anweisen, einweisen*, etc.), as well as with the chain of *richten* (*sich richten nach, die Richte, Richtigkeit*, etc.). Heidegger does not link these different chains together in a "conceptual" knot by means of which the enabling conditions of accordance would have become articulated in a most economic torsion. As far as the question of *Bestimmung* is concerned, Heidegger does not achieve anything comparable to the notions of *Gestell* or *Ereignis*. The most he will venture to do is to think *Bestimmung* in the direction of a more originary *Gestimmtheit*, or to make some use of hyphenation to demarcate metaphysical *Bestimmung* from one that is open to the *Stimme des Sein* (see in this context Martin Heidegger, *What Is Philosophy?* trans. W. Kluback and J. T. Wilde [Estover: Vision Press, 1989]). What is the reason for such hesitance? Is it that the Heideggerian gathering gesture still presupposes (linguistic, etymological) homogeneity, and thus does not permit inclusion of heterogeneous chains (such as *stimmen, richten, weisen*) in *one* terminological construct?

6. This twice-double accord is not chiastic, strictly speaking, since the two accords that seem to produce the crisscross effect are not homogeneous. The accord that constitutes the inner possibility of accordance, and the one that grounds it, occur on very distinct levels of thought.

7. In section 4 of "The Essence of Truth," Heidegger had already shown that engagement with disclosedness is the more essential ground not only of the traditional concept of truth as accordance but also of history. Engagement with disclosedness (as opposed to the freedom for something opened up as such in its singularity) takes place, Heidegger writes, as "a distinctive relatedness to a being as a whole [*zu einem Seinenden im Ganzen als einem solchen*] which first founds all history" (p. 129, translation slightly modified). Engagement with beings as such, as a whole, occurs in a particular way each time, and is constitutive of the very manner in which a people relates to "its essential possibilities" that are conserved (*ver-wahrt*) in such dis-closure (p. 130). The more essential ground of truth as accordance (of *Übereinstimmung* and of its subsequent function of logical determination, *Bestimmung*) is thus as well the ground for the *Bestimmung* of

a historical mankind, that is, for its vocation, its teleology, its *Geschick*. Heidegger's attempt to foreground the classical conception of truth thus lays the groundwork for accounting for the (modern) distinction of logical and historical determination, and the exchanges between the two. Heidegger's developments toward what we have seen to amount to a "fundamental" theory of accord lead in such a direction.

8. See Birault, *Heidegger et l'expérience de la pensée*, p. 496.

9. This eclipse is also the reason for the inevitable plurality of, and hence discord between, the goals or ends (*Bestimmungen*) to which all particular truth claims (*Übereinstimmungen*) must yield.

10. Heidegger touches here on the limits of phenomenology, on what one could call a constitutive blind spot of a philosophy of appearing as such.

CHAPTER 7

1. Here I follow Michael Murray's distinctions in his essay "Philosophical Canon as Series, Score, and Scepter" (forthcoming).

2. See, for instance, Ernst Robert Curtius, *European Literature and the Latin Middle Ages*, trans. W. R. Trask (Princeton, N.J.: Princeton University Press, 1973), pp. 256–72.

3. Immanuel Kant, *Logik*, in *Kants gesammelte Schriften (Akademie-Ausgabe)*, (Berlin: de Gruyter), 11: 13.

4. See Hermann Krings, "Denken," in *Handbuch philosophischer Grundbegriffe* (Munich: Kösel, 1973), 1: 274–88.

5. As Reiner Schürmann has forcefully argued in *Heidegger on Being and Acting: From Principles to Anarchy*, trans. C.-M. Gros (Bloomington: Indiana University Press, 1987), philosophy, since Aristotle discovered that the *pros hen* could be applied to all regions of the world, has spoken "with the voice of a physicist" (pp. 42–43). See Chapter 8 below, "Like the Rose—Without Why."

6. Martin Heidegger, "On the Essence of Truth," in *Basic Writings*, ed. D. F. Krell (New York: Harper and Row, 1977), pp. 140–41.

7. Martin Heidegger, " ... Poetically Man Dwells ... ," in his *Poetry, Language, Thought*, trans. A. Hofstadter (New York: Harper and Row, 1971), pp. 214–15. All page references in the text of this chapter refer to this edition.

8. Werner Marx, *Gibt es auf Erden ein Mass?* (Frankfurt am Main: Fischer 1986), p. 25. My translation.

9. Martin Heidegger, "A Letter on Humanism," in *Basic Writings*, pp. 240–41.

10. Ibid., p. 242

11. Jean-François Lyotard, *The Differend: Phrases in Dispute*, trans. G. Van Den Abbeele (Minneapolis: University of Minnesota Press, 1988), p. xiv.

CHAPTER 8

1. Martin Heidegger, "Letter on Humanism," in *Basic Writings*, ed. D. F. Krell (New York: Harper and Row, 1977), p. 231.

2. Reiner Schürmann, *Heidegger on Being and Acting: From Principles to Anarchy*, trans. C.-M. Gros (Bloomington: Indiana University Press, 1987). All page references in the text of this chapter are to this work.

3. Martin Heidegger, *Being and Time*, trans. J. Macquarrie and E. Robinson (New York: Harper and Row, 1962), pp. 79–80.

4. Schürmann makes a clear distinction between "deconstruction" and "dismantling" (in a Marxian and Nietzschean sense).

5. See, for instance, Jacques Derrida, "The Principle of Reason: The University in the Eyes of Its Pupils," *Diacritics* 13 (Fall 1983): 18–19.

6. For instance, on p. 6, where Schürmann writes, "Still a principle, but a principle of anarchy."

7. I put the word in quotation marks to distinguish the sense intended here from the systematicity of metaphysical systems.

CHAPTER 9

1. Gottfried Wilhelm Friedrich Hegel, "Wie der gemeine Menschenverstand die Philosophie nehme—dargestellt an den Werken des Herrn Krug," in *Werke in zwanzig Bänden* (Frankfurt am Main: Suhrkamp, 1970), 2: 201. Wilhelm Traugott Krug became the successor of Kant at the University of Königsberg.

2. Ibid.

3. Jacob and Wilhelm Grimm, *Deutsches Wörterbuch* (Leipzig: Hirzel, 1854).

4. Hegel, "Wie der gemeine Menschenverstand die Philosophie nehme," p. 202.

5. Ibid., p. 189.

6. Martin Heidegger, "The Nature of Language," in *On the Way to Language*, trans. P. D. Hertz (San Francisco: Harper and Row, 1971), p. 92. All page references in the text of this chapter are to this edition of Heidegger's essays on language.

7. Ute Guzzoni, *Identität oder nicht: Zur Kritischen Theorie der Ontologie* (Freiburg: Alber, 1981), p. 222.

8. This is the case in particular with Heidegger's interpretation of the Stefan George poem in "The Nature of Language." See, for instance, pp. 66–67, 85.

9. Any more extensive exploration of the philosophical implications of the notion of *Vermutung* within Heidegger's work will have to return to Nicholas of Cusa's *De conjecturis*.

10. Another example suggesting the merely provisional role of presupposition occurs in "The Way to Language," when Heidegger states, "a thinking that pur-

sues the *Appropriation* can still only surmise it [*dieses erst vermuten*], and yet can experience it even now in the nature of modern technology" (p. 131).

11. Martin Heidegger, *Poetry, Language, Thought*, trans. A. Hofstadter (New York: Harper and Row, 1971), pp. 190–91.

12. Let me also invoke here Hans Blumenberg's call, undoubtedly gesturing in the direction of Nicholas of Cusa, upon the courage to conjecture (*Mut zur Vermutung*). Hans Blumenberg, *Paradigmen zu einer Metaphorologie* (Frankfurt am Main: Suhrkamp, 1998), p. 13; see also p. 39.

13. The poem by George, "The Word," which Heidegger discusses at length in "The Nature of Language," represents for the latter a turning point in George's poetry, more precisely, the point where his poetry becomes lyric song (*Gesang*), in other words, great poetry. This poem has not only "turned out well," as the translator suggests, but has succeeded in becoming a lyric song of language (*das zum singenden Lied von der Sprache geglückt ist*, p. 69). This, too, is a matter of luck.

14. *Befremdung*, in addition, means astonishment, surprise. It might thus be interesting to link it to the question of the *thaumazein* and the pleasure of *theoria*, and to show that the thinking experience envisioned by Heidegger is a philosophical experience of a kind altogether different from the one at the heart of the Western tradition.

15. Although "Other" in the context of "The Nature of Language" refers only to the address, grant, or promise of language, the structure of "relating" developed here can be extended to all kinds of Others, human and divine Others included. Such is the case, for instance, in Emmanuel Levinas's essay from 1965, "Enigme et phénomène," in which *perhaps* is shown to be the "new modality" for the enigma, irreducible to the modalities of being and certitude. Emmanuel Levinas, *En décrouvant l'existence avec Husserl et Heidegger* (Paris: Vrin, 1974), pp. 209, 214. For a discussion of the status of the *perhaps* in Levinas, see Krzysztof Ziarek, "Semantics of Proximity: Language and the Other in the Philosophy of Emmanuel Levinas," *Research in Phenomenology* 29 (1989): 242–43.

CHAPTER 10

1. Martin Heidegger, *Being and Time*, trans. J. Macquarrie and E. Robinson (New York: Harper and Row, 1962), p. 244. Page references given with the abbreviation *BT* in the text of this chapter are to this edition.

2. Martin Heidegger, *Identity and Difference*, trans. J. Stambaugh (New York: Harper and Row, 1969), p. 66. Page references given with the abbreviation *ID* in the text of this chapter are to this edition.

3. Martin Heidegger, *Poetry, Language, Thought*, trans. A. Hofstadter (New York: Harper and Row, 1971), p. 105. Page references given with the abbreviation *PLT* in the text of this chapter are to this edition.

4. Martin Heidegger, *Basic Writings*, ed. D. F. Krell (New York: Harper and Row, 1977), pp. 203–4. Page references given with the abbreviation *BW* in the text of this chapter are to this edition.

5. Martin Heidegger, *Gesamtausgabe, Wegmarken*, vol. 9 (Frankfurt am Main: Klostermann, 1996), p. 332. My translation.

6. Heidegger, *Gesamtausgabe*, 9: 184. My translation.

7. To distinguish the Earth that Heidegger opposes to the world in "The Origin of the Work of Art" from the earth that appears in the fourfold, I use upper case "E" when the first is meant and lowercase "e" when the second is meant. The French translations of Heidegger make such a distinction and therefore warrant my doing so.

8. Martin Heidegger, *Existence and Being*, ed. W. Brock (Chicago: Regnery Gateway, 1949), p. 274.

9. Martin Heidegger, *Early Greek Thinking*, trans. D. F. Krell and F. A. Capuzzi (New York: Harper and Row, 1975), p. 25. Page references given with the abbreviation *EGT* in the text of this chapter are to this edition.

10. Martin Heidegger, *Pathmarks*, trans. W. McNeil (New York: Cambridge University Press, 1998), p. 213.

11. Ibid., pp. 213–14.

12. Heidegger, *Existence and Being*, p. 281.

13. Heidegger, *Pathmarks*, pp. 212–13.

14. Martin Heidegger, *Erläuterungen zu Hölderlins Dichtung* (Frankfurt am Main: Klostermann, 1971), p. 68. Page references given with the abbreviation *EHD* in the text of this chapter are to this edition; the translations are mine.

15. Martin Heidegger, *On Time and Being*, trans. J. Stambaugh (New York: Harper and Row, 1972), pp. 11–12.

16. Heidegger, *Gesamtausgabe*, 9: 213.

17. Heidegger, *Pathmarks*, pp. 226–27.

18. Ibid., p. 228.

CHAPTER 11

1. Jacques Derrida, "The *Retrait* of Metaphor," trans. F. Gasdner et al., *Enclitic* 2, no. 2 (Fall 1978): 19. See also the translator's note on the word *retrait* (p. 5); the translator, to preserve as much as possible the variety of meanings this word has in French, decided to leave it untranslated.

2. Ibid., p. 22.   3. Ibid., p. 29.

4. Ibid., p. 31.   5. Ibid., p. 33.

6. "If we are inquiring about the meaning of Being, our investigation does not then become a 'deep' one [*tiefsinnig*], nor does it puzzle out what stands behind Being. It asks about Being itself insofar as Being enters into the intelligibil-

ity of Dasein. The meaning of Being can never be contrasted with entities, or with Being as the 'ground' which gives entities support" (Martin Heidegger, *Being and Time*, trans. J. Macquarrie and E. Robinson [New York: Harper and Row, 1962], pp. 193–94). What remains is a deepening of this very *question*, a systematic exploration of what according to Heidegger is equiprimordial (*gleichursprünglich*) with this question.

7. If Heidegger, as Henri Birault has demonstrated in "Heidegger et la pensée de la finitude" (*Revue internationale de philosophie*, 1960, no. 52), progressively abandons the concept of finitude, it is to avert the theological implications of this concept. However, what Heidegger originally aimed at when using the concept of finitude continued to preoccupy his thought in the form of the idea of a historicity (*Geschichtlichkeit*) and destiny (*Geschick*) of Being.

8. No doubt, this critique of the transcendental and of the romantic chiasm is far from unequivocal. Yet such Heideggerian notions as "coming forth," "setting forth," "belonging to," etc., and in particular the notion of the gift (*Gabe*) of Being or of the Word, have to be understood as such an attempt to think more originally and to reinscribe the idea of constitution or of engenderment.

9. "The Anaximander Fragment," in Martin Heidegger, *Early Greek Thinking*, trans. D. F. Krell and F. A. Capuzzi (New York: Harper and Row, 1975), p. 26.

10. Cf. Ernst Tugendhat, *Selbstbewusstsein und Selbstbestimmung* (Frankfurt am Main: Suhrkamp, 1979).

11. Martin Heidegger, *Logik: Die Frage nach der Wahrheit*, vol. 21 of *Gesamtausgabe* (Frankfurt am Main: Klostermann, 1976), pp. 127–61.

12. The doctrine of an analogy of Being and its meanings, a doctrine that seems to go back to Thomas Aquinas's Aristotle exegeses, may be contrary to the spirit and the letter of Aristotle's text and represent a "Platonization" of Aristotle, as Pierre Aubenque argues in *Le problème de l'être chez Aristote* (Paris: P.U.F., 1966), pp. 198–206. Nonetheless, it is important to realize that Heidegger's question of the meaning of Being originated in his 1907 reading of Franz Brentano's dissertation, *On the Several Senses of Being in Aristotle* (1862), which pursued precisely the Aquinian exegesis of Aristotle.

13. Gérard Granel's excellent review of Derrida's *Of Grammatology*, published in 1967 in *Critique*, has remained one of the very few commentaries to address pertinent questions to the work of Derrida. Here Granel already asked Derrida about the difference between the question of writing (*écriture*) and the question of Being. Indeed, the attentive reader of both Heidegger and Derrida will not be able to avoid recognizing the striking structural similarities between writing and Being, and between text and Being. Gérard Granel, "Jacques Derrida et la rature de l'origine," reprinted in Gérard Granel, *Traditionis Traditio* (Paris: Gallimard, 1972).

14. Vincent Descombes, *Modern French Philosophy*, trans. L. Scott-Fox and J. M. Harding (Cambridge, Eng.: Cambridge University Press, 1980), p. 150.

15. Jacques Derrida, *Of Grammatology*, trans. G. C. Spivak (Baltimore: The Johns Hopkins University Press, 1976), p. 62.

16. See, for instance, Jacques Derrida, "The Law of Genre," trans. A. Ronell, in *Glyph 7* (Baltimore: The Johns Hopkins University Press, 1980), and "Living On: *Border Lines*," in *Deconstruction and Criticism*, ed. H. Bloom et al. (New York: Seabury Press, 1979).

17. Another way to approach this notion of text is to conceive of it in terms of a radical empiricism, that is, as an empiricism that undoes its own philosophical foundations. Cf. Derrida, *Of Grammatology*, p. 162.

18. Stéphane Mallarmé, *Oeuvres complètes* (Paris: Gallimard, 1945), p. 345. I thank Maria Assad for translating this and the following Mallarmé passages for me.

19. These quotations are from Martin Heidegger, *Identity and Difference*, trans. J. Stambough (New York: Harper and Row, 1969), and *On the Way to Language*, trans. P. D. Hertz (San Francisco: Harper and Row, 1971).

20. Heidegger, *On the Way to Language*, p. 149.

21. Émile Benveniste, *Problèmes de linguistique générale*, vol. 1 (Paris: Gallimard, 1966), pp. 327–35.

22. See also the essay by Philippe Lacoue-Labarthe, "The Echo of the Subject," in *Typography*, trans. C. Fynsk (Stanford, Calif.: Stanford University Press, 1998), particularly from p. 196 on.

23. Mallarmé, p. 333.

24. Ibid., p. 345.

25. "Which does not take place insofar as that of any existing object," writes Mallarmé (p. 333). "What is peculiar to Being is not anything having the character of Being" ("Das Eigentümliche des Seins ist nichts Seinsartiges"), writes Martin Heidegger in *On Time and Being*, trans. J. Stambaugh (New York: Harper and Row, 1972), p. 10.

26. Jacques Derrida, *Dissemination*, trans. B. Johnson (Chicago: University of Chicago Press, 1981), p. 193. All page references in the text of this chapter are to this edition.

27. Heidegger, *Being and Time*, p. 51.

28. Granel, p. 168.

29. Ibid., p. 156.

30. Jacques Derrida, *Writing and Difference*, trans. A. Bass (Chicago: University of Chicago Press, 1978), p. 148. The essay "On a Newly Arisen Apocalyptic Tone in Philosophy" is to be found in *Raising the Tone of Philosophy: Late Essays by Immanuel Kant: Transformative Critique by Jacques Derrida*, ed. P. Fenves (Bal-

timore: The Johns Hopkins University Press, 1993), pp. 117–71. As to the problem of eschatology in Heidegger, see, for instance, Heidegger's comment, "As something fateful (*geschickliches*), Being itself is inherently eschatological." Heidegger, "The Anaximander Fragment," p. 18.

31. Derrida, "The *Retrait* of Metaphor," p. 24.

32. Granel, pp. 126–27.

33. Jacques Derrida, "Ousia and Gramme," in *Margins of Philosophy*, trans. A. Bass (Chicago: University of Chicago Press, 1982), pp. 51–52, 63.

34. See the last pages of Derrida, "Ousia and Gramme." See also Jacques Derrida, *Spurs: Nietzsche's Styles*, trans. B. Harlow (Chicago: University of Chicago Press, 1979), especially on how, according to Derrida, the issue of propriation and appropriation (*Ereignis*) bears on the question and the meaning of Being (pp. 119–21).

CHAPTER 12

1. Edmund Husserl, *Logical Investigations*, trans. J. N. Findlay, vol. 1 (New Jersey: Humanities Press, 1970), p. 261. Page numbers given with the abbreviation *LI* in the text refer to this edition.

2. Edmund Husserl, *The Crisis of European Sciences and Transcendental Philosophy*, trans. D. Carr (Evanston, Ill.: Northwestern University Press, 1970), p. 58.

3. Walter Benjamin, "Central Park," trans. L. Spencer and M. Harrington, *New German Critique*, no. 34., (Winter 1989): 33, translation modified.

4. Leonard Lawlor, *Imagination and Chance: The Difference Between the Thought of Ricoeur and Derrida* (Albany: SUNY Press, 1993), p. 2. See also Leonard Lawlor, "Political Risks: On Derrida's Notion of Différance," *Research in Phenomenology* 21 (1991): 88.

5. Lawlor, *Imagination and Chance*, p. 93.

6. Ibid., p. 96.

7. Ibid., p. 102.

8. Ibid., p. 25. See also p. 46.

9. Jacques Derrida, *"Speech and Phenomena" and Other Essays on Husserl's Theory of Signs*, trans. D. B. Allison (Evanston, Ill.: Northwestern University Press, 1973), p. 88. Page numbers given with the abbreviation *SP* in the text refer to this edition.

10. Jacques Derrida, *Le problème de la genèse dans la philosophie de Husserl* (Paris: Presses Universitaires de France, 1990), p. 179. Page numbers given with the abbreviation *PG* in the text refer to this edition.

11. This was the title of Derrida's seminar at the Ecole Normal Supérieure in 1969–70.

12. In the *Avertissement* to *Le problème de la genèse*, written almost 30 years af-

ter the book itself to preface its long-delayed publication, Derrida claims that "to distance [himself] from either phenomenology or dialectics has never been for . . . [him] without remorse" (*PG*, p. vii). Undoubtedly this means that the break is not only with phenomenology properly speaking but with the kind of philosophy with which he had hoped, at the time, to be able to solve Husserl's dilemmas. It also implies quite powerfully that a reading bent on exiting from the text of phenomenology is not simply a breaking with it.

    13. Rudolf Bernet, "Derrida et la Voix de son Maître," *Revue Philosophique de la France et de l'Etranger*, special issue on Derrida, 2 (1990): 166.

    14. Ibid., p. 159.

    15. From everything laid out, it should be obvious that representation in all senses of the word is not a "negative" value for Derrida. Even though infinite re-peatability in the form of representation and its modifications destroys the possi-bility of pure expressivity in simple self-identity, it is the finite condition for the upsurge of the primordial impression, as well as for its "ever renewed upsurge and virginity" (*SP*, pp. 65–66). Representation is neither discredited in the name, for instance, of immediacy, nor valorized as a reason for simply relinquishing all claims at originarity, primordiality, or self-identical presence. In his opening ad-dress to the eighteenth meeting of the French-speaking philosophical societies in Strasbourg, France, in 1980, entitled "Sending: On Representation," Derrida makes this point once again quite forcefully. After acknowledging that the con-cept of representation has been attacked from many places, and that representa-tion is often considered bad, he holds that determining language, for example, as representation, is not something that "came about one day and of which we could rid ourselves by a decision when the time comes." On the contrary, he continues, "the authority of representation constrains us, imposing itself on our thought through a whole dense, enigmatic, and heavily stratified history. It programs us and precedes us and warns us too severely for us to make a mere object of it, a representation, an object of representation confronting us, before us like a theme" (*Social Research* 49, no. 2 [Summer 1982]: 304). As Derrida shows in this talk, the attacks on representation are intimately linked to the dominant status that repre-sentation has achieved in modernity, where "everything which becomes present, everything which happens or presents itself is apprehended within the form of representation. The experience of what-is becomes essentially representation. *Representation* becomes the most general category to determine the apprehension of whatever it is that is of concern or interest in any relation at all" (p. 310, trans. slightly modified). Indeed, since with modernity the category of representation serves to articulate "all the modifications of the subject in its relationship with an object," the "great question" for this epoch becomes necessarily one regarding "the *value* of representation, of its truth or its adequacy to what it represents"

(ibid.). The criticism of representation and even blunt opposition to it, as can be found, respectively, in Hegel and Nietzsche, are called forth by the category of representation itself. In addition, such criticism and opposition are carried out with the help and within the system of representation, that is, in the name "of immediacy, of original simplicity, of presence without repetition or delegation." A deconstruction of representation, Derrida adds, must thus differ from criticism of representation that combines with "the worst regressions" (p. 311). A deconstruction cannot consist in an attempt to overcome representation. First, because all the concepts by means of which one would seek to get beyond it are "essentially marked by the structure and the closure of representation" (p. 304). Second, because "representation" might not have a unifying semantic meaning that would allow it to be confronted and overcome as such. If "Sending: On Representation" does, indeed, attempt to deconstruct representation, it does so precisely by establishing the linguistic (i.e., idiomatic) as well as the lexical and nominal limits that prohibit the constitution of a semantic unity of the word or concept in question. On one hand, in *Speech and Phenomena* Derrida seeks to draw out, via Husserl's distinctions concerning presentation and re-presentation, a representative structure that accounts for the possibility (and eventual purity-limits) of these distinct differences On the other hand, the 1980 Strasbourg address inquires into the singularizing differences resulting from the historical developments of the notion of representation, its Latino-Germanic translation (such as the relation between *repraesentatio* and *Vorstellung* and *Darstellung*), and the multiple and irreducible uses within one idiom of the word "representation" and all its modifications. In the 1980 address, Derrida, more attentive than ever to the differences between the uses and the concepts of representation, hopes to establish the necessary and nonsuppressible reference (*renvoi*) to other idioms that restricts knowing what representation is within the limits of one single idiom.

CHAPTER 13

1. Andrzej Warminski, *Readings in Interpretation: Hölderlin, Hegel, Heidegger* (Minneapolis: University of Minnesota Press, 1987). All page references in the text of this chapter are to this edition.

2. Jacques Derrida, *Of Grammatology*, trans. G. C. Spivak (Baltimore: The Johns Hopkins University Press, 1976), p. 200.

3. Pierre Aubenque, *Le problème de l'être chez Aristote* (Paris: P. U. F., 1966), pp. 460–72.

4. Wolfgang Iser, *The Act of Reading* (Baltimore: The Johns Hopkins University Press, 1980), pp. 130–31.

5. Philippe Lacoue-Labarthe, *Typography*, trans. C. Fynsk (Stanford, Calif.: Stanford University Press, 1998), p. 235.

6. Henri Morier, *Dictionnaire de poétique et de rhétorique* (Paris: P.U.F., 1961), p. 77.

7. John W. Welch, Introduction, in *Chiasmus in Antiquity: Structures, Analyses, Exegesis*, ed. J. W. Welch (Hildesheim: Gerstenberg, 1981), p. 11.

8. John W. Welch, "Chiasmus in Ancient Greek and Latin Literatures," in *Chiasmus in Antiquity*, p. 251.

9. Ibid., p. 252.

10. Samuel E. Bassett, "Hysteron Proteron Homerikos," *Harvard Studies in Classical Philology* 31 (1920): 45.

11. Emmanuel Levinas, quoted from Jean Greisch, *Herméneutique et grammatologie* (Paris: Editions du CNRS, 1977), p. 216.

12. Kathleen Freeman, *Ancilla to the Pre-Socratic Philosophers* (Cambridge, Mass.: Harvard University Press, 1983), p. 25.

13. Plato, *The Collected Dialogues*, ed. E. Hamilton and H. Cairns (Princeton, N.J.: Princeton University Press, 1980), p. 540 (187 a–b).

14. Paul de Man, *Allegories of Reading: Figural Language in Rousseau, Nietzsche, Rilke and Proust* (New Haven, Conn.: Yale University Press, 1979), p. 113.

15. Jacques Derrida, *Positions*, trans. A. Bass (Chicago: Chicago University Press, 1981), p. 70.

16. Jacques Derrida, *Dissemination*, trans. B. Johnson (Chicago: University of Chicago Press, 1981), pp. 127–28.

17. Jacques Derrida, *Archaeology of the Frivolous*, trans. John P. Leavy (Pittsburgh: Duquesne University Press, 1980), p. 134.

18. Derrida, *Dissemination*, p. 127.

19. Jacques Derrida, "The *Retrait* of Metaphor," trans. F. Gasdner et al., *Enclitic* 2, no. 2 (Fall 1978): 14.

20. Jacques Derrida, "Living On: *Border Lines*," in *Deconstruction and Criticism*, ed. H. Bloom et al. (New York: Seabury, 1979), pp. 100–101.

21. Ibid., p. 97.   22. Ibid., p. 166.

23. Ibid., p. 100.   24. Ibid., p. 103.

25. Maurice Merleau-Ponty, *The Visible and the Invisible*, trans. A. Lingis (Evanston, Ill.: Northwestern University Press, 1968), pp. 268, 193, and 130.

26. Ibid., pp. 139–40.   27. Ibid., p. 152.

28. Ibid., p. 147.   29. Ibid., pp. 155 and 147.

30. Whereas for Merleau-Ponty, the sensible (visible and tactile) qualities of the chiastic reversal limit the synthesizing power of the prereflexive opening toward the world (without limiting its generality), for Gaston Bachelard, the elementary opening on the world that he calls "rêverie," which also relies on chiastic crisscrossing, gives rise to effectively integrated totalities. The prerational and prereflexive states of experiential plenitude that Bachelard thematizes are, there-

fore, distinguished by repose, happiness, fullness, and so on. Although the synthesizing power of chiastic reversal in reverie is not put into question by Bachelard—to the contrary, he forcefully emphasizes it—the unbreached totalities it engenders are, for him, always concrete, particular, and finite openings. But as in Merleau-Ponty, in Bachelard this finitude does not impinge on the generality of these openings toward the world. See Gaston Bachelard, *The Poetics of Reverie*, trans. D. Russell (Boston: Beacon Press, 1971).

31. Jacques Derrida, "The Law of the Genre," trans. A. Ronell, in *Glyph* 7 (Baltimore: Johns Hopkins University Press, 1980), p. 219.

32. On several occasions, let us also note, Derrida has pointed to the fact that the logic that rules philosophy's desire to achieve closure and continuity resembles the "sophistry" of the borrowed kettle Freud refers to in *Interpretation of Dreams* and in *Jokes and Their Relation to the Unconscious*. But does the contradictory coherence designated by the "sophistry" in question not represent a kind of perversion of chiastic totalization and, thus, a "symptom" of the impossibility of philosophy's ever achieving its goal? Since deconstruction must be understood as the attempt to account for philosophy's contradictory coherence, its critical relation to chiasm as a device productive of philosophical continuity may well be much broader and more essential than we have outlined here.

33. For a discussion of chiasm in Heidegger, see François Mattèi, *La métaphysique à la limite* (Paris: P.U.F., 1983), pp. 49–162.

34. "The essence of a riddle consists in describing a fact by an impossible combination of words" (Aristotle, *Poetics*, trans. W. H. Fyfe [Cambridge, Mass.: Harvard University Press, 1927], 1458a 24–30). Let us recall here that the riddle called either *ainigma* or *griphos* in Greek takes its name from a specific kind of fishnet. Indeed, the riddle is braided in the same way as a fishnet, that is, through intertwinement of opposite terms. See Konrad Ohlert, *Rätsel und Gesellschaftsspiele der alten Griechen* (Berlin: Mayer and Miller, 1886).

35. De Man, *Allegories of Reading*, p. 49.

CHAPTER 14

1. Jürgen Habermas, *Nachmetaphysisches Denken: Philosophische Aufsätze* (Frankfurt am Main: Suhrkamp, 1992), pp. 242–44; translations from this edition are mine. For a more detailed discussion of Habermas's contention that deconstruction conflates rhetoric and logic, see my *Inventions of Difference: On Jacques Derrida* (Cambridge, Mass.: Harvard University Press, 1994), pp. 109–15.

2. Habermas, p. 247. 3. Ibid., p. 260.
4. Ibid., p. 247. 5. Ibid., p. 255.

6. This is not the place for a detailed critique of Habermas's reductive presentation of Derrida's thought. One hint about how and where such a critical de-

370 Notes to Chapter 14

bate ought to take place must suffice here. Habermas contends that "Derrida works on Husserl and Saussure not differently than on Artaud" (p. 243). Since *The Origin of Geometry*, Derrida has been working in light of the difference between the literary and the philosophical text. When confronting Husserl's and Joyce's enterprises, Derrida makes the point in *The Origin of Geometry* that Joyce's generalization and totalization of all equivocalities is not possible without universal univocality in the Husserlian sense. When confronting Genet and Hegel, Derrida asserts in *Glas* that the singular literary work of Genet presupposes, as a condition of its uniqueness, a minimal kind of universally shareable intelligibility (under the form of the *gl*) that makes it partake, in spite of all its difference, in Hegel's attempt to determine the intelligibility of the entirety of all conceivable Others to the system. In Derrida's writings on Artaud, Ponge, or Kafka, one finds a similar respect for the difference between discourses, but such respect does not exclude an investigation into the condition that underwrites such difference.

7. An Other must always be invented for something to be, but by the same token, such inevitable invention also means that no being can ever be taken for granted, for being what it is.

8. As Derrida's reference in the essay "Before the Law" to Heidegger's talk of Being as the "transcendent" demonstrates, his concern is not limited to questioning the Kantian concept of transcendence and transcendental conditions of possibility. Jacques Derrida, *Acts of Literature*, ed. D. Attridge (New York: Routledge, 1992), p. 206. All page references in the text of this chapter are to this edition.

9. The virtual inscription of the Other in the pure law can also manifest itself through a certain theatricality of the law. In "Plato's Pharmacy" (in Jacques Derrida, *Dissemination*, trans. B. Johnson [Chicago: University of Chicago Press, 1981]), for instance, Derrida shows to what extent Plato's philosophical discourse on truth is inevitably linked to a theatrical play, a family scene about legitimate descent and bastardy. Since the possibility of presentation and singularization is inscribed in the philosophical notion of an intelligibility free from all sensibility, the trace of the philosophical discourse's other within itself affects the intelligibility and purity it aspires to, and thus solicits a rethinking of the concepts themselves.

10. An extended version of "Before the Law" was presented by Derrida as a lecture in 1982 at a colloquium in Cerisy (Normandy) on the work of Jean-François Lyotard. The title of the lecture then was "Préjugés: Devant la loi" (Prejudgments: Before the law). It was published in Jacques Derrida et al., *La faculté de Juger* (Paris: Minuit, 1985), pp. 87–139.

11. In *The Other Heading*, Derrida writes: "Whatever the answer may be, the question remains. I would even say this is necessary: it should remain, even beyond all answers." Jacques Derrida, *The Other Heading: Reflections on Today's Eu-*

rope, trans. P.-A. Brault and M. Naas (Bloomington: Indiana University Press, 1992), pp. 16–17.

12. Habermas, p. 45. After giving his definition of "the abyss of irrationality" (pp. 159–60), Habermas avers that irrationality characterizes not only Heidegger's "mystical thought of Being," Wittgenstein's "therapeutical treatment of language," Derrida's "deconstructive activity," and Adorno's "negative dialectic" but many others as well.

13. Maurice Blanchot, *The Work of Fire*, trans. C. Mandell (Stanford, Calif.: Stanford University Press, 1995), p. 54.

14. For a more refined understanding of why the possibility of the Other, with respect to which an identity is the identity that it is, necessarily inhabits this identity, see the various analyses that Derrida has devoted to the notion of the trait, particularly in Jacques Derrida, "The *Retrait* of Metaphor," trans. F. Gasdner et al., *Enclitic* 2, no. 2 (Fall 1978): 6–33.

15. The reasons for this futural dimension of literature and philosophy are structural, and not because these disciplines would be ideals to be infinitely approximated. Hence, there is nothing romantic about the temporality of *à venir*.

CHAPTER 15

1. Maurice Blanchot, *The Work of Fire*, trans. C. Mandell (Stanford, Calif.: Stanford University Press, 1995), p. 302. All page references in the text of this chapter are to this edition.

2. Roger Laporte, *Etudes* (Paris: P.O.L., 1990), p. 23.

3. The concepts borrowed from Hegel do not simply project their dialectical power upon Blanchot's developments; they also suffer a significant mutation *within* Blanchot's text, thus exhibiting possibilities that Hegel might not have accounted for. Let me also refer here to Andrzej Warminski's *Readings in Interpretation: Hölderlin, Hegel, Heidegger* (Minneapolis: University of Minnesota Press, 1987), where he argues that Blanchot, in his readings of Hegel in the 1940s, rewrites Hegel's concepts, "in particular, the concepts of the negative and death) in another place, to the side" (p. 185).

4. Maurice Blanchot, *The Space of Literature*, trans. A. Smock (Lincoln: University of Nebraska Press, 1983), p. 109.

5. To substantiate this point, a careful parallel reading of Blanchot's essay and Hegel's *Phenomenology* would of course be required. Such a comparison would have to determine the exact points of Blanchot's departure from Hegel. Here let me only note that there is never anything marvelous about a dialectical inversion. It occurs with necessity, in all logical rigor.

6. G. W. F. Hegel, *Phenomenology of Spirit*, trans. A. V. Miller (Oxford: Oxford University Press, 1977), pp. 240–41.

7. In his analysis of how consciousness deceives itself and others, Hegel distinguishes different ways in which things happen to it independently of its own making, but which consciousness claims nonetheless for itself. Hegel writes, "an event of historical importance [*Weltbegebenheit*] which does not really concern him, he makes . . . his own; and an interest for which he has done nothing is, in his own eyes, a party interest which *he* has favoured or opposed, and even combated or supported." Ibid., p. 248.

8. See also Blanchot, *Work of Fire*, p. 80.

9. The writer is a stoic if he endures his condition, a condition that, however, allows him to acquire not personal but universal freedom. He is a skeptic, or nihilist, as Blanchot also calls him, if "he negates everything at once, and he is obliged to negate everything, since he deals only with everything." Finally, he is an unhappy consciousness "since he is a writer only by virtue of his fragmented consciousness divided into irreconcilable moments." *Work of Fire*, p. 318.

10. To suspect that Blanchot's discussion of revolutionary terror refers covertly to his own association with right-wing movements in prewar France and that it is a late attempt to come to grips with it misreads completely the status of the fourth temptation. Blanchot takes up the theme of terror for the same reason that he has discussed the three temptations of stoicism, skepticism, and unhappy consciousness and the dialectic between talent and work, work and individual, namely, because he borrows his themes from Hegel's *Phenomenology*, following at times even the latter's order of exposition. If indeed the theme of terror enjoys a special privilege over all the other themes, this is not because it stands in for a personal past of guilt but because, deriving from the conflicts previously discussed, it becomes the place *par excellence* for exemplifying all the paradoxes that make up literature and literary activity. Moreover, the theme of revolutionary terror in question concerns terror in the name of freedom, not the terror of the far Right. To take this discussion as an implicit acknowledgment by Blanchot of his own political past is not only to give in to arbitrary association but also to spell out a whole "philosophy" of the literary text. Whatever the critical methods are, including the seemingly progressive ones of structuralism, by means of which associations of this kind are made, the literary text is reduced to the expression of, in this case, a shameful experience. A literary criticism thus limited to hunting down in the literary text the signs of scandalous political involvement is indeed nothing but a pretext for a return to an autobiographical and anecdotal understanding of literature. Apart from foreclosing all reflection on how the "universally" valid medium of literature relates to empirical (and in particular to private, secret, hidden) factuality, such an approach trivializes history by reducing its constituting agents or forces, its course, and its disasters to the simple effects of individual actions. A commonsense or, rather, vulgar con-

ception of work, writer, and history presides over such an approach. This is, of course, not to disqualify all sociopolitical contextualization of the text, nor even to deny encrypted within it a reference to a secret. Such analyses, however, require that the text be first recognized as text.

11. In 1941, Jean Paulhan, in *Les fleurs de Tarbes, ou La Terreur dans les lettres*, compared the violently antirhetorical and subjectivist literary criticism that begins with Sainte-Beuve, and that finds in Henri Bergson its metaphysical legitimization, to the Terror during the French Revolution. This criticism is bent on reading literature as coinciding with the spirit of the creator, oblivious to the fact that literature requires rhetorical skills, in other words, that it is made of words. The first victims of the French Terror, as Paulhan argues, were also those distinguished by their talents. See Jean Paulhan, *Les fleurs de Tarbes, ou La Terreur dans les lettres* (Paris: Gallimard, 1990), pp. 61–77. Blanchot's designation of literature as the "Reign of the Terror" refers, of course, to this work by Jean Paulhan.

12. It has been remarked with barely restrained indignation that in "Literature and the Right to Death," Blanchot's main example illustrating the destructive power of language is that of a woman: "For me to be able to say, 'This woman,' I must somehow take her flesh-and-blood reality away from her, cause her to be absent, annihilate her" (*Work of Fire*, p. 322). The choice of the example is not fortuitous, of course. In question are indeed the linguistic and ontological conditions under which a thing in general, an animal (the cat), and a human being can become an Other to begin with. To elaborate on how something can become an Other is also to inquire into the conditions of possibility of relation, communication, exchange. It would seem that this can be done most poignantly by taking "woman" as the example.

13. Françoise Collin, *Maurice Blanchot et la question de l'écriture* (Paris: Gallimard, 1971), p. 92.

14. Henri Meschonnic, in a essay entitled "Maurice Blanchot ou l'écriture hors langage" (*Les Cahiers du Chemin* 20 [1974]: 79–116), has taken Blanchot to task for his linkage of language, as a medium of ideality and universality, to destruction, negation, and death. Meschonnic, who opposes a scientific, or semiotico-semantic, interpretation of language to what he deems to be a "mythology of langage" (p. 90) whose dualism reveals its metaphysical postulates (p. 95), primarily objects to Blanchot's privileging of the word as characteristic of language as a whole. No doubt, in "Literature and the Right to Death," Blanchot approaches language (and its idealizing function) primarily from the name. But the name is, for Blanchot, clearly and first of all a word. Where language becomes conceived in its materiality, the "name ceases to be the ephemeral passing of nonexistence and becomes a concrete ball, a solid mass of existence" (Blanchot, *Work of Fire*, p. 327). Here the name is shown to regress to the word. It is the

words that for Blanchot make up language, and the word is not thought from the name. "The meaning for the meaning of words," which can be that of either materiality or negativity, springs from "an ambiguous indeterminacy that wavers between yes and no," and which as the end of the essay demonstrates is that of death (p. 343). Moreover, in his analysis of the word, he draws on a variety of implications that come with the traditional concept of the word itself, and that thoroughly displace its metaphysical status, as well as its potential for giving rise to what Meschonnic terms a "mysticism of lost unity and of the end to come" (p. 100). As an example of such emphasis on potentially dislocating traits of the word, I quote the following from Blanchot's essay: "Take the trouble to listen to a single word: in that word, nothingness is struggling and toiling away, it digs tirelessly, doing its utmost to find a way out, nullifying what encloses it—it is infinite disquiet, formless and nameless [*sans nom*] vigilance" (p. 326).

Index

Cultural Memory | in the Present

Library of Congress Cataloging-in-Publication Data

Gasché, Rodolphe.
    Of minimal things : studies on the notion of relation / Rodolphe Gasché.
        p.   cm. — (Cultural memory in the present)
    Includes bibliographical references and index.
    ISBN 0-8047-3676-6 (alk. paper) — ISBN 0-8047-3677-4 (pbk. : alk. paper)
    1. Relation (Philosophy)   I. Title.   II. Series.
BI32.R43 G37   1999

                                                        99-038672

⊚   This book is printed on acid-free, archival quality paper.

Original printing 1999

Last figure below indicates the year of this printing:
08   07   06   05   04   03   02   01   00   99

Typeset by James P. Brommer in 11/13.5 Garamond